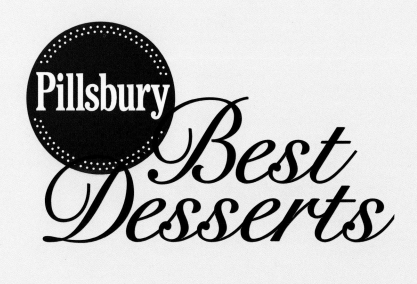

Pillsbury Best Desserts

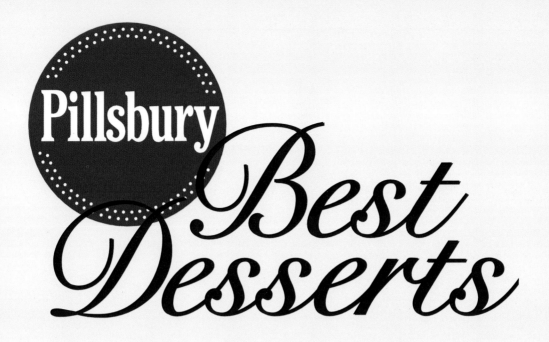

Pillsbury Best Desserts

More than 350 Recipes from America's Most-Trusted Kitchen

The Pillsbury Company

Clarkson Potter/Publishers
New York

Credits

PILLSBURY: BEST DESSERTS COOKBOOK
THE PILLSBURY COMPANY

Publisher: Sally Peters
Publication Manager: Diane B. Anderson
Senior Editors: Jackie Sheehan, Betsy Wray
Senior Food Editor: Andi Bidwell
Recipe Editors: Nancy Lilleberg, Grace Wells
Contributing Writer: Mary Caldwell
Photography: Glenn Peterson Photography,
    Graham Brown Photography, Hedstrom/Blessing Photo,
    Tad Ware Photography
Food Stylists: Lynn Boldt, JoAnn Cherry, Sharon Harding,
    Barb Standal
Recipe Typist: Michelle Barringer

PILLSBURY PUBLICATIONS

Publisher: Sally Peters
Publication Managers: Diane B. Anderson, William Monn
Senior Editors: Jackie Sheehan, Betsy Wray
Senior Food Editor: Andi Bidwell
Test Kitchen Coordinator: Pat Peterson
Circulation Manager: Karen Goodsell
Circulation Coordinator: Rebecca Bogema
Recipe System Administrator: Bev Gustafson
Recipe System Coordinator: Nolan Vaughan
Recipe Production Specialists: Mary Prokott
Publication Secretary: Jackie Ranney

Bake-Off is a registered trademark of The Pillsbury Company.
Bundt is a registered trademark of Northland Aluminum
    Company.

CLARKSON POTTER/PUBLISHERS
THE CROWN PUBLISHING GROUP

President and Publisher: Chip Gibson
Vice President-Editorial Director: Lauren Shakely
Senior Editor: Katie Workman
Assistant Editor: Erica Youngren
Designer: Julie Baker Schroeder
Executive Managing Editor: Laurie Stark
Managing Editor: Amy Boorstein
Senior Production Manager: Jane Searle
Publicist: Wendy Schuman

Published by Clarkson Potter / Publishers,
New York, New York.
Member of the Crown Publishing Group.

Random House, Inc.
New York, Toronto, London, Sydney, Auckland
www.randomhouse.com

Clarkson N. Potter is a trademark and Potter and colophon
are registered trademarks of Random House, Inc.

Printed in Japan
Design by Julie Baker Schroeder

Library of Congress Cataloging-in-Publication Data
Pillsbury, best desserts / the Pillsbury Company.
    1. Desserts. I. The Pillsbury Company.
TX773.P573   1998
641.8'6—dc21   98-9183

ISBN   0-609-60285-3

10 9 8 7

COVER: FUDGY ORANGE CAPPUCCINO TORTE, PAGE 265
FRONTISPIECE: CHOCOLATE SOUFFLÉ, PAGE 134

CONTENTS

DESSERT BASICS

Ah, sweet endings. A homemade treat can brighten a gray day or heighten the joy of a special occasion. Among the 350 desserts featured in this book, there's something for every sweet tooth, whether you are partial to elegant layer cakes, two-crust pies or the homestyle comfort of apple crisp or bread pudding.

RASPBERRY-CHERRY PIE, PAGE 75

ACH RECIPE made its way into this collection as a worthy answer to the all-important question—what's for dessert? You'll find simple sweets to whip up while the rest of dinner cooks and more elaborate showpieces for leisurely baking. Some start from scratch, while others get a head start from packaged puddings and cakes. We've even included twenty-five of the all-time best desserts from America's most famous cooking event, the Pillsbury Bake-Off® Contest.

EQUIPMENT

Making dessert is easier if you have the right tools for the job. A list of specific equipment for each type of dessert appears in the introduction to each chapter. Some of the basics you'll need for any kind of dessert include:

MIXING BOWLS IN VARIOUS SIZES. Microwave-safe ceramic bowls are handy for melting chocolate or butter; stainless steel bowls are unbreakable and a good choice for most recipes. Avoid plastic bowls for beating egg whites, as even clean plastic may retain traces of grease that will impede whipping.

ELECTRIC MIXER. This appliance is used for mixing, creaming and whipping ingredients. A portable hand-held mixer is great for light mixtures. A free-standing electric mixer works best for larger quantities and longer mixing times.

MEASURING SPOONS. Use a properly calibrated set for accurate measurement; do not rely on ordinary silverware or estimates.

LIQUID AND DRY MEASURING CUPS. Yes, you do need both to ensure the accurate measurements that are critical for baking.

LIQUID MEASURING CUPS. These are made out of transparent glass or plastic, with calibrations marked on the side. Set the cup on a flat surface, fill it, then check it at eye level; the top of the liquid should be even with the top of the measuring line. Add or take away liquid as necessary to achieve the right amount.

DRY MEASURING CUPS. Dry measuring cups, available in nesting sets made of metal or plastic, typically include cups for $1/4$ cup, $1/3$ cup, $1/2$ cup and 1 cup (sometimes $1/8$ cup, too, which is also known as a coffee measure). For most accurate measurement, do not use the measuring cup as a scoop, which can result in air pockets. Instead, spoon the dry ingredient into the measuring cup, and then level off the top with the flat side of a knife or metal spatula.

WIRE COOLING RACKS. Air circulating around the entire dessert—whether it's a cookie, cake or pie—will hasten cooling and also prevent sogginess.

INGREDIENTS

It's fascinating to think about how the same basic shopping list—flour, milk, sugar, eggs, butter—can yield foods as different as cookies, pie pastry, custard and biscuits. Here's a look at some fundamental ingredients. For best results, use the ingredients in the recipes as written.

FLOUR. Most dessert recipes call for all-purpose flour. Either bleached or unbleached may be used. Don't substitute bread flour, which has a higher gluten content that will toughen desserts. Whole wheat flour is sometimes added to cookies but is not recommended for most desserts because it produces a heavier, more compact texture.

FATS. Fat provides tenderness and moisture for cookies, cakes, pie crusts and more.

• BUTTER offers the most flavor in addition to the moistening and tenderizing properties common to all fats. If a recipe specifies butter only, rather than "margarine or butter," then you'll know that butter is essential for the best performance and/or flavor in the finished recipe.

• MARGARINE, though it has little flavor of its own, will yield good results in most recipes in this book, except where it is not listed as an option.

• VEGETABLE SHORTENING can produce a flaky pie crust, a pure white cake or fine-textured cookies, but it doesn't contribute flavor.

• WHIPPED MARGARINES OR BUTTERS incorporate air for a lighter-textured, easier-to-spread topping. They're great for spreading, but don't substitute them for regular butter in baking because they contain more air, and therefore less weight, than regular butter.

• LOW-FAT SPREADS contain a higher proportion of water and air, and their performance as a dessert ingredient is not so predictable. In general, as fat is reduced in cookies, the dough becomes more soft and sticky. Cookies are less crisp and more cakelike, with a slightly tougher texture. Cakes have a thinner batter, and the texture becomes more gummy and the surface more porous.

• VEGETABLE OIL does not allow for the proper incorporation of air as the dough is beaten and should not be used in desserts unless it's called for.

BAKING POWDER is a traditional leavening agent for cakes, cookies, muffins and more. It works by creating bubbles of gas that cause the batter or dough to expand, yielding a multitude of tiny air pockets and a light texture. Old-fashioned baking powder began to work its magic as soon as it was combined with liquid, meaning batters had to be baked in short order so the leavening power would not be expended prematurely. Modern double-acting baking powders, on the other hand, get two bursts: The baking powder begins to work when it's combined with liquid but puts forth most leavening when exposed to the heat of the oven.

BAKING SODA, alone or in combination with baking powder, is the leavening agent of choice when the recipe includes acidic ingredients such as citrus, vinegar, buttermilk, molasses and, surprisingly, chocolate. The acid activates the baking soda's bubbling action, causing the dough or batter to rise; the baking soda, in turn, has a neutralizing effect on the acid.

EMERGENCY SUBSTITUTIONS

INGREDIENT	SUBSTITUTE
Baking powder, 1 teaspoon	1/4 teaspoon baking soda plus 1/2 teaspoon cream of tartar
Buttermilk, 1 cup	1 tablespoon vinegar or lemon juice plus enough milk to make 1 cup
Dairy sour cream, 1 cup	1 cup plain yogurt
Honey, 1 cup	1 1/4 cups sugar plus 1/4 cup liquid
Semi-sweet chocolate, 1 ounce	1 ounce unsweetened chocolate plus 1 tablespoon sugar OR 3 tablespoons semi-sweet chocolate chips
Unsweetened chocolate, 1 ounce	3 tablespoons unsweetened cocoa plus 1 tablespoon shortening or margarine

CHOCOLATE. Chocolate is made from the bitter-flavored "beans" of the cacao tree. The beans are fermented, roasted, shelled, then ground to produce a substance known as chocolate liquor, which contains cocoa solids and cocoa butter and forms the basis for all the various types of chocolate. Lecithin, an emulsifier, may be added to the finished sweetened chocolate to give it a smoother texture.

UNSWEETENED BAKING CHOCOLATE, made from solidified chocolate liquor, is usually sold in the supermarket in 8-ounce packages that contain individually wrapped 1- or 2-ounce blocks. Although the aroma of melted unsweetened chocolate is enticing, the flavor is quite bitter until sweetener is added.

SEMI-SWEET CHOCOLATE is made from chocolate liquor plus additional cocoa butter, sweetener and usually a flavoring such as vanilla or vanillin. Most chocolate chips are made of semi-sweet chocolate.

MILK CHOCOLATE consists of sweetened chocolate with the addition of milk solids.

WHITE CHOCOLATE is popular but not really accurately named. Because it contains no chocolate liquor, it's not really chocolate. It's made from cocoa butter, sweetened milk and flavorings.

COCOA POWDER, used in many baking recipes, is a special favorite with low-fat bakers because it provides chocolate flavor with little fat. Cocoa is made from dried, ground chocolate liquor from which the cocoa butter has been removed. For baking, always use unsweetened cocoa powder, not drink mix with dried milk and sugar. "Dutch-process" or alkalized cocoa is preferred by some bakers because they feel it is smoother and has less acidity.

EGGS. The recipes in this book have been tested using large eggs. If you use a different size, your results may differ. Since raw eggs have a slight possibility of being contaminated with salmonella bacteria, which are destroyed by cooking, we do not recommend licking the spoon of doughs or batters that contain raw eggs.

Eggs are easiest to separate when cold, but whites whip best at room temperature. When whipping egg whites, be sure to use a nonplastic bowl and beaters that are absolutely dry and free of grease. Don't even put lotion on your hands before beginning. If both whites and yolks will be beaten, whip the whites first, then the yolks to avoid getting any speck of yolk into the whites; the fat in yolks also impedes whipping.

MILK. Stove-top puddings may taste a little less rich and be prone to scorching when made with skim milk, but most other recipes will

tolerate whatever milk you happen to have on hand. Powdered skim milk is a breeze to use in cookies and cakes. Simply stir in the correct amount of skim milk powder with the dry ingredients and add the corresponding amount of water along with the wet ingredients. If you're looking for ways to boost protein or calcium intake (such as for children who don't like to drink milk, pregnant or nursing women, or people with osteoporosis), double the amount of dry milk powder but keep the amount of liquid the same.

SWEETENERS. Sweetness may be added to a recipe in one or more of many forms. You'll have the best results if you use the sweetener called for in a recipe. If, however, you do use substitutes, keep in mind that the flavor and possibly the texture of the resulting recipe will not be the same as the original's. In general, you can use brown sugar (packed) for an equal quantity of white granulated sugar; the resulting flavor will be reminiscent of molasses.

There is no direct substitute for honey and granulated sugar. If you'd like to experiment, use these guidelines: If the recipe calls for 1 cup of honey, substitute 1 1/4 cups granulated sugar plus 1/4 cup liquid; if the recipe calls for 1 cup of sugar, substitute 3/4 cup honey.

• SUGAR. Recipes that simply call for "sugar" mean white, granulated sugar. It adds sweetness, tenderness and moisture to recipes and aids in browning. Measure it in a dry measuring cup and level off the top with a metal spatula or the flat side of a knife.

• BROWN SUGAR. A mixture of granulated sugar and molasses, it contributes moistness, color and flavor to recipes. The dark version has a more pronounced flavor. Pack brown sugar firmly into a dry measuring cup, until it is level with the top of the cup.

• POWDERED SUGAR. Made from granulated sugar that has been ground extra fine, powdered sugar (also known as confectioners' sugar) dissolves more readily than granulated sugar. It's most often used in icings and as a garnish, though some cookie recipes use it in the dough itself. Sift it before using to get rid of lumps.

• HONEY. Like sugar, honey adds moistness and sweetness, but it also contributes a distinct flavor.

• MOLASSES. A by-product of sugar refining, molasses is a thick, sweet liquid available in light and dark varieties. The bitterness of a third type, blackstrap molasses, makes it unsuitable for baking.

• CORN SYRUP. This thick, sweet liquid comes in dark and light varieties. It's widely used as a sweetener in commercial products, and occasionally in cookie recipes, too.

WHIPPED TOPPINGS. It's a snap to use commercially prepared whipped toppings, whether you opt for real whipped cream in a pressurized can or frozen whipped topping. To make your own whipped cream, prechill the mixing bowl and beaters. Use whipping cream or the slightly higher-fat heavy cream; light cream or half-and-half won't whip. The cream will whip more easily if it is chilled.

TIPS FOR SUCCESS

MEASURING DRY INGREDIENTS. Use plastic or metal dry measuring cups so you can level off the top with a metal spatula or the flat side of a knife. To measure flour: Spoon the flour into a dry measuring cup—rather than dipping the cup into the flour—then smooth off the top with the flat side of a knife. Do not pack the flour. There is no need to sift the flour.

MEASURING LIQUID INGREDIENTS. Use a glass liquid measuring cup with space above the top printed measure. Check the contents at eye level for accuracy.

PREPARING PANS. Many recipes call for greasing—or greasing and flouring—the baking pan to prevent sticking. For best results, use solid vegetable shortening. Use a paper towel or piece of waxed paper to rub a thin, even layer of shortening over the pan. Grease the pan before baking the first batch only.

If the recipe requires flouring, too, spoon a teaspoon or two of flour into the greased pan, then tilt it from side to side as you tap the edges to distribute the flour evenly.

If you use nonstick cooking spray instead of shortening, spray it on the pan in a light, even layer; use a paper towel, if necessary, to distribute the layer more evenly or to remove excess shortening. Doughs with a high proportion of fat may not require greased pans, while meringues and other nonfat egg white—based recipes require ungreased pans so they can rise properly.

BAKING DESSERTS. Always preheat the oven before you put the cookies, cakes, pies and other baked desserts into the oven. Allow 10 to

15 minutes for it to reach the desired heat; use an oven thermometer for accuracy.

In general, desserts will bake most evenly on the center rack of the oven. If you're baking one pan, center it on the shelf. If more than one pan is being used, space them evenly. Pans should not touch each other or the sides of the oven.

Unless you have a convection oven, which circulates the hot air evenly, your oven may have "hot spots." If pans of cookies brown more quickly at one end than the other, try reversing the sheets halfway through cooking time. However, don't open the door on a cake before the minimum baking time specified in the recipe, or it may fall.

REDUCED-FAT DESSERTS

Many desserts are naturally low in fat—sorbets, angel food cake and fruit compotes, for example. And of course, portion control plays a big role in maintaining a low-fat or low-calorie diet. A sliver of your favorite rich cheesecake or chocolate pie may cost you fewer calories than a binge on low-fat cookies.

If you wish to experiment with lower-fat alternatives to your favorite rich desserts, make gradual changes to the recipe and see how you like the results. Flaky pie pastry is difficult to modify successfully, but you could compromise by making a one-crust pie instead of using a double crust, or by substituting a low-fat crumb crust for a pastry crust.

Cakes, cookies and other desserts can be modified with varying degrees of success. Try substituting some plain nonfat yogurt, applesauce or prune puree for part of the fat in cake or cookies. Reduce or eliminate nuts. Use low- or nonfat versions of milk, sour cream and cream cheese.

Reduced-fat cookies will probably be less crisp, more cakelike, slightly tougher, smoother on top and less brown. Reduced-fat cakes may be a bit drier and may benefit from being served with a fruit puree or dessert sauce. You may enjoy lower-fat desserts better if you modify a new

EQUIVALENT MEASURES AND WEIGHTS

Dash = less than $\frac{1}{8}$ teaspoon

3 teaspoons = 1 tablespoon

2 tablespoons = $\frac{1}{8}$ cup or 1 fluid ounce

4 tablespoons = $\frac{1}{4}$ cup

5 $\frac{1}{3}$ tablespoons = $\frac{1}{3}$ cup

8 tablespoons = $\frac{1}{2}$ cup

12 tablespoons = $\frac{3}{4}$ cup

16 tablespoons = 1 cup

1 cup = 8 fluid ounces

2 cups = 1 pint or 16 fluid ounces

4 cups = 1 quart

4 quarts = 1 gallon

16 ounces = 1 pound

recipe rather than a family favorite, which may be disappointing in an altered form.

HIGH-ALTITUDE DESSERTS

Tried-and-true recipes may yield less than perfect results when baked at high altitudes (over 3,500 feet above sea level). As altitude increases, air pressure decreases, causing water to have a lower boiling point and altering the way leavening agents, sweeteners and liquids act.

Cakes are especially sensitive to altitude and take longer to bake, but other desserts may react, too. All of the baked recipes in this book have been tested at high altitude. If a specific change is recommended, it is noted at the end of the recipe. If you have trouble with a particular recipe that doesn't specify high altitude adjustments, try adding 2 to 4 tablespoons of flour or reducing the sugar by 3 tablespoons per cup.

ABOUT THE RECIPES

PREP TIMES. Each recipe states a "Prep Time," which includes the time necessary for mixing and baking or cooking the entire quantity being made. If the recipe requires additional unattended time (for steps such as freezing, chilling or cooling), a "Ready In" time also is noted.

NUTRITION INFORMATION. The nutrition information that accompanies each recipe can help you estimate how specific recipes contribute to your overall meal plan. Included are figures for calories, fat, cholesterol, sodium and dietary fiber.

You'll also find dietary exchanges, the nutritional accounting system commonly used by people with diabetes. This information is based on 1995 Exchange Lists for Meal Planning by the American Diabetes Association and the American Dietetic Association. (These are different from Weight Watchers exchanges.) Two lists of exchanges are provided: The first list uses the traditional method of figuring dietary exchanges; the second reflects the newer system of carbohydrate counting. If you have questions about the exchanges, consult your doctor or registered dietitian, or call the American Dietetic Association at (800) 366-1655.

To calculate nutrition we:

• Use the first ingredient mentioned, when the recipe gives options. For example, if "eggs or egg substitute" is listed, eggs would be calculated.

• Use the larger amount of an ingredient when the recipe gives a range.

• Include garnishing or "if desired" ingredients if they are included in the ingredient list.

CAKES AND FROSTINGS

✦ ✦ ✦

Cakes hold an undeniable spot in the limelight at weddings, birthday parties and other celebrations. Whether you prefer to start from scratch or welcome the shortcut of a packaged mix (doctored up to make it more special), this chapter offers something for your next special occasion—or no occasion at all.

GERMAN CHOCOLATE CAKE WITH COCONUT-PECAN FROSTING, PAGE 13

Measure accurately and mix carefully, and you'll be well on your way to turning out scrumptious, beautiful cakes.

TIPS FOR SUCCESS

MEASURING. Baking a cake may be an art, but science plays a major role, too. We're talking chemistry here—the mingling of molecules to produce cakes with good texture. Slight mismeasurements may hurt the results, much more so than with breads, for example. Always measure carefully with calibrated measuring cups and spoons; don't rely on approximate measures.

MIXING. Most cake recipes call for creaming the butter—that is, mixing with an electric mixer to soften it into a smooth, creamy mass. It's easiest if you soften the butter at room temperature for about an hour or heat it very briefly (a few seconds) on medium power in the microwave. Watch it carefully, as melted butter will not incorporate air the same way that creamed butter does. Oil is used with many cake mixes, but don't substitute oil for butter in a from-scratch cake.

PREHEATING. Don't skip this step. Most ovens take 10 to 15 minutes to reach the proper temperature. Turn on the oven when you start mixing the batter so it will be ready when you are.

PAN SIZES. You'll have the best results if you use the pan size specified in the recipe. Round and square pans of the same size may be interchanged, but don't substitute a pan that's smaller than the one called for or the batter may overflow in the oven. Don't fill the pan more than three-fourths full of batter. In a pinch, you can use a pan that's slightly larger than the one called for—a 9-inch round cake pan instead of the 8-inch pan called for—but the baking time will probably be a little shorter since the batter will be in a thinner layer.

Pans called for in this chapter include:

+ 13 × 9 × 2-inch rectangular pan

+ 10-inch tube pan (also known as an angel food pan)

+ 12-cup Bundt® pan (similar to a tube pan but with a ridged design)

+ 8-inch and 9-inch round cake pans

+ 8-inch and 9-inch square pans

+ 8 × 4-inch and 9 × 5-inch loaf pans

+ 8-inch, 9-inch and 10-inch springform pans (the bottom and sides of a springform pan are separate pieces—a clip holds the sides of the pan tightly together during baking; removing the clip after baking releases the sides and makes it easy to remove the cake from the pan)

Bundt® is a registered trademark of Northland Aluminum Products, Inc., Minneapolis, MN.

+ 15 × 10 × 1-inch pan (also known as a jelly roll pan; a large cookie sheet with a 1-inch-high rim may be used)

PREPARING THE PAN. Angel food cake, made of beaten egg whites, bakes in an ungreased pan so that the whites can cling to the sides of the pan and give the cake its characteristic airy texture. Most other pans must be greased (shortening is preferred—butter, margarine or nonfat cooking spray may be used) to prevent the cake from sticking, and sometimes floured. To flour the pan, sprinkle in a teaspoon or two of flour, then tap the pan from side to side to coat the greased surface evenly.

TESTING FOR DONENESS. While all recipes include baking times, your oven thermostat may not be perfectly accurate. Variations in temperature and humidity can also affect baking times. As the cake bakes, it will shrink slightly from the sides of the pans and, in most cases, rise gently to a dome in the center. Most cakes are done if a toothpick inserted into the center comes out clean (that is, not coated with batter or crumbs) and if the top springs back when gently pressed with a fingertip.

COOLING AND REMOVING FROM THE PAN. Once the cake is removed from the oven, set it on top of a wire cooling rack for about 10 minutes. Run a knife around the edge of the pan. Place another rack on top of the cake pan, invert the racks and gently tap on the bottom of the pan to loosen any sticky areas. Carefully remove the pan. Place the first rack back on the cake and invert the layer again so it's right side up on the cooling rack.

FROSTING. Some glazes may be poured or spread onto a cake that is still hot, but most frostings work best if they're spread onto a completely cooled cake. With a table knife or flat-bladed metal spatula, frost the sides first. Finish with the top.

STORING. Delicate "plain" cakes with little fat are best eaten the day they're made. Cakes made with a high percentage of fat or other moist ingredients—such as crushed or pureed fruit, or sour cream—will usually keep well for several days. If you don't have a "cake keeper," you can improvise by inverting a large mixing bowl over the cake plate. If you're worried about soft frosting sticking to plastic wrap, stick a few toothpicks or birthday candles into the cake first; for a tube or Bundt® cake, you can insert a drinking glass or pillar candle into the center hole to lift the wrap above the frosting.

FREEZING. Many cakes freeze well. Put the unwrapped whole cake or slices on a plate and into the freezer. When the surface has become hard, wrap the cake tightly in plastic freezer wrap, then pop the wrapped cake into a self-sealing plastic freezer bag labeled with the date and contents. Use the cake within a month or so. Defrost plain cakes on the counter in the wrapper; unwrap frosted cakes. Forget any romantic notions about saving frozen cake for an anniversary a year later. All foods dry out and pick up odors in the freezer no matter how careful you are about wrapping. While this isn't harmful to your health, it *is* disappointing.

DECORATING. Here's a chance to let your creativity shine and enhance the mood of the occasion. Cake decorating can be simple enough for a beginner to complete in 5 or 10 minutes or elaborate enough to keep a professional baker busy for hours. Here are some ideas:

• Sprinkle the surface of the cake with chocolate or colored sprinkles, flaked coconut, grated chocolate or miniature chocolate chips.

• Create a "mosaic" design or spell out the name of the guest of honor with candy-coated chocolates, jelly beans, gumdrops, walnuts, miniature mints or another favorite sweet.

• Use purchased tubes of decorator icing—or homemade icing in a pastry bag—to pipe decorations on the top. Use a plain tip to write a name or a message; use a star tip to create simple flowers or pipe a border around the edge. You can improvise a pastry bag with a cone of parchment paper or waxed paper or a plastic freezer bag with a hole cut in the corner; insert a decorator tip, fill the bag with icing and decorate away.

• Garnish the top of each slice, or the whole cake, with dollops of whipped cream topped with a few fresh berries and a sprig of fresh mint.

• Instead of, or in addition to, frosting, ladle chocolate sauce, berry puree or another sweet topping around a slice of cake on a dessert plate.

• Simple texture variations are easy and pretty. Use a butter knife to create swirls all over the top, or use a dinner fork alternately dragged horizontally and vertically in inch-long segments to create a basket-weave appearance.

• Try contrasting frosting: Frost the top of a round layer cake with chocolate and the sides with vanilla; or spread the contrasting icings in concentric circles on the top for a delicious "bull's eye."

• Kids can make decorations by attaching small hearts, stars or character stickers to toothpicks; remove before serving them to little ones!

• Melt semi-sweet chocolate chips in the microwave in a small self-sealing plastic bag. Cut a tiny hole in a bottom corner of the bag and use to pipe script or designs onto cakes.

HOLIDAY CAKES

+ NEW YEAR'S CELEBRATION. Sprinkle the top of the cake with multicolored sprinkles to imitate confetti.

+ VALENTINE'S DAY. To make a heart shape, bake a two-layer cake in one square pan and one round. Place the square layer, positioned to look like a diamond, at the end of a large cake platter. Cut the round layer in half to make two semicircles. Place the cut edges of each semicircle against the adjoining sides at the top of the diamond to make a heart shape; frost the whole thing to hide the seams.

HEART CAKE

+ ST. PATRICK'S DAY. Frost a sheet cake with green-tinted icing. Use arcs of colored icing to make a rainbow; arrange some chocolate coins at the end of the rainbow to make an edible pot of gold.

+ EASTER. To make a bunny cake, bake 2 round layers. One will become the rabbit's face. From the second layer, cut a bow-tie shape from the center, leaving two rabbit ears on either side. Place the bow tie under the rabbit's chin and the ears in the logical spots; use very creamy-textured frosting to avoid spreading crumbs across the surface. Let the kids decorate the rabbit's face with jelly beans, purchased icing tubes or whatever strikes your fancy.

+ INDEPENDENCE DAY. Frost your favorite cake with whipped cream or vanilla icing. Decorate with blueberries and raspberries or strawberries.

+ HALLOWEEN. Bake a batch or two of cupcakes. Frost some with orange icing and use candy corn to mimic jack-o'-lantern faces. Frost others with chocolate icing. To make cats: Use candy corn for ears, round candies or flower-shaped sprinkles for eyes and nose, and piped icing or shoestring licorice for whiskers.

+ THANKSGIVING. As an alternative (or complement) to traditional pies, try a turkey cake: Bake an 8-inch or 9-inch round cake, plus 12 large cupcakes and 24 miniature cupcakes. To make the turkey, place the large round layer in the center of a very large platter and frost with chocolate. To make the tail feathers, use rows of chocolate-frosted cupcakes (largest close to the body, fanning out to miniature cupcakes for the tips). Use a large chocolate-frosted cupcake for the head and a small one frosted red for the "wattle." Use additional cupcakes for legs. Use tubes of purchased decorator icing or homemade icing tinted yellow or orange to pipe chevron designs onto the "feathers."

+ WINTER HOLIDAYS. Place a purchased paper doily over a cake and sift powdered sugar or cocoa (whichever will show up better on the particular cake) onto the top; carefully lift off the doily to reveal an intricate and beautiful "snowflake." This is best done just before serving so the design doesn't melt into the frosting and disappear. You can vary this technique by cutting your own stencil (holiday stars, candles) from a piece of waxed paper.

TYPES OF CAKES

Among the recipes in this chapter you'll find the following:

BUTTER CAKE, the moist, light, fine-textured cake commonly made with butter, but sometimes made with margarine or solid shortening. Butter cakes usually are baked into the following two forms:

LAYER CAKE, the old-fashioned birthday favorite, consists of rounds or squares (or other shapes) of cake stacked on top of each other with filling or frosting in between. To fill a single layer, use a long, sharp knife held parallel to the work surface and cut the cake into two separate layers.

SHEET CAKE, a flat rectangular cake typically baked in a 13 × 9-inch or 15 × 10-inch pan is a good choice for a crowd because it's easy to serve.

ANGEL FOOD CAKE is light textured and fat-free, as it's made only from egg whites, flour, sugar and flavoring. It lends itself to a variety of toppings (fruit, dessert sauces, whipped cream, frostings) and is an especially good choice for someone trying to limit fat intake or someone who can't tolerate milk products.

PUDDING CAKE is an almost magical kind of homestyle dessert in which the batter separates while it's baking in the oven to create a cake layer and moist layer that serves as a sauce for the cake.

FRUITCAKE uses a relatively large amount of fresh or dried fruit to add moistness, natural sweetness and flavor. Carrot cakes, zucchini bread and the like are cousins of this genre. Although they contain "healthy" ingredients, some versions are among the richest of desserts.

CHIFFON CAKE, like angel food cake, relies on beaten eggs to achieve lofty heights, but the batter also includes some fat.

SPONGE CAKE batter includes eggs but no butter, shortening or oil. It's richer and higher-fat than angel food cakes, but generally lower-fat and less rich than many other cakes.

◆ ◆ ◆

GERMAN CHOCOLATE CAKE WITH COCONUT-PECAN FROSTING

PICTURED ON PAGE 9.

◆

Yield: 16 servings; Prep Time: 30 minutes
(Ready in 2 hours 50 minutes)

This cake takes its name from the German brand sweet cooking chocolate with which it was developed.

CAKE
4 oz. sweet cooking chocolate, cut into pieces
1/2 cup water
2 cups sugar
1 cup margarine or butter, softened
4 eggs
2 1/2 cups all-purpose flour
1 teaspoon baking soda
1/2 teaspoon salt
1 cup buttermilk*
1 teaspoon vanilla

FROSTING
1 cup sugar
1 cup evaporated milk
1/2 cup margarine or butter
3 eggs, beaten
1 1/3 cups flaked coconut
1 cup chopped pecans or walnuts
1 teaspoon vanilla

1. Heat oven to 350°F. Grease and lightly flour three 9-inch round cake pans. In small saucepan over low heat, melt chocolate with water; cool.

2. In large bowl, combine 2 cups sugar and 1 cup margarine; beat until light and fluffy. Add 4 eggs, 1 at a time, beating well after each addition. Stir in chocolate mixture. Add all remaining cake ingredients; beat at low speed until well combined. Pour batter into greased and floured pans.

3. Bake at 350°F. for 35 to 45 minutes or until toothpick inserted in center comes out clean. Cool 5 minutes. Remove from pans. Cool 1 hour or until completely cooled.

4. In medium saucepan, combine 1 cup sugar, evaporated milk, 1/2 cup margarine and 3 eggs; mix well. Cook over medium heat until mixture begins to bubble, stirring constantly. Remove from heat; stir in coconut, pecans and 1 teaspoon vanilla. Cool 30 minutes or until completely cooled.

5. Place 1 cake layer, top side down, on serving plate. Spread with 1/3 of frosting. Repeat with remaining cake layers and frosting, ending with frosting.

Tip: To substitute for buttermilk, use 1 tablespoon vinegar or lemon juice plus enough milk to make 1 cup.

High Altitude (Above 3,500 feet): Decrease sugar in cake to 1 3/4 cups; decrease baking soda to 3/4 teaspoon. Bake at 375°F. for 25 to 30 minutes.

Nutrition per Serving: Serving Size: 1/16 of Recipe. Calories 560; Calories from Fat 270; Total Fat 30g; Saturated Fat 8g; Cholesterol 100mg; Sodium 420mg; Dietary Fiber 2g

Dietary Exchange: 3 Starch, 1 1/2 Fruit, 5 Fat OR 4 1/2 Carbohydrate, 5 Fat

YELLOW CAKE

◆

Yield: 12 servings; Prep Time: 20 minutes
(Ready in 1 hour 55 minutes)

Sprinkle the cooled layers with sifted powdered sugar for an easy-pack lunch-box treat, or spread the stacked layers with your favorite flavor of Buttercream Frosting (page 60) for the perfect birthday cake.

2 1/2 cups all-purpose flour
3 teaspoons baking powder
1/4 teaspoon salt
1 1/4 cups sugar
3/4 cup margarine or butter, softened
1 teaspoon vanilla
3 eggs
1 cup milk

1. Heat oven to 350°F. Grease and flour two 8 or 9-inch round cake pans.* In medium bowl, combine flour, baking powder and salt; mix well.

2. In large bowl, combine sugar and margarine; beat until light and fluffy. Add vanilla and eggs; blend well. Alternately add dry ingredients and milk, beating well after each addition. Pour batter into greased and floured pans.

3. Bake at 350°F. for 27 to 35 minutes or until toothpick inserted in center comes out clean. Cool 10 minutes. Remove from pans. Cool 1 hour or until completely cooled. Fill and frost as desired.

Tip: Cake can be baked in greased and floured 13 × 9-inch pan. Bake at 350°F. for 33 to 40 minutes. Cool 1 hour or until completely cooled.

High Altitude (Above 3,500 feet): Decrease sugar to 1 cup. Bake as directed above.

Nutrition per Serving: Serving Size: 1/12 of Recipe. Calories 310; Calories from Fat 120; Total Fat 13g; Saturated Fat 3g; Cholesterol 55mg; Sodium 330mg; Dietary Fiber 1g

Dietary Exchange: 1 1/2 Starch, 1 1/2 Fruit, 2 Fat OR 3 Carbohydrate, 2 Fat

WHITE CAKE

◆

Yield: 12 servings; Prep Time: 15 minutes
(Ready in 2 hours)

What's the occasion? Team this pure white cake with Mallow Frosting (page 60), Chocolate Buttercream Frosting (page 60) or Ganache (page 60).

2 cups all-purpose flour
1 1/2 cups sugar
3 teaspoons baking powder
1/2 teaspoon salt
1 cup milk
1/2 cup shortening
1 teaspoon vanilla or 1/2 teaspoon almond extract
5 egg whites

1. Heat oven to 350°F. Grease and flour two 9-inch round cake pans.* In large bowl, combine flour, sugar, baking powder, salt, milk and shortening; beat at low speed until moistened. Beat 2 minutes at medium speed. Add vanilla and egg whites; beat an additional 2 minutes. Pour into greased and floured pans.

2. Bake at 350°F. for 27 to 35 minutes or until toothpick inserted in center comes out clean. Cool 10 minutes. Remove from pans. Cool 1 hour or until completely cooled. Fill and frost as desired.

Tip: Cake can be baked in greased and floured 13 × 9-inch pan. Bake at 350°F. for 33 to 40 minutes. Cool 1 hour or until completely cooled.

High Altitude (Above 3,500 feet): Decrease sugar to 1 1/4 cups. Bake as directed above.

Nutrition per Serving: Serving Size: 1/12 of Recipe. Calories 270; Calories from Fat 80; Total Fat 9g; Saturated Fat 2g; Cholesterol 0mg; Sodium 330mg; Dietary Fiber 1g

Dietary Exchange: 1 1/2 Starch, 1 1/2 Fruit, 1 1/2 Fat OR 3 Carbohydrate, 1 1/2 Fat

VARIATIONS

Coconut Cake: Stir 1 cup flaked coconut into batter before pouring into greased and floured pans.

Poppy Seed Cake: Combine 1/4 cup poppy seed with an additional 1/4 cup milk; let stand 30 minutes. Add to batter with vanilla and egg whites.

Yellow Cake

COCONUT CAKE WITH LEMON FILLING

Yield: 12 servings; **Prep Time:** 30 minutes
(Ready in 2 hours 10 minutes)

This old-fashioned favorite brings back memories of Grandmother's kitchen. A cloud of fluffy coconut frosting around the top and sides conceals the sweet surprise inside: smooth, lemony filling.

CAKE

2 cups all-purpose flour
1 1/2 cups sugar
3 teaspoons baking powder
1 teaspoon salt
1 cup milk
1/2 cup shortening
2 teaspoons coconut extract or
   vanilla
4 egg whites

FILLING

3/4 cup sugar
3 tablespoons cornstarch
1/4 teaspoon salt
2/3 cup cold water
2 egg yolks
1 tablespoon margarine or butter
2 teaspoons grated lemon peel
3 tablespoons lemon juice

FROSTING

1/2 cup sugar
2 tablespoons water
2 egg whites
1 (7-oz.) jar marshmallow creme
1 cup coconut

1. Heat oven to 350°F. Grease and flour two 9-inch round cake pans. In large bowl, combine flour, 1 1/2 cups sugar, baking powder, 1 teaspoon salt, milk and shortening; beat at low speed until moistened. Beat 2 minutes at medium speed. Add coconut extract and 4 egg whites; beat an additional 2 minutes. Pour into greased and floured pans.

2. Bake at 350°F. for 20 to 30 minutes or until toothpick inserted in center comes out clean. Cool 10 minutes. Remove from pans. Cool 1 hour or until completely cooled.

3. Meanwhile, in small saucepan, combine 3/4 cup sugar, cornstarch and 1/4 teaspoon salt. Gradually stir in water until smooth. Cook over medium heat, stirring constantly, until mixture boils. Boil 1 minute, stirring constantly. Remove from heat.

4. In small bowl, beat egg yolks. Stir about 1/4 cup of hot mixture into egg yolks. Gradually stir yolk mixture into hot mixture. Cook over medium heat until mixture boils. Boil 1 minute, stirring constantly. Remove from heat; stir in margarine, lemon peel and lemon juice. Cool 30 minutes or until completely cooled.

5. In medium saucepan, combine 1/2 cup sugar, 2 tablespoons water and 2 egg whites. Cook over low heat, beating continuously with electric hand mixer at high speed until soft peaks form. Add marshmallow creme; beat until stiff peaks form.

6. Place 1 cake layer, top side down, on serving plate; spread with cooled filling. Top with remaining cake layer, top side up; frost sides and top of cake with frosting. Sprinkle coconut on top of cake.

High Altitude (Above 3,500 feet): Decrease flour to 1 3/4 cups; decrease sugar in cake to 1 1/4 cups. Bake at 375°F. for 25 to 30 minutes.

Nutrition per Serving: Serving Size: 1/12 of Recipe. Calories 470; Calories from Fat 120; Total Fat 13g; Saturated Fat 5g; Cholesterol 40mg; Sodium 420mg; Dietary Fiber 1g

Dietary Exchange: 2 Starch, 3 1/2 Fruit, 2 Fat OR 5 1/2 Carbohydrate, 2 Fat

Coconut Cake with Lemon Filling

ELEGANT SOUTHERN JAM CAKE

Yield: 16 servings; **Prep Time:** 40 minutes
(Ready in 2 hours 30 minutes)

Get out the best china and serve wedges of this very pretty four-layer specialty for an afternoon tea, wedding shower or garden party.

CAKE
1 (1 lb. 2.25-oz.) pkg. pudding-included French vanilla or white cake mix
1 (3.4-oz.) pkg. instant French vanilla pudding and pie filling mix
1 cup water
¼ cup oil
4 eggs

FROSTING AND FILLING
½ cup sugar
2 tablespoons water
2 egg whites
1 (7-oz.) jar (1½ cups) marshmallow creme
1 cup seedless blackberry or raspberry jam
Shredded coconut or additional blackberry or raspberry jam, if desired

1. Heat oven to 350°F. Grease and flour two 9-inch round cake pans. In large bowl, combine all cake ingredients; beat at low speed until moistened. Beat 2 minutes at medium speed. Pour batter into greased and floured pans.

2. Bake at 350°F. for 25 to 35 minutes or until toothpick inserted in center comes out clean. Cool 15 minutes. Remove from pans. Cool 1 hour or until completely cooled.

3. Meanwhile, in small, heavy saucepan, combine sugar, 2 tablespoons water and egg whites. Cook over low heat, beating continuously with electric hand mixer at high speed until soft peaks form. Remove from heat. Add marshmallow creme; beat until stiff peaks form.

4. To assemble cake, split each layer in half horizontally to form 4 layers. Place 1 layer, cut side up, on serving plate. Spread with ⅓ cup of the blackberry jam. Top with second cake layer, cut side down; spread with ⅓ cup jam. Top with third cake layer, cut side up; spread with remaining ⅓ cup jam. Top with remaining cake layer. Frost sides and top of cake with frosting. Sprinkle cake with coconut or swirl small dollops of jam in frosting on top of cake. Store in refrigerator.

High Altitude (Above 3,500 feet): Add ⅓ cup flour to dry cake mix; increase water in cake to 1¼ cups. Bake as directed above.

Nutrition per Serving: Serving Size: 1⁄16 of Recipe. Calories 350; Calories from Fat 80; Total Fat 9g; Saturated Fat 3g; Cholesterol 55mg; Sodium 340mg; Dietary Fiber 1g

Dietary Exchange: 1½ Starch, 2½ Fruit, 2 Fat OR 4 Carbohydrate, 2 Fat

BANANA CREAM TORTE

Yield: 12 servings; **Prep Time:** 25 minutes
(Ready in 2 hours 15 minutes)

So luscious and so easy! To intensify the flavor of the nuts, toast them on a cookie sheet in a 350°F. oven, stirring occasionally, until the nuts are fragrant and lightly browned; watch carefully to make sure they don't burn. Cool the nuts before sprinkling onto the cake.

CAKE
1 (1 lb. 2.25-oz.) pkg. pudding-included banana cake mix
1 cup water
½ cup margarine or butter, softened
3 eggs

FILLING
1 (3.4-oz.) pkg. instant banana cream pudding and pie filling mix
1½ cups cold milk
2 cups frozen whipped topping, thawed

GARNISH
¼ cup chopped walnuts

1. Heat oven to 350°F. Grease and flour two 9-inch round cake pans. In large bowl, combine all cake ingredients; beat at low speed until moistened. Beat 2 minutes at medium speed. Pour batter into greased and floured pans.

2. Bake at 350°F. for 30 to 40 minutes or until cake springs back when touched lightly in center. Cool 15 minutes. Remove from pans. Cool 1 hour or until completely cooled.

3. In large bowl, combine pudding mix and milk; beat 2 minutes at low speed. Let stand 5 minutes. Fold in whipped topping.

4. To assemble cake, split each cake layer in half horizontally to form 4 layers. Place 1 cake layer, cut side up, on serving plate. Spread with 1/4 of filling. Top with second cake layer, cut side down; spread with another 1/4 of filling. Repeat with remaining cake layers and filling, ending with filling. Sprinkle with walnuts. Store in refrigerator.

High Altitude (Above 3,500 feet): Add 3 tablespoons flour to dry cake mix. Bake at 350°F. for 25 to 35 minutes.

Nutrition per Serving: Serving Size: 1/12 of Recipe. Calories 370; Calories from Fat 160; Total Fat 18g; Saturated Fat 6g; Cholesterol 55mg; Sodium 510mg; Dietary Fiber 1g

Dietary Exchange: 1 1/2 Starch, 1 1/2 Fruit, 3 1/2 Fat OR 3 Carbohydrate, 3 1/2 Fat

DEVIL'S FOOD CAKE

Yield: 12 servings; **Prep Time:** 15 minutes
(Ready in 2 hours)

For many people, young and old alike, devil's food is the chocolate cake, perfect to celebrate any occasion. This American tradition may get its name from the slightly reddish color of some recipes, owing to the addition of red food color.

2 cups all-purpose flour

1 1/4 teaspoons baking soda

1/2 teaspoon salt

1 1/2 cups sugar

1/2 cup margarine or butter, softened

1 teaspoon vanilla

2 eggs

4 oz. unsweetened chocolate, cut into pieces, melted

1 cup milk

1. Heat oven to 350°F. Grease and flour two 8 or 9-inch round cake pans.* In medium bowl, combine flour, baking soda and salt; mix well.

2. In large bowl, combine sugar and margarine; beat until light and fluffy. Add vanilla and eggs; blend well. Stir in chocolate. Alternately add dry ingredients and milk, beating well after each addition. Pour batter into greased and floured pans.

3. Bake at 350°F. for 27 to 35 minutes or until toothpick inserted in center comes out clean. Cool 10 minutes. Remove from pans. Cool 1 hour or until completely cooled. Fill and frost as desired.

*Tip: Cake can be baked in greased and floured 13 × 9-inch pan. Bake at 350°F. for 33 to 40 minutes. Cool 1 hour or until completely cooled.

High Altitude (Above 3,500 feet): Decrease sugar to 1 1/4 cups. Bake as directed above.

Nutrition per Serving: Serving Size: 1/12 of Recipe. Calories 330; Calories from Fat 130; Total Fat 14g; Saturated Fat 5g; Cholesterol 35mg; Sodium 330mg; Dietary Fiber 2g

Dietary Exchange: 1 1/2 Starch, 1 1/2 Fruit, 2 1/2 Fat OR 3 Carbohydrate, 2 1/2 Fat

BLACK FOREST CAKE

✦

Yield: 12 servings; **Prep Time:** 30 minutes
(Ready in 2 hours 30 minutes)

A German tradition, Black Forest Cake pairs rich chocolate cake with cherries. With its topping of whipped cream and chocolate curls, it makes a stunning company dessert.

CAKE
1 (1 lb. 2.25-oz.) pkg. pudding-included dark chocolate cake mix
1 1/4 cups water
1/3 cup oil
2 eggs

FILLING
1 (21-oz.) can cherry pie filling
1/2 teaspoon almond extract

FROSTING
1 pint (2 cups) whipping cream
1/2 cup powdered sugar
2 tablespoons brandy
Chocolate curls, if desired

1. Heat oven to 350°F. Grease and flour two 8 or 9-inch round cake pans. In large bowl, combine all cake ingredients; beat at low speed until moistened. Beat 2 minutes at medium speed. Pour batter into greased and floured pans.

2. Bake at 350°F. for 35 to 45 minutes or until cake springs back when touched lightly in center. Cool 15 minutes. Remove from pans. Cool 1 hour or until completely cooled.

3. In small bowl, combine filling ingredients; mix well.

4. In medium bowl, beat whipping cream at high speed until slightly thickened. Gradually add powdered sugar, beating until stiff peaks form. Fold in brandy.

5. Place 1 cake layer, top side down, on serving plate; spread 1 cup filling to within 1 inch of edge. Top with second cake layer, top side up. Frost sides and top with whipped cream. Spoon remaining filling in center of top of cake. Garnish with chocolate curls. Store in refrigerator.

High Altitude (Above 3,500 feet): Add 1/4 cup flour to dry cake mix; increase water to 1 1/3 cups. Bake as directed above.

Nutrition per Serving: Serving Size: 1/12 of Recipe. Calories 480; Calories from Fat 230; Total Fat 26g; Saturated Fat 12g; Cholesterol 90mg; Sodium 420mg; Dietary Fiber 2g

Dietary Exchange: 1 Starch, 3 Fruit, 5 Fat OR 4 Carbohydrate, 5 Fat

Black Forest Cake

QUICK RED VELVET CAKE

Yield: 16 servings; Prep Time: 30 minutes
(Ready in 2 hours 20 minutes)

Red food color keeps the color of this festive cake deep, even after the mix is enriched with sour cream. The butter-rich, intensely vanilla frosting gains extra smoothness from the cooked flour-milk base.

CAKE

1 (1 lb. 2.25-oz.) pkg. pudding-included German chocolate cake mix
1 cup sour cream
½ cup water
¼ cup oil
1 (1-oz.) bottle red food color
3 eggs

FROSTING

½ cup all-purpose flour
1½ cups milk
1½ cups sugar
1½ cups margarine or butter, softened
1 tablespoon vanilla

1. Heat oven to 350°F. Grease and flour two 9-inch round cake pans. In large bowl, combine all cake ingredients; beat at low speed until moistened. Beat 2 minutes at medium speed. Pour batter into greased and floured pans.

2. Bake at 350°F. for 25 to 35 minutes or until cake springs back when touched lightly in center. Cool 15 minutes. Remove from pans. Cool 1 hour or until completely cooled.

3. Meanwhile, in medium saucepan, combine flour and milk. Cook over medium heat until mixture is very thick, stirring constantly. Cover surface with plastic wrap; cool 30 minutes or until completely cooled.

4. In large bowl, combine sugar and margarine; beat until light and fluffy. Gradually add flour mixture by tablespoonfuls, beating at high speed until smooth. Beat in vanilla.

5. Place 1 cake layer, top side down, on serving plate; spread with 1 cup frosting. Top with second layer, top side up. Frost sides and top of cake with frosting. Store in refrigerator.

High Altitude (Above 3,500 feet): Add ¼ cup flour to dry cake mix. Bake as directed above.

Nutrition per Serving: Serving Size: ¹⁄₁₆ of Recipe. Calories 460; Calories from Fat 250; Total Fat 28g; Saturated Fat 7g; Cholesterol 50mg; Sodium 430mg; Dietary Fiber 1g

Dietary Exchange: 1½ Starch, 2 Fruit, 5 Fat OR 3½ Carbohydrate, 5 Fat

COOKIES 'N CREAM CAKE

Yield: 12 servings; Prep Time: 25 minutes
(Ready in 2 hours 15 minutes)

Here's the perfect cake for a potluck supper, school party or birthday celebration. Crushed cookies spike an ordinary white cake mix with flavor and fun.

CAKE

1 (1 lb. 2.25-oz.) pkg. pudding-included white cake mix
1¼ cups water
¼ cup oil
3 egg whites
1 cup coarsely crushed creme-filled chocolate sandwich cookies

FROSTING

3 cups powdered sugar
¾ cup shortening
¼ cup milk
1 teaspoon vanilla

1. Heat oven to 350°F. Grease and flour two 9 or 8-inch round cake pans.* In large bowl, combine all cake ingredients except crushed cookies; beat at low speed until moistened. Beat 2 minutes at medium speed. With spoon, stir in cookies. Pour batter into greased and floured pans.

2. Bake at 350°F. for 25 to 35 minutes or until toothpick inserted in center comes out clean. Cool 15 minutes. Remove from pans. Cool 1 hour or until completely cooled.

3. In small bowl, combine all frosting ingredients; beat until smooth. To assemble cake, place 1 cake layer, top side down, on serving plate; spread evenly with about ¼ of frosting. Top with remaining cake layer, top side up. Spread sides and top of cake with remaining frosting. Garnish as desired.

Tip: Cake can be baked in greased and floured 13×9-inch pan. Bake at 350°F. for 30 to 40 minutes. Cool 1 hour or until completely cooled.

High Altitude (Above 3,500 feet): Add 3 tablespoons flour to dry cake mix; increase water to 1⅓ cups. Bake at 375°F. for 20 to 30 minutes.

Nutrition per Serving: Serving Size: ¹⁄₁₂ of Recipe. Calories 520; Calories from Fat 220; Total Fat 24g; Saturated Fat 5g; Cholesterol 0mg; Sodium 380mg; Dietary Fiber 1g

Dietary Exchange: 1 Starch, 4 Fruit, 4½ Fat OR 5 Carbohydrate, 4½ Fat

Cookies 'n Cream Cake

S'MORE SNACK CAKE

♦

Yield: 16 servings; **Prep Time:** 25 minutes
(Ready in 2 hours 15 minutes)

Anyone who's ever had a cookout with kids is probably familiar with "s'mores" (so named because everyone always asks for "some more, please"). A toasted marshmallow is placed atop a graham cracker and a square of chocolate, melting the whole thing into a delightfully gooey campfire dessert. Re-create those special flavors indoors with this easy sheet cake.

1 cup all-purpose flour
1 1/2 cups graham cracker crumbs
    (24 squares)
1 teaspoon baking powder
1/2 teaspoon baking soda
1/2 teaspoon salt
1 cup firmly packed brown sugar
1/2 cup shortening
3 eggs
1 cup milk
1 cup miniature semi-sweet
    chocolate chips
1 (7-oz.) jar (1 1/2 cups)
    marshmallow creme

1. Heat oven to 350°F. Grease and flour 13×9-inch pan. In medium bowl, combine flour, graham cracker crumbs, baking powder, baking soda and salt; mix well.

2. In large bowl, combine brown sugar, shortening and eggs; beat until well blended. Add dry ingredients and milk; beat at low speed until well blended. Beat 1 minute at medium speed. Stir in 2/3 cup of the chocolate chips. Spoon and spread batter evenly into greased and floured pan.

3. Bake at 350°F. for 25 to 35 minutes or until toothpick inserted in center comes out clean. Cool 15 minutes.

4. Meanwhile, in small saucepan over low heat, melt remaining 1/3 cup chocolate chips. Spoon teaspoonfuls of marshmallow creme onto top of warm cake; carefully spread with knife dipped in hot water. Drizzle with melted chocolate; swirl chocolate through marshmallow creme to marble. Cool 1 hour or until completely cooled.

High Altitude (Above 3,500 feet): Increase flour to 1 cup plus 2 tablespoons. Bake at 375°F. for 20 to 30 minutes.

Nutrition per Serving: Serving Size: 1/16 of Recipe. Calories 300; Calories from Fat 110; Total Fat 12g; Saturated Fat 4g; Cholesterol 40mg; Sodium 220mg; Dietary Fiber 1g

Dietary Exchange: 1 1/2 Starch, 1 1/2 Fruit, 2 Fat OR 3 Carbohydrate, 2 Fat

HOT FUDGE SWIRL CAKE

♦

Yield: 36 servings; **Prep Time:** 30 minutes
(Ready in 2 hours)

Here's one of those crowd-pleasing desserts that's sure to draw "oohs" and "ahs," with a fancy-looking but deceptively easy topping of marbleized vanilla frosting and hot fudge sauce.

1 (1 lb. 2.25-oz.) pkg. pudding-
    included devil's food cake mix
1 1/4 cups water
1/4 cup oil
3 eggs
1/2 cup miniature semi-sweet
    chocolate chips
1 (16-oz.) jar (1 1/2 cups) hot fudge
    ice cream topping, warmed
1 (16-oz.) can vanilla frosting

1. Heat oven to 350°F. Grease and flour 15×10×1-inch baking pan. In large bowl, combine cake mix, water, oil and eggs; beat at low speed until moistened. Beat 2 minutes at medium speed. Stir in chocolate chips. Pour into greased and floured pan.

2. Bake at 350°F. for 18 to 28 minutes or until cake springs back when touched lightly in center. Cool 5 minutes. Gently spoon and spread 1 1/4 cups of the warm fudge topping evenly over cake. Cool 1 hour or until completely cooled.

Hot Fudge Swirl Cake

3. Carefully spoon vanilla frosting onto fudge layer on cake; spread evenly to edges. Spoon remaining ¼ cup warm fudge topping in teaspoonfuls over frosting; swirl with back of spoon to marble.

High Altitude (Above 3,500 feet): Add ¼ cup flour to dry cake mix. Bake as directed above.

Nutrition per Serving: Serving Size: ¹⁄₃₆ of Recipe. Calories 200; Calories from Fat 70; Total Fat 8g; Saturated Fat 2g; Cholesterol 20mg; Sodium 160mg; Dietary Fiber 1g

Dietary Exchange: 1 Starch, 1 Fruit, 1 ½ Fat OR 2 Carbohydrate, 1 ½ Fat

MISSISSIPPI MUD CAKE

Yield: 16 servings; **Prep Time:** 20 minutes
(Ready in 1 hour 15 minutes)

Marshmallow creme, spread onto the cake while warm, forms a delicious layer of sweetness swirled into the fudge frosting.

CAKE
1 (1 lb. 2.25-oz.) pkg. pudding-
   included devil's food cake mix
1 ¼ cups water
½ cup oil
3 eggs
1 cup chopped pecans
1 (7-oz.) jar (1 ½ cups)
   marshmallow creme

FROSTING
1 (16-oz.) can chocolate fudge
   frosting
1 to 2 tablespoons milk

1. Heat oven to 350°F. Grease and flour bottom only of 13×9-inch pan. In large bowl, combine cake mix, water, oil and eggs; beat at low speed until moistened. Beat 2 minutes at medium speed. Pour batter into greased and floured pan. Sprinkle pecans evenly over batter.

2. Bake at 350°F. for 30 to 40 minutes or until toothpick inserted in center comes out clean. Remove cake from oven. Spoon marshmallow creme evenly over top of hot cake; carefully spread to cover cake. Cool cake 15 minutes.

3. In small bowl, combine frosting and enough milk for desired spreading consistency; blend well. Drop frosting by spoonfuls onto cake; spread gently to cover. Lightly swirl to marble. Cool 1 hour or until completely cooled.

High Altitude (Above 3,500 feet): Add ¼ cup flour to dry cake mix; increase water to 1 ⅓ cups. Bake as directed above.

Nutrition per Serving: Serving Size: 1/16 of Recipe. Calories 410; Calories from Fat 180; Total Fat 20g; Saturated Fat 4g; Cholesterol 40mg; Sodium 330mg; Dietary Fiber 2g

Dietary Exchange: 2 Starch, 1 ½ Fruit, 3 ½ Fat OR 3 ½ Carbohydrate, 3 ½ Fat

FROSTED BANANA SNACK CAKE

Yield: 9 servings; **Prep Time:** 30 minutes
(Ready in 2 hours)

Sweet spices complement the natural sweetness of banana; buttermilk imparts both flavor and tenderness.

CAKE
¾ cup sugar
⅓ cup margarine or butter,
   softened
¾ cup mashed ripe bananas
¼ cup buttermilk*
1 teaspoon vanilla
1 egg
1 ¼ cups all-purpose flour
1 teaspoon baking powder
½ teaspoon baking soda
½ teaspoon salt
½ teaspoon cinnamon
⅛ teaspoon cloves
⅛ teaspoon nutmeg
¼ cup chopped walnuts or pecans

FROSTING
2 cups powdered sugar
1 (3-oz.) pkg. cream cheese,
   softened
2 tablespoons margarine or butter,
   softened
1 tablespoon milk
½ teaspoon vanilla

1. Heat oven to 350°F. Grease and flour 8 or 9-inch square pan. In large bowl, combine sugar and ⅓ cup margarine; beat until light and fluffy. Add bananas, buttermilk, vanilla and egg; blend well. Add all remaining cake ingredients except walnuts; mix well. Stir in walnuts. Pour batter into greased and floured pan.

2. Bake at 350°F. for 25 to 30 minutes or until cake is golden brown and toothpick inserted in center comes out clean. Cool 1 hour or until completely cooled.

3. In medium bowl, combine all frosting ingredients; beat until smooth and creamy. Spread over cooled cake. Store in refrigerator.

*Tip: To substitute for buttermilk, use ¾ teaspoon vinegar or lemon juice plus milk to make ¼ cup.

High Altitude (Above 3,500 feet): Decrease sugar to ½ cup. Bake as directed above.

Nutrition per Serving: Serving Size: 1/9 of Recipe. Calories 410; Calories from Fat 140; Total Fat 16g; Saturated Fat 4g; Cholesterol 35mg; Sodium 400mg; Dietary Fiber 1g

Dietary Exchange: 1 Starch, 3 Fruit, 3 Fat OR 4 Carbohydrate, 3 Fat

PINEAPPLE-COCONUT CAKE SQUARES

Yield: 16 servings; **Prep Time:** 20 minutes
(Ready in 2 hours)

Sweet pineapple and coconut bring tropical flavor to purchased cake mix.

CAKE
1 (1 lb. 2.25-oz.) pkg. pudding-included white cake mix
1 (20-oz.) can crushed pineapple, well drained, reserving 1 cup liquid
1/3 cup oil
3 eggs

TOPPING
1 (3.4-oz.) pkg. instant vanilla pudding and pie filling mix
1 1/2 cups cold milk
2 cups frozen whipped topping, thawed
1 cup coconut
Reserved drained pineapple

1. Heat oven to 350°F. Grease and flour 13×9-inch pan. In large bowl, combine cake mix, 1 cup reserved pineapple liquid, oil and eggs; beat at low speed until moistened. Beat 2 minutes at medium speed. With spoon, stir in 1/2 cup of the drained pineapple. Pour batter into greased and floured pan.

2. Bake at 350°F. for 30 to 40 minutes or until cake springs back when touched lightly in center. Cool 1 hour or until completely cooled.

3. In large bowl, combine pudding mix and milk; beat at low speed just until blended. Fold in whipped topping; spread over cooled cake. Top with coconut and remaining pineapple. Store in refrigerator.

High Altitude (Above 3,500 feet): Add 1/3 cup flour to dry cake mix. Bake as directed above.

Nutrition per Serving: Serving Size: 1/16 of Recipe. Calories 300; Calories from Fat 120; Total Fat 13g; Saturated Fat 6g; Cholesterol 40mg; Sodium 330mg; Dietary Fiber 1g

Dietary Exchange: 1 Starch, 2 Fruit, 2 1/2 Fat OR 3 Carbohydrate, 2 1/2 Fat

FUDGY CREME DE MENTHE CAKE

Yield: 16 servings; **Prep Time:** 20 minutes
(Ready in 2 hours)

The coolness of mint is so refreshing paired with the flavor of fudge.

CAKE
1 (1 lb. 2.25-oz.) pkg. pudding-included chocolate cake mix
1 1/4 cups water
1/4 cup oil
2 eggs
3 tablespoons creme de menthe syrup

TOPPING
1 (16-oz.) jar (1 1/2 cups) hot fudge ice cream topping, slightly warmed
2 cups whipping cream, whipped
1/4 cup creme de menthe syrup
20 foil-wrapped rectangular mints, coarsely chopped

1. Heat oven to 350°F. Grease and flour 13×9-inch pan. In large bowl, combine all cake ingredients; beat at low speed until moistened. Beat 2 minutes at medium speed. Pour into greased and floured pan.

2. Bake at 350°F. for 30 to 40 minutes or until toothpick inserted in center comes out clean. Cool 1 hour or until completely cooled.

3. Gently spread hot fudge topping over cooled cake. In small bowl, gently fold together whipped cream and 1/4 cup creme de menthe syrup. Spread over ice cream topping. Top with chopped mints. Store in refrigerator.

High Altitude (Above 3,500 feet): Add 1/4 cup flour to dry cake mix. Bake as directed above.

Nutrition per Serving: Serving Size: 1/16 of Recipe. Calories 440; Calories from Fat 210; Total Fat 23g; Saturated Fat 11g; Cholesterol 70mg; Sodium 260mg; Dietary Fiber 1g

Dietary Exchange: 1 1/2 Starch, 2 Fruit, 4 1/2 Fat OR 3 1/2 Carbohydrate, 4 1/2 Fat

OLD-FASHIONED CARROT CAKE

✦

Yield: 16 servings; **Prep Time:** 20 minutes
(Ready in 2 hours 10 minutes)

When you don't have time to grate carrots from scratch, doctor up a carrot cake mix with crushed pineapple, raisins and nuts. Blending extra cream cheese with purchased frosting makes a smooth, less-sweet frosting that's just right for the moist cake.

CAKE

1 (1 lb. 2.25-oz.) pkg. pudding-
  included carrot cake mix
3/4 cup water
2/3 cup oil
4 eggs
1/2 cup coconut
1/2 cup finely chopped nuts
1/2 cup raisins
1 (8-oz.) can crushed pineapple in
  unsweetened juice, drained

FROSTING

1 (16-oz.) can vanilla or cream
  cheese frosting
1 (3-oz.) pkg. cream cheese,
  softened

1. Heat oven to 350°F. Grease and flour 13 × 9-inch pan. In large bowl, combine cake mix, water, oil and eggs; beat at low speed until moistened. Beat 2 minutes at medium speed. Add coconut, nuts, raisins and pineapple; mix well. Pour batter into greased and floured pan.

2. Bake at 350°F. for 40 to 50 minutes or until toothpick inserted in center comes out clean. Cool 1 hour or until completely cooled.

3. In small bowl, combine frosting and cream cheese; beat until smooth and fluffy. Spread over cooled cake. Store in refrigerator.

High Altitude (Above 3,500 feet): Add 1/4 cup flour to dry cake mix. Increase water to 1 cup; decrease oil to 1/3 cup. Bake as directed above. (Cake may crumble slightly when cut.)

Nutrition per Serving: Serving Size: 1/16 of Recipe. Calories 420; Calories from Fat 200; Total Fat 22g; Saturated Fat 5g; Cholesterol 55mg; Sodium 290mg; Dietary Fiber 1g

Dietary Exchange: 1 1/2 Starch, 2 Fruit, 4 Fat OR 3 1/2 Carbohydrate, 4 Fat

CARROT CAKE WITH CREAMY COCONUT FROSTING

Yield: 24 servings; **Prep Time:** 30 minutes
(Ready in 2 hours 30 minutes)

This is a wonderful cake, brimming with texture thanks to crushed pineapple, raisins, nuts and, of course, grated carrots. Coconut gives a special twist to the classic cream cheese frosting, which has just enough tang to balance the cake's sweetness.

CAKE

2 1/2 cups all-purpose flour
2 teaspoons baking soda
1 teaspoon salt
1 teaspoon cinnamon, if desired
2 cups sugar
1 cup oil
2 teaspoons vanilla
2 eggs
2 cups shredded carrots
1 (8 1/4-oz.) can crushed pineapple,
  well drained
1/2 cup raisins
1/2 cup chopped nuts

FROSTING

1 (8-oz.) pkg. cream cheese,
  softened
2 1/2 cups powdered sugar
6 tablespoons margarine or butter,
  softened
2 teaspoons vanilla
1 cup coconut
1/2 cup chopped nuts

Carrot Cake with Creamy Coconut Frosting

1. Heat oven to 350°F. Grease and flour 13×9-inch pan. In medium bowl, combine flour, baking soda, salt and cinnamon; mix well.

2. In large bowl, combine sugar, oil, 2 teaspoons vanilla and eggs; beat well. Add flour mixture; mix well. Stir in carrots, pineapple, raisins and ¹/₂ cup nuts. Pour and spread batter into greased and floured pan.

3. Bake at 350°F. for 50 to 60 minutes or until cake springs back when touched lightly in center. Cool 1 hour or until completely cooled.

4. In large bowl, combine cream cheese, powdered sugar, margarine and 2 teaspoons vanilla; beat until smooth. Stir in coconut and ¹/₂ cup nuts. Spread over cooled cake.

High Altitude (Above 3,500 feet): Increase flour to 2 ³/₄ cups; decrease sugar in cake to 1 ¹/₂ cups. Bake as directed above.

Nutrition per Serving: Serving Size: ¹/₂₄ of Recipe. Calories 380; Calories from Fat 180; Total Fat 20g; Saturated Fat 5g; Cholesterol 30mg; Sodium 270mg; Dietary Fiber 1g

Dietary Exchange: 1 Starch, 2 Fruit, 4 Fat OR 3 Carbohydrate, 4 Fat

LEMON-ORANGE PICNIC CAKE

Yield: 9 servings; Prep Time: 15 minutes
(Ready in 1 hour 50 minutes)

Easy-to-pack cakes are always welcome additions to the picnic basket or lunch box. Here, a citrusy sugar topping provides a touch of sweetness without the worry of frosting melting or sticking to the wrapping.

CAKE
1 cup all-purpose flour
3/4 cup sugar
1 1/2 teaspoons grated orange peel
1 teaspoon grated lemon peel
1 teaspoon baking powder
1/4 teaspoon salt
1/3 cup skim milk
1/4 cup shortening
2 tablespoons orange juice
3 egg whites

TOPPING
1/4 cup sugar
2 teaspoons lemon juice
1 teaspoon orange juice

1. Heat oven to 350°F. Spray bottom only of 8-inch square pan with nonstick cooking spray. In large bowl, combine all cake ingredients; beat at low speed until moistened. Beat 2 minutes at medium speed. Pour into sprayed pan.

2. Bake at 350°F. for 25 to 32 minutes or until cake is light golden brown and toothpick inserted in center comes out clean.

3. In small bowl, combine all topping ingredients; spread over warm cake. Cool 1 hour or until completely cooled.

High Altitude (Above 3,500 feet): Decrease sugar in cake to 2/3 cup. Bake as directed above.

Nutrition per Serving: Serving Size: 1/9 of Recipe. Calories 200; Calories from Fat 50; Total Fat 6g; Saturated Fat 1g; Cholesterol 0mg; Sodium 135mg; Dietary Fiber 0g

Dietary Exchange: 1 Starch, 1 Fruit, 1 Fat OR 2 Carbohydrate, 1 Fat

BLUEBERRY CAKE

Yield: 16 servings; Prep Time: 15 minutes
(Ready in 1 hour 55 minutes)

Serve squares of this cinnamon-scented cake as a change of pace from muffins at brunch. Tossing the blueberries with a small amount of flour before they're folded into the batter keeps the berries evenly distributed as the cake bakes.

1 3/4 cups all-purpose flour
1 1/2 teaspoons baking soda
1 teaspoon cinnamon
3/4 cup sugar
1/2 cup margarine or butter, softened
1/3 cup buttermilk*
1 teaspoon vanilla
2 eggs
1 cup fresh or frozen blueberries (do not thaw)
1 tablespoon all-purpose flour
1/2 teaspoon powdered sugar

1. Heat oven to 375°F. Grease and flour 9-inch square pan. In medium bowl, combine 1 3/4 cups flour, baking soda and cinnamon; mix well.

2. In large bowl, combine sugar and margarine; beat well. Add buttermilk, vanilla, eggs and flour mixture; beat at low speed until moistened. Beat 1 to 2 minutes at medium speed or until batter is smooth.

3. In small bowl, combine blueberries and 1 tablespoon flour; gently fold into cake batter. Pour and spread batter in greased and floured pan.

4. Bake at 375°F. for 30 to 40 minutes or until toothpick inserted in center comes out clean. Cool 1 hour or until completely cooled. Sprinkle with powdered sugar.

Tip: To substitute for buttermilk, use 1 teaspoon vinegar or lemon juice plus milk to make 1/3 cup.

High Altitude (Above 3,500 feet): Increase flour in batter to 2 cups. Bake as directed above.

Nutrition per Serving: Serving Size: 1/16 of Recipe. Calories 160; Calories from Fat 60; Total Fat 7g; Saturated Fat 1g; Cholesterol 25mg; Sodium 200mg; Dietary Fiber 1g

Dietary Exchange: 1 Starch, 1/2 Fruit, 1 Fat OR 1 1/2 Carbohydrate, 1 Fat

Blueberry Cake

BURNT SUGAR-ALMOND CAKE

✦

Yield: 24 servings; **Prep Time:** 20 minutes
(Ready in 2 hours 15 minutes)

A cake mix becomes a bakery-style delicacy with a nutty brown sugar topping that browns to bubbly goodness under the broiler.

1 (1 lb. 2.25-oz.) pkg. pudding-included yellow cake mix
1 ¼ cups water
¼ cup oil
1 teaspoon almond extract
3 eggs
1 ¼ cups firmly packed brown sugar
1 cup butter
2 cups sliced almonds

1. Heat oven to 350°F. Grease and lightly flour 13×9-inch pan. In large bowl, combine cake mix, water, oil, almond extract and eggs; beat at low speed until moistened. Beat 2 minutes at medium speed. Pour batter into greased and floured pan.

2. Bake at 350°F. for 30 to 40 minutes or until toothpick inserted in center comes out clean. Cool 10 minutes.

3. Meanwhile, in medium saucepan, combine brown sugar and butter; melt over low heat, stirring constantly. Stir in almonds. Spread evenly over cake.

4. Broil 4 to 6 inches from heat for 1 to 2 minutes or until bubbly and golden brown. Cut into squares while still warm. Cool 1 hour or until completely cooled.

High Altitude (Above 3,500 feet): Add ⅓ cup flour to dry cake mix. Bake as directed above.

Nutrition per Serving: Serving Size: ¹⁄₂₄ of Recipe. Calories 290; Calories from Fat 150; Total Fat 17g; Saturated Fat 6g; Cholesterol 45mg; Sodium 230mg; Dietary Fiber 1g

Dietary Exchange: 1 Starch, 1 Fruit, 3 Fat OR 2 Carbohydrate, 3 Fat

CARAMEL-APPLE-RAISIN CAKE

✦

Yield: 24 servings; **Prep Time:** 20 minutes
(Ready in 2 hours 30 minutes)

Popular flavors combine in this family favorite.

CAKE
2 ½ cups all-purpose flour
2 teaspoons baking powder
4 teaspoons pumpkin pie spice
¾ teaspoon salt
1 ½ cups sugar
¾ cup shortening
1 ½ teaspoons vanilla
2 eggs
1 cup milk
2 Granny Smith apples, peeled, chopped (about 2 ½ cups)
½ cup raisins

GLAZE
1 cup firmly packed brown sugar
½ cup whipping cream
1 ½ cups powdered sugar

1. Heat oven to 350°F. Grease and lightly flour 13×9-inch pan. In medium bowl, combine flour, baking powder, pumpkin pie spice and salt; mix well.

2. In large bowl, combine sugar, shortening and vanilla; beat until light and fluffy. Add eggs 1 at a time, beating well after each addition. Alternately add dry ingredients and milk to shortening mixture, beginning and ending with dry ingredients. Stir in apples and raisins. Pour and spread batter into greased and floured pan.

3. Bake at 350°F. for 45 to 55 minutes or until toothpick inserted in center comes out clean. Cool 10 minutes.

4. Meanwhile, in medium saucepan, combine brown sugar and cream. Bring to a rolling boil over high heat, stirring constantly. Remove from heat; stir in powdered sugar until smooth. Cool 5 minutes, stirring occasionally. Pour glaze over cake; spread evenly. Cool 1 hour or until completely cooled.

High Altitude (Above 3,500 feet): Decrease sugar to 1 ¼ cups. Bake as directed above.

Nutrition per Serving: Serving Size: ¹⁄₂₄ of Recipe. Calories 250; Calories from Fat 80; Total Fat 9g; Saturated Fat 3g; Cholesterol 25mg; Sodium 125mg; Dietary Fiber 1g

Dietary Exchange: ½ Starch, 2 Fruit, 2 Fat OR 2 ½ Carbohydrate, 2 Fat

**Burnt Sugar-Almond Cake,
Caramel-Apple-Raisin Cake**

OLD-FASHIONED OATMEAL CAKE WITH BROILED TOPPING

◆

Yield: 16 servings; **Prep Time:** 30 minutes
(Ready in 2 hours 15 minutes)

Oatmeal gives this cake the slightly chewy texture of a country farmhouse dessert.

CAKE
1½ cups quick-cooking rolled oats
1¼ cups boiling water
1 cup sugar
1 cup firmly packed brown sugar
½ cup margarine or butter, softened
1 teaspoon vanilla
3 eggs
1½ cups all-purpose flour
1 teaspoon baking soda
½ teaspoon baking powder
½ teaspoon salt
1½ teaspoons cinnamon
½ teaspoon nutmeg

TOPPING
⅔ cup firmly packed brown sugar
¼ cup margarine or butter, melted
3 tablespoons half-and-half or milk
1 cup coconut
½ cup chopped nuts

1. In small bowl, combine rolled oats and boiling water; let stand 20 minutes.

2. Meanwhile, heat oven to 350°F. Grease and flour 13×9-inch pan. In large bowl, combine sugar, 1 cup brown sugar and ½ cup margarine; beat until light and fluffy. Add vanilla and eggs; blend well. Add oatmeal and all remaining cake ingredients; mix well. Pour batter into greased and floured pan.

3. Bake at 350°F. for 35 to 45 minutes or until toothpick inserted in center comes out clean.

4. In small bowl, combine ⅔ cup brown sugar, ¼ cup margarine and half-and-half; beat at high speed until smooth. Stir in coconut and nuts. Spoon over warm cake; spread to cover.

5. Broil 4 to 6 inches from heat for 1 to 2 minutes or until bubbly and light golden brown. Cool 1 hour or until completely cooled.

High Altitude (Above 3,500 feet): Decrease brown sugar in cake to ¾ cup; increase flour to 1½ cups plus 3 tablespoons. Bake at 375°F. for 30 to 40 minutes.

Nutrition per Serving: Serving Size: 1/16 of Recipe. Calories 350; Calories from Fat 130; Total Fat 14g; Saturated Fat 4g; Cholesterol 40mg; Sodium 300mg; Dietary Fiber 2g

Dietary Exchange: 1½ Starch, 2 Fruit, 2½ Fat OR 3½ Carbohydrate, 2½ Fat

PUMPKIN GINGERBREAD WITH CARAMEL SAUCE

Yield: 12 servings; **Prep Time:** 20 minutes
(Ready in 1 hour 10 minutes)

Cinnamon, ginger and cloves provide a sweet fragrance as the pumpkin cake bakes. For this recipe, purchase plain canned pumpkin rather than "pumpkin pie filling," which contains spices.

GINGERBREAD
2¼ cups all-purpose flour
½ cup sugar
⅔ cup margarine or butter
¾ cup coarsely chopped pecans
1 teaspoon baking soda
1½ teaspoons ginger
½ teaspoon cinnamon
¼ teaspoon salt
¼ teaspoon cloves
¾ cup buttermilk*
½ cup light molasses
½ cup canned pumpkin
1 egg

SAUCE
½ cup margarine or butter
1¼ cups firmly packed brown sugar
2 tablespoons light corn syrup
½ cup whipping cream

1. Heat oven to 350°F. In large bowl, combine flour and sugar; mix well. With pastry blender or fork, cut in ⅔ cup margarine until mixture resembles fine crumbs. Stir in pecans. Press 1¼ cups crumb mixture in bottom of ungreased 9-inch square pan.

2. To remaining crumb mixture, add all remaining gingerbread ingredients; mix well. Pour evenly into crust-lined pan.

3. Bake at 350°F. for 40 to 50 minutes or until toothpick inserted in center comes out clean.

4. Melt ½ cup margarine in medium saucepan. Stir in brown sugar and corn syrup. Bring to a boil. Cook about 1 minute or until sugar dissolves, stirring constantly. Stir in whipping cream; return to a boil. Remove from heat. Serve warm sauce over warm gingerbread. If desired, top with ice cream and sprinkle with chopped pecans.

*Tip: To substitute for buttermilk, use 2¼ teaspoons vinegar or lemon juice plus milk to make ¾ cup.

High Altitude (Above 3,500 feet): Add 3 tablespoons flour to remaining crumb mixture. Bake as directed above.

Nutrition per Serving: Serving Size: ¹⁄₁₂ of Recipe. Calories 520; Calories from Fat 240; Total Fat 27g; Saturated Fat 6g; Cholesterol 30mg; Sodium 400mg; Dietary Fiber 2g

Dietary Exchange: 1½ Starch, 3 Fruit, 5 Fat OR 4½ Carbohydrate, 5 Fat

Pumpkin Gingerbread with Caramel Sauce

GINGERBREAD WITH LEMON SAUCE

✦

Yield: 9 servings; **Prep Time:** 20 minutes
(Ready in 50 minutes)

Nothing fancy, nothing phony about this warm dessert. It's just honest-to-goodness cake-style gingerbread with a pleasing lemon topping. Serve piping hot tea with lemon alongside.

GINGERBREAD
1 cup all-purpose flour
⅓ cup wheat germ
¼ cup firmly packed brown sugar
¾ teaspoon ginger
¾ teaspoon cinnamon
½ teaspoon baking powder
½ teaspoon baking soda
½ teaspoon allspice
½ cup unsweetened apple juice
⅓ cup molasses
¼ cup oil
¼ cup refrigerated or frozen fat-free egg product, thawed, or 1 egg

SAUCE
¼ cup sugar
2 teaspoons cornstarch
½ cup hot water
1 tablespoon lemon juice
1 teaspoon grated lemon peel

1. Heat oven to 350°F. Grease bottom only of 8-inch square pan. In large bowl, combine flour, wheat germ, brown sugar, ginger, cinnamon, baking powder, baking soda and allspice; mix well. Add all remaining gingerbread ingredients; blend well. Pour into greased pan.

2. Bake at 350°F. for 30 to 40 minutes or until toothpick inserted in center comes out clean.

3. Meanwhile, in medium saucepan, combine sugar and cornstarch. Gradually stir in hot water. Cook over medium heat until mixture comes to a boil and is slightly thickened and clear, stirring constantly. Stir in lemon juice and lemon peel. Serve warm sauce over warm gingerbread.

High Altitude (Above 3,500 feet): Increase flour to 1 cup plus 2 tablespoons. Bake as directed above.

Nutrition per Serving: Serving Size: ⅑ of Recipe. Calories 220; Calories from Fat 60; Total Fat 7g; Saturated Fat 1g; Cholesterol 0mg; Sodium 115mg; Dietary Fiber 1g

Dietary Exchange: 1 Starch, 1½ Fruit, 1 Fat OR 2½ Carbohydrate, 1 Fat

UPSIDE-DOWN GINGERBREAD

Yield: 9 servings; **Prep Time:** 30 minutes
(Ready in 1 hour 55 minutes)

Turn your traditional notions of gingerbread topsy-turvy with a spicy cake topped with pecans, pineapple and cranberries.

TOPPING
½ cup firmly packed brown sugar
¼ cup margarine or butter, melted
1 (8-oz.) can pineapple chunks in unsweetened juice, drained
¾ cup fresh or frozen cranberries
¼ cup chopped pecans

GINGERBREAD
1⅓ cups all-purpose flour
½ teaspoon baking powder
½ teaspoon baking soda
¼ teaspoon salt
¾ teaspoon cinnamon
¾ teaspoon ginger
½ teaspoon allspice
½ cup firmly packed brown sugar
½ cup margarine or butter, softened
½ cup boiling water
½ cup molasses
1 egg, slightly beaten

Upside-Down Gingerbread

1. Heat oven to 350°F. In small bowl, combine ¹/₂ cup brown sugar and ¹/₄ cup margarine; blend well. Spread in bottom of ungreased 8 or 9-inch square pan. Arrange pineapple in 3 diagonal rows over sugar mixture; sprinkle cranberries and pecans around pineapple.

2. In large bowl, combine flour, baking powder, baking soda, salt, cinnamon, ginger and allspice; mix well. Add all remaining gingerbread ingredients; blend well. Pour batter evenly over pineapple, cranberries and pecans.

3. Bake at 350°F. for 45 to 55 minutes or until toothpick inserted in center comes out clean. Cool upright in pan for 2 minutes. Run knife around edge of pan; invert onto serving plate. Cool at least 30 minutes. If desired, serve warm with whipped cream.

High Altitude (Above 3,500 feet): Increase flour to 2 cups. Bake at 375°F. for 40 to 50 minutes.

Nutrition per Serving: Serving Size: ¹/₉ of Recipe. Calories 390; Calories from Fat 160; Total Fat 18g; Saturated Fat 3g; Cholesterol 25mg; Sodium 360mg; Dietary Fiber 1g

Dietary Exchange: 1 Starch, 2 ¹/₂ Fruit, 3 ¹/₂ Fat OR 3 ¹/₂ Carbohydrate, 3 ¹/₂ Fat

RUM RING CAKE

✦

Yield: 16 servings; **Prep Time:** 30 minutes
(Ready in 2 hours 25 minutes)

A simple cooked sugar syrup flavored with rum or orange juice keeps this ring cake moist even if made the day ahead of serving. As an alternative to the apricot glaze, dust the cooled cake with sifted powdered sugar just before serving.

CAKE
2 cups all-purpose flour
1 cup sugar
4 teaspoons baking powder
¼ teaspoon salt
½ cup milk
¼ cup margarine or butter, melted
1 teaspoon vanilla
4 eggs

SYRUP
1 cup sugar
1 cup water
¼ cup rum or orange juice

GLAZE
½ cup apricot preserves
2 cups cut-up fresh fruit

1. Heat oven to 350°F. Generously grease 12-cup Bundt® pan or 8-cup ring mold. In large bowl, combine all cake ingredients; beat at low speed until moistened. Beat 2 minutes at medium speed. Pour into greased pan.

2. Bake at 350°F. for 30 to 40 minutes or until toothpick inserted in center comes out clean.

3. Meanwhile, in medium saucepan, combine 1 cup sugar and water. Bring to a boil, stirring constantly until sugar dissolves. Remove from heat; stir in rum. Cool slightly.

4. Using long-tined fork, pierce hot cake in pan at 1-inch intervals; immediately pour syrup over cake. Cool cake in pan 15 minutes. Invert onto serving plate. Cool 1 hour or until completely cooled.

5. In small saucepan, heat apricot preserves. Press preserves through strainer into bowl to remove large apricot pieces. Drizzle glaze over cooled cake. Just before serving, fill center of cake with cut-up fruit.

High Altitude (Above 3,500 feet): Increase flour to 2 cups plus 3 tablespoons. Bake at 375°F. for 25 to 35 minutes.

Nutrition per Serving: Serving Size: ¹⁄₁₆ of Recipe. Calories 250; Calories from Fat 35; Total Fat 4g; Saturated Fat 1g; Cholesterol 55mg; Sodium 210mg; Dietary Fiber 1g

Dietary Exchange: 1½ Starch, 1½ Fruit, 1 Fat OR 3 Carbohydrate, 1 Fat

Rum Ring Cake

APPLESAUCE FRUITCAKE

♦

Yield: 20 servings; **Prep Time:** 30 minutes
(Ready in 3 hours 15 minutes)

Serve this rich dessert with mugs of hot coffee or tea. For variety, substitute chopped dried apricots for the raisins or spread slices of the cooled cake with whipped cream cheese.

1 ½ cups sugar

1 cup shortening

2 eggs

3 ¼ cups all-purpose flour

1 ½ teaspoons baking soda

2 teaspoons cinnamon

1 teaspoon allspice

1 teaspoon cloves

½ teaspoon salt

1 ½ cups chopped nuts

1 ½ cups raisins

1 ½ cups coarsely chopped dates

½ cup coarsely chopped red
   maraschino cherries, drained*

2 cups applesauce

6 red maraschino cherries, halved*

6 pecan halves

1. Heat oven to 325°F. Grease 10-inch tube pan; line bottom with waxed paper or foil and grease again. In large bowl, combine sugar and shortening; beat until light and fluffy. Add eggs; blend well. Reserve ½ cup flour. Add remaining 2 ¾ cups flour, baking soda, cinnamon, allspice, cloves and salt to egg mixture; blend at low speed until moistened. Beat 2 minutes at medium speed.

2. In another large bowl, combine ½ cup reserved flour with nuts, raisins, dates and ½ cup cherries; stir until nuts and fruit are lightly coated. With spoon, stir nut-fruit mixture and applesauce into batter; mix well. Pour and spread batter into greased and waxed paper–lined pan; top with cherry halves and pecans.

3. Bake at 325°F. for 1 ¼ to 1 ¾ hours or until toothpick inserted in center comes out clean. Cool upright in pan 5 minutes. Remove from pan; remove waxed paper. Turn upright onto wire rack. Cool 1 hour or until completely cooled. Wrap cake in plastic wrap or foil to keep moist. Store in refrigerator.

*Tip: Candied cherries can be substituted for maraschino cherries.

High Altitude (Above 3,500 feet): No change.

Nutrition per Serving: Serving Size: ⅟₂₀ of Recipe. Calories 410; Calories from Fat 150; Total Fat 17g; Saturated Fat 3g; Cholesterol 20mg; Sodium 160mg; Dietary Fiber 3g

Dietary Exchange: 2 Starch, 2 Fruit, 3 Fat OR 4 Carbohydrate, 3 Fat

APPLE BRANDY CAKE

Yield: 16 servings; **Prep Time:** 20 minutes
(Ready in 2 hours 30 minutes)

McIntosh, Cortland or Rome apples work well in this moist, nutty cake. If you wish, fold in ½ cup of raisins along with the nuts and use apple brandy (Calvados), pear brandy (Poire William) or even Grand Marnier in place of the regular brandy.

CAKE

2 ½ cups all-purpose flour

1 cup sugar

1 cup firmly packed brown sugar

2 teaspoons baking soda

1 teaspoon salt

2 teaspoons cinnamon

1 cup oil

¼ cup brandy or apple cider

2 teaspoons vanilla

3 eggs

3 cups chopped peeled apples

1 cup chopped nuts, if desired

BROWN BUTTER GLAZE

¼ cup butter (do not use
   margarine)

1 cup powdered sugar

2 to 4 tablespoons apple cider or
   milk

1. Heat oven to 350°F. Grease and flour 12-cup Bundt® or 10-inch tube pan. In large bowl, combine flour, sugar, brown sugar, baking soda, salt and cinnamon; mix well. Add oil, brandy, vanilla and eggs. With spoon, stir until well blended. (Mixture will be very thick.) Fold in apples and nuts. Pour and spread batter into greased and floured pan.

2. Bake at 350°F. for 50 to 60 minutes or until toothpick inserted in center comes out clean. Cool cake in pan 10 minutes. Invert cake onto serving plate. Cool 1 hour or until completely cooled.

3. In small saucepan over medium heat, cook butter until light golden brown, stirring constantly. Remove from heat. Add powdered sugar and 2 tablespoons apple cider; blend well. Add additional apple cider until glaze is of desired drizzling consistency. Spoon glaze over cake, allowing some to run down sides.

High Altitude (Above 3,500 feet): Decrease granulated sugar to ¾ cup. Bake as directed above.

Nutrition per Serving: Serving Size: 1/16 of Recipe. Calories 440; Calories from Fat 200; Total Fat 22g; Saturated Fat 4g; Cholesterol 50mg; Sodium 340mg; Dietary Fiber 1g

Dietary Exchange: 1 ½ Starch, 2 Fruit, 4 ½ Fat OR 3 ½ Carbohydrate, 4 ½ Fat

PUDDING RICH FUNFETTI® RING CAKE

Yield: 16 servings; Prep Time: 20 minutes (Ready in 2 hours 45 minutes)

Enrich a boxed cake with extra pudding to create an extra-moist dessert that kids will love.

CAKE
1 (1 lb. 2.25-oz.) pkg. pudding-included white cake mix with candy bits
1 (3.4-oz.) pkg. instant vanilla pudding and pie filling mix
1 cup water
¼ cup oil
4 eggs
2 tablespoons powdered sugar
1 tablespoon vanilla

GLAZE
½ cup vanilla frosting with candy bits (from 16-oz. can)

1. Heat oven to 350°F. Generously grease and flour 12-cup Bundt® pan or 10-inch tube pan. In large bowl, combine all cake ingredients; beat at low speed until moistened. Beat 2 minutes at medium speed. Pour batter into greased and floured pan.

2. Bake at 350°F. for 45 to 55 minutes or until toothpick inserted in center comes out clean. Cool 30 minutes. Invert onto serving plate. Cool 1 hour or until completely cooled.

3. Remove candy bits packet from frosting. Heat frosting in small saucepan just until melted. Spoon glaze over cake, allowing some to run down sides. If desired, sprinkle with some of the candy bits.

High Altitude (Above 3,500 feet): Add ⅓ cup flour to dry cake mix. Bake as directed above.

Nutrition per Serving: Serving Size: 1/16 of Recipe. Calories 250; Calories from Fat 80; Total Fat 9g; Saturated Fat 2g; Cholesterol 55mg; Sodium 320mg; Dietary Fiber 0g

Dietary Exchange: 1 Starch, 1 ½ Fruit, 1 ½ Fat OR 2 ½ Carbohydrate, 1 ½ Fat

TOFFEE POUND CAKE TORTE

✦

Yield: 12 servings; **Prep Time:** 25 minutes
(Ready in 2 hours 45 minutes)

At its narrowest definition, a torte is a flourless cake; taken more loosely, the term refers to a rich cake such as this toffee-studded loaf.

CAKE
½ cup sugar
½ cup firmly packed brown sugar
1 cup butter, softened
5 eggs
2 teaspoons vanilla
2 cups all-purpose flour
½ teaspoon baking powder
½ teaspoon salt
2 (1.4-oz.) bars chocolate-covered English toffee candy, chopped, or ½ cup chocolate-coated toffee bits

FROSTING
1 (8-oz.) container frozen whipped topping, thawed
1 (1.4-oz.) bar chocolate-covered English toffee candy, coarsely chopped, or ¼ cup chocolate-coated toffee bits

1. Heat oven to 325°F. Grease and flour 9 × 5-inch loaf pan. In large bowl, combine sugar, brown sugar and butter; beat until light and fluffy. Add eggs 1 at a time, beating well after each addition. Add vanilla; blend well.

2. In small bowl, combine flour, baking powder and salt; mix well. Add dry ingredients to butter mixture; beat just until smooth. Stir in 2 chopped candy bars. Spoon and spread batter into greased and floured pan.

3. Bake at 325°F. for 60 to 70 minutes or until toothpick inserted in center comes out clean. Cool 10 minutes. Remove from pan. Cool on wire rack for 1 hour or until completely cooled.

4. Just before serving, frost sides and top of cake with whipped topping. Sprinkle with coarsely chopped candy bar. Store in refrigerator.

High Altitude (Above 3,500 feet): No change.

Nutrition per Serving: Serving Size: ¹⁄₁₂ of Recipe. Calories 430; Calories from Fat 230; Total Fat 26g; Saturated Fat 14g; Cholesterol 135mg; Sodium 320mg; Dietary Fiber 1g

Dietary Exchange: 2 Starch, 1 Fruit, 5 Fat OR 3 Carbohydrate, 5 Fat

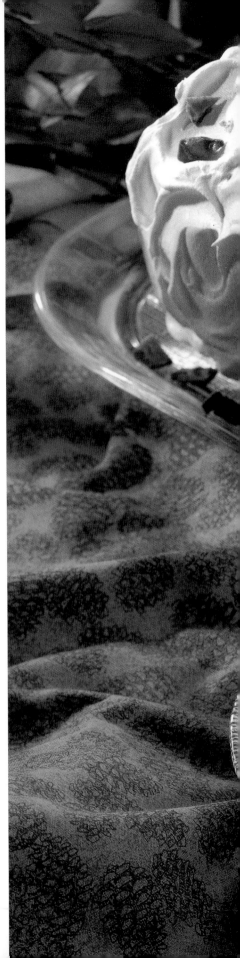

Toffee Pound Cake Torte

SOUR CREAM POUND CAKE

✦

Yield: 16 servings; **Prep Time:** 15 minutes
(Ready in 2 hours 35 minutes)

Rich pound cake is moist enough to fly solo, with no frosting. Serve it with fresh fruit for a satisfying afternoon snack with coffee.

2 ¾ cups sugar
1 ½ cups butter, softened
1 teaspoon vanilla
6 eggs
3 cups all-purpose flour
1 teaspoon grated orange or lemon peel
½ teaspoon baking powder
½ teaspoon salt
1 cup sour cream

1. Heat oven to 350°F. Generously grease and flour 12-cup Bundt® pan. In large bowl, combine sugar and butter; beat until light and fluffy. Beat in vanilla. Add eggs 1 at a time, beating well after each addition.

2. In medium bowl, combine flour, orange peel, baking powder and salt; mix well. Add dry ingredients alternately with sour cream, beating well after each addition. Pour batter into greased and floured pan.

3. Bake at 350°F. for 55 to 65 minutes or until toothpick inserted in center comes out clean. Cool 15 minutes. Invert onto serving plate. Cool 1 hour or until completely cooled.

High Altitude (Above 3,500 feet): Decrease sugar to 2 ½ cups. Bake at 375°F. for 55 to 65 minutes.

Nutrition per Serving: Serving Size: ¹⁄₁₆ of Recipe. Calories 440; Calories from Fat 210; Total Fat 23g; Saturated Fat 13g; Cholesterol 135mg; Sodium 290mg; Dietary Fiber 1g

Dietary Exchange: 1 ½ Starch, 2 Fruit, 4 ½ Fat OR 3 ½ Carbohydrate, 4 ½ Fat

CRANBERRY-ORANGE POUND CAKE

✦

Yield: 16 servings; **Prep Time:** 15 minutes
(Ready in 1 hour 45 minutes)

A classic American duo, cranberry and orange, tastes especially good at holiday time. The cake and the sauce can be made up to several days in advance; store in the refrigerator, return the cake to room temperature and reheat the sauce briefly before serving. Substitute plain nonfat sour cream for the regular sour cream to cut calories and fat without affecting flavor or texture.

CAKE
2 ¾ cups sugar
1 ½ cups butter, softened
1 teaspoon vanilla
1 teaspoon grated orange peel
6 eggs
3 cups all-purpose flour
1 teaspoon baking powder
½ teaspoon salt
1 (8-oz.) container sour cream
1 ½ cups chopped fresh or frozen cranberries (do not thaw)*

BUTTER RUM SAUCE
1 cup sugar
1 tablespoon all-purpose flour
½ cup half-and-half
½ cup butter
4 teaspoons light rum or ¼ teaspoon rum extract

1. Heat oven to 350°F. Generously grease and lightly flour 12-cup Bundt® pan. In large bowl, combine 2 ¾ cups sugar and 1 ½ cups butter; beat until light and fluffy. Add vanilla and orange peel; blend well. Add eggs 1 at a time, beating well after each addition.

2. In medium bowl, combine 3 cups flour, baking powder and salt; mix well. Add to butter mixture alternately with sour cream, beating well after each addition. Gently stir in cranberries. Pour and spread batter into greased and floured pan.

Cranberry-Orange Pound Cake

3. Bake at 350°F. for 65 to 75 minutes or until toothpick inserted in center comes out clean. Cool 15 minutes. Remove from pan.

4. Meanwhile, in small saucepan, combine 1 cup sugar and 1 tablespoon flour. Stir in half-and-half and ½ cup butter. Cook over medium heat until bubbly and thickened, stirring constantly. Remove from heat; stir in rum. Serve warm sauce over cake.

Tip: To easily chop frozen cranberries, use food processor with metal blade.

High Altitude (Above 3,500 feet): Decrease sugar in cake to 2½ cups. Bake as directed above.

Nutrition per Serving: Serving Size: ¹⁄₁₆ of Recipe. Calories 560; Calories from Fat 260; Total Fat 29g; Saturated Fat 17g; Cholesterol 150mg; Sodium 370mg; Dietary Fiber 1g

Dietary Exchange: 2 Starch, 2½ Fruit, 5½ Fat OR 4½ Carbohydrate, 5½ Fat

INDIVIDUAL HOT FUDGE SUNDAE CAKES

Yield: 6 servings; **Prep Time:** 10 minutes
(Ready in 35 minutes)

Here's a chocolate-lover's version of pudding cake, an old-time recipe in which the cake makes its own sauce as it bakes. If you choose to decorate the top with a stenciled powdered sugar design, don't dust the cake tops with the powdered sugar until just before serving to keep the design from melting into the cake top.

1 cup all-purpose flour
1/2 cup sugar
2 tablespoons unsweetened cocoa
1 1/2 teaspoons baking powder
2/3 cup skim milk
2 tablespoons margarine or butter, melted
1 teaspoon vanilla
3/4 cup firmly packed brown sugar
1/4 cup unsweetened cocoa
1 1/2 cups hot water

1. Heat oven to 350°F. In small bowl, combine flour, sugar, 2 tablespoons cocoa and baking powder. Add milk, margarine and vanilla; blend well. Spoon evenly into 6 ungreased 10-oz. custard cups. Place cups in 15 × 10 × 1-inch baking pan.

2. In small bowl, combine brown sugar and 1/4 cup cocoa; mix well. Spoon 2 to 3 tablespoons mixture evenly over batter in each cup. Pour 1/4 cup hot water evenly over sugar mixture in each cup.

3. Bake at 350°F. for 20 to 25 minutes or until center is set and firm to the touch. Serve warm. If desired, sprinkle with powdered sugar, or serve with frozen nonfat yogurt or light whipped topping.*

*Tip: To decorate top of each dessert with powdered sugar, cut stencil of favorite holiday shape from paper, or use paper doily. Place stencil on dessert; dust with powdered sugar. Remove stencil.

High Altitude (Above 3,500 feet): No change.

Nutrition per Serving: Serving Size: 1/6 of Recipe. Calories 320; Calories from Fat 45; Total Fat 5g; Saturated Fat 1g; Cholesterol 0mg; Sodium 150mg; Dietary Fiber 2g

Dietary Exchange: 1 1/2 Starch, 2 1/2 Fruit, 1 Fat OR 4 Carbohydrate, 1 Fat

LEMON PUDDING CAKE

Yield: 6 (1/2-cup) servings;
Prep Time: 15 minutes
(Ready in 50 minutes)

As the ingredients bake, the cake rises to the top above a pool of lemony sauce.

3 eggs, separated
1/2 cup milk
1/4 cup lemon juice
1 teaspoon grated lemon peel
1/2 cup sugar
1/3 cup all-purpose flour
1/8 teaspoon salt

1. Heat oven to 350°F. Grease 1-quart casserole. In small bowl, beat egg yolks; stir in milk, lemon juice and lemon peel. Add sugar, flour and salt; beat until smooth.

2. In another small bowl, beat egg whites until stiff peaks form. Gently fold yolk mixture into beaten egg whites. DO NOT OVERMIX. Pour into greased casserole. Place casserole in 13 × 9-inch pan; place in oven. Pour hot water into pan around casserole to a depth of 1 inch.

3. Bake at 350°F. for 25 to 35 minutes or until light golden brown. Serve warm or cool.

Nutrition per Serving: Serving Size: 1/2 Cup. Calories 140; Calories from Fat 25; Total Fat 3g; Saturated Fat 1g; Cholesterol 110mg; Sodium 90mg; Dietary Fiber 0g

Dietary Exchange: 1/2 Starch, 1 Fruit, 1/2 Medium-Fat Meat OR 1 1/2 Carbohydrate, 1/2 Medium-Fat Meat

SPONGE CAKE

Yield: 12 servings; **Prep Time:** 15 minutes
(Ready in 2 hours)

True sponge cakes gain richness from eggs but do not contain any butter, shortening or oil. Consequently, they're lower in fat than some other cakes, and are usually at their best within a day or so of being baked.

6 eggs, separated
¾ teaspoon cream of tartar
1 ½ cups sugar
1 ½ cups all-purpose flour
1 tablespoon grated orange peel
1 teaspoon baking powder
½ teaspoon salt
½ cup apricot nectar or water
1 teaspoon rum extract or vanilla

1. Heat oven to 350°F. In large bowl, combine egg whites and cream of tartar; beat until mixture forms soft peaks. Gradually add ¾ cup of the sugar, beating at high speed until stiff peaks form.

2. In small bowl, combine egg yolks, remaining ¾ cup sugar, flour, orange peel, baking powder, salt, nectar and rum extract; beat at low speed until moistened. Beat 1 minute at medium speed. Pour over egg white mixture; fold in gently just until blended. Pour batter into ungreased 10-inch tube pan.

3. Bake at 350°F. for 35 to 45 minutes or until top springs back when touched lightly in center. Immediately invert cake onto funnel or soft drink bottle; let hang 1 hour or until completely cooled. To remove cake from pan, run edge of knife around outer edge of pan and tube.

High Altitude (Above 3,500 feet): Decrease total sugar to 1¼ cups. Bake at 375°F. for 35 to 45 minutes.

Nutrition per Serving: Serving Size: ¹/₁₂ of Recipe. Calories 200; Calories from Fat 25; Total Fat 3g; Saturated Fat 1g; Cholesterol 105mg; Sodium 160mg; Dietary Fiber 1g

Dietary Exchange: 1½ Starch, 1 Fruit, ½ Fat OR 2½ Carbohydrate, ½ Fat

CHIFFON CAKE

Yield: 12 servings; **Prep Time:** 30 minutes
(Ready in 2 hours 45 minutes)

Beaten egg whites give Chiffon Cake its trademark lightness, reminiscent of the sheer fabric of the same name. Make sure to use an ungreased tube pan so the batter can "climb" up the sides and achieve maximum height.

2 cups all-purpose flour
1 ½ cups sugar
3 teaspoons baking powder
¼ teaspoon salt
¾ cup cold water
½ cup oil
7 eggs, separated
½ teaspoon vanilla
4 teaspoons finely grated lemon
    peel
½ teaspoon cream of tartar

1. Heat oven to 325°F. In large bowl, combine flour, sugar, baking powder and salt; mix well. Add water, oil, egg yolks and vanilla; beat at low speed until moistened. Beat at high speed for 5 minutes or until very smooth, scraping sides of bowl occasionally. Fold in lemon peel. Transfer to another large bowl. Thoroughly wash bowl and beaters.

2. In same large bowl, combine egg whites and cream of tartar; beat 3 minutes or until stiff peaks form. Gradually add egg yolk mixture to egg whites, folding gently to combine. Pour into ungreased 10-inch tube pan.

3. Bake at 325°F. for 60 to 75 minutes or until top springs back when lightly touched. Immediately invert cake onto funnel or soft drink bottle; let hang 1 hour or until completely cooled. To remove cake from pan, run edge of knife around outer edge of pan and tube.

High Altitude (Above 3,500 feet): Bake at 350°F. for 55 to 60 minutes.

Nutrition per Serving: Serving Size: ¹/₁₂ of Recipe. Calories 300; Calories from Fat 110; Total Fat 12g; Saturated Fat 2g; Cholesterol 125mg; Sodium 200mg; Dietary Fiber 1g

Dietary Exchange: 2 Starch, 1 Fruit, 2 Fat OR 3 Carbohydrate, 2 Fat

ANGEL FOOD CAKE

◆

Yield: 12 servings; **Prep Time:** 20 minutes
(Ready in 2 hours)

This cake gets its name from its characteristic light, ethereal sweetness. For best results, use a metal or china mixing bowl (not plastic) and make sure the bowl, beaters and even your hands are free of any trace of grease, which can prevent the egg whites from reaching their highest volume. Cut the cake gently with a serrated knife, using a back-and-forth sawing motion to avoid squashing its delicate texture.

¾ cup all-purpose flour
¾ cup sugar
1 ½ cups (about 12) egg whites,
    room temperature
1 ½ teaspoons cream of tartar
¼ teaspoon salt
1 ½ teaspoons vanilla
½ teaspoon almond extract
¾ cup sugar

1. Place oven rack at lowest position. Heat oven to 375°F. In small bowl, combine flour and ¾ cup sugar.

2. In large bowl, combine egg whites, cream of tartar, salt, vanilla and almond extract; beat until mixture forms soft peaks. Gradually add ¾ cup sugar, beating at high speed until stiff peaks form. Spoon flour-sugar mixture ¼ cup at a time over beaten egg whites; gently fold in just until blended. Pour batter into ungreased 10-inch tube pan. With knife, cut gently through batter to remove large air bubbles.

3. Bake at 375°F. on lowest oven rack for 30 to 40 minutes or until crust is golden brown and cracks are very dry. Immediately invert cake onto funnel or soft drink bottle; let hang 1 hour or until completely cooled. To remove cake from pan, run edge of knife around outer edge of pan and tube.

Tip: To make loaves, bake in 2 ungreased 9 × 5-inch loaf pans for 25 to 30 minutes.

High Altitude (Above 3,500 feet): Increase flour to 1 cup; increase egg whites to 1 ¾ cups (about 13). Bake at 400°F. for 30 to 35 minutes.

Nutrition per Serving: Serving Size: ¹⁄₁₂ of Recipe. Calories 140; Calories from Fat 0; Total Fat 0g; Saturated Fat 0g; Cholesterol 0mg; Sodium 100mg; Dietary Fiber 0g

Dietary Exchange: 1 Starch, 1 Fruit OR 2 Carbohydrate

VARIATION

Chocolate-Cherry Angel Food Cake: Fold ⅓ cup well-drained, chopped maraschino cherries and 1 oz. grated semisweet chocolate into batter. Bake as directed above. In small saucepan over low heat, melt 2 tablespoons margarine or butter and 1 oz. semisweet chocolate with 1 tablespoon corn syrup. Stir in 1 cup powdered sugar and 2 to 3 tablespoons maraschino cherry liquid until smooth and of desired drizzling consistency. Immediately drizzle over cooled cake.

**Angel Food Cake,
Chocolate-Cherry Variation**

WARM VANILLA CAKE WITH RASPBERRY SAUCE

Yield: 8 servings; **Prep Time**: 15 minutes
(Ready in 45 minutes)

For a weeknight treat, whip together this easy little cake and let it bake while you eat supper; thaw the raspberries for the sauce at the same time. The sauce also makes a good nonfat topping for purchased pound cake or a scoop of sorbet with fresh fruit.

CAKE

2/3 cup sugar
1/4 cup margarine or butter, softened
2 teaspoons vanilla
1 egg
1 cup all-purpose flour
1 teaspoon baking powder
1/2 cup skim milk

SAUCE

1 (10-oz.) pkg. frozen raspberries in syrup, thawed
2 tablespoons powdered sugar
1 teaspoon vanilla

1. Heat oven to 350°F. Spray 8-inch round cake pan with non-stick cooking spray.* In medium bowl, combine sugar and margarine; beat with electric mixer until well blended. Add 2 teaspoons vanilla and egg; beat well. Add flour and baking powder; mix at low speed until combined.

Add milk; blend well. Pour batter evenly into sprayed pan.

2. Bake at 350°F. for 25 to 30 minutes or until toothpick inserted in center comes out clean.

3. Meanwhile, place all sauce ingredients in blender container or food processor bowl with metal blade; blend until smooth. Press sauce through strainer into bowl to remove seeds; discard seeds.

4. To serve, cut warm cake into wedges; place on individual dessert plates. Top each with sauce.

*Tip: If desired, cake can be baked in sprayed 9-inch round cake pan. Bake at 350°F. for 20 to 25 minutes.

High Altitude (Above 3,500 feet): Decrease sugar to 1/2 cup. Bake as directed above.

Nutrition per Serving: Serving Size: 1/8 of Recipe. Calories 240; Calories from Fat 60; Total Fat 7g; Saturated Fat 1g; Cholesterol 25mg; Sodium 140mg; Dietary Fiber 2g

Dietary Exchange: 1 Starch, 1 1/2 Fruit, 1 1/2 Fat OR 2 1/2 Carbohydrate, 1 1/2 Fat

CHOCOLATE CHUNK CHRISTMAS CAKE

Yield: 3 (20-slice) loaves;
Prep Time: 30 minutes
(Ready in 3 hours 15 minutes)

Economize on baking time by making three loaves at once: one to slice for a beautiful holiday buffet, one to wrap and give away, and one to tuck into the freezer for unexpected company.

2 cups raisins
2 cups golden raisins
2 cups red and green candied cherries
1 cup cut-up candied pineapple
1 cup cut-up dates
1 cup slivered blanched almonds
16 oz. semi-sweet chocolate, chopped
3 cups all-purpose flour
1 1/2 teaspoons baking powder
1 1/2 teaspoons cinnamon
1 teaspoon ginger
3/4 teaspoon salt
1/2 teaspoon nutmeg
1/2 teaspoon cloves
1 1/4 cups firmly packed brown sugar
1 cup butter, softened
6 eggs
1/4 cup molasses
1/3 cup cold strong coffee

1. Heat oven to 300°F. Generously grease and flour three 8×4-inch loaf pans. In very large bowl, combine raisins, golden raisins, cherries, pineapple, dates, almonds and chocolate; mix well.

2. In medium bowl, combine flour, baking powder, cinnamon, ginger, salt, nutmeg and cloves; mix well. Sprinkle over fruit; stir to coat and separate fruit. Set aside.

Chocolate Chunk Christmas Cake

3. In large bowl, combine brown sugar and butter; beat until light and fluffy. Add eggs 1 at a time, beating well after each addition. Stir in molasses. (Mixture may look curdled.) Pour over fruit mixture; mix well. Stir in coffee until well mixed. Spoon and spread into greased and floured pans.

4. Bake at 300°F. for 1 1/4 to 1 1/2 hours or until loaves are deep golden brown and toothpick inserted in center comes out clean. Cool 15 minutes. Remove from pans. Cool 1 hour or until completely cooled. Wrap tightly in plastic wrap or foil. Store in refrigerator for up to 1 month or freeze for up to 3 months.

High Altitude (Above 3,500 feet): No change.

Nutrition per Serving: Serving Size: 1 Slice. Calories 200; Calories from Fat 60; Total Fat 7g; Saturated Fat 4g; Cholesterol 30mg; Sodium 105mg; Dietary Fiber 1g

Dietary Exchange: 1 Starch, 1 Fruit, 1 1/2 Fat OR 2 Carbohydrate, 1 1/2 Fat

DELICIOUS WHITE FRUITCAKE

◆

Yield: 2 (20-slice) loaves;
Prep Time: 15 minutes
(Ready in 3 hours 15 minutes)

Try this change of pace from traditional dark fruitcakes; white cake shows off the colorful candied cherries and pineapple to good advantage.

1 ¾ cups all-purpose flour
1 cup sugar
½ teaspoon salt
½ teaspoon baking powder
1 ½ cups margarine or butter, softened
1 tablespoon vanilla
1 tablespoon lemon extract
5 eggs
1 lb. (4 cups) pecan halves
1 lb. (2 cups) cut-up candied pineapple
¾ lb. (1 ½ cups) whole or cut-up candied cherries

1. Heat oven to 300°F. Generously grease and lightly flour two 8×4-inch loaf pans. In large bowl, combine all ingredients except pecans and fruit; beat at low speed until moistened. Beat 2 minutes at medium speed. Stir in pecans and fruit. Spoon and spread batter into greased and floured pans.

2. Bake at 300°F. for 1¼ to 1¾ hours or until toothpick inserted in center comes out clean. Cool 15 minutes. Remove from pans. Cool 1 hour or until completely cooled. Wrap tightly in plastic wrap or foil. Store in refrigerator for up to 1 month or freeze for up to 3 months.

Tip: Fruitcake can be wrapped in cheesecloth that has been soaked in brandy or fruit juice. Wrap with plastic wrap or foil. Store in refrigerator. Moisten cloth every 2 weeks.

High Altitude (Above 3,500 feet): No change.

Nutrition per Serving: Serving Size: 1 Slice. Calories 260; Calories from Fat 140; Total Fat 15g; Saturated Fat 2g; Cholesterol 25mg; Sodium 180mg; Dietary Fiber 1g

Dietary Exchange: ½ Starch, 1 ½ Fruit, 3 Fat OR 2 Carbohydrate, 3 Fat

JELLY ROLL

◆

Yield: 10 servings; **Prep Time:** 30 minutes
(Ready in 1 hour 45 minutes)

Jelly roll (called "Swiss Roll" by the British) is a flat, airy sponge cake spread with a filling and rolled into a spiral. Vanilla or chocolate pudding makes a delicious substitute for the jelly filling.

2 teaspoons powdered sugar
4 eggs
¾ cup sugar
¼ cup cold water
1 teaspoon vanilla
1 cup all-purpose flour
1 teaspoon baking powder
¼ teaspoon salt
¾ cup any flavor jelly or preserves

1. Heat oven to 375°F. Lightly sprinkle clean towel with powdered sugar; set aside. Generously grease and lightly flour 15×10×1-inch baking pan.

2. In large bowl, beat eggs at high speed for 5 minutes or until thick and lemon colored. Gradually add sugar, beating until light and fluffy. Stir in water and vanilla. Add flour, baking powder and salt; blend at low speed just until dry ingredients are moistened. Spread batter evenly in greased and floured pan.

3. Bake at 375°F. for 8 to 12 minutes or until cake springs back when touched lightly in center. Loosen edges of cake; immediately invert onto sugared side of towel. Remove pan.

4. Starting with short side, roll up cake in towel; cool on wire rack for 1 hour or until completely cooled.

5. Unroll cake; remove towel. Spread cake with jelly; reroll loosely to incorporate filling. Wrap in foil or waxed paper. Store in refrigerator. If desired, sprinkle with powdered sugar just before serving.

High Altitude (Above 3,500 feet): No change.

Nutrition per Serving: Serving Size: 1/10 of Recipe. Calories 200; Calories from Fat 20; Total Fat 2g; Saturated Fat 1g; Cholesterol 85mg; Sodium 135mg; Dietary Fiber 1g

Dietary Exchange: 1 ½ Starch, 1 Fruit, ½ Fat OR 2 ½ Carbohydrate, ½ Fat

Jelly Roll

ITALIAN PLUM CAKE

✦

Yield: 8 servings; **Prep Time:** 20 minutes
(Ready in 1 hour 15 minutes)

Sit outside on the patio and imagine the breeze is wafting in from the Mediterranean while you enjoy wedges of plum cake with tall glasses of iced tea or demitasse cups of espresso. "Secret" ingredients here include cornmeal, which gives a hearty texture to the cake, and crushed cookies, which make an easy sweet-crumb topping.

²⁄₃ cup sugar
¹⁄₃ cup margarine or butter,
    softened
1 teaspoon vanilla
¹⁄₂ cup refrigerated or frozen fat-
    free egg product, thawed, or
    2 eggs
1 cup all-purpose flour
¹⁄₂ cup yellow cornmeal
1 teaspoon baking powder
1 (16¹⁄₂-oz.) can purple plums,
    drained, pitted and halved
³⁄₄ cup crushed amaretti cookies or
    almond biscotti
¹⁄₂ teaspoon powdered sugar, if
    desired

1. Heat oven to 350°F. Spray bottom only of 8-inch springform pan with nonstick cooking spray. In large bowl, combine sugar, margarine and vanilla; beat until light and fluffy. Add egg product; blend well.

2. Add flour, cornmeal and baking powder; mix well. Spoon and spread batter into sprayed pan. Arrange plum halves over batter, leaving 1-inch border. Sprinkle with crushed cookies.

3. Bake at 350°F. for 35 to 45 minutes or until toothpick inserted in center comes out clean. Cool in pan 10 minutes. Remove sides of pan. Sprinkle cake with powdered sugar. Serve warm or cool.

High Altitude (Above 3,500 feet): Decrease sugar to ¹⁄₂ cup. Bake as directed above.

Nutrition per Serving: Serving Size: ¹⁄₈ of Recipe. Calories 280; Calories from Fat 70; Total Fat 8g; Saturated Fat 1g; Cholesterol 0mg; Sodium 180mg; Dietary Fiber 2g

Dietary Exchange: 1 ¹⁄₂ Starch, 1 ¹⁄₂ Fruit, 1 ¹⁄₂ Fat OR 3 Carbohydrate, 1 ¹⁄₂ Fat

CHOCOLATE VELVET CAKE WITH DESSERT SAUCES

✦

Yield: 12 servings; **Prep Time:** 35 minutes
(Ready in 2 hours 25 minutes)

Emulate professional dessert chefs with this unbelievably delicious, dense chocolate cake made with only six ingredients. Use your imagination when "painting" the white chocolate and raspberry dessert sauces on the plate: Swirl the two together or make alternating zigzags.

Or, spoon some of the white sauce onto the plate and add dots of raspberry sauce. Drag a toothpick or the tip of a knife through the raspberry to create crosshatches or decorative spirals.

CAKE
3 eggs
²⁄₃ cup sugar
¹⁄₄ cup all-purpose flour
4 oz. semi-sweet chocolate,
    melted
2 oz. unsweetened chocolate,
    melted
¹⁄₂ cup butter, melted

WHITE CHOCOLATE SAUCE
1 ¹⁄₂ cups whipping cream
2 tablespoons powdered sugar
¹⁄₂ cup white vanilla chips

RASPBERRY SAUCE
1 (10-oz.) pkg. frozen raspberries
    in syrup, thawed and drained
¹⁄₄ cup seedless raspberry jam
1 tablespoon cherry-flavored
    liqueur, if desired

1. Heat oven to 350°F. Grease 9-inch springform pan. In large bowl, combine eggs and sugar; beat at high speed for 2 minutes or until lemon colored. Fold in flour until well blended. Add semi-sweet and unsweetened chocolate and butter; stir just until combined. Pour into greased pan.

2. Bake at 350°F. for 25 to 35 minutes or until toothpick inserted in center comes out clean.

Cool 15 minutes. Carefully remove sides of pan. Cool 1 hour or until completely cooled.

3. While cake is baking, in small saucepan, combine whipping cream and powdered sugar; mix well. Bring just to a boil. Remove from heat; stir in vanilla chips until smooth. Refrigerate until thickened, about 2 hours. Store in refrigerator.

4. In blender container, puree raspberries. Press pureed raspberries through strainer into bowl to remove seeds; discard seeds. Stir in jam and liqueur. Store in refrigerator.

5. Just before serving, spoon 2 tablespoons white chocolate sauce onto each dessert plate. Drizzle 2 teaspoons raspberry sauce over white chocolate sauce on each plate to create desired design. Cut cake into wedges; place cake wedge on each plate over sauces. Garnish as desired.

High Altitude (Above 3,500 feet): Decrease sugar to ½ cup. Bake as directed above.

Nutrition per Serving: Serving Size: 1/12 of Recipe. Calories 420; Calories from Fat 250; Total Fat 28g; Saturated Fat 17g; Cholesterol 115mg; Sodium 115mg; Dietary Fiber 2g

Dietary Exchange: 1 Starch, 1½ Fruit, 5½ Fat OR 2½ Carbohydrate, 5½ Fat

Chocolate Velvet Cake with Dessert Sauces

NORWEGIAN HAZELNUT CAKE

♦

Yield: 16 servings; **Prep Time:** 30 minutes
(Ready in 1 hour 45 minutes)

Hazelnuts impart rich flavor and texture. For best results, grind the nuts with on/off turns of the food processor or blender; watch carefully to make sure they don't turn into paste.

CAKE
2 (2 ½-oz.) pkg. hazelnuts (filberts)
   or pecans
½ cup butter
3 eggs
1 ½ cups sugar
1 teaspoon vanilla
2 cups all-purpose flour
2 teaspoons baking powder
¼ teaspoon salt

GLAZE
½ cup whipping cream
1 (6-oz.) pkg. (1 cup) semi-sweet
   chocolate chips
½ teaspoon vanilla

1. Heat oven to 350°F. Lightly grease bottom only of 10-inch springform pan.* Reserve 8 whole nuts for garnish. In food processor bowl with metal blade or blender container, process nuts until ground (about 1 ⅓ cups); reserve 1 tablespoon for garnish.

2. Melt butter in small saucepan over low heat; cool. In large bowl, combine eggs, sugar and 1 teaspoon vanilla; beat 2 to 3 minutes or until thick and lemon colored. Add flour, baking powder, salt and ground nuts; mix well. Continue beating, gradually adding cooled, melted butter until well blended. (Mixture will be thick.) Spoon and spread batter into greased pan.

3. Bake at 350°F. for 35 to 45 minutes or until toothpick inserted in center comes out clean. Cool 15 minutes. Remove sides of pan. Run long knife under cake to loosen from pan bottom; invert onto serving plate. Cover with a cloth towel. Cool 30 minutes.

4. In medium saucepan, bring whipping cream just to a boil; remove from heat. Add chocolate chips; stir until melted and smooth. Stir in ½ teaspoon vanilla. Spread glaze over top of cake, allowing some to run down sides. Sprinkle reserved ground nuts around top edge of cake; arrange reserved whole nuts over ground nuts.

Tip: A 9-inch round cake pan can be used. Line pan with foil; grease well. Bake at 350°F. for 45 to 55 minutes.

High Altitude (Above 3,500 feet): Increase flour to 2 cups plus 2 tablespoons. Bake at 375°F. for 30 to 40 minutes.

Nutrition per Serving: Serving Size: ¹⁄₁₆ of Recipe. Calories 340; Calories from Fat 160; Total Fat 18g; Saturated Fat 8g; Cholesterol 65mg; Sodium 170mg; Dietary Fiber 2g

Dietary Exchange: 1 ½ Starch, 1 Fruit, 3 ½ Fat OR 2 ½ Carbohydrate, 3 ½ Fat

Norwegian Hazelnut Cake

CRANBERRY UPSIDE-DOWN CAKE

Yield: 9 servings; **Prep Time:** 20 minutes
(Ready in 1 hour 50 minutes)

A glistening cranberry topping sets a festive mood for a holiday buffet.

TOPPING
⅔ cup sugar

2 cups fresh or frozen cranberries

CAKE
1 ¼ cups all-purpose flour

1 cup sugar

1 ½ teaspoons baking powder

½ teaspoon salt

1 teaspoon grated lemon peel

⅔ cup milk

¼ cup shortening

¼ teaspoon vanilla

1 egg

1. Heat oven to 350°F. Grease 8-inch square pan. Sprinkle ⅓ cup of the sugar evenly in bottom of pan. Arrange cranberries over sugar; sprinkle with ⅓ cup sugar. Cover with foil. Bake at 350°F. for 30 minutes. Remove foil; cool 10 minutes.

2. Meanwhile, in large bowl, combine all cake ingredients; beat at low speed until moistened. Beat 2 minutes at medium speed. Pour batter evenly over cranberries.

3. Bake at 350°F. for 40 to 50 minutes or until toothpick in-serted in center comes out clean. Run knife around edge of pan; invert onto serving plate, leaving pan over cake for 2 minutes. Remove pan. Serve warm or cool.

High Altitude (Above 3,500 feet): Decrease sugar in cake to ¾ cup. Bake as directed above.

Nutrition per Serving: Serving Size: ⅑ of Recipe. Calories 290; Calories from Fat 60; Total Fat 7g; Saturated Fat 2g; Cholesterol 25mg; Sodium 220mg; Dietary Fiber 1g

Dietary Exchange: 1 Starch, 2 ½ Fruit, 1 ½ Fat OR 3 ½ Carbohydrate, 1 ½ Fat

COUNTRY PEAR CAKE

Yield: 8 servings; **Prep Time:** 15 minutes
(Ready in 1 hour 40 minutes)

In the tradition of a country "cottage pudding," slices of the warm cake are served with a simple sauce.

CAKE
3 eggs

1 cup sugar

1 ½ cups all-purpose flour

3 tablespoons oil

2 teaspoons grated lemon peel

1 teaspoon baking powder

¼ teaspoon allspice

2 large or 3 small pears, peeled, thinly sliced

TOPPING
2 teaspoons sugar

⅛ teaspoon cinnamon

SAUCE
1 cup nonfat sour cream

½ cup powdered sugar

½ cup skim milk

1 teaspoon vanilla

1. Heat oven to 350°F. Spray 9-inch springform pan with non-stick cooking spray. In large bowl, combine eggs and 1 cup sugar; beat at medium speed for 3 to 5 minutes or until fluffy and lemon colored. Add all remaining cake ingredients except pears; beat at low speed just until mixed.

2. Reserve 12 pear slices for top; fold remaining slices into batter. Spread batter in sprayed pan. Arrange reserved pear slices in circular pattern on top of batter.

3. In small bowl, combine topping ingredients; mix well. Sprinkle over batter.

4. Bake at 350°F. for 55 to 70 minutes or until toothpick inserted in center comes out clean. Cool 15 minutes.

5. Meanwhile, in medium bowl, combine all sauce ingredients; mix until smooth. Serve sauce with warm cake. Store in refrigerator.

High Altitude (Above 3,500 feet): Increase flour to 1 ⅔ cups. Bake as directed above.

Nutrition per Serving: Serving Size: ⅛ of Recipe. Calories 360; Calories from Fat 60; Total Fat 7g; Saturated Fat 1g; Cholesterol 80mg; Sodium 150mg; Dietary Fiber 2g

Dietary Exchange: 2 ½ Starch, 2 Fruit, 1 Fat OR 4 ½ Carbohydrate, 1 Fat

Country Pear Cake

BUTTERCREAM FROSTING

◆

Yield: Frosts 2-layer or 13 × 9-inch cake;
Prep Time: 10 minutes

Sweet and simple, this basic frosting is easy to "customize" with various flavorings and is ideal for almost any layer cake, sheet cake or cupcakes. The recipe is easy enough for junior bakers to help mix and spread.

²⁄₃ cup butter, softened
4 cups powdered sugar
1 teaspoon vanilla
2 to 4 tablespoons half-and-half or
   milk

1. In large bowl, beat butter until light and fluffy. Gradually add powdered sugar, beating well.

2. Beat in vanilla and enough half-and-half for desired spreading consistency.

Nutrition per Serving: Serving Size: ¹⁄₁₂ of Recipe. Calories 260; Calories from Fat 100; Total Fat 11g; Saturated Fat 7g; Cholesterol 30mg; Sodium 105mg; Dietary Fiber 0g

Dietary Exchange: 2 ¹⁄₂ Fruit, 2 ¹⁄₂ Fat OR 2 ¹⁄₂ Carbohydrate, 2 ¹⁄₂ Fat

VARIATIONS

Browned Butter Frosting: In large saucepan over medium heat, cook butter until light golden brown, stirring constantly. Gradually add powdered sugar, beating well. Continue as directed above.

Chocolate Buttercream Frosting: Add ¹⁄₃ cup unsweetened cocoa, 2 envelopes premelted unsweetened chocolate or 2 oz. unsweetened chocolate, melted, to butter; blend well. Continue as directed above.

Chocolate-Cherry Buttercream Frosting: Add 3 tablespoons drained chopped maraschino cherries to Chocolate Buttercream Frosting; mix well.

Coffee Buttercream Frosting: Dissolve 1 ¹⁄₂ teaspoons instant coffee granules or crystals in 2 tablespoons of the half-and-half.

Lemon Buttercream Frosting: Substitute 2 to 4 tablespoons lemon juice for the half-and-half and 1 teaspoon grated lemon peel for the vanilla.

Nut Buttercream Frosting: Stir in ¹⁄₄ cup chopped nuts.

Orange Buttercream Frosting: Substitute 2 to 4 tablespoons orange juice for the half-and-half and 1 teaspoon grated orange peel for the vanilla.

Peanut Butter Frosting: Add 3 tablespoons peanut butter to the butter; blend well. Continue as directed above.

MALLOW FROSTING

Yield: Frosts 2-layer or 13 × 9-inch cake;
Prep Time: 15 minutes

An electric hand mixer makes it much easier to achieve the billowy results.

¹⁄₂ cup sugar
2 tablespoons water
2 egg whites
1 (7-oz.) jar (1 ¹⁄₂ cups)
   marshmallow creme
1 teaspoon vanilla

1. In top of double boiler, combine sugar, water and egg whites. Cook over simmering water, beating until soft peaks form.

2. Add marshmallow creme; beat until stiff peaks form. Remove from heat; beat in vanilla.

Nutrition per Serving: Serving Size: ¹⁄₁₂ of Recipe. Calories 90; Calories from Fat 0; Total Fat 0g; Saturated Fat 0g; Cholesterol 0mg; Sodium 15mg; Dietary Fiber 0g

Dietary Exchange: 1 ¹⁄₂ Fruit OR 1 ¹⁄₂ Carbohydrate

GANACHE

Yield: Frosts 2-layer or 13 × 9-inch cake;
Prep Time: 15 minutes
(Ready in 1 hour 15 minutes)

"Ganache" just happens to rhyme with "panache," and this cream-and-chocolate topping is in fact a way to elevate a simple cake into a finale worthy of those tempting dessert carts in elegant restaurants.

6 oz. semi-sweet chocolate, cut
   into pieces, or 1 cup semi-sweet
   chocolate chips
¹⁄₂ cup whipping cream
1 tablespoon butter

1. In small saucepan, combine chocolate and whipping cream; heat over low heat until chocolate is melted and mixture is smooth and creamy, stirring constantly. Remove from heat; stir in butter. Refrigerate 1 to 1 ¹⁄₂ hours or until cold, stirring occasionally.

2. With wooden spoon or electric hand mixer, beat chilled mixture until thick and creamy and of desired spreading consistency.

Nutrition per Serving: Serving Size: $1/12$ of Recipe. Calories 120; Calories from Fat 80; Total Fat 9g; Saturated Fat 5g; Cholesterol 15mg; Sodium 15mg; Dietary Fiber 1g

Dietary Exchange: $1/2$ Starch, 2 Fat OR $1/2$ Carbohydrate, 2 Fat

BASIC POWDERED SUGAR GLAZE

✦

Yield: 1 $1/2$ cups; Prep Time: 10 minutes

This is one of the most versatile glazes in the baker's repertoire, as it takes only a few minutes to prepare and can be flavored to complement the particular cake. Use it on one of your homemade specialties or as a quick "dress up" for purchased pound cake.

2 cups powdered sugar
2 tablespoons margarine or butter, softened
1 teaspoon vanilla
3 to 4 tablespoons milk or half-and-half

1. In medium bowl, combine all ingredients until smooth, adding enough milk for desired glaze consistency.

2. Use to glaze cakes, coffee cakes or pastries.

Nutrition per Serving: Serving Size: $1/12$ of Recipe. Calories 100; Calories from Fat 20; Total Fat 2g; Saturated Fat 0g; Cholesterol 0mg; Sodium 25mg; Dietary Fiber 0g

Dietary Exchange: 1 Fruit, $1/2$ Fat OR 1 Carbohydrate, $1/2$ Fat

VARIATIONS

Chocolate Glaze: Add 2 oz. unsweetened chocolate, melted, or 2 envelopes premelted unsweetened chocolate.
Coffee Glaze: Substitute hot water for milk. Dissolve 1 teaspoon instant coffee granules or crystals in the hot water.
Lemon Glaze: Substitute 2 tablespoons lemon juice for part of milk and add 1 teaspoon grated lemon peel.
Maple Glaze: Add $1/2$ teaspoon maple extract or flavor.
Orange Glaze: Substitute orange juice for milk and add 1 teaspoon grated orange peel.
Spice Glaze: Combine $1/4$ teaspoon cinnamon and $1/8$ teaspoon nutmeg with powdered sugar.

BUTTERY DECORATOR ICING

Yield: 3 cups; Prep Time: 10 minutes

Using a combination of vegetable shortening and butter yields a fluffy texture and delicately pale color, while still allowing the flavor of the butter to come through.

$1/2$ cup butter, softened
$1/4$ cup shortening
1 teaspoon vanilla
$1/8$ teaspoon salt
4 cups powdered sugar
2 to 4 tablespoons milk

1. In large bowl, combine butter and shortening; beat until light and fluffy. Add vanilla and salt; mix well.

2. Add powdered sugar 1 cup at a time, beating well after each addition. Beat in enough milk at high speed until light and fluffy and of desired spreading consistency.

Tip: Icing can be made up to 2 weeks in advance and stored in a tightly covered container in the refrigerator. Bring to room temperature and rewhip before using.

Nutrition per Serving: Serving Size: $1/12$ of Recipe. Calories 270; Calories from Fat 110; Total Fat 12g; Saturated Fat 6g; Cholesterol 20mg; Sodium 105mg; Dietary Fiber 0g

Dietary Exchange: 3 Fruit, 2 Fat OR 3 Carbohydrate, 2 Fat

PIES AND TARTS

✦ ✦ ✦

If the thought of preparing
pie dough from scratch makes you
nervous, relax. We'll take you
through the basics, step-by-step.
If you're still reluctant, or pressed
for time, you can substitute a
refrigerated pie crust or shell for
any of the recipes in this chapter.
Likewise, if you're a pastry pro,
feel free to substitute a homemade
crust in any recipe that calls for
store-bought pastry.

SOUTHERN PEACH PIE WITH BERRY SAUCE, PAGE 74

In this chapter, you'll find a pie for every occasion, from a casual summer picnic to an elegant formal dinner.

CHOOSING A PIE PAN

Several types of pie pans are available. Some, such as tart pans with removable bottoms, are required for certain recipes; others can be used interchangeably.

REMOVABLE-BOTTOM PANS. The bottom is a separate piece that fits into a rim. These pans make it easy to transfer the pie to an attractive serving platter and make it easier to cut and serve the dessert, too.

GLASS PIE PANS. A classic choice, glass pie pans retain heat more than other pans.

METAL PANS. Dark or dull-finish metal pans, which many experts like better than glass, absorb heat better than shiny aluminum and so are less likely to result in a soggy bottom crust.

ALUMINUM PANS. The disposable pans that come with purchased pies are convenient to reuse for baking and taking pies to bake sales or potlucks.

PIE PASTRY BASICS

MIXING THE PASTRY. Classic rolled pastry is flaky and tender. Instead of the creaming technique that thoroughly mixes butter and dry ingredients for cakes, pie dough requires the shortening (or other solid fat) to remain in distinct little pieces. As the shortening melts in the oven, steam rises and creates air pockets, yielding the characteristic flakiness.

To mix the dough, cut the shortening into the flour mixture with a pastry blender or a fork. Continue cutting until the mixture resembles coarse crumbs with a few pea-sized pieces remaining. Add liquid a tablespoon at a time (ice water is preferred; it prevents the shortening from melting), pressing the dough into a ball with your hand or a utensil. As long as the dough can be formed into a ball without it crumbling to pieces, the less liquid used, the better.

You can also mix pastry dough in a food processor. Cut in the shortening with on/off pulses. Then add the ice water a little at a time, and use on/off pulses to form the dough without toughening it, stopping just as soon as it can be gathered into a ball.

CHILLING THE PASTRY. Once the dough has been formed, flatten it into a disk shape and wrap it in plastic wrap. Refrigerate it for at least 30 minutes to firm it up enough for rolling. Disks wrapped tightly in moisture- and vapor-proof wrap

can also be frozen and stored up to two months.

ROLLING THE DOUGH. Pastry dough must be chilled for most effective rolling, but the shortening may be too hard right after the dough has been removed from the refrigerator. Let it stand at room temperature for a few minutes. Lightly flour a work surface and warm the dough slightly with your hands. (Professional bakers favor marble surfaces for pastry work as the surface remains cool.) Flour the rolling pin, too, and roll the dough gently to the desired size. Always roll from the center to the edge, and lift the dough a couple of times during rolling to prevent it from sticking to the board. If necessary, run a knife blade under the dough to loosen it. Treat the dough gently and handle it as little as possible to prevent it from getting tough.

PUTTING THE PASTRY IN THE PAN. To transfer the rolled dough to the pie pan, gently fold it into quarters, place it into the pie pan and delicately unfold it and fit it into the pan. Or loosely wrap the dough circle around the rolling pin, then unroll it gently into place on the pan. Don't stretch the dough, or it will shrink more during baking.

For a top crust, cut steam vents in the dough before it goes on the pie. These can be simple slits, initials such as "A" for apple or decorative shapes cut with mini cookie cutters.

FLUTING THE EDGE. Fluting is functional, as it prevents the filling from oozing out of the edges of the pie during baking, but it also can be decorative. See "Finishing Touches for Pies."

MAKING A DECORATIVE TOP. For a change of pace from conventional rolled tops or lattice tops, use cookie cutters to cut the rolled dough into shapes and top the pie with an assortment of dough cutouts.

USING LEFTOVER DOUGH. Don't throw away dough scraps. Sprinkle scraps with cinnamon sugar and bake. Or reroll the scraps into a circle or rectangle, sprinkle with cinnamon sugar (perhaps with a few raisins or chopped walnuts), roll it up lengthwise and bake it on a piece of foil or small baking dish in the oven or toaster oven until the dough is golden brown, about 15 minutes.

PREBAKING PIE SHELLS. If you prebake a pie shell, you'll notice it tends to shrink from the edges. The solution is to butter a piece of foil or parchment paper about the same size as the pie pan. Put the crust into the pan and prick it all over the bottom with a fork, then press the foil, buttered side down, into the shell. Fill the shell with pie weights (small pieces of metal, available at specialty bake shops), dried beans or rice. About 10 minutes before the end of baking time, care-

fully remove the pie weights, beans or rice (they can be reused), take off the foil and continue baking until the crust is golden brown and flaky.

TESTING FOR DONENESS. A pie is done when the pastry crust is light golden brown and flaky and the fruit filling is tender and bubbly. Custard fillings should be set and a knife inserted into the center should come out clean. If the edges start to get too brown before the center of the pie is done, cover the edges lightly with strips of aluminum foil. Cool baked pies on a wire cooling rack.

CRUMB CRUSTS. Crumb crusts, usually made from crushed graham crackers or cookies plus melted butter and sugar, are especially good with custard fillings, cheesecake mixtures, and other creamy-textured pies. Make your own (see chart, page 68) or purchase them ready-made at the supermarket.

FINISHING TOUCHES FOR PIES

Make pies extra-special with fancy edges and crusts. With tools as simple as a knife, a fork or your fingertips, you can dress up your pies. For finishing touches from latticework crusts to herringbone edges, just follow the easy step-by-step instructions and illustrations on these pages.

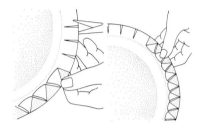

STARBURST EDGE

Trim dough even with edge of pan. Cut edge of crust at about $1/2$-inch intervals, making each cut $1/2$ inch long. Fold each piece in half diagonally to form a triangle, pressing lightly to seal dough.

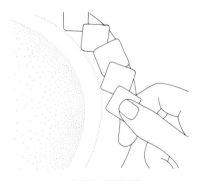

CUT-OUT EDGE

Trim dough even with edge of pan. Using canape cutter of desired shape, cut shapes from additional dough. Brush edge of crust with egg white. Overlap cutouts on edge of crust, pressing lightly to secure.

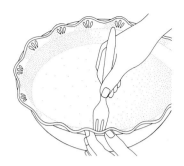

SCALLOPED EDGE

Trim dough even with edge of pan. Form a stand-up rim. Place left thumb and index finger about ³/₄ inch apart on outside of raised edge. With right thumb, push pastry toward outside to form a scalloped edge.

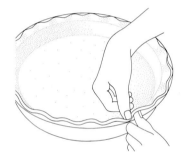

SCALLOPED EDGE VARIATION

Complete a scalloped edge, making scallops wide enough to accommodate width of fork. Dip fork in flour; press fork tines in center of each scallop, but do not press tines through the pastry.

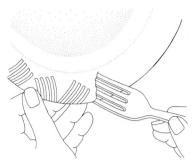

HERRINGBONE EDGE

Trim dough even with edge of pan. Dip fork tines in flour; press fork tines diagonally onto edge of dough. Angle tines and press next to previous marks, creating herringbone pattern. Continue around rim.

WOVEN LATTICE

Prepare crust for two-crust pie, leaving ¹/₂ inch of bottom crust extending beyond edge of pan. Cut remaining dough into about ¹/₂-inch-wide strips (for a decorative edge, use a pastry wheel). Lay part of strips across filling in parallel rows about ³/₄ inch apart, twisting if desired. Use longest strips for the center and shortest strips on the sides.

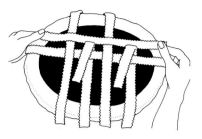

WOVEN LATTICE

Add strips at right angles, lifting every other strip as the cross strips are added to form a woven lattice.

WOVEN LATTICE

Trim ends even with edge of dough. Form a stand-up rim; flute.

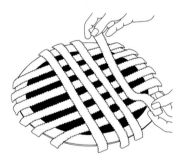

EASY LATTICE

Follow directions for Woven Lattice but do not weave lattice strips. Lay half the strips in 1 direction. Rotate pan 1 quarter turn and lay remaining strips at right angles directly over first strips. Trim ends even with edge of dough. Form a stand-up rim; flute.

◆   ◆   ◆

PASTRY FOR PIES AND TARTS

✦

Yield: One-crust pastry;
Prep Time: 20 minutes

Perfect pie pastry is light and flaky. For best results, treat the dough gently. Add just enough ice water so the dough sticks together and handle it as little as possible.

ONE-CRUST PIE
1 cup all-purpose flour
1/2 teaspoon salt
1/3 cup shortening
2 to 4 tablespoons ice water

1. In medium bowl, combine flour and salt; mix well. With pastry blender or fork, cut in shortening until mixture resembles coarse crumbs. Sprinkle with water 1 tablespoon at a time, while tossing and mixing lightly with fork. Add water until dough is just moist enough to form a ball when lightly pressed together. (Too much water causes dough to become sticky and tough; too little water causes edges to crack and pastry to tear easily while rolling.)

2. Shape dough into a ball. Flatten ball to 1/2-inch thickness, rounding and smoothing edges. On floured surface, roll lightly from center to edge into 11-inch round. Fold pastry in half; place in 9-inch pie pan, or 9 or 10-inch tart pan. Unfold; gently press in bottom and up sides of pan. Do not stretch.

3. If using pie pan, fold edge under to form a standing rim; flute edges. If using tart pan, trim pastry edges if necessary.

For One-Crust Filled Pie: Fill and bake as directed in recipe.

For One-Crust Baked Pie Shell (Unfilled): Prick bottom and sides of pastry generously with fork. Bake at 450°F. for 9 to 12 minutes or until light golden brown. Cool. Continue as directed in recipe.

Nutrition per Serving: Serving Size: 1/8 of Recipe. Calories 140; Calories from Fat 80; Total Fat 9g; Saturated Fat 2g; Cholesterol 0mg; Sodium 135mg; Dietary Fiber 0g

Dietary Exchange: 1 Starch, 1 1/2 Fat OR 1 Carbohydrate, 1 1/2 Fat

---

Yield: Two-crust pastry

TWO-CRUST PIE
2 cups all-purpose flour
1 teaspoon salt
2/3 cup shortening
5 to 7 tablespoons ice water

1. In medium bowl, combine flour and salt; mix well. With pastry blender or fork, cut in shortening until mixture resembles coarse crumbs. Sprinkle with water 1 tablespoon at a time, while tossing and mixing lightly with fork. Add water until dough is just moist enough to form a ball when lightly pressed together. (Too much water causes dough to become sticky and tough; too little water causes edges to crack and pastry to tear easily while rolling.)

2. Shape dough into 2 balls. Flatten 1 ball to 1/2-inch thickness, rounding and smoothing edges. On floured surface, roll lightly from center to edge into 11-inch round. Fold pastry in half; place in 9-inch pie pan, or 9 or 10-inch tart pan. Unfold; gently press in bottom and up sides of pan. Do not stretch.

3. Trim pastry even with pan edge. Roll out remaining pastry; set aside. Continue as directed in recipe.

Nutrition per Serving: Serving Size: 1/8 of Recipe. Calories 260; Calories from Fat 150; Total Fat 17g; Saturated Fat 4g; Cholesterol 0mg; Sodium 270mg; Dietary Fiber 1g

Dietary Exchange: 1 1/2 Starch, 3 Fat OR 1 1/2 Carbohydrate, 3 Fat

VARIATIONS

Cheese Pastry: For one-crust pastry, add 1/4 to 1/2 cup shredded Cheddar or American cheese to flour. Omit salt. (For two-crust pastry, use 1/2 to 1 cup.)

Extra Flaky Pastry: For one-crust pastry, add 1 teaspoon sugar with flour and 1 teaspoon vinegar with water. (For two-crust pastry, use 2 teaspoons sugar and 2 teaspoons vinegar.)

Whole Wheat Pastry: For one-crust pastry, substitute up to 1/2 cup whole wheat flour for all-purpose flour. Additional water may be necessary. (For two-crust pastry, use up to 1 cup whole wheat flour.)

PRESS-IN-THE-PAN OIL PIE CRUST

Yield: 9-inch baked pie crust;
Prep Time: 10 minutes
(Ready in 1 hour)

Here's an easier way to make pie crust. No cutting in of shortening or rolling—just mix the ingredients and press them in the pan.

1 ¾ cups all-purpose flour
1 teaspoon sugar
1 teaspoon salt
½ cup oil
¼ cup milk

1. Heat oven to 425°F. In medium bowl, combine flour, sugar and salt; mix well. In small bowl, combine oil and milk; blend well. Pour over flour mixture. Stir with fork until well mixed. Press in bottom and up sides of 9-inch pie pan; flute edge. (If desired, crust can be rolled out between 2 sheets of waxed paper.) Prick bottom and sides of crust generously with fork.

2. Bake at 425°F. for 12 to 17 minutes or until light golden brown. Cool 30 minutes or until completely cooled. Fill with desired filling.

1. **Microwave Directions:** Prepare crust as directed above using 9-inch microwave-safe pie pan; flute edge. Prick bottom and sides of crust generously with fork.

2. Microwave on HIGH for 6 to 8 minutes, rotating pan ½ turn every 2 minutes. Crust is done when surface appears dry and flaky. Cool 30 minutes or until completely cooled.

Nutrition per Serving: Serving Size: ⅛ of Recipe. Calories 230; Calories from Fat 130; Total Fat 14g; Saturated Fat 2g; Cholesterol 0mg; Sodium 270mg; Dietary Fiber 1g

Dietary Exchange: 1 ½ Starch, 1 ½ Fat OR 1 ½ Carbohydrate, 1 ½ Fat

CRUMB PIE CRUSTS

♦

Prep Time: 20 minutes (Ready in 50 minutes)

Pie crusts made with crushed crumbs are delicious and foolproof.

COOKIE OR CRACKER	AMOUNT OF CRUMBS	SUGAR	MARGARINE OR BUTTER, MELTED
Chocolate Wafer	1 ¼ cups (20 wafers)	¼ cup	¼ cup
Creme-Filled Choco/Vanilla Cookie	1 ½ cups (15 cookies)	None	¼ cup
Crisp Macaroon Cookie	1 ½ cups	None	¼ cup
Gingersnap Cookie	1 ½ cups	None	¼ cup
Graham Cracker*	1 ½ cups (24 squares)	¼ cup	⅓ cup
Granola (coarsely crushed)	1 ½ cups	None	¼ cup
Pretzel**	1 ¼ cups	¼ cup	½ cup
Vanilla Wafer	1 ½ cups (30 wafers)	None	¼ cup

1. Heat oven to 375°F. In medium bowl, combine crumbs, sugar and melted margarine; blend well. Press mixture firmly in bottom and up sides of 8 or 9-inch pie pan or in bottom of 9-inch springform pan.

2. Bake at 375°F. for 8 to 10 minutes. Cool at least 30 minutes or until completely cooled. Fill with ice cream or pudding. Freeze or refrigerate.

*Tips: * One-half teaspoon cinnamon can be added, if desired.*
*   ** For easier serving, butter pan before preparing crust.*

Nutrition Information: Not possible to calculate because of recipe variables.

PERFECT APPLE PIE

Yield: 8 servings; Prep Time: 35 minutes
(Ready in 1 hour 20 minutes)

Tart apples, such as Granny Smith, McIntosh or Pippin, make the most flavorful pies. Serve warm from the oven, with a scoop of vanilla ice cream, homemade whipped cream and a sprinkle of fresh nutmeg or a slice of Cheddar cheese that's traditional in some households.

CRUST

1 (15-oz.) pkg. refrigerated pie crusts or Pastry for Two-Crust Pie (page 67)

FILLING*

6 cups (6 medium) thinly sliced, peeled apples
¾ cup sugar
2 tablespoons all-purpose flour
¾ teaspoon cinnamon
¼ teaspoon salt
⅛ teaspoon nutmeg
1 tablespoon lemon juice

1. Prepare pie crust for *two-crust pie* using 9-inch pie pan.

2. Heat oven to 425°F. In large bowl, combine all filling ingredients; toss gently to mix. Spoon into crust-lined pan. Top with second crust; seal edges and flute. Cut slits or shapes in several places in top crust.

3. Bake at 425°F. for 40 to 45 minutes or until apples are tender and crust is golden brown.

Tip: Two 21-oz. cans apple pie filling can be substituted for filling.

Nutrition per Serving: Serving Size: ⅛ of Recipe. Calories 370; Calories from Fat 140; Total Fat 15g; Saturated Fat 6g; Cholesterol 15mg; Sodium 340mg; Dietary Fiber 2g

Dietary Exchange: 1 Starch, 3 Fruit, 2½ Fat OR 4 Carbohydrate, 2½ Fat

VARIATIONS

Caramel Pecan Apple Pie: Immediately after removing pie from oven, drizzle with ⅓ cup caramel ice cream topping. Sprinkle with 2 to 4 tablespoons chopped pecans.
Cheese Crust Apple Pie: Substitute Cheese Pastry (page 67) for crust.

APPLE PRALINE PIE

Yield: 8 servings; Prep Time: 40 minutes
(Ready in 2 hours 25 minutes)

A rich brown sugar–pecan praline mixture puts the crowning touch on a two-crust pie.

CRUST

1 (15-oz.) pkg. refrigerated pie crusts or Pastry for Two-Crust Pie (page 67)

FILLING*

6 cups (6 medium) sliced peeled apples
¾ cup sugar
¼ cup all-purpose flour
1 teaspoon cinnamon
¼ teaspoon salt
2 tablespoons margarine or butter

TOPPING

¼ cup margarine or butter
½ cup firmly packed brown sugar
2 tablespoons milk or half-and-half
½ cup chopped pecans

1. Prepare pie crust for *two-crust pie* using 9-inch pie pan.

2. Heat oven to 425°F. In large bowl, combine apples, sugar, flour, cinnamon and salt; toss gently to mix. Spoon mixture into crust-lined pan. Dot with 2 tablespoons margarine. Top with second crust; seal edges and flute. Cut slits in several places in top crust.

3. Bake at 425°F. for 35 to 45 minutes or until apples are tender and crust is golden brown. Cover edge of crust with strips of foil after 15 to 20 minutes of baking to prevent excessive browning. Remove from oven.

4. In small saucepan, melt ¼ cup margarine. Stir in brown sugar and milk. Bring to a boil over medium heat. Remove from heat; stir in pecans. Spread over top of hot pie. *Place pie on cookie sheet.* Return to oven; bake an additional 2 to 3 minutes or until topping bubbles. Cool at least 1 hour before serving.

Tip: Two 21-oz. cans apple pie filling can be substituted for filling.

Nutrition per Serving: Serving Size: ⅛ of Recipe. Calories 560; Calories from Fat 250; Total Fat 28g; Saturated Fat 8g; Cholesterol 15mg; Sodium 450mg; Dietary Fiber 3g

Dietary Exchange: 1 Starch, 4 Fruit, 5½ Fat OR 5 Carbohydrate, 5½ Fat

FRENCH CRANBERRY-APPLE PIE

Yield: 8 servings; **Prep Time:** 35 minutes
(Ready in 1 hour 30 minutes)

Welcome cooler weather with a pie that offers two of autumn's delights: apples and cranberries.

CRUST
1 refrigerated pie crust (from
   15-oz. pkg.) or Pastry for
   One-Crust Pie (page 67)

FILLING
4 cups (4 medium) sliced peeled
   apples
2 cups fresh or frozen cranberries
½ cup sugar
¼ cup all-purpose flour
¼ cup firmly packed brown sugar
½ teaspoon cinnamon
¼ teaspoon nutmeg

TOPPING
½ cup all-purpose flour
⅓ cup firmly packed brown sugar
¼ teaspoon cinnamon
Dash nutmeg
¼ cup margarine or butter
⅓ cup chopped pecans

1. Prepare pie crust for *one-crust filled pie* using 9-inch pie pan.

2. Heat oven to 375°F. In large bowl, combine apples and cranberries. In small bowl, combine all remaining filling ingredients; mix well. Add dry ingredients to fruit; toss to coat. Pour filling into crust-lined pan.

3. In small bowl, combine all topping ingredients except margarine and pecans. With pastry blender or fork, cut in margarine until crumbly. Stir in pecans. Sprinkle evenly over top of pie.

4. Bake at 375°F. for 45 to 55 minutes or until apples are tender and crust and topping are golden brown. Cover edge of crust with strips of foil after 15 to 20 minutes of baking to prevent excessive browning. If desired, serve warm with whipped cream or ice cream.

Nutrition per Serving: Serving Size: ⅛ of Recipe. Calories 410; Calories from Fat 150; Total Fat 17g; Saturated Fat 4g; Cholesterol 5mg; Sodium 210mg; Dietary Fiber 3g

Dietary Exchange: 1 Starch, 3 Fruit, 3½ Fat OR 4 Carbohydrate, 3½ Fat

French Cranberry-Apple Pie

MAPLE FROSTED APPLE PAN-TART

Yield: 8 servings; **Prep Time:** 35 minutes
(Ready in 1 hour 30 minutes)

You don't need a pie pan to bake this delicious apple pie. It's quickly shaped, then baked on a cookie sheet. A maple glaze adds a sweet finish.

CRUST
1 (15-oz.) pkg. refrigerated pie crusts or Pastry for Two-Crust Pie (page 67)
1 teaspoon all-purpose flour
1 egg white, beaten

FILLING
1 ½ cups corn flakes cereal
6 cups (6 medium) thinly sliced, peeled apples
1 cup sugar
1 teaspoon cinnamon

GLAZE
½ cup powdered sugar
3 tablespoons maple-flavored syrup

1. Prepare pie crust for *two-crust pie.* Heat oven to 350°F. Sprinkle 1 pie crust with ½ teaspoon of the flour. Place crust flour side down on ungreased cookie sheet.

2. Sprinkle cereal over crust to within ½ inch of edge. Top with apples. Sprinkle with sugar and cinnamon. Brush edge of crust with beaten egg white. Place second crust over filling. Fold edge of bottom crust over top crust; pinch edges to seal and flute. Cut slits in several places in top crust. Brush top crust with egg white.

3. Bake at 350°F. for 45 to 55 minutes or until crust is golden brown and apples are tender.

4. In small bowl, combine glaze ingredients; beat until smooth. Drizzle over warm crust. Serve warm or cool.

Nutrition per Serving: Serving Size: ⅛ of Recipe. Calories 460; Calories from Fat 140; Total Fat 15g; Saturated Fat 6g; Cholesterol 15mg; Sodium 330mg; Dietary Fiber 2g

Dietary Exchange: 1 Starch, 4 Fruit, 3 Fat OR 5 Carbohydrate, 3 Fat

FRESH BLUEBERRY PIE

Yield: 8 servings; **Prep Time:** 35 minutes
(Ready in 1 hour 30 minutes)

This old-fashioned summertime pie will remind you of country fairs and church picnics. Before mixing the fruit with the sugar, pick out any stems and wilted blueberries.

CRUST
1 (15-oz.) pkg. refrigerated pie crusts or Pastry for Two-Crust Pie (page 67)

FILLING
4 cups fresh blueberries*
¾ cup sugar
¼ cup all-purpose flour
¼ teaspoon cinnamon
2 teaspoons lemon juice
2 tablespoons margarine or butter

TOPPING
1 to 2 tablespoons milk
2 teaspoons sugar
Dash cinnamon

1. Prepare pie crust for *two-crust pie* using 9-inch pie pan.

2. Heat oven to 425°F. In large bowl, combine blueberries, ¾ cup sugar, flour, ¼ teaspoon cinnamon and lemon juice; toss gently to mix. Spoon into crust-lined pan. Dot with margarine. Top with second crust; seal edges and flute. Cut slits in several places in top crust. Brush crust with milk; sprinkle with 2 teaspoons sugar and dash cinnamon.

3. Bake at 425°F. for 45 to 55 minutes or until crust is golden brown. Cover edge of crust with strips of foil after 15 to 20 minutes of baking to prevent excessive browning.

Tip: Frozen blueberries, thawed and well drained, can be substituted for fresh blueberries.

Nutrition per Serving: Serving Size: ⅛ of Recipe. Calories 400; Calories from Fat 160; Total Fat 18g; Saturated Fat 6g; Cholesterol 15mg; Sodium 320mg; Dietary Fiber 3g

Dietary Exchange: ½ Starch, 3 ½ Fruit, 3 ½ Fat OR 4 Carbohydrate, 3 ½ Fat

Maple Frosted Apple Pan-Tart

SOUTHERN PEACH PIE WITH BERRY SAUCE

PICTURED ON PAGE 63.

Yield: 8 servings; Prep Time: 45 minutes
(Ready in 1 hour 50 minutes)

Lemon and nutmeg bring out the flavor of the peaches in a tasty pie that has the colors of a summer sunset.

CRUST
1 (15-oz.) pkg. refrigerated pie crusts or Pastry for Two-Crust Pie (page 67)

FILLING
5 ½ to 6 cups (6 to 8 medium) sliced peeled peaches
1 tablespoon lemon juice
1 cup sugar
¼ cup cornstarch
¼ teaspoon nutmeg
¼ teaspoon salt

SAUCE
¼ cup sugar
1 tablespoon cornstarch
1 (12-oz.) pkg. frozen whole raspberries or blackberries, thawed, drained and reserving liquid
½ teaspoon almond extract

1. Prepare pie crust for *two-crust pie* using 9-inch pie pan.

2. Heat oven to 400°F. In large bowl, combine peaches and lemon juice. Add 1 cup sugar, ¼ cup cornstarch, nutmeg and salt; toss gently to mix. Spoon into crust-lined pan. Top with second crust; seal edges and flute. Cut slits in several places in top crust.

3. Bake at 400°F. for 35 to 45 minutes or until golden brown. Cover edge of crust with strips of foil after 15 to 20 minutes of baking to prevent excessive browning.

4. Meanwhile, in medium saucepan, combine ¼ cup sugar and 1 tablespoon cornstarch; mix well. If necessary, add water to reserved raspberry liquid to measure ½ cup; add liquid to sugar mixture. Cook over medium heat until thickened, stirring constantly. Stir in almond extract. Gently fold in raspberries. Cool 30 minutes. To serve, spoon sauce over individual servings.

Nutrition per Serving: Serving Size: ⅛ of Recipe. Calories 490; Calories from Fat 140; Total Fat 15g; Saturated Fat 6g; Cholesterol 15mg; Sodium 340mg; Dietary Fiber 5g

Dietary Exchange: 1 Starch, 4 ½ Fruit, 3 Fat OR 5 ½ Carbohydrate, 3 Fat

CHERRY PIE

Yield: 8 servings; Prep Time: 30 minutes
(Ready in 1 hour 15 minutes)

Fresh tart cherries make a splendid pie, though pitting them is labor-intensive. Don't be tempted to substitute sweet red Bing or golden Rainier cherries. Though lovely to eat out of hand, they lack the acidity to remain flavorful when baked.

CRUST
1 (15-oz.) pkg. refrigerated pie crusts or Pastry for Two-Crust Pie (page 67)

FILLING*
2 (16-oz.) cans pitted tart red cherries in syrup, drained**
1 ¼ cups sugar
¼ cup all-purpose flour
2 tablespoons margarine or butter

1. Prepare pie crust for *two-crust pie* using 9-inch pie pan.

2. Heat oven to 425°F. In large bowl, combine cherries, sugar and flour; toss gently to mix. Spoon into crust-lined pan.*** Dot with margarine. Top with second crust; seal edges and flute. Cut slits in several places in top crust.

3. Bake at 425°F. for 35 to 45 minutes or until juice begins to bubble through slits in crust.

Tips: Two 21-oz. cans cherry pie filling can be substituted for filling.

***Four cups pitted fresh tart red cherries can be substituted for canned cherries.*

****If desired, sprinkle cherries with ¼ teaspoon almond extract before dotting with margarine.*

Nutrition per Serving: Serving Size: ⅛ of Recipe. Calories 450; Calories from Fat 160; Total Fat 18g; Saturated Fat 6g; Cholesterol 15mg; Sodium 320mg; Dietary Fiber 2g

Dietary Exchange: 1 Starch, 3 ½ Fruit, 3 ½ Fat OR 4 ½ Carbohydrate, 3 ½ Fat

RASPBERRY-CHERRY PIE

PICTURED ON PAGE 1.

Yield: 8 servings; **Prep Time:** 30 minutes
(Ready in 1 hour 15 minutes)

The combination of raspberries and cherries provides stunning color and delicious flavor in a simple-to-make pie.

CRUST

1 (15-oz.) pkg. refrigerated pie crusts or Pastry for Two-Crust Pie (page 67)

FILLING

2 cups fresh or frozen whole raspberries (do not thaw)
¼ to ½ cup sugar
1 tablespoon all-purpose flour
1 (21-oz.) can cherry fruit pie filling

1. Prepare pie crust for *two-crust pie* using 9-inch pie pan.

2. Heat oven to 400°F. In large bowl, combine all filling ingredients; stir gently to mix. Spoon into crust-lined pan. Top with second crust; seal edges and flute. Cut slits or shapes in several places in top crust.

3. Bake at 400°F. for 40 to 45 minutes or until crust is golden brown and filling is bubbly. (Place foil or cookie sheet on lowest oven rack during baking to guard against spillage.)

Nutrition per Serving: Serving Size: ⅛ of Recipe. Calories 400; Calories from Fat 140; Total Fat 15g; Saturated Fat 6g; Cholesterol 15mg; Sodium 280mg; Dietary Fiber 3g

Dietary Exchange: 1 Starch, 3 Fruit, 3 Fat OR 4 Carbohydrate, 3 Fat

CRANBERRY-PEACH PIE

Yield: 8 servings; **Prep Time:** 40 minutes
(Ready in 1 hour 20 minutes)

An inspired duo: Tart red cranberries balance the sweetness of the peach filling and offer beautiful color contrast, too.

CRUST

1 (15-oz.) pkg. refrigerated pie crusts or Pastry for Two-Crust Pie (page 67)

FILLING

2 cups fresh or frozen cranberries
½ cup sugar
2 tablespoons cornstarch
1 (21-oz.) can peach pie filling

TOPPING

1 egg yolk
1 teaspoon water

1. Prepare pie crust for *two-crust pie* using 9-inch pie pan.

2. Heat oven to 425°F. In large bowl, combine cranberries, sugar and cornstarch; mix well. Add pie filling; stir gently. Spoon into crust-lined pan.

3. Unfold second crust. Using star-shaped canapé or cookie cutter, cut pattern of stars in dough, cutting to within 1½ inches of edge.* Reserve cutouts. Place crust over filling; fold edge of top crust under bottom crust. Press together to seal. Dip fork tines in flour; press fork tines diagonally on edge of dough. Rotate tines 90 degrees and press next to first set of marks. Continue around rim.

4. In small bowl, combine egg yolk and water; beat well. Brush over top crust. Arrange star cutouts on top crust; brush with egg yolk mixture.

5. Bake at 425°F. for 30 to 40 minutes or until crust is deep golden brown and filling is bubbly. Cover edge of crust with strips of foil after 15 to 20 minutes of baking to prevent excessive browning.

Tip: Any shape canapé or cookie cutter can be used.

Nutrition per Serving: Serving Size: ⅛ of Recipe. Calories 380; Calories from Fat 140; Total Fat 15g; Saturated Fat 6g; Cholesterol 40mg; Sodium 290mg; Dietary Fiber 2g

Dietary Exchange: 1 Starch, 3 Fruit, 2½ Fat OR 4 Carbohydrate, 2½ Fat

CRANBERRY-APRICOT PIE

Yield: 8 servings; **Prep Time:** 30 minutes
(Ready in 3 hours 20 minutes)

With canned pie filling in the pantry and cranberries in the freezer, you don't have to plan ahead to make this scrumptious pie. If you wish, substitute cherry or apple pie filling for the apricot.

CRUST
1 (15-oz.) pkg. refrigerated pie
    crusts or Pastry for Two-Crust Pie
    (page 67)

FILLING
1/2 cup sugar
1 tablespoon cornstarch
1 (21-oz.) can apricot pie filling
1 1/2 cups fresh or frozen
    cranberries
1/2 teaspoon cinnamon

GARNISH
Water
2 teaspoons sugar

1. Prepare pie crust for *two-crust pie* using 9-inch pie pan.

2. Heat oven to 425°F. In large bowl, combine 1/2 cup sugar and cornstarch; mix well. Stir in pie filling, cranberries and cinnamon until well mixed. Spoon into crust-lined pan.

3. With fluted pastry cutter, cut remaining pie crust into 1/2-inch-wide strips. Place strips over filling, overlapping to make a lattice design; flute edge. Brush with water; sprinkle with 2 teaspoons sugar.

4. Bake at 425°F. for 40 to 50 minutes or until crust is golden brown. Cover edge of crust with strips of foil after 15 to 20 minutes of baking to prevent excessive browning. Cool 2 hours or until completely cooled.

Nutrition per Serving: Serving Size: 1/8 of Recipe. Calories 400; Calories from Fat 140; Total Fat 15g; Saturated Fat 6g; Cholesterol 15mg; Sodium 280mg; Dietary Fiber 3g

Dietary Exchange: 1 Starch, 3 Fruit, 3 Fat OR 4 Carbohydrate, 3 Fat

SLICES OF LEMON PIE

♦

Yield: 8 servings; **Prep Time:** 35 minutes
(Ready in 2 hours 20 minutes)

Pucker up if you love lemon! This pie uses whole slices of the golden fruit, not just a few drops of the juice. Use a sharp paring knife to peel the lemons right down to the flesh so all traces of the white pith (which is bitter) are removed. If you want the pie even more intensely lemon, add some grated lemon peel along with the orange peel.

CRUST
1 (15-oz.) pkg. refrigerated pie
    crusts or Pastry for Two-Crust Pie
    (page 67)

FILLING
2 cups sugar
1/3 cup all-purpose flour
1/4 teaspoon salt
2/3 cup water
2 tablespoons margarine or butter,
    softened
2 to 3 teaspoons grated orange
    peel
3 eggs
1 to 2 lemons, peeled, sliced
    1/8 inch thick

1. Prepare pie crust for *two-crust pie* using 9-inch pie pan.

2. Heat oven to 400°F. In large bowl, combine sugar, flour and salt; mix well. Add water, margarine, orange peel and eggs; beat until well blended. Stir in lemon slices. Pour into crust-lined pan. Top with second crust; seal edges and flute. Cut slits in several places in top crust.

3. Bake at 400°F. for 35 to 45 minutes or until golden brown. Cool 1 hour or until completely cooled. Store in refrigerator.

Nutrition per Serving: Serving Size: 1/8 of Recipe. Calories 510; Calories from Fat 170; Total Fat 19g; Saturated Fat 7g; Cholesterol 95mg; Sodium 400mg; Dietary Fiber 1g

Dietary Exchange: 1 1/2 Starch, 4 Fruit, 3 1/2 Fat OR 5 1/2 Carbohydrate, 3 1/2 Fat

Cranberry-Apricot Pie

NEW-FASHIONED RHU-BERRY PIE

Yield: 8 servings; Prep Time: 40 minutes
(Ready in 1 hour 25 minutes)

Rhubarb and strawberries are an expected twosome; here, blueberries are a refreshing change of pace with the spring stalks. To prepare fresh rhubarb, trim the ends and discard all traces of the leaves (rhubarb leaves are poisonous). Scrub the stalks and cut into pieces about 1 inch in length.

CRUST
1 (15-oz.) pkg. refrigerated pie
   crusts or Pastry for Two-Crust Pie
   (page 67)

FILLING
2 cups cut-up fresh rhubarb
2 cups fresh blueberries
¾ cup sugar
¼ cup all-purpose flour
⅛ teaspoon nutmeg
Dash salt

1. Prepare pie crust for *two-crust pie* using 9-inch pie pan.

2. Heat oven to 400°F. In large bowl, combine all filling ingredients; toss gently to mix. Spoon into crust-lined pan. Top with second crust; seal edges and flute. Cut slits in several places in top crust.

3. Bake at 400°F. for 40 to 45 minutes or until golden brown. Cover edge of crust with strips of foil after 15 to 20 minutes of baking to prevent excessive browning.

Nutrition per Serving: Serving Size: ⅛ of Recipe. Calories 360; Calories from Fat 140; Total Fat 15g; Saturated Fat 6g; Cholesterol 15mg; Sodium 300mg; Dietary Fiber 2g

Dietary Exchange: ½ Starch, 3 Fruit, 3 Fat OR 3 ½ Carbohydrate, 3 Fat

CRUMBLEBERRY PEAR PIE

Yield: 8 servings; Prep Time: 30 minutes
(Ready in 1 hour 30 minutes)

Five separate layers—flaky pastry, almond filling, sliced pears, berries and crumbly topping—join forces for an exquisite pie.

CRUST
1 refrigerated pie crust (from
   15-oz. pkg.) or Pastry for
   One-Crust Pie (page 67)

FILLING
½ cup butter
½ cup sugar
2 eggs
1 cup finely ground almonds
¼ cup all-purpose flour
1 firm large pear, peeled, thinly
   sliced
1 cup fresh or frozen raspberries
   and/or blueberries, thawed

TOPPING
¾ cup all-purpose flour
⅓ cup firmly packed brown sugar
½ teaspoon almond extract
⅓ cup butter

1. Prepare pie crust for *one-crust filled pie* using 9-inch pie pan.

2. Heat oven to 350°F. In large bowl, combine ½ cup butter and sugar; beat until light and fluffy. Add eggs 1 at a time, beating well after each addition. Stir in almonds and ¼ cup flour just until evenly moistened. Spread mixture in crust-lined pan. Arrange pear slices on top of filling, overlapping slightly.

3. Bake at 350°F. for 20 to 30 minutes or until filling and pears are light golden brown.

4. Meanwhile, in medium bowl, combine ¾ cup flour, brown sugar and almond extract; mix well. With pastry blender or fork, cut in ⅓ cup butter until mixture resembles coarse crumbs.

5. Remove pie from oven. Sprinkle raspberries over pears; sprinkle with topping. Return to oven; bake an additional 18 to 28 minutes or until topping is golden brown. Serve warm. Store in refrigerator.

Nutrition per Serving: Serving Size: ⅛ of Recipe. Calories 550; Calories from Fat 310; Total Fat 34g; Saturated Fat 16g; Cholesterol 110mg; Sodium 350mg; Dietary Fiber 4g

Dietary Exchange: 2 Starch, 1 ½ Fruit, 6 ½ Fat OR 3 ½ Carbohydrate, 6 ½ Fat

FRESH RASPBERRY LATTICE PIE

◆

Yield: 8 servings; **Prep Time:** 50 minutes
(Ready in 2 hours 35 minutes)

Raspberries are delicate and highly perishable, so they nearly always command a steep price in the market. The red or black varieties are equally good in this pie, or combine them for colorful contrast.

FILLING

4 1/2 cups fresh raspberries*
1 1/4 cups sugar
5 tablespoons cornstarch
Dash salt
1 tablespoon margarine or butter

CRUST

1 (15-oz.) pkg. refrigerated pie
   crusts or Pastry for Two-Crust Pie
   (page 67)

1. In medium saucepan, combine raspberries, sugar, cornstarch and salt. Cook over medium heat for about 15 minutes or until mixture boils and thickens, stirring constantly. Refrigerate 1 hour or until completely cooled.

2. Prepare pie crust for *two-crust pie* using 9-inch pie pan. Heat oven to 425°F. Pour filling into crust-lined pan. Dot with margarine.

3. To make lattice top, cut second crust into 1/2-inch-wide strips. Arrange strips in lattice design over filling. Trim edges and flute. With any remaining crust, form small pea-sized balls; place over crossings in lattice pattern.

4. Bake at 425°F. for 35 to 45 minutes or until golden brown. If desired, sprinkle with powdered sugar before serving.

Tip: Frozen whole raspberries, thawed and well drained, can be substituted for fresh raspberries.

Nutrition per Serving: Serving Size: 1/8 of Recipe. Calories 420; Calories from Fat 140; Total Fat 16g; Saturated Fat 6g; Cholesterol 15mg; Sodium 310mg; Dietary Fiber 5g

Dietary Exchange: 1/2 Starch, 4 Fruit, 3 Fat OR 4 1/2 Carbohydrate, 3 Fat

SWEET POTATO PIE

◆

Yield: 8 servings; **Prep Time:** 20 minutes
(Ready in 2 hours)

A touch of dry sherry adds a subtle nuance to this Dixieland treasure.

CRUST

1 refrigerated pie crust (from
   15-oz. pkg.) or Pastry for
   One-Crust Pie (page 67)

FILLING

1 1/2 cups mashed canned sweet
   potatoes
2/3 cup firmly packed brown sugar
1 cup half-and-half
1 teaspoon cinnamon
1/2 teaspoon allspice
1 tablespoon dry sherry or lemon
   juice
2 eggs, beaten

TOPPING

1 cup whipping cream
2 tablespoons sugar
1 teaspoon vanilla
Pecan halves

1. Prepare pie crust for *one-crust filled pie* using 9-inch pie pan.

2. Heat oven to 425°F. In blender container or food processor bowl with metal blade, combine all filling ingredients; blend well. Pour into crust-lined pan.

3. Bake at 425°F. for 15 minutes. Reduce oven temperature to 350°F.; bake an additional 30 to 40 minutes or until center is set. Cool 45 minutes or until completely cooled.

4. In small bowl, combine whipping cream, sugar and vanilla; beat until soft peaks form. Garnish pie with whipped cream and pecan halves. Store in refrigerator.

Nutrition per Serving: Serving Size: 1/8 of Recipe. Calories 420; Calories from Fat 220; Total Fat 24g; Saturated Fat 12g; Cholesterol 110mg; Sodium 230mg; Dietary Fiber 1g

Dietary Exchange: 1 1/2 Starch, 1 1/2 Fruit, 4 1/2 Fat OR 3 Carbohydrate, 4 1/2 Fat

CUSTARD PIE

✦

Yield: 8 servings; Prep Time: 25 minutes
(Ready in 1 hour 25 minutes)

This simple old-fashioned pie is comfort food, pure and simple, perfect to finish a cozy family supper.

CRUST
1 refrigerated pie crust (from 15-oz. pkg.) or Pastry for One-Crust Pie (page 67)

FILLING
3 eggs
¾ cup sugar
¼ teaspoon salt
¼ teaspoon nutmeg or cinnamon
1 teaspoon vanilla
2½ cups hot milk

1. Prepare pie crust for *one-crust filled pie* using 9-inch pie pan.

2. Heat oven to 400°F. In large bowl, beat eggs. Add sugar, salt, nutmeg and vanilla; mix well. Gradually blend in hot milk. Pour into crust-lined pan.

3. Bake at 400°F. for 25 to 30 minutes or until knife inserted near center comes out clean. Cool 30 minutes. Serve slightly warm or cold. Store in refrigerator.

Nutrition per Serving: Serving Size: ⅛ of Recipe. Calories 260; Calories from Fat 100; Total Fat 11g; Saturated Fat 4g; Cholesterol 90mg; Sodium 270mg; Dietary Fiber 0g

Dietary Exchange: 2 Starch, 2 Fat OR 2 Carbohydrate, 2 Fat

HONEYED PUMPKIN PIE WITH BROILED PRALINE TOPPING

✦

Yield: 10 servings; Prep Time: 25 minutes
(Ready in 3 hours 20 minutes)

The classic holiday dessert gets a sweet twist with honey-laced filling and Southern-style pecan–brown sugar topping. Serve with coffee or tea.

CRUST
1 refrigerated pie crust (from 15-oz. pkg.) or Pastry for One-Crust Pie (page 67)

FILLING
1 (16-oz.) can (2 cups) pumpkin
1 cup honey
¾ teaspoon salt
¾ teaspoon nutmeg
¼ teaspoon allspice
4 eggs
¾ cup evaporated milk

TOPPING
⅓ cup chopped pecans
¼ cup firmly packed brown sugar
2 tablespoons margarine or butter, melted

1. Prepare pie crust for *one-crust filled pie* using 10-inch deep dish pie pan.

2. Heat oven to 375°F. In large bowl, combine pumpkin, honey, salt, nutmeg and allspice; mix well. Add eggs; blend well. Gradually add milk, beating at low speed until well blended. Pour into crust-lined pan.

3. Bake at 375°F. for 45 to 55 minutes or until edges are set. Cool on wire rack for 2 hours or until completely cooled.

4. In small bowl, combine all topping ingredients; sprinkle over top of cooled pie. Broil 4 to 6 inches from heat for 2 to 3 minutes or until topping is bubbly. Store in refrigerator.

Nutrition per Serving: Serving Size: ⅒ of Recipe. Calories 350; Calories from Fat 130; Total Fat 14g; Saturated Fat 5g; Cholesterol 95mg; Sodium 350mg; Dietary Fiber 2g

Dietary Exchange: 1½ Starch, 2 Fruit, 2½ Fat OR 3½ Carbohydrate, 2½ Fat

LEMON CHESS PIE

Yield: 8 servings; Prep Time: 25 minutes
(Ready in 4 hours 35 minutes)

Butter in the filling makes this Southern favorite richer than other custard pies. Garnish each slice with a sprig of fresh mint or a couple of fresh raspberries.

CRUST
1 refrigerated pie crust (from 15-oz. pkg.) or Pastry for One-Crust Pie (page 67)

FILLING

- ⅓ cup margarine or butter, softened
- 1 cup sugar
- 3 eggs
- 2 tablespoons all-purpose flour
- ¼ cup lemon juice
- 1 tablespoon grated lemon peel
- ½ cup milk
- ¼ teaspoon nutmeg

1. Heat oven to 450°F. Prepare pie crust for *one-crust filled pie* using 9-inch pie pan. Bake at 450°F. for 5 to 8 minutes or until light brown. Reduce oven temperature to 325°F.

2. Meanwhile, in large bowl, combine margarine, sugar and eggs; beat well. Add flour, lemon juice, lemon peel and milk; blend well. (Mixture may look curdled.) Pour into partially baked crust. Sprinkle with nutmeg.

3. Bake at 325°F. for 40 to 45 minutes or until edges of filling begin to brown and center is almost set. Cover edge of crust with strips of foil after 15 to 20 minutes of baking to prevent excessive browning. Cool 30 minutes. Refrigerate at least 3 hours before serving. If desired, serve with whipped cream. Store in refrigerator.

Nutrition per Serving: Serving Size: ⅛ of Recipe. Calories 330; Calories from Fat 150; Total Fat 17g; Saturated Fat 5g; Cholesterol 90mg; Sodium 260mg; Dietary Fiber 0g

Dietary Exchange: 1 Starch, 1½ Fruit, 3½ Fat OR 2½ Carbohydrate, 3½ Fat

Lemon Chess Pie

RHUBARB CREAM PIE

Yield: 8 servings; Prep Time: 25 minutes
(Ready in 2 hours 30 minutes)

Bring a springtime meal to a sweet close with this lovely pie.

CRUST

1 refrigerated pie crust (from 15-oz. pkg.) or Pastry for One-Crust Pie (page 67)

FILLING

2 cups cut-up fresh rhubarb (do not use frozen rhubarb)

3 egg yolks

1/2 cup half-and-half

1 cup sugar

2 tablespoons all-purpose flour

1/2 teaspoon salt

MERINGUE

3 egg whites

1/4 teaspoon cream of tartar

1/2 teaspoon vanilla

6 tablespoons sugar

1. Prepare pie crust for *one-crust filled pie* using 9-inch pie pan.

2. Heat oven to 400°F. Place rhubarb in crust-lined pan. In small bowl, beat egg yolks until thick and lemon colored. Stir in half-and-half. Add all remaining filling ingredients; blend well. Pour egg mixture over rhubarb.

Rhubarb Cream Pie

3. Bake at 400°F. for 10 minutes. Reduce oven temperature to 350°F.; bake an additional 40 minutes.

4. In small, deep bowl, combine egg whites, cream of tartar and vanilla; beat at medium speed until soft peaks form. Add 6 tablespoons sugar, 1 tablespoon at a time, beating at high speed until stiff glossy peaks form and sugar is dissolved. Spoon meringue onto hot filling; spread to edge of crust to seal well and prevent shrinkage.

5. Bake at 350°F. for 15 to 20 minutes or until meringue is light golden brown. Cool 1 hour or until completely cooled. Store in refrigerator.

Nutrition per Serving: Serving Size: 1/8 of Recipe. Calories 320; Calories from Fat 100; Total Fat 11g; Saturated Fat 5g; Cholesterol 95mg; Sodium 300mg; Dietary Fiber 1g

Dietary Exchange: 1 1/2 Starch, 2 Fruit, 2 Fat OR 3 1/2 Carbohydrate, 2 Fat

OLD-FASHIONED PUMPKIN PIE

Yield: 8 servings; Prep Time: 25 minutes
(Ready in 4 hours)

Thanksgiving just wouldn't be the same without a slice of pumpkin pie.

CRUST

1 refrigerated pie crust (from 15-oz. pkg.) or Pastry for One-Crust Pie (page 67)

FILLING

3/4 cup sugar

1 1/2 teaspoons pumpkin pie spice

1/2 teaspoon salt

1 (16-oz.) can (2 cups) pumpkin

1 (12-oz.) can (1 1/2 cups) evaporated milk

2 eggs, beaten

TOPPING

1/2 cup whipping cream, whipped

1. Prepare pie crust for *one-crust filled pie* using 9-inch pie pan.

2. Heat oven to 425°F. In large bowl, combine all filling ingredients; blend well. Pour into crust-lined pan.

3. Bake at 425°F. for 15 minutes. Reduce oven temperature to 350°F.; bake an additional 40 to 50 minutes or until knife inserted near center comes out clean. Cool 30 minutes. Refrigerate at least 2 hours or until serving time. Just before serving, top with whipped cream. Store in refrigerator.

Nutrition per Serving: Serving Size: 1/8 of Recipe. Calories 340; Calories from Fat 150; Total Fat 17g; Saturated Fat 9g; Cholesterol 95mg; Sodium 340mg; Dietary Fiber 2g

Dietary Exchange: 2 Starch, 1/2 Fruit, 3 1/2 Fat OR 2 1/2 Carbohydrate, 3 1/2 Fat

VARIATION

Maple Pumpkin Pie: Substitute 1/2 cup maple-flavored syrup for 1/2 cup of the evaporated milk.

LEMON MERINGUE PIE

Yield: 8 servings; Prep Time: 1 hour
(Ready in 5 hours 15 minutes)

Eggs separate most easily when they are cold, but the whites will whip best at room temperature. To take off the chill, set the bowl of whites into a larger pan filled with warm water.

CRUST
1 refrigerated pie crust (from 15-oz. pkg.) or Pastry for One-Crust Pie (page 67)

FILLING
1 1/4 cups sugar
1/3 cup cornstarch
1/2 teaspoon salt
1 1/2 cups cold water
3 egg yolks
2 tablespoons margarine or butter
1 tablespoon grated lemon peel
1/2 cup fresh lemon juice

MERINGUE
3 egg whites
1/4 teaspoon cream of tartar
1/2 teaspoon vanilla
1/4 cup sugar

1. Heat oven to 450°F. Prepare pie crust for *one-crust baked shell* using 9-inch pie pan. Bake at 450°F. for 9 to 11 minutes or until light golden brown. Cool 30 minutes or until completely cooled.

2. Meanwhile, in medium saucepan, combine 1 1/4 cups sugar, cornstarch and salt; mix well. Gradually stir in water until smooth. Cook over medium heat until mixture boils, stirring constantly. Boil 1 minute, stirring constantly. Remove from heat.

3. In small bowl, beat egg yolks. Stir about 1/4 cup of hot mixture into egg yolks. Gradually stir yolk mixture into hot mixture. Cook over low heat until mixture boils, stirring constantly. Boil 1 minute, stirring constantly.

4. Remove from heat; stir in margarine, lemon peel and lemon juice. Cool slightly, about 15 minutes. Pour into cooled baked shell.

5. Reduce oven temperature to 350°F. In small deep bowl, combine egg whites, cream of tartar and vanilla; beat at medium speed for about 1 minute or until soft peaks form. Add sugar 1 tablespoon at a time, beating at high speed until stiff glossy peaks form and sugar is dissolved. Spoon meringue onto hot filling; spread to edge of crust to seal well and prevent shrinkage.

6. Bake at 350°F. for 12 to 15 minutes or until meringue is light golden brown. Cool 1 hour or until completely cooled. Refrigerate 3 hours or until filling is set. Store in refrigerator.

Nutrition per Serving: Serving Size: 1/8 of Recipe. Calories 230; Calories from Fat 45; Total Fat 5g; Saturated Fat 1g; Cholesterol 80mg; Sodium 190mg; Dietary Fiber 0g

Dietary Exchange: 1 Starch, 2 Fruit, 1/2 Fat OR 3 Carbohydrate, 1/2 Fat

CHOCOLATE CASHEW PIE

Yield: 10 servings; Prep Time: 25 minutes
(Ready in 3 hours 20 minutes)

Nut lovers will rave over this decadent combination of cashews and chocolate, garnished with additional chocolate-covered cashews.

CRUST
1 refrigerated pie crust (from 15-oz. pkg.) or Pastry for One-Crust Pie (page 67)

FILLING AND TOPPING
3/4 cup light corn syrup
1/2 cup sugar
3 tablespoons margarine or butter, melted
1 teaspoon vanilla
3 eggs
1 (6-oz.) pkg. (1 cup) semi-sweet chocolate chips
1 cup cashew halves
10 whole cashews
Whipped cream, if desired*

1. Prepare pie crust for *one-crust filled pie* using 9-inch pie pan.

2. Heat oven to 325°F. In large bowl, combine corn syrup, sugar, margarine, vanilla and eggs; beat with wire whisk until well blended. Reserve 2 tablespoons chocolate chips for topping. Stir in remaining chocolate chips and cashew halves. Spread evenly in crust-lined pan.

3. Bake at 325°F. for 45 to 55 minutes or until pie is deep golden brown and filling is set. Cover edge of crust with strips of foil after 15 to 20 minutes of baking to prevent excessive browning. Cool 2 hours or until completely cooled.

4. Meanwhile, line cookie sheet with waxed paper. In small saucepan, melt reserved 2 tablespoons chocolate chips over low heat. Dip each whole cashew in chocolate. Place on lined cookie sheet. Refrigerate 15 to 20 minutes or until chocolate is set. Garnish pie with whipped cream and chocolate-dipped cashews. Store in refrigerator.

Tip: To flavor whipped cream, fold in sweetened cocoa mix, grated citrus peel, spices or a favorite liqueur.

Nutrition per Serving: Serving Size: 1/10 of Recipe. Calories 500; Calories from Fat 250; Total Fat 28g; Saturated Fat 11g; Cholesterol 90mg; Sodium 290mg; Dietary Fiber 2g

Dietary Exchange: 1 1/2 Starch, 2 Fruit, 5 1/2 Fat OR 3 1/2 Carbohydrate, 5 1/2 Fat

Chocolate Cashew Pie

GOLDEN PECAN PIE

Yield: 8 servings; **Prep Time:** 25 minutes
(Ready in 3 hours 15 minutes)

One of the most treasured desserts from the American South, pecan pie is sweetly seductive. Cut it into thin slivers: It's very rich!

CRUST
1 refrigerated pie crust (from 15-oz. pkg.) or Pastry for One-Crust Pie (page 67)

FILLING
1/3 cup firmly packed brown sugar
1 1/2 teaspoons all-purpose flour
1 1/4 cups light corn syrup
1 1/4 teaspoons vanilla
3 eggs
1 1/2 cups pecan halves or broken pecans
2 tablespoons margarine or butter, melted

1. Prepare pie crust for *one-crust filled pie* using 9-inch pie pan.

2. Heat oven to 375°F. In large bowl, combine brown sugar, flour, corn syrup, vanilla and eggs; beat well. Stir in pecans and margarine. Pour into crust-lined pan.

3. Bake at 375°F. for 40 to 50 minutes or until filling is puffed and pie is golden brown. Cool 2 hours or until completely cooled. Store in refrigerator.

Nutrition per Serving: Serving Size: 1/8 of Recipe. Calories 510; Calories from Fat 230; Total Fat 25g; Saturated Fat 5g; Cholesterol 85mg; Sodium 260mg; Dietary Fiber 2g

Dietary Exchange: 1 1/2 Starch, 3 Fruit, 4 1/2 Fat OR 4 1/2 Carbohydrate, 4 1/2 Fat

VARIATION

Orange Pecan Pie: Add 1/2 teaspoon grated orange peel to filling. If desired, garnish with candied orange peel.

MAPLE NUTCRACKER PIE

◆

Yield: 8 servings; **Prep Time:** 40 minutes
(Ready in 1 hour 25 minutes)

Maple syrup and walnuts collaborate for a sweet variation on pecan pie, decorated with a galaxy of pastry star cutouts.

CRUST
1 (15-oz.) pkg. refrigerated pie crusts or Pastry for Two-Crust Pie (page 67)
1 egg, slightly beaten

FILLING
1 cup firmly packed brown sugar
1 cup butter maple–flavored syrup
1/3 cup margarine or butter, melted
1 teaspoon vanilla
3 eggs
1 cup chopped walnuts or pecans

TOPPING
1/2 cup whipping cream, whipped

1. Prepare pie crust for *one-crust filled pie* using 9-inch pie pan. Trim crust even with edge of pan. Using 2-inch star-shaped canapé or cookie cutter, cut 22 stars from second crust.*

2. Heat oven to 375°F. Place 8 star cutouts on ungreased cookie sheet. Brush with beaten egg. Reserve remaining beaten egg. Bake at 375°F. for 8 to 11 minutes or until golden brown.

3. Meanwhile, in large bowl, combine brown sugar, syrup, margarine, vanilla and 3 eggs; blend well. Stir in walnuts. Pour into crust-lined pan. Brush edge of crust with beaten egg. Arrange remaining 14 star cutouts over crust edge, extending over filling. Brush with reserved beaten egg.

4. Bake at 375°F. for 35 to 45 minutes or until center is set and crust is deep golden brown. Cover edge of pie crust with strips of foil after 15 to 20 minutes of baking to prevent excessive browning.

5. Just before serving, top each serving with dollop of whipped cream and star cutout. Store in refrigerator.

Tip: Any shape canapé or cookie cutter can be used.

Nutrition per Serving: Serving Size: 1/8 of Recipe. Calories 680; Calories from Fat 330; Total Fat 37g; Saturated Fat 11g; Cholesterol 130mg; Sodium 460mg; Dietary Fiber 1g

Dietary Exchange: 2 Starch, 3 1/2 Fruit, 7 Fat OR 5 1/2 Carbohydrate, 7 Fat

RAISIN-WALNUT PIE

Yield: 8 servings; Prep Time: 25 minutes
(Ready in 1 hour 25 minutes)

When you're in the mood for pure indulgence, bake up a country-style Raisin-Walnut Pie.

CRUST
1 refrigerated pie crust (from
   15-oz. pkg.) or Pastry for
   One-Crust Pie (page 67)

FILLING
1 cup raisins
1 cup chopped walnuts
¼ cup firmly packed brown sugar
2 teaspoons grated orange peel
¼ teaspoon salt
1½ cups light corn syrup
1 teaspoon orange extract or
   vanilla
3 eggs

1. Prepare pie crust for *one-crust filled pie* using 9-inch pie pan.

2. Heat oven to 425°F. In medium bowl, combine all filling ingredients; mix well. Pour into crust-lined pan.

3. Bake at 425°F. for 10 minutes. Reduce oven temperature to 350°F.; bake an additional 25 to 35 minutes or until knife inserted 1 inch from edge comes out clean. (Center will be slightly soft.) Cover edge of crust with strips of foil after 15 to 20 minutes of baking to prevent excessive browning. Cool 15 minutes before serving. If desired, serve with whipped cream.

Nutrition per Serving: Serving Size: ⅛ of Recipe. Calories 530; Calories from Fat 170; Total Fat 19g; Saturated Fat 4g; Cholesterol 85mg; Sodium 310mg; Dietary Fiber 2g

Dietary Exchange: 2 Starch, 3½ Fruit, 3½ Fat OR 5½ Carbohydrate, 3½ Fat

FROSTY MINT ICE CREAM PIES

Yield: 2 pies; 12 servings;
Prep Time: 25 minutes
(Ready in 2 hours 50 minutes)

Think creatively. Baked with fudge frosting and just a little water, a chocolate cake mix makes two fudgy shells for ice cream pies.

1 (1 lb. 2.25-oz.) pkg. pudding-
   included devil's food or dark
   chocolate cake mix
1 (16-oz.) can chocolate fudge
   frosting
¾ cup water
1½ quarts (6 cups) mint chocolate
   chip or any flavor ice cream,
   slightly softened

1. Heat oven to 350°F. Generously grease bottom, sides and rim of two 9-inch pie pans. DO NOT SUBSTITUTE 8-INCH PIE PANS.

2. In large bowl, combine cake mix, ¾ cup of the frosting and water; beat at low speed until moistened. Beat 2 minutes at high speed. Spread half of batter (2¼ cups) in bottom of each greased pan. DO NOT SPREAD UP SIDES OF PAN.

3. Bake at 350°F. for 20 to 25 minutes or just until center is set. DO NOT OVERBAKE. Cakes will collapse to form shells. Cool 1 hour or until completely cooled.

4. Spoon ice cream evenly into each shell. In small saucepan, heat remaining frosting over low heat just until melted, stirring occasionally. Drop by teaspoonfuls over ice cream; lightly swirl with tip of knife to marble. Freeze about 1 hour or until firm.

5. Serve immediately, or cover and freeze until serving time. If necessary, let pie stand at room temperature for 10 to 15 minutes before serving.

High Altitude (Above 3,500 feet): Add ¼ cup flour to dry cake mix. Bake as directed above.

Nutrition per Serving: Serving Size: 1/12 of Recipe. Calories 470; Calories from Fat 160; Total Fat 18g; Saturated Fat 8g; Cholesterol 30mg; Sodium 510mg; Dietary Fiber 2g

Dietary Exchange: 2 Starch, 3 Fruit, 3 Fat OR 5 Carbohydrate, 3 Fat

CHOCOLATE-COVERED NUTTY ICE CREAM PIE

◆

Yield: 8 servings; **Prep Time:** 15 minutes
(Ready in 4 hours 15 minutes)

Vanilla ice cream, chopped peanuts and maraschino cherries make a frosty, crunchy filling for a graham cracker crust. The "frosting" on the pie is a hot fudge sauce given a twist with coffee liqueur or strong brewed coffee.

1 quart (4 cups) vanilla ice cream, slightly softened
½ cup chopped peanuts
¼ cup chopped maraschino cherries, well drained
1 (6 or 9-oz.) graham cracker crumb crust

1 cup hot fudge ice cream topping
1 to 2 tablespoons coffee-flavored liqueur or strong coffee
8 whole maraschino cherries, if desired

1. In large bowl, combine ice cream, peanuts and ¼ cup maraschino cherries; blend well. Spoon into crumb crust. Freeze at least 4 hours or until firm.

Chocolate-Covered Nutty Ice Cream Pie

2. Just before serving, let pie stand at room temperature for 10 minutes. In small saucepan, combine ice cream topping and liqueur; mix well. Heat over low heat just until warm, stirring constantly. Spoon sauce over individual servings. Garnish each serving with whole maraschino cherry.

Nutrition per Serving: Serving Size: 1/8 of Recipe. Calories 540; Calories from Fat 230; Total Fat 25g; Saturated Fat 9g; Cholesterol 35mg; Sodium 360mg; Dietary Fiber 2g

Dietary Exchange: 2 1/2 Starch, 2 1/2 Fruit, 4 Fat OR 5 Carbohydrate, 4 Fat

FROZEN CAPPUCCINO PIE

Yield: 8 servings; **Prep Time:** 20 minutes
(Ready in 1 hour 20 minutes)

This satisfying and rich-tasting dessert has surprisingly little fat—just 2 grams per serving. Make it ahead for a special celebration dinner.

2 tablespoons instant espresso powder or dark-roast coffee granules

1 tablespoon boiling water

15 chocolate wafer cookies

6 fat-free devil's food cookie cakes, cut up

1 quart (4 cups) frozen nonfat vanilla yogurt

1/4 cup powdered sugar

Dash nutmeg or cinnamon, if desired

1. Heat oven to 375°F. Spray 9-inch pie pan with nonstick cooking spray. In small bowl, dissolve espresso powder in boiling water. Set aside to cool.

2. Place wafer cookies in food processor bowl with metal blade; process 10 to 15 seconds or until fine crumbs form. Add cut-up cookie cakes; process 10 to 15 seconds or until fine. Place crumbs in sprayed pan. With spoon, press in bottom and up sides of pan. Bake at 375°F. for 5 minutes. Cool in freezer or refrigerator.

3. Meanwhile, spoon frozen yogurt and powdered sugar into food processor bowl with metal blade; process 10 to 15 seconds or until yogurt is slightly softened. While machine is running, gradually pour dissolved espresso through feed tube and process an additional 10 seconds or just until blended.

4. Quickly spoon mixture into cooled crust; spread evenly. Sprinkle with nutmeg. Freeze at least 1 hour or until firm. If desired, garnish with chocolate-covered coffee beans.

Nutrition per Serving: Serving Size: 1/8 of Recipe. Calories 210; Calories from Fat 20; Total Fat 2g; Saturated Fat 0g; Cholesterol 0mg; Sodium 150mg; Dietary Fiber 1g

Dietary Exchange: 1 1/2 Starch, 1 1/2 Fruit OR 3 Carbohydrate

ICE CREAM PIE WITH FRUIT

Yield: 8 servings; **Prep Time:** 10 minutes
(Ready in 1 hour 25 minutes)

This frozen pie would also be delightful with strawberries or blueberries; you can substitute another favorite flavor of ice cream, too.

1 quart (4 cups) vanilla fudge or vanilla ice cream, slightly softened

1 (6-oz.) chocolate flavor crumb crust

2 cups fresh raspberries

2 tablespoons powdered sugar

2 tablespoons amaretto or
    1 teaspoon almond extract plus
    2 teaspoons water

1. Spoon ice cream into crumb crust, mounding slightly. Freeze 1 hour or until firm.

2. Meanwhile, in small bowl, combine all remaining ingredients; mix gently. Cover; refrigerate.

3. Just before serving, let pie stand at room temperature for 15 minutes. Spoon fruit mixture over individual servings.

Nutrition per Serving: Serving Size: 1/8 of Recipe. Calories 310; Calories from Fat 140; Total Fat 16g; Saturated Fat 6g; Cholesterol 30mg; Sodium 240mg; Dietary Fiber 3g

Dietary Exchange: 1 Starch, 1 1/2 Fruit, 3 Fat OR 2 1/2 Carbohydrate, 3 Fat

LEMON LAYERED ICE CREAM PIE

◆

Yield: 8 servings; **Prep Time:** 25 minutes
(Ready in 2 hours 35 minutes)

If desired, serve slices of this yellow-and-white-striped pie atop a pool of Raspberry Dessert Sauce (page 329).

CRUST
9 (2-inch) gingersnap cookies
1/2 cup corn flake crumbs
1/4 cup sugar
2 tablespoons margarine or butter
1 teaspoon water

FILLING
1 (15.75-oz.) can lemon pie filling
1 tablespoon lemon juice
1 quart (4 cups) low-fat vanilla ice cream, slightly softened
1 teaspoon grated lemon peel

1. Place cookies in food processor bowl with metal blade or blender container; process 20 to 30 seconds or until very fine crumbs form. Reserve 2 teaspoons crumbs for garnish.

2. To remaining crumbs in food processor bowl, add corn flake crumbs, sugar and margarine. With machine running, add water, processing until blended. Press mixture firmly in bottom and up sides of 9-inch pie pan. Set aside.

3. In small bowl, combine pie filling and lemon juice; blend well. Set aside.

4. In large bowl, combine ice cream and lemon peel; stir just until mixed. Quickly spread half of ice cream mixture in crust-lined pan. Top with pie filling mixture, spreading evenly. Spoon remaining ice cream mixture over top; spread evenly to cover. Sprinkle with reserved crumbs. Freeze at least 2 hours or until firm in center.

5. To serve, let pie stand at room temperature for 10 to 15 minutes.

Nutrition per Serving: Serving Size: 1/8 of Recipe. Calories 290; Calories from Fat 35; Total Fat 4g; Saturated Fat 1g; Cholesterol 0mg; Sodium 280mg; Dietary Fiber 0g

Dietary Exchange: 2 Starch, 2 Fruit OR 4 Carbohydrate

FROZEN YOGURT COOKIE PIE

Yield: 8 servings; **Prep Time:** 15 minutes
(Ready in 2 hours 35 minutes)

Peach ice cream or frozen yogurt is a seasonal specialty in some regions, available only in the summertime. Garnish slices of the pie with chopped fresh peaches or nectarines tossed with a little orange juice and Grand Marnier.

CRUST
24 bite-sized pecan shortbread cookies, crushed (1 cup)
2 tablespoons margarine or butter, melted
18 bite-sized pecan shortbread cookies

FILLING
1/2 gallon (8 cups) peach frozen yogurt or ice cream, softened
2 tablespoons chopped pecans or cookie crumbs

1. In small bowl, combine crushed cookies and margarine; mix well. Press mixture evenly in bottom only of 9-inch pie pan. Stand whole cookies up around edges, pressing slightly into crust mixture. Freeze 20 minutes or until cold.

2. Carefully spread frozen yogurt in crust. Sprinkle with pecans. Cover; freeze at least 2 hours before serving.

Nutrition per Serving: Serving Size: 1/8 of Recipe. Calories 620; Calories from Fat 250; Total Fat 28g; Saturated Fat 6g; Cholesterol 25mg; Sodium 350mg; Dietary Fiber 1g

Dietary Exchange: 1 Starch, 4 Fruit, 1 Skim Milk, 4 1/2 Fat OR 6 Carbohydrate, 4 1/2 Fat

Lemon Layered Ice Cream Pie

MARGARITA PIE

Yield: 8 servings; **Prep Time:** 30 minutes
(Ready in 2 hours 30 minutes)

Translate the sugar-salt-lime-tequila zing of a favorite summer drink into a frosty summer dessert. Garnish each serving with additional shredded lime peel or a thin slice of fresh lime slit to the center and given a twist.

2 cups miniature pretzel twists

2 tablespoons sugar

2 tablespoons margarine or butter

1 (6-oz.) can frozen limeade concentrate

1 quart (4 cups) low-fat vanilla ice cream, slightly softened

1 teaspoon grated lime peel

3 tablespoons tequila

1 tablespoon orange-flavored liqueur

1. Heat oven to 375°F. Spray 9-inch pie pan with nonstick cooking spray.

2. In food processor bowl with metal blade or blender container, process pretzels until crumbs form. Add sugar; process with on/off turns to mix. Add margarine; mix well. With machine running, add 2 tablespoons of the limeade concentrate, processing until well mixed. Place mixture in sprayed pan. With back of spoon, press mixture firmly in bottom and up sides of pan.

3. Bake at 375°F. for 5 to 7 minutes or until set. Cool baked shell in freezer or refrigerator for 10 to 15 minutes.

4. Meanwhile, in food processor bowl with metal blade or large bowl for electric mixer, combine remaining limeade concentrate, ice cream, lime peel, tequila and liqueur; process or mix just until blended. Spoon into cooled baked shell. Freeze 2 hours or until firm.

Nutrition per Serving: Serving Size: 1/8 of Recipe. Calories 340; Calories from Fat 50; Total Fat 6g; Saturated Fat 2g; Cholesterol 20mg; Sodium 390mg; Dietary Fiber 1g

Dietary Exchange: 3 Starch, 1 Fruit, 1 Fat OR 4 Carbohydrate, 1 Fat

BERRY-CHERRY PIE

Yield: 8 servings; **Prep Time:** 30 minutes
(Ready in 3 hours)

The pie shell bakes briefly, but the crimson-pretty filling itself requires no time in the oven.

CRUST

1 refrigerated pie crust (from 15-oz. pkg.) or Pastry for One-Crust Pie (page 67)

FILLING

1 (8-oz.) pkg. cream cheese, softened

1/3 cup sugar

1 teaspoon vanilla

1/2 teaspoon grated lemon peel

1 pint (2 cups) fresh whole strawberries

1 (21-oz.) can cherry pie filling

1. Heat oven to 450°F. Prepare pie crust for *one-crust baked shell* using 9-inch pie pan. Bake at 450°F. for 9 to 11 minutes or until light golden brown. Cool 30 minutes or until completely cooled.

2. In small bowl, combine cream cheese, sugar, vanilla and lemon peel; beat until smooth and well blended. Spread evenly in cooled baked shell.

3. Arrange strawberries over cream cheese mixture; press in lightly. Spoon pie filling over strawberries. Refrigerate at least 2 hours before serving. If desired, garnish with whipped cream.

Nutrition per Serving: Serving Size: 1/8 of Recipe. Calories 310; Calories from Fat 110; Total Fat 12g; Saturated Fat 6g; Cholesterol 20mg; Sodium 280mg; Dietary Fiber 2g

Dietary Exchange: 1 Starch, 2 Fruit, 2 1/2 Fat OR 3 Carbohydrate, 2 1/2 Fat

RASPBERRY-CHOCOLATE CREAM PIE

Yield: 8 servings; **Prep Time:** 10 minutes
(Ready in 2 hours 25 minutes)

Easily made in advance (it requires at least 2 hours of chilling), this showpiece is fancy enough for an elegant party and easy enough for a family supper. If you wish, decorate the top with chocolate curls or additional raspberries instead of chocolate chips.

Raspberry-Chocolate Cream Pie

1 cup milk chocolate chips
2 teaspoons oil
4 cups frozen whipped topping, thawed
2 cups fresh raspberries
1 (6-oz.) chocolate-flavored crumb crust

1. Reserve 2 tablespoons chocolate chips. In medium microwave-safe bowl or small saucepan, combine remaining chocolate chips and oil. Microwave on HIGH for 1 1/2 to 2 minutes or heat over low heat until melted, stirring frequently. Cool 15 minutes or until completely cooled.

2. Fold whipped topping into cooled chocolate mixture. Gently fold in 1 cup of the raspberries. Spoon filling into crumb crust. Arrange remaining 1 cup raspberries over top.

3. Chop reserved chocolate chips; sprinkle evenly over top of pie. Refrigerate at least 2 hours or until set. Store in refrigerator.

Nutrition per Serving: Serving Size: 1/8 of Recipe. Calories 380; Calories from Fat 220; Total Fat 24g; Saturated Fat 14g; Cholesterol 5mg; Sodium 170mg; Dietary Fiber 3g

Dietary Exchange: 1 Starch, 1 1/2 Fruit, 4 1/2 Fat OR 2 1/2 Carbohydrate, 4 1/2 Fat

BLUEBERRY-LEMON CHEESECAKE PIE

Yield: 8 servings; **Prep Time:** 25 minutes
(Ready in 1 hour 55 minutes)

Dessert doesn't get much easier than this luscious cheesecake-flavored filling crowned with blueberries and whipped cream.

CRUST
1 refrigerated pie crust (from 15-oz. pkg.) or Pastry for One-Crust Pie (page 67)

FILLING
½ cup whipping cream
1 (8-oz.) pkg. cream cheese, softened
⅓ cup sugar
1 to 2 teaspoons grated lemon peel

TOPPING
1 (21-oz.) can blueberry pie filling

1. Heat oven to 450°F. Prepare pie crust for *one-crust baked shell* using 9-inch pie pan. Bake at 450°F. for 9 to 11 minutes or until light golden brown. Cool 30 minutes or until completely cooled.

2. In small bowl, beat whipping cream until stiff peaks form. In another small bowl, combine cream cheese, sugar and lemon peel; beat until light and fluffy.

Fold in whipped cream. Spread evenly in cooled baked shell.

3. Spoon pie filling evenly over lemon filling. Refrigerate at least 1 hour before serving. Just before serving, garnish with whipped cream, if desired. Store in refrigerator.

Nutrition per Serving: Serving Size: ⅛ of Recipe. Calories 440; Calories from Fat 240; Total Fat 27g; Saturated Fat 15g; Cholesterol 70mg; Sodium 230mg; Dietary Fiber 1g

Dietary Exchange: 1 Starch, 2 Fruit, 5½ Fat OR 3 Carbohydrate, 5½ Fat

LEMON SILK PIE WITH BLUEBERRY SAUCE

Yield: 10 servings; **Prep Time:** 30 minutes
(Ready in 3 hours 30 minutes)

The smooth, smooth texture of the filling gives this pie its name; the sweetness of the briefly cooked fresh blueberry topping balances the lemony tartness.

PIE
1 cup sugar
¾ cup butter, softened (do not use margarine)
1 tablespoon grated lemon peel
2 tablespoons lemon juice
¾ cup refrigerated or frozen fat-free egg product, thawed (do not use eggs)

1 (6-oz.) graham cracker crumb crust or vanilla wafer crumb crust

SAUCE
⅓ cup sugar
⅓ cup water
1 tablespoon cornstarch
1½ cups fresh or frozen blueberries, thawed

1. In small bowl, combine 1 cup sugar and butter; beat at medium speed until well blended, scraping bowl frequently. Add lemon peel and lemon juice; beat until well mixed. (Mixture will look curdled.) Gradually add egg product; beat 5 minutes or until light and fluffy, scraping bowl frequently. Spoon mixture into crumb crust. Refrigerate at least 3 hours or until set.

2. Meanwhile, in small saucepan, combine ⅓ cup sugar, water and cornstarch; mix well. Add blueberries; cook over medium-high heat until mixture comes to a boil, stirring constantly. Boil 1 minute. Cool 15 minutes. Cover; refrigerate at least 2 hours before serving.

3. To serve, spoon sauce over individual servings. Store in refrigerator.

Nutrition per Serving: Serving Size: ⅒ of Recipe. Calories 380; Calories from Fat 180; Total Fat 20g; Saturated Fat 10g; Cholesterol 35mg; Sodium 310mg; Dietary Fiber 1g

Dietary Exchange: 1 Starch, 2 Fruit, 4 Fat OR 3 Carbohydrate, 4 Fat

RUM-COCONUT-KEY LIME PIE

Yield: 10 servings; **Prep Time:** 20 minutes
(Ready in 3 hours 50 minutes)

Toasted coconut intensifies the tropical character of the Florida Keys' signature dessert. True Key limes— small round citrus grown in Florida —are hard to come by outside of the Sunshine State, but any lime juice will contribute the appropriate tang. You may find bottled Key lime juice in some specialty stores.

CRUST
1 cup coconut, toasted*
6 tablespoons margarine or butter, melted
12 creme-filled vanilla sandwich cookies, finely crushed (about 1 1/2 cups)

FILLING
1 (14-oz.) can sweetened condensed milk (not evaporated)
1 (8-oz.) pkg. cream cheese, softened
1/2 cup Key lime juice or lime juice
1/2 teaspoon rum extract

1. Reserve 1 tablespoon toasted coconut for topping. In 9-inch pie pan, combine remaining coconut, margarine and cookie crumbs; mix well. Press in bottom and up sides of pan. Refrigerate 30 minutes or until set.

2. In large bowl, combine sweetened condensed milk and cream cheese; beat until smooth and fluffy. Add lime juice and rum extract; mix well. Pour into crust-lined pan. Top with reserved coconut. Refrigerate at least 3 hours or until set. Store in refrigerator.

*Tip: To toast coconut, spread on cookie sheet; bake at 350°F. for 6 to 8 minutes or until light golden brown, stirring occasionally.

Nutrition per Serving: Serving Size: 1/10 of Recipe. Calories 380; Calories from Fat 220; Total Fat 24g; Saturated Fat 12g; Cholesterol 40mg; Sodium 240mg; Dietary Fiber 1g

Dietary Exchange: 2 Starch, 5 Fat OR 2 Carbohydrate, 5 Fat

STRAWBERRIES AND CREAM PIE

Yield: 10 servings; **Prep Time:** 30 minutes
(Ready in 2 hours)

Inspired by recipes for cheesecake and cream pies, this heavenly whipped cream–cream cheese filling nestles beneath fresh strawberries and drizzled chocolate. If you wish, substitute raspberries or blueberries, or a combination.

CRUST
1 refrigerated pie crust (from 15-oz. pkg.) or Pastry for One-Crust Pie (page 67)

FILLING
1 (8-oz.) pkg. cream cheese, softened
1/3 cup sugar
1/4 to 1/2 teaspoon almond extract
1 cup whipping cream, whipped
2 pints (4 cups) fresh whole strawberries

GARNISH
1/2 cup semi-sweet chocolate chips
1 tablespoon shortening

1. Heat oven to 450°F. Prepare pie crust for *one-crust baked shell* using 9-inch pie pan or 10-inch tart pan with removable bottom. Bake at 450°F. for 9 to 11 minutes or until light golden brown. Cool 30 minutes or until completely cooled.

2. In large bowl, beat cream cheese until fluffy. Gradually add sugar and almond extract, blending well. Fold in whipped cream. Spoon into cooled baked shell. Arrange strawberries, pointed side up, over filling. Refrigerate.

3. In small saucepan, melt chocolate chips and shortening over low heat, stirring constantly until smooth. Drizzle over strawberries and filling. Refrigerate 1 hour or until set. Store in refrigerator.

Nutrition per Serving: Serving Size: 1/10 of Recipe. Calories 370; Calories from Fat 240; Total Fat 27g; Saturated Fat 15g; Cholesterol 65mg; Sodium 190mg; Dietary Fiber 2g

Dietary Exchange: 1 1/2 Starch, 1/2 Fruit, 5 Fat OR 2 Carbohydrate, 5 Fat

SOUR CREAM RAISIN PIE

♦

Yield: 8 servings; **Prep Time:** 25 minutes
(Ready in 2 hours 55 minutes)

Sour cream enriches a custard-style pie filled with plump raisins and sweet spices. To add a contrasting crunch to the smooth pie, sprinkle each serving with a spoonful of finely chopped toasted walnuts.

CRUST
1 refrigerated pie crust (from 15-oz. pkg.) or Pastry for One-Crust Pie (page 67)

FILLING
1 1/2 cups raisins
3/4 cup sugar
1/4 cup cornstarch
1/2 teaspoon cinnamon
1/4 teaspoon salt
1/4 teaspoon nutmeg
2 cups milk
3 egg yolks, beaten
1 cup sour cream
1 tablespoon lemon juice

TOPPING
1 cup whipping cream, whipped

1. Heat oven to 450°F. Prepare pie crust for *one-crust baked shell* using 9-inch pie pan. Bake at 450°F. for 9 to 11 minutes or until light golden brown. Cool 30 minutes or until completely cooled.

2. Meanwhile, in medium saucepan, combine raisins, sugar, cornstarch, cinnamon, salt and nutmeg; mix well. Stir in milk until smooth. Cook over medium heat until mixture boils, stirring constantly. Boil 1 minute. Remove from heat.

3. Stir about 1/4 cup hot raisin mixture into egg yolks. Gradually stir yolk mixture into hot mixture. Add sour cream; mix well. Cook just until mixture begins to bubble, stirring constantly.

4. Remove from heat; stir in lemon juice. Cool 10 minutes. Pour into cooled baked shell. Refrigerate 2 hours or until set. Top with whipped cream. Store in refrigerator.

Nutrition per Serving: Serving Size: 1/8 of Recipe. Calories 520; Calories from Fat 250; Total Fat 28g; Saturated Fat 15g; Cholesterol 145mg; Sodium 270mg; Dietary Fiber 1g

Dietary Exchange: 2 Starch, 2 Fruit, 5 1/2 Fat OR 4 Carbohydrate, 5 1/2 Fat

VARIATION

Sour Cream Raisin Meringue Pie: Heat oven to 350°F. Substitute meringue for 1 cup whipping cream. After pouring filling into cooled baked shell, in small bowl, combine 3 egg whites and 1/4 teaspoon cream of tartar; beat at medium speed for about 1 minute or until soft peaks form. Gradually add 1/4 cup sugar 1 tablespoon at a time, beating at high speed until stiff peaks form and sugar is dissolved. Spoon meringue onto hot filling; spread to edge of crust to seal well and prevent shrinkage. Bake at 350°F. for 10 to 15 minutes or until meringue is light golden brown. Cool completely. Store in refrigerator.

BLACK FOREST CREAM PIE

Yield: 8 servings; **Prep Time:** 30 minutes
(Ready in 2 hours 30 minutes)

The flavors of Black Forest cake—cherries and chocolate—unite in an easy, make-ahead pie. Keep it refrigerated until ready to serve.

CRUST
1 refrigerated pie crust (from 15-oz. pkg.) or Pastry for One-Crust Pie (page 67)

FILLING
6 oz. semi-sweet chocolate, chopped
2 tablespoons margarine or butter
1/4 cup powdered sugar
1 (8-oz.) pkg. cream cheese, softened
1 (21-oz.) can cherry pie filling

TOPPING
1 cup whipping cream, whipped
1 oz. semi-sweet chocolate, grated

1. Heat oven to 450°F. Prepare pie crust for *one-crust baked shell* using 9-inch pie pan or 10-inch tart pan with removable bottom. Bake at 450°F. for 9 to 11 minutes or until light golden brown. Cool 30 minutes or until completely cooled.

2. In small saucepan, combine 6 oz. chocolate and margarine; melt over low heat, stirring constantly. Remove from heat.

Black Forest Cream Pie

3. In small bowl, combine powdered sugar and cream cheese; beat until smooth. Stir in melted chocolate mixture; beat until smooth. Fold in 1 cup of the pie filling. Spread chocolate filling evenly into cooled baked shell. Refrigerate 1 hour.

4. In small bowl, combine topping ingredients. Spread evenly over cooled chocolate layer. Spoon remaining pie filling evenly around outer edge of pie. Refrigerate at least 30 minutes before serving. If desired, garnish with chocolate curls. Store in refrigerator.

Nutrition per Serving: Serving Size: $\frac{1}{8}$ of Recipe. Calories 590; Calories from Fat 350; Total Fat 39g; Saturated Fat 21g; Cholesterol 80mg; Sodium 280mg; Dietary Fiber 2g

Dietary Exchange: 1 $\frac{1}{2}$ Starch, 2 Fruit, 7 $\frac{1}{2}$ Fat OR 3 $\frac{1}{2}$ Carbohydrate, 7 $\frac{1}{2}$ Fat

SLIM CHOCOLATE CHEESECAKE PIE

Yield: 16 servings; **Prep Time:** 25 minutes
(Ready in 4 hours 50 minutes)

If you're trying to watch your waist-line and satisfy a sweet tooth at the same time, try a slice of this delectable cheesecake—just 5 grams of fat per serving!

CRUST
1 cup graham cracker crumbs
  (16 squares)
1 tablespoon sugar

FILLING
1 (15-oz.) container light ricotta
  cheese
1 cup sugar
½ cup unsweetened cocoa
1 (8-oz.) pkg. ⅓-less-fat cream
  cheese (Neufchatel),
  softened

½ cup refrigerated or frozen fat-
  free egg product, thawed, or
  2 egg whites
⅓ cup skim milk
2 teaspoons vanilla

TOPPING
1 cup orange juice
4 teaspoons cornstarch
2 (11-oz.) cans mandarin orange
  segments, drained
2 kiwi fruit, peeled, sliced
1 cup sliced fresh strawberries

Slim Chocolate Cheesecake Pie

1. Heat oven to 325°F. Spray 9-inch pie pan thoroughly (6 to 8 seconds) with nonstick cooking spray. In small bowl, combine graham cracker crumbs and 1 tablespoon sugar; mix well. Add crumb mixture to pan; tilt pan to coat evenly. (Avoid tapping pan, which will loosen crumbs from sides.) Gently press crumbs against sides and bottom of pan. (Crumbs will stick loosely together but will be held firmly in place when filling is added.) Set aside.

2. In food processor bowl with metal blade, process ricotta cheese until smooth.* Add 1 cup sugar, cocoa and cream cheese; process until smooth. Add egg product, milk and vanilla; process until blended. Carefully pour mixture into crust.

3. Bake at 325°F. for 45 to 55 minutes or until edges are firm. (Center will be soft.) Turn oven off; open door at least 4 inches. Let pie sit in oven for 30 minutes.

4. Remove pie from oven; cool on wire rack for 1 hour or until cooled. Cover; refrigerate at least 2 hours before serving.

5. Meanwhile, in small saucepan, combine orange juice and cornstarch; cook over medium heat until mixture thickens and comes to a full boil. Remove from heat; cool 1 hour or until completely cooled. Fold in orange segments, kiwi fruit and strawberries. Serve topping over individual servings. Store in refrigerator.

*Tip: Ricotta cheese can be pureed in blender container in 2 batches, using half of the milk for each batch. Transfer pureed ricotta mixture to large bowl. Continue as directed using an electric mixer.

Nutrition per Serving: Serving Size: 1/16 of Recipe. Calories 190; Calories from Fat 45; Total Fat 5g; Saturated Fat 3g; Cholesterol 15mg; Sodium 150mg; Dietary Fiber 2g

Dietary Exchange: 2 Starch, 1/2 Fat OR 2 Carbohydrate, 1/2 Fat

VANILLA CREAM PIE

Yield: 8 servings; **Prep Time:** 25 minutes
(Ready in 3 hours 55 minutes)

Here's proof that "plain vanilla" can be every bit as luscious as any other flavor. This basic recipe is also easy to vary with the flavors of banana, butterscotch, chocolate or coconut.

CRUST
1 refrigerated pie crust (from 15-oz. pkg.) or Pastry for One-Crust Pie (page 67)

FILLING
3/4 cup sugar
1/4 cup cornstarch
1/4 teaspoon salt
3 cups milk
3 egg yolks, slightly beaten
2 tablespoons margarine or butter
2 teaspoons vanilla

1. Heat oven to 450°F. Prepare pie crust for *one-crust baked shell* using 9-inch pie pan. Bake at 450°F. for 9 to 11 minutes or until light golden brown. Cool 30 minutes or until completely cooled.

2. In medium saucepan, combine sugar, cornstarch and salt; mix well. Stir in milk until smooth. Cook over medium heat until mixture boils and thickens, stirring constantly. Boil 2 minutes. Remove from heat.

3. Stir about 1/4 cup hot mixture into egg yolks. Gradually stir yolk mixture into hot mixture. Cook just until mixture begins to bubble, stirring constantly.

4. Remove from heat; stir in margarine and vanilla. Pour into cooled baked shell. Refrigerate 3 hours or until set. If desired, top with whipped cream. Store in refrigerator.

Nutrition per Serving: Serving Size: 1/8 of Recipe. Calories 300; Calories from Fat 130; Total Fat 14g; Saturated Fat 5g; Cholesterol 95mg; Sodium 290mg; Dietary Fiber 0g

Dietary Exchange: 1 1/2 Starch, 1 Fruit, 2 1/2 Fat OR 2 1/2 Carbohydrate, 2 1/2 Fat

VARIATIONS

Banana Cream Pie: Cool filling in saucepan to lukewarm. Slice 2 or 3 bananas into cooled baked shell. Pour filling over bananas.

Chocolate Cream Pie: Increase sugar to 1 cup and add 2 oz. unsweetened chocolate to filling mixture before cooking.

Coconut Cream Pie: Stir 1 cup coconut into cooked filling with margarine and vanilla.

HONEY NUT TART

Yield: 12 servings; **Prep Time:** 25 minutes
(Ready in 3 hours 30 minutes)

Luxury in a pie pan: crunchy, slightly salty nuts bathe in a rich filling.

CRUST
1 refrigerated pie crust (from 15-oz. pkg.) or Pastry for One-Crust Pie (page 67)

FILLING
2 cups low-salt or lightly salted mixed cocktail nuts, coarsely chopped
½ cup firmly packed brown sugar
½ cup honey
¼ cup margarine or butter, melted
½ teaspoon grated orange peel
1 teaspoon vanilla
3 eggs

TOPPING
Whipped cream or topping

1. Heat oven to 450°F. Prepare pie crust for *one-crust baked shell* using 10-inch tart pan with removable bottom. Bake at 450°F. for 9 to 11 minutes or until light golden brown. Cool 30 minutes or until completely cooled.

2. Reduce oven temperature to 375°F. Spread chopped nuts evenly in partially baked shell. In medium bowl, combine all remaining filling ingredients; blend well. Pour over nuts.

3. Bake at 375°F. for 25 to 35 minutes or until filling is puffed and tart is golden brown. Cool 2 hours or until completely cooled. To serve, top with whipped cream. Store in refrigerator.

Nutrition per Serving: Serving Size: ¹⁄₁₂ of Recipe. Calories 400; Calories from Fat 240; Total Fat 27g; Saturated Fat 7g; Cholesterol 70mg; Sodium 260mg; Dietary Fiber 2g

Dietary Exchange: 2 Starch, ½ Fruit, 4 ½ Fat OR 2 ½ Carbohydrate, 4 ½ Fat

AMARETTO PEACH TART

Yield: 10 servings; **Prep Time:** 35 minutes
(Ready in 2 hours 40 minutes)

This cheesecake-like filling is topped with a beautiful fresh peach topping.

CRUST
1 refrigerated pie crust (from 15-oz. pkg.) or Pastry for One-Crust Pie (page 67)

FILLING
1 (8-oz.) pkg. cream cheese, softened
⅓ cup sugar
2 tablespoons amaretto
¼ teaspoon almond extract
2 eggs

TOPPING
2 cups (2 to 3 medium) thinly sliced, peeled peaches or 1 (16-oz.) pkg. frozen sliced peaches without syrup, thawed, well drained
2 tablespoons peach preserves
1 tablespoon amaretto
Mint leaves, if desired

1. Heat oven to 450°F. Prepare pie crust for *one-crust baked shell* using 10-inch tart pan with removable bottom. Place crust in pan; press in bottom and up sides of pan. Trim edges if necessary. Generously prick crust with fork. Bake at 450°F. for 9 to 11 minutes or until light golden brown. Cool 30 minutes or until completely cooled.

2. Reduce oven temperature to 375°F. In medium bowl, combine cream cheese and sugar; beat until light and fluffy. Add 2 tablespoons amaretto, almond extract and eggs; blend well. Pour into cooled baked shell. Bake at 375°F. for 18 to 22 minutes or until filling is set. Cool 10 minutes. Refrigerate at least 1 hour or until completely cooled and set.

3. Just before serving, arrange peach slices over tart. In small saucepan, combine preserves and 1 tablespoon amaretto; heat until melted. Cool 5 minutes. If desired, strain mixture. Brush mixture over peaches. Garnish with mint leaves. Store in refrigerator.

Nutrition per Serving: Serving Size: ¹⁄₁₀ of Recipe. Calories 260; Calories from Fat 140; Total Fat 15g; Saturated Fat 8g; Cholesterol 75mg; Sodium 190mg; Dietary Fiber 1g

Dietary Exchange: 1 Starch, ½ Fruit, 3 Fat OR 1 ½ Carbohydrate, 3 Fat

Amaretto Peach Tart

TRIPLE CHOCOLATE-RASPBERRY TART

◆

Yield: 8 servings; Prep Time: 25 minutes

Melted spreadable fruit is an ingenious substitute for fat in this pie's chocolate crust. "Spreadable fruit" is preserves made with no added sweetener to supplement the natural sugars of the fruit.

1 ¼ cups chocolate wafer cookie
    crumbs (20 cookies)
5 tablespoons raspberry
    spreadable fruit, melted
2 tablespoons semi-sweet
    chocolate chips
½ teaspoon oil
2 tablespoons white vanilla chips
2 cups fresh raspberries

1. Heat oven to 400°F. Spray 9-inch tart pan with removable bottom with nonstick cooking spray. In small bowl, combine cookie crumbs and 2 tablespoons of the melted spreadable fruit; mix well. Spray hands with nonstick cooking spray. Press mixture evenly in bottom of sprayed pan.

2. Bake at 400°F. for 5 minutes. Remove from oven; spread remaining 3 tablespoons spreadable fruit over crust. Freeze 5 to 8 minutes or until cool.

3. While crust is cooling, in small microwave-safe cup, combine chocolate chips and ¼ teaspoon of the oil.* Microwave on HIGH for 40 to 60 seconds or until melted. In another microwave-safe cup, combine vanilla chips and remaining ¼ teaspoon oil. Microwave on HIGH for 30 to 40 seconds or until melted.

4. Arrange raspberries over cooled crust; drizzle with melted chocolate chips and vanilla chips. Serve immediately or refrigerate until serving time.

5. To serve, remove outer ring from tart pan; do not remove bottom of pan.

*Tip: To melt chips in separate small saucepans, combine each kind of chip with ¼ teaspoon oil; heat and stir over low heat until melted.

Nutrition per Serving: Serving Size: ⅛ of Recipe. Calories 150; Calories from Fat 35; Total Fat 4g; Saturated Fat 2g; Cholesterol 0mg; Sodium 95mg; Dietary Fiber 3g

Dietary Exchange: ½ Starch, 1 Fruit, 1 Fat OR 1½ Carbohydrate, 1 Fat

Triple Chocolate-Raspberry Tart

CHOCOLATE-PEANUT BUTTER PIE

Yield: 10 servings; **Prep Time:** 25 minutes
(Ready in 4 hours 40 minutes)

Leave it to the Americans to develop such a fortuitous linking of two rich ingredients: peanut butter and chocolate. The peanutty-chocolate crust would also be great for an ice cream pie.

CRUST
1 refrigerated pie crust (from 15-oz. pkg.) or Pastry for One-Crust Pie (page 67)
1 cup peanuts, finely chopped
½ cup miniature semi-sweet chocolate chips

FILLING
1 ¼ cups whipping cream
¼ cup powdered sugar
1 tablespoon vanilla
1 (8-oz.) pkg. cream cheese, softened
½ cup creamy peanut butter
1 cup powdered sugar
¼ cup milk

TOPPING
2 tablespoons finely chopped peanuts
2 tablespoons miniature semi-sweet chocolate chips

1. Heat oven to 450°F. Prepare pie crust for *one-crust baked shell* using 9-inch pie pan. Gently press 1 cup peanuts into bottom and up sides of crust. Prick crust with fork. Bake at 450°F. for 10 to 14 minutes or until light golden brown. Cool 10 minutes. Sprinkle with ½ cup chocolate chips.

2. In medium bowl, combine whipping cream, ¼ cup powdered sugar and vanilla; beat until soft peaks form.

3. In large bowl, combine cream cheese and peanut butter; beat until light and fluffy. Add 1 cup powdered sugar and milk; beat until smooth and creamy. Fold in 1 ½ cups of the whipped cream. Spread evenly in cooled baked shell. Refrigerate at least 4 hours before serving.

4. To serve, garnish with remaining whipped cream. Sprinkle with 2 tablespoons peanuts and 2 tablespoons chocolate chips. Store in refrigerator.

Nutrition per Serving: Serving Size: ¹⁄₁₀ of Recipe. Calories 590; Calories from Fat 390; Total Fat 43g; Saturated Fat 19g; Cholesterol 70mg; Sodium 320mg; Dietary Fiber 3g

Dietary Exchange: 2 Starch, ½ Fruit, ½ High-Fat Meat, 8 Fat OR 2 ½ Carbohydrate, ½ High-Fat Meat, 8 Fat

APRICOT-PEAR LATTICE TART

Yield: 10 servings; **Prep Time:** 45 minutes
(Ready in 2 hours 10 minutes)

A touch of lemon adds a bright flavor amid the sweetness of apricots, pears and brown sugar. For a fancier lattice top, cut the strips with a fluted pastry cutter.

CRUST
1 (15-oz.) pkg. refrigerated pie crusts or Pastry for Two-Crust Pie (page 67)

FILLING
1 (16-oz.) can apricot halves in light syrup, drained
1 (16-oz.) can pear slices in light syrup, drained
⅓ cup firmly packed brown sugar
3 tablespoons chopped pecans or walnuts
½ teaspoon cinnamon
¼ to ½ teaspoon grated lemon peel

TOPPING
1 egg yolk
1 teaspoon water

GLAZE
⅓ cup apricot preserves

1. Prepare pie crust for *two-crust pie* using 9-inch tart pan with removable bottom or 9-inch pie pan. Place 1 crust in pan; press in bottom and up sides of pan. Trim edges if necessary.

2. Heat oven to 400°F. Arrange apricots and pears in crust-lined pan. In small bowl, combine brown sugar, pecans, cinnamon and lemon peel; mix well. Sprinkle evenly over fruit.

3. To make lattice top, cut second crust into ½-inch-wide strips. Arrange strips in lattice design over filling. Trim and seal edges. In small bowl, combine egg yolk and water; beat well. Brush over lattice.

4. Bake at 400°F. for 45 to 55 minutes or until golden brown. Cover tart with foil during last 15 to 20 minutes of baking to prevent excessive browning. Cool 30 minutes.

5. In small saucepan, heat apricot preserves over low heat. Brush preserves over tart.

Nutrition per Serving: Serving Size: ¹⁄₁₀ of Recipe. Calories 290; Calories from Fat 130; Total Fat 14g; Saturated Fat 5g; Cholesterol 35mg; Sodium 230mg; Dietary Fiber 2g

Dietary Exchange: ½ Starch, 2 Fruit, 3 Fat OR 2½ Carbohydrate, 3 Fat

ALMOND FRUIT TART

Yield: 10 servings; Prep Time: 45 minutes (Ready in 2 hours 15 minutes)

For an elegant restaurant-style presentation, arrange colorful summer fruit in concentric circles on top of the almond cream. Kiwi fruit slices, pitted fresh cherry halves, raspberries or seedless red grapes could also be used.

CRUST
1 refrigerated pie crust (from 15-oz. pkg.) or Pastry for One-Crust Pie (page 67)

FILLING
1 (8-oz.) pkg. cream cheese, softened
3½ oz. (⅓ cup) almond paste
¼ teaspoon almond extract
2 tablespoons sugar

TOPPING
1 cup halved fresh strawberries
1 cup fresh blueberries
½ cup halved seedless green grapes
2 tablespoons apple jelly, melted

1. Heat oven to 450°F. Prepare pie crust for *one-crust baked shell* using 9 or 10-inch tart pan with removable bottom. Place crust in pan; press in bottom and up sides of pan. Trim edges if necessary. Prick crust with fork. Bake at 450°F. for 9 to 11 minutes or until light golden brown. Cool 30 minutes or until completely cooled.

2. In food processor bowl with metal blade or blender container, combine all filling ingredients; process until smooth. Spread evenly in cooled baked shell.*

3. Top with fruit; brush with jelly. Refrigerate 1 to 2 hours before serving. Store in refrigerator.

Tip: Recipe can be prepared ahead to this point. Cover tart with plastic wrap; refrigerate overnight. Continue as directed above.

Nutrition per Serving: Serving Size: ¹⁄₁₀ of Recipe. Calories 270; Calories from Fat 150; Total Fat 17g; Saturated Fat 8g; Cholesterol 30mg; Sodium 180mg; Dietary Fiber 2g

Dietary Exchange: ½ Starch, 1 Fruit, 4 Fat OR 1½ Carbohydrate, 4 Fat

FRESH FRUIT TARTS

Yield: 10 tarts; **Prep Time:** 30 minutes
(Ready in 1 hour 30 minutes)

These attractive individual tart shells are created with an ordinary muffin pan. Rounds of pie pastry are draped over the backs of muffins cups and pinched to make the pleats.

CRUST
1 (15-oz.) pkg. refrigerated pie
　crusts or Pastry for Two-Crust Pie
　(page 67)

FILLING
5 cups fresh fruit (blueberries,
　sliced strawberries and/or
　bananas)
1 (16-oz.) jar strawberry glaze
½ cup frozen whipped topping,
　thawed

1. Prepare pie crust for *two-crust pie.* Heat oven to 450°F. With fluted round cookie cutter, cut five 4-inch rounds from each pie crust. Fit rounds floured side down over backs of ungreased muffin cups. Pinch 5 equally spaced pleats around sides of each cup. Prick each pastry generously with fork.

2. Bake at 450°F. for 9 to 13 minutes or until light golden brown. Cool 30 minutes or until completely cooled. Remove from muffin cups.

Fresh Fruit Tarts

3. Meanwhile, in large bowl, combine fruit and strawberry glaze. Refrigerate 30 minutes or until thoroughly chilled.

4. Just before serving, spoon ½ cup fruit mixture into each cooled tart shell. Top with whipped topping.

Nutrition per Serving: Serving Size: 1 Tart. Calories 300; Calories from Fat 120; Total Fat 13g; Saturated Fat 6g; Cholesterol 10mg; Sodium 230mg; Dietary Fiber 2g

Dietary Exchange: 1 Starch, 2 Fruit, 2 Fat OR 3 Carbohydrate, 2 Fat

STRAWBERRY-KIWI TART

Yield: 8 servings; **Prep Time:** 20 minutes
(Ready in 1 hour 50 minutes)

The red strawberry–green kiwi fruit topping makes a festive holiday presentation. For an Independence Day celebration, substitute raspberries and blueberries.

CRUST
1 refrigerated pie crust (from
　15-oz. pkg.) or Pastry for
　One-Crust Pie (page 67)

FILLING
1½ cups nonfat plain yogurt
1 (8-oz.) container light sour cream
1 (3.4-oz.) pkg. instant vanilla
　pudding and pie filling mix
2 tablespoons orange-flavored
　liqueur or orange juice

TOPPING
1 cup halved fresh strawberries
2 kiwi fruit, peeled, thinly sliced
2 tablespoons orange marmalade

1. Heat oven to 450°F. Prepare pie crust for *one-crust baked shell* using 9-inch tart pan with removable bottom or 9-inch pie pan. Bake at 450°F. for 9 to 11 minutes or until light golden brown. Cool 30 minutes or until completely cooled.

2. In medium bowl, combine all filling ingredients; mix until well blended. Pour into cooled baked shell. Arrange strawberries on filling around outer edge of pie; arrange kiwi fruit in center.

3. Place marmalade in small microwave-safe bowl. Microwave on HIGH for 5 to 10 seconds or until melted. Brush over fruit. Refrigerate 1 hour or until set. Store in refrigerator.

Nutrition per Serving: Serving Size: ⅛ of Recipe. Calories 260; Calories from Fat 80; Total Fat 9g; Saturated Fat 4g; Cholesterol 15mg; Sodium 370mg; Dietary Fiber 1g

Dietary Exchange: 1½ Starch, 1 Fruit, 2 Fat OR 2½ Carbohydrate, 2 Fat

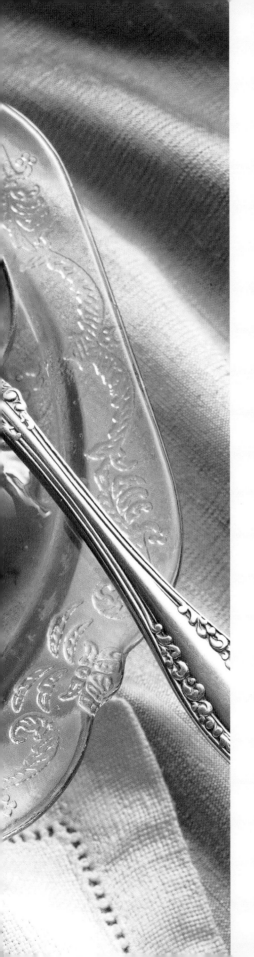

BAKED DESSERTS

◆ ◆ ◆

Warm from the oven and straight
from the heart, baked desserts
offer a homey, comforting ending
to the meal. This chapter includes
crisps, cobblers, bread puddings
and other old-fashioned favorites
that you'll want to make for the
family time and time again. Most
are more forgiving than their deli-
cate pastry and cake counterparts,
making them good choices for
time-pressed or beginning cooks.

APPLE-RASPBERRY COBBLER, PAGE 115

OLD-FASHIONED FRUIT DESSERTS

There's a whole family of desserts in which fruit bakes with a simple topping. In general, these desserts are easy and flexible, and most will still be delicious if you substitute a different fruit or mix and match toppings.

BETTY. Buttered bread crumbs above and below the fruit serve as bottom crust and topping.

COBBLER. Baking-powder biscuit dough forms the topping for the fruit mixture. The dough can be cut into plain or fancy shapes to top individual portions, or rolled into a solid piece to cover the entire top. Even easier, skip rolling out the dough and simply drop spoonfuls of the biscuit mixture directly on top of the fruit mixture. The topping will have a somewhat bumpier top—delightfully old-fashioned. If you wish, sprinkle the biscuit mixture with a little sugar before baking.

CRISP. The most popular crisp topping blends oatmeal, brown sugar and butter. In the oven, the brown sugar and butter melt to enrich the fruit and also sweeten the oatmeal, which becomes crisp.

CRUMBLE. This variation of a crisp omits the oatmeal and uses a mixture of butter and sugar, and sometimes sweet spices or a little flour, to yield a topping similar to that of many coffee cakes.

BAKED CUSTARD DESSERTS

BAKED CUSTARD. A basic custard combines egg, sugar and milk (and flavorings) into a delicate semi-solid dessert with a silken texture. Many recipes call for setting the pan of custard mixture into a larger pan partially filled with water. To check for doneness, insert a knife blade into the center; if the custard is set, the knife will come out clean.

BREAD PUDDING, RICE PUDDING AND NOODLE PUDDING. All are heartier variations of baked custard in which the creamy-textured egg mixture surrounds the title ingredient. Raisins or other small or chopped dried fruits are tasty additions to any of these.

MERINGUES AND SOUFFLÉS

Starting with beaten egg whites and sugar, you can arrive at two different types of lofty baked desserts.

MERINGUE. Baked meringue comes in two basic forms. Soft-textured meringues crown pies, baked Alaska and cookies relatively quickly; crisp, melt-in-your mouth meringues require lengthier baking at a low oven temperature plus additional time with the oven door closed and no peeking. Don't attempt to make meringue on a humid day because moisture in the air may cause the baked whites to "weep" and not set properly.

SOUFFLÉ. Time and soufflés wait for no one. This classic preparation is made by folding delicate beaten egg whites into a sweetened liquid mixture that may or may not include egg yolks. The baked dessert has an ethereal texture that is very fragile; the soufflé must be served immediately after it emerges from the oven before it collapses.

◆   ◆   ◆

SNAPPY BAKED FRUIT

◆

Yield: 6 (½-cup) servings;
Prep Time: 25 minutes

Crushed gingersnaps become a quick and zesty topping for baked peaches and pears.

1 (16-oz.) can sliced peaches, drained
1 (16-oz.) can pear halves, drained, chopped
½ teaspoon grated lemon peel, if desired

1 cup finely crushed gingersnaps
(about 14 cookies)
1 tablespoon margarine or butter,
melted

1. Heat oven to 375°F. In medium bowl, combine peaches, pears and lemon peel; mix well. Divide fruit mixture evenly into 6 ungreased 6-oz. custard cups.

2. In small bowl, combine crushed gingersnaps and margarine; mix well. Sprinkle evenly over fruit.

3. Bake at 375°F. for 12 to 15 minutes or until hot and bubbly.

Nutrition per Serving: Serving Size: ½ Cup. Calories 130; Calories from Fat 35; Total Fat 4g; Saturated Fat 1g; Cholesterol 0mg; Sodium 135mg; Dietary Fiber 3g

Dietary Exchange: 1 ½ Fruit, 1 Fat OR 1 ½ Carbohydrate, 1 Fat

SIMPLE FRUIT CRISP

✦

Yield: 8 servings; **Prep Time**: 10 minutes
(Ready in 40 minutes)

Tonight's dessert shortcut: top purchased pie filling with a quick from-scratch crumble for a delicious homemade dessert assembled in only 10 minutes.

FRUIT
1 (21-oz.) can fruit pie filling
(apple, apricot, cherry,
blueberry, peach or raspberry)

TOPPING
¾ cup all-purpose flour
⅓ cup firmly packed brown sugar
½ teaspoon cinnamon, if desired
½ teaspoon nutmeg, if desired
¼ cup margarine or butter,
softened

1. Heat oven to 375°F. Spread pie filling in ungreased 8-inch square (2-quart) baking dish.

2. In medium bowl, combine all topping ingredients; mix until crumbly. Sprinkle over pie filling.

3. Bake at 375°F. for 25 to 30 minutes or until bubbly and golden brown. If desired, serve warm with frozen yogurt or whipped topping.

Nutrition per Serving: Serving Size: ⅛ of Recipe. Calories 220; Calories from Fat 50; Total Fat 6g; Saturated Fat 1g; Cholesterol 0mg; Sodium 75mg; Dietary Fiber 1g

Dietary Exchange: 1 Starch, 1 ½ Fruit, 1 Fat OR 2 ½ Carbohydrate, 1 Fat

MIXED BERRY FRUIT CRISP

✦

Yield: 8 servings; **Prep Time**: 15 minutes
(Ready in 45 minutes)

Vary the proportions of berries to suit what's available in the market or your garden. If you wish, substitute sliced nectarines for any of the berries.

FRUIT MIXTURE
1 ½ cups fresh or frozen
blackberries
1 ½ cups fresh or frozen
blueberries
1 ½ cups fresh or frozen
raspberries
¼ cup sugar
3 tablespoons cornstarch

TOPPING
⅓ cup all-purpose flour
⅓ cup quick-cooking rolled oats
⅓ cup firmly packed brown sugar
1 teaspoon cinnamon
¼ cup margarine or butter, melted

1. Heat oven to 400°F. In large bowl, combine all fruit mixture ingredients; toss gently. Spoon evenly into ungreased 8-inch square (2-quart) baking dish.

2. In small bowl, combine all topping ingredients; mix until crumbly. Sprinkle over fruit mixture.

3. Bake at 400°F. for 25 to 30 minutes or until edges are lightly browned and fruit mixture is bubbly. Cool slightly. Serve warm or at room temperature. If desired, top with vanilla ice cream.

Nutrition per Serving: Serving Size: ⅛ of Recipe. Calories 200; Calories from Fat 50; Total Fat 6g; Saturated Fat 4g; Cholesterol 15mg; Sodium 65mg; Dietary Fiber 4g

Dietary Exchange: 1 Starch, 1 Fruit, 1 ½ Fat OR 2 Carbohydrate, 1 ½ Fat

OLD-FASHIONED PEACH CRISP

✦

Yield: 12 servings; Prep Time: 10 minutes
(Ready in 45 minutes)

A simple mixture of brown sugar, rolled oats, butter and flour bakes up into a crisp topping that's a delightful complement to tender baked peaches.

FRUIT MIXTURE
6 cups fresh or frozen sliced peeled peaches, thawed (8 to 10 medium)
1 teaspoon cinnamon, if desired

TOPPING
1 cup rolled oats
¾ cup all-purpose flour
¾ cup firmly packed brown sugar
½ cup margarine or butter, softened

1. Heat oven to 375°F. Place peaches in ungreased 12 × 8-inch (2-quart) baking dish. Sprinkle with cinnamon.

2. In large bowl, combine all topping ingredients; mix until crumbly. Sprinkle crumb mixture evenly over peaches.

3. Bake at 375°F. for 25 to 35 minutes or until peaches are tender and topping is golden brown. If desired, serve warm with cream, ice cream or whipped cream.

Nutrition per Serving: Serving Size: ¹⁄₁₂ of Recipe. Calories 300; Calories from Fat 70; Total Fat 8g; Saturated Fat 2g; Cholesterol 0mg; Sodium 105mg; Dietary Fiber 3g

Dietary Exchange: 1 Starch, 2 ½ Fruit, 1 ½ Fat OR 3 ½ Carbohydrate, 1 ½ Fat

CRANBERRY-APPLE CRISP

Yield: 10 servings; Prep Time: 15 minutes
(Ready in 55 minutes)

A wonderful family dessert, this crisp adds cranberries to the classic apple recipe. If you like cooked apples to retain a bit of firmness, use Granny Smiths; if you prefer a softer baked texture, McIntosh apples would be a good choice.

FRUIT MIXTURE
5 cups (5 medium) sliced peeled apples
1 ½ cups fresh or frozen cranberries
1 cup sugar
2 tablespoons all-purpose flour
1 teaspoon cinnamon

TOPPING
1 cup rolled oats
½ cup firmly packed brown sugar
⅓ cup all-purpose flour
⅓ cup margarine or butter
½ cup chopped nuts

1. Heat oven to 375°F. Grease 12 × 8-inch (2-quart) baking dish. In large bowl, combine all fruit mixture ingredients; toss to coat. Spoon into greased baking dish.

2. In small bowl, combine rolled oats, brown sugar and ⅓ cup flour. With pastry blender or fork, cut in margarine until crumbly. Stir in nuts. Sprinkle topping evenly over fruit.

3. Bake at 375°F. for 30 to 40 minutes or until topping is golden brown and apples are tender. If desired, serve with ice cream, whipped cream or whipped topping.

Nutrition per Serving: Serving Size: ¹⁄₁₀ of Recipe. Calories 320; Calories from Fat 100; Total Fat 11g; Saturated Fat 2g; Cholesterol 0mg; Sodium 75mg; Dietary Fiber 3g

Dietary Exchange: 1 Starch, 2 ½ Fruit, 2 Fat OR 3 ½ Carbohydrate, 2 Fat

Old-Fashioned Peach Crisp

BLUEBERRY CRUMBLE

Yield: 6 servings; **Prep Time:** 10 minutes
(Ready in 40 minutes)

Crumbly brown sugar topping turns an irresistible golden brown as it bakes over a blueberry-raisin melange.

FRUIT MIXTURE
4 cups fresh or frozen blueberries
¼ cup raisins
2 tablespoons cornstarch
1 teaspoon grated lemon peel
1 tablespoon lemon juice
⅓ cup apricot preserves

TOPPING
½ cup all-purpose flour
½ cup firmly packed brown sugar
1 teaspoon cinnamon
¼ cup margarine or butter, softened

1. Heat oven to 400°F. Grease 10 × 6-inch (1 ½-quart) or 8-inch square (2-quart) baking dish. In large bowl, combine blueberries, raisins, cornstarch, lemon peel and lemon juice. Spoon mixture evenly into greased baking dish. Dot with apricot preserves.

2. In medium bowl, combine flour, brown sugar and cinnamon; mix well. With pastry blender or fork, cut in margarine until mixture is crumbly. Sprinkle topping evenly over fruit mixture.

3. Bake at 400°F. for 20 to 30 minutes or until topping is golden brown. Serve warm or at room temperature. If desired, top with whipped topping or ice cream.

Nutrition per Serving: Serving Size: ⅙ of Recipe. Calories 320; Calories from Fat 70; Total Fat 8g; Saturated Fat 1g; Cholesterol 0mg; Sodium 110mg; Dietary Fiber 4g

Dietary Exchange: 1 Starch, 3 Fruit, 1 ½ Fat OR 4 Carbohydrate, 1 ½ Fat

CARAMEL APPLE BAKED DESSERT

Yield: 6 servings; **Prep Time:** 20 minutes
(Ready in 45 minutes)

Dry-roasted peanuts in this sweetly sauced dessert offer a welcome change of pace from the walnuts or pecans more typically linked with apples.

TOPPING
⅓ cup corn flake crumbs
¼ cup firmly packed brown sugar
¼ cup chopped dry-roasted peanuts
3 tablespoons all-purpose flour
2 tablespoons margarine or butter, melted

FRUIT MIXTURE
4 medium red baking apples, unpeeled, cut into ½-inch cubes (4 cups)
⅔ cup nonfat caramel ice cream topping
2 teaspoons lemon juice

1. Heat oven to 400°F. Spray 8-inch square (2-quart) baking dish with nonstick cooking spray.

2. In small bowl, combine corn flake crumbs, brown sugar, peanuts and flour; mix well. Add melted margarine; stir until well mixed.

3. In large bowl, combine all fruit mixture ingredients; mix well. Spoon evenly into sprayed baking dish; sprinkle with topping.

4. Bake at 400°F. for 20 to 25 minutes or until apples are tender and mixture is bubbly. Cool slightly before serving. (Apple layer will be saucy.)

Nutrition per Serving: Serving Size: ⅙ of Recipe. Calories 310; Calories from Fat 60; Total Fat 7g; Saturated Fat 1g; Cholesterol 0mg; Sodium 250mg; Dietary Fiber 3g

Dietary Exchange: 1 Starch, 3 Fruit, 1 Fat OR 4 Carbohydrate, 1 Fat

APPLE-RASPBERRY COBBLER

PICTURED ON PAGE 108.

Yield: 6 servings; Prep Time: 15 minutes
(Ready in 40 minutes)

Who doesn't love a homey cobbler, comfort food at its best? As the slightly sweet biscuit topping bakes, the tops become golden brown and crisp while the bottoms remain soft as they mingle with the juices from the apples and raspberries.

FRUIT MIXTURE
1 (21-oz.) can apple pie filling
1 ½ cups fresh or frozen
    raspberries

TOPPING
¾ cup all-purpose flour
¼ cup sugar
1 teaspoon baking powder
3 tablespoons milk
2 tablespoons margarine or butter,
    melted
1 egg

1. Heat oven to 400°F. In medium saucepan, combine pie filling and raspberries. Cook and stir over medium heat until hot and bubbly. Pour into ungreased 8-inch square (2-quart) baking dish.

2. In small bowl, combine flour, sugar and baking powder; mix well. Add milk, margarine and egg; mix until batter is smooth. Drop 6 spoonfuls of batter onto hot fruit mixture.

3. Bake at 400°F. for 15 to 22 minutes or until topping is light golden brown. If desired, top with warm milk or half-and-half.

High Altitude (Above 3,500 feet): No change.

Nutrition per Serving: Serving Size: ⅙ of Recipe. Calories 260; Calories from Fat 45; Total Fat 5g; Saturated Fat 1g; Cholesterol 35mg; Sodium 160mg; Dietary Fiber 4g

Dietary Exchange: 1 Starch, 2 ½ Fruit, ½ Fat OR 3 ½ Carbohydrate, ½ Fat

RASPBERRY-PEACH COBBLER

Yield: 9 servings; Prep Time: 15 minutes
(Ready in 1 hour)

Sour cream enhances the tenderness of the biscuit topping.

BISCUITS
1 cup all-purpose flour
½ cup sugar
1 teaspoon baking powder
¼ teaspoon salt
¾ cup sour cream
2 tablespoons margarine or butter,
    melted
1 egg
1 tablespoon sugar

FRUIT MIXTURE
¾ cup sugar
3 tablespoons cornstarch
1 (10-oz.) pkg. frozen raspberries
    in syrup, thawed, drained,
    reserving liquid

1 (16-oz.) pkg. frozen sliced
    peaches, thawed, drained

1. Heat oven to 375°F. In medium bowl, combine flour, ½ cup sugar, baking powder and salt; mix well. Stir in sour cream, margarine and egg until well blended. Set aside.

2. In medium saucepan, combine ¾ cup sugar, cornstarch and reserved raspberry liquid. Cook over medium heat until mixture comes to a boil. Boil 1 minute, stirring constantly. Add raspberries and peaches; cook 1 minute. Pour into ungreased 2-quart casserole.

3. Spoon biscuit mixture over hot fruit mixture, forming 9 biscuits around edge of casserole. Sprinkle biscuits with 1 tablespoon sugar.

4. Bake at 375°F. for 35 to 45 minutes or until biscuits are golden brown. Serve warm.

High Altitude (Above 3,500 feet): No change.

Nutrition per Serving: Serving Size: ⅑ of Recipe. Calories 340; Calories from Fat 70; Total Fat 8g; Saturated Fat 3g; Cholesterol 30mg; Sodium 170mg; Dietary Fiber 3g

Dietary Exchange: 1 Starch, 3 Fruit, 2 Fat OR 4 Carbohydrate, 2 Fat

COUNTRY PEACH COBBLER

Yield: 8 servings; **Prep Time:** 15 minutes
(Ready in 35 minutes)

Enjoy homey, from-scratch flavor without all the work of peeling peaches.

FRUIT MIXTURE
1 (21-oz.) can peach pie filling
1/2 cup apricot preserves
1/4 teaspoon almond extract

TOPPING
1 cup all-purpose flour
2 tablespoons sugar
2 teaspoons baking powder
1/4 teaspoon salt
1/4 cup margarine or butter
2 to 3 tablespoons milk
1 egg
1/2 teaspoon sugar

1. Heat oven to 425°F. In medium saucepan, combine pie filling, preserves and almond extract. Cook over medium-high heat for 2 to 3 minutes or until mixture boils, stirring occasionally. Pour mixture into ungreased 8-inch square pan; spread evenly.

2. In large bowl, combine flour, 2 tablespoons sugar, baking powder and salt; mix well. With pastry blender or fork, cut in margarine until crumbly.

3. In small bowl, combine 2 tablespoons milk and egg; beat well. Stir into flour mixture to form a stiff dough, adding additional milk if necessary. Drop dough by spoonfuls evenly over fruit mixture. Sprinkle with 1/2 teaspoon sugar.

4. Bake at 425°F. for 12 to 17 minutes or until fruit bubbles around edges and topping is golden brown. Serve warm.

High Altitude (Above 3,500 feet): No change.

Nutrition per Serving: Serving Size: 1/8 of Recipe. Calories 260; Calories from Fat 60; Total Fat 7g; Saturated Fat 1g; Cholesterol 25mg; Sodium 290mg; Dietary Fiber 1g

Dietary Exchange: 1 1/2 Starch, 1 1/2 Fruit, 1 Fat OR 3 Carbohydrate, 1 Fat

OLD-FASHIONED BERRY COBBLER

Yield: 8 servings; **Prep Time:** 25 minutes
(Ready in 45 minutes)

Even if you grew up in the city, old-fashioned cobblers evoke images of life on the farm and family dinners around tables spread with red-checked cloths. If you prefer, top the fruit with the dough rectangle in a single piece, being sure to cut a few slits for the steam to escape.

FRUIT MIXTURE
4 cups fresh or frozen berries (raspberries, blackberries, boysenberries and/or loganberries)
1/2 cup seedless raspberry jam
2 tablespoons quick-cooking tapioca or cornstarch
2 tablespoons sugar
2 tablespoons margarine or butter

BISCUITS
1 cup all-purpose flour
2 tablespoons sugar
2 teaspoons baking powder
1/4 teaspoon salt
1/4 cup margarine or butter
2 to 4 tablespoons milk
1 egg
1/2 teaspoon sugar

1. Heat oven to 425°F. Grease 10 × 6-inch (1 1/2-quart) baking dish or 1 1/2-quart casserole. In large bowl, combine berries, jam, tapioca and 2 tablespoons sugar; mix gently. Spread in greased baking dish. Dot with 2 tablespoons margarine. Bake at 425°F. for 15 to 20 minutes or until berries begin to bubble.

2. Meanwhile, in large bowl, combine flour, 2 tablespoons sugar, baking powder and salt; mix well. With pastry blender or fork, cut in 1/4 cup margarine until crumbly. In small bowl, combine 2 tablespoons milk and egg; beat well. Stir into flour mixture until stiff dough forms, adding additional milk if necessary.

Old-Fashioned Berry Cobbler

3. On lightly floured surface, roll out dough to ¹/₂-inch thickness. With 2-inch cookie cutter, cut out hearts, rounds or diamonds. Stir hot fruit mixture; top with dough cutouts. Sprinkle cutouts with ¹/₂ teaspoon sugar.

4. Bake at 425°F. for 10 to 20 minutes or until fruit bubbles around edges and biscuits are light golden brown. If desired, serve warm with cream or ice cream.

High Altitude (Above 3,500 feet): No change.

Nutrition per Serving: Serving Size: ¹/₈ of Recipe. Calories 310; Calories from Fat 90; Total Fat 10g; Saturated Fat 2g; Cholesterol 25mg; Sodium 310mg; Dietary Fiber 5g

Dietary Exchange: 1 Starch, 2 ¹/₂ Fruit, 2 Fat OR 3 ¹/₂ Carbohydrate, 2 Fat

PEAR-CRANBERRY-APRICOT COBBLER

Yield: 10 servings; **Prep Time:** 15 minutes
(Ready in 1 hour 5 minutes)

Whip up this cobbler with classic autumn ingredients and let it bake while you serve the main course.

FRUIT MIXTURE
4 cups (4 to 5 medium) sliced
    peeled pears
1 cup fresh or frozen cranberries
1 (16-oz.) can apricot halves,
    undrained
½ cup sugar
¾ teaspoon cinnamon
2 to 3 teaspoons grated orange
    peel

TOPPING
1¼ cups all-purpose flour
½ cup sugar
1 teaspoon baking powder
¼ teaspoon salt
¼ cup milk
1 tablespoon margarine or butter,
    melted
2 eggs

1. Heat oven to 350°F. Grease 2-quart casserole. In medium saucepan, combine all fruit mixture ingredients. Cook over medium heat for 10 to 15 minutes or until mixture is hot, stirring occasionally.

2. Meanwhile, in medium bowl, combine flour, ½ cup sugar, baking powder and salt; blend well. Add milk, margarine and eggs; mix until batter is smooth.

3. Pour hot fruit mixture into greased casserole; spoon topping over fruit.

4. Bake at 350°F. for 30 to 40 minutes or until topping is golden brown. Serve warm.

High Altitude (Above 3,500 feet): No change.

Nutrition per Serving: Serving Size: 1/10 of Recipe. Calories 260; Calories from Fat 25; Total Fat 3g; Saturated Fat 1g; Cholesterol 45mg; Sodium 120mg; Dietary Fiber 3g

Dietary Exchange: 1½ Starch, 2 Fruit, ½ Fat OR 3½ Carbohydrate, ½ Fat

PEACH BROWN BETTY

Yield: 6 servings; **Prep Time:** 15 minutes
(Ready in 45 minutes)

Peaches are slightly less traditional but every bit as good as apples for a crumb-topped betty. Whole wheat bread gives the dessert a bit more character than white crumbs.

3 cups fresh or frozen thinly
    sliced, peeled peaches, thawed
    (4 to 5 medium)
2 tablespoons sugar
5 slices whole wheat bread, torn
    into small pieces

¼ cup firmly packed brown sugar
1 teaspoon cinnamon
3 tablespoons margarine or butter,
    melted

1. Heat oven to 375°F. In medium bowl, combine peaches and sugar; toss to coat. Set aside.

2. In food processor bowl with metal blade, process bread pieces to make about 3 cups crumbs.* Add brown sugar and cinnamon; process to mix well. With machine running, slowly add margarine until well mixed.

3. Sprinkle ⅓ of crumb mixture evenly in bottom of 8-inch square (2-quart) baking dish. Layer half of peach mixture on top of crumb mixture. Repeat layers. Top with remaining crumbs.

4. Bake at 375°F. for 20 to 30 minutes or until peaches are tender when pierced with fork. If desired, serve warm with milk.

Tip: If food processor is unavailable, a blender can be used. Blend 2 slices of bread at a time until crumbs form. In medium bowl, combine bread crumbs, brown sugar and cinnamon; mix well. Add melted margarine; stir until moistened.

Nutrition per Serving: Serving Size: 1/6 of Recipe. Calories 210; Calories from Fat 60; Total Fat 7g; Saturated Fat 1g; Cholesterol 0mg; Sodium 190mg; Dietary Fiber 4g

Dietary Exchange: 1 Starch, 1½ Fruit, 1 Fat OR 2½ Carbohydrate, 1 Fat

APPLE BROWN BETTY

Yield: 8 servings; **Prep Time:** 10 minutes
(Ready in 1 hour 20 minutes)

Apple Brown Betty has been a favorite home-style dessert in America dating back to colonial days. Buttered bread crumbs serve both as a quick crust and a crumbly topping for the spiced apple filling.

5 cups (5 medium) sliced peeled apples
½ cup firmly packed brown sugar
1 teaspoon grated lemon peel
¼ teaspoon nutmeg
1 tablespoon lemon juice
1 cup unseasoned dry bread crumbs
½ cup margarine or butter, melted
Half-and-half, if desired

1. Heat oven to 375°F. Grease 8-inch square (2-quart) baking dish. In large bowl, combine apples, brown sugar, lemon peel, nutmeg and lemon juice; mix well.

2. In medium bowl, combine bread crumbs and margarine; sprinkle ½ cup bread crumb mixture in greased baking dish. Spoon apple mixture over crumb mixture; top with remaining bread crumb mixture. Cover with foil.

3. Bake at 375°F. for 45 to 50 minutes or until apples are almost tender. Uncover; bake an additional 15 to 20 minutes or until top is crisp and golden brown. Serve warm with half-and-half.

Nutrition per Serving: Serving Size: ⅛ of Recipe. Calories 300; Calories from Fat 140; Total Fat 16g; Saturated Fat 5g; Cholesterol 10mg; Sodium 270mg; Dietary Fiber 2g

Dietary Exchange: 1 Starch, 1 ½ Fruit, 3 Fat OR 2 ½ Carbohydrate, 3 Fat

MAPLE BAKED APPLES

Yield: 6 servings; **Prep Time:** 20 minutes
(Ready in 1 hour 10 minutes)

Make this country-style dessert in autumn when crisp, fresh apples are plentiful. Rome Beauty, Cortland or McIntosh would all be good choices to complement the maple syrup. If you wish, add ¼ cup finely chopped nuts to the filling, too.

6 large baking apples
2 tablespoons lemon juice
½ cup raisins
½ teaspoon cinnamon
1 cup maple or maple-flavored syrup
¼ cup water

1. Heat oven to 350°F. Core apples and remove a 1-inch strip of peel around top to prevent splitting. Brush tops and insides with lemon juice. Place apples in 8-inch square (2-quart) baking dish.

2. In small bowl, combine raisins and cinnamon; fill center of each apple with mixture. Pour maple syrup over apples. Add ¼ cup water to baking dish.

3. Bake at 350°F. for 45 to 50 minutes or until apples are tender, occasionally spooning syrup mixture over apples.

Nutrition per Serving: Serving Size: ⅙ of Recipe. Calories 320; Calories from Fat 10; Total Fat 1g; Saturated Fat 0g; Cholesterol 0mg; Sodium 5mg; Dietary Fiber 6g

Dietary Exchange: 5 ½ Fruit OR 5 ½ Carbohydrate

FRUITED PEARS WITH RUM SAUCE

◆

Yield: 6 servings; **Prep Time:** 20 minutes

Fruit desserts bring a meal to a sweet conclusion without the heaviness of many other desserts. This dessert is also scrumptious made with canned peaches or apricots.

PEARS
1 (16-oz.) can pear halves in heavy or light syrup, drained, reserving ½ cup liquid
¼ cup prepared mincemeat

SAUCE
½ cup reserved pear liquid
2 teaspoons cornstarch
1 tablespoon rum or ¼ teaspoon rum extract
1 tablespoon margarine or butter

1. Heat oven to 375°F. Place pear halves, cut side up, in ungreased 8-inch square (2-quart) baking dish. Spoon about 1 tablespoon mincemeat into each pear half. Bake at 375°F. for 15 minutes or until thoroughly heated.

2. Meanwhile, in small saucepan, combine reserved pear liquid and cornstarch; blend well. Cook over medium heat until mixture comes to a boil, stirring constantly. Remove from heat; stir in rum and margarine. Serve warm over pears.

Nutrition per Serving: Serving Size: ⅙ of Recipe. Calories 130; Calories from Fat 20; Total Fat 2g; Saturated Fat 1g; Cholesterol 0mg; Sodium 95mg; Dietary Fiber 2g

Dietary Exchange: 2 Fruit OR 2 Carbohydrate

APPLE MYSTERY DESSERT

◆

Yield: 8 servings; **Prep Time:** 25 minutes
(Ready in 55 minutes)

The puzzle here is whether to classify this cinnamon-apple dessert as a cake, a pudding or a pie. Let others debate while you dig into slices of the moist dessert, topped with a pat of sweet Cinnamon Hard Sauce that's more like icing than what we usually think of as "sauce."

DESSERT
¾ cup all-purpose flour
1 cup firmly packed brown sugar
1 ½ teaspoons baking powder
½ teaspoon salt
Dash mace, if desired
Dash cinnamon
1 ½ teaspoons vanilla
2 eggs
2 cups chopped peeled tart apples
¾ cup chopped walnuts

CINNAMON HARD SAUCE
¼ cup margarine or butter, softened
1 cup powdered sugar
½ teaspoon cinnamon
Dash salt
1 tablespoon milk
1 teaspoon vanilla

1. Heat oven to 350°F. Grease 9-inch pie pan. In large bowl, combine flour, brown sugar, baking powder, ½ teaspoon salt, mace and dash of cinnamon; mix well. Stir in 1 ½ teaspoons vanilla and eggs; blend well. Add apples and walnuts; mix well. Pour into greased pan.

2. Bake at 350°F. for 20 to 30 minutes or until browned and firm to the touch.

3. Meanwhile, in small bowl, combine all hard sauce ingredients. Beat at high speed until well blended. Shape into 2-inch-thick roll or spread into butter molds. Wrap in plastic wrap; refrigerate until firm.

4. To serve, cut hard sauce into slices. Top each serving of dessert with slice of hard sauce.

Nutrition per Serving: Serving Size: ⅛ of Recipe. Calories 380; Calories from Fat 130; Total Fat 14g; Saturated Fat 2g; Cholesterol 55mg; Sodium 340mg; Dietary Fiber 2g

Dietary Exchange: 2 Starch, 2 Fruit, 2 Fat OR 4 Carbohydrate, 2 Fat

Apple Mystery Dessert

FINNISH BLUEBERRY SQUARES

✦

Yield: 12 servings; **Prep Time:** 25 minutes
(Ready in 2 hours 5 minutes)

Serve this blueberry-packed dessert, with the purple filling peeping through the lattice top, slightly warm from the oven with a dollop of whipped cream or ice cream.

PASTRY

1 cup margarine or butter, softened
1/2 cup sugar
2 3/4 cups all-purpose flour
1/4 teaspoon salt
1/2 teaspoon vanilla
1 egg

FILLING

3 cups fresh or frozen blueberries
1 cup sugar
3 tablespoons cornstarch

1 teaspoon powdered sugar

1. In large bowl, combine margarine and 1/2 cup sugar; beat well. Add flour, salt, vanilla and egg; mix well. Cover; refrigerate until firm, about 2 hours.

2. Meanwhile, in medium saucepan, combine blueberries, 1 cup sugar and cornstarch; mix well. Cook over medium heat until mixture comes to a boil, stirring constantly. Boil 3 minutes or until thickened, stirring constantly. Remove from heat; cool.

3. Heat oven to 375°F. Pat 2/3 of chilled pastry dough into ungreased 13 × 9-inch pan, pressing 1/2 inch up sides. Spread blueberry mixture evenly over dough. Roll out remaining dough to 1/4-inch thickness. With fluted wheel, cut dough into 1/2-inch-wide strips. Arrange strips in lattice design over filling. (Strips may break apart but will bake together.) Trim and seal edges.

4. Bake at 375°F. for 30 to 40 minutes or until top is golden brown. Cool slightly. Sprinkle with powdered sugar; cut into squares. If desired, serve with ice cream or whipped topping.

Nutrition per Serving: Serving Size: 1/12 of Recipe.
Calories 380; Calories from Fat 140; Total Fat 16g;
Saturated Fat 3g; Cholesterol 20mg; Sodium 230mg;
Dietary Fiber 2g

Dietary Exchange: 1 1/2 Starch, 2 Fruit, 3 Fat OR
3 1/2 Carbohydrate, 3 Fat

Finnish Blueberry Squares

LIME DESSERT SQUARES

Yield: 9 servings; **Prep Time:** 20 minutes
(Ready in 2 hours 40 minutes)

This tangy dessert is a cross between a lemon bar and lemon meringue pie, with lime as the flavoring.

CRUST
¾ cup all-purpose flour
⅓ cup powdered sugar
5 tablespoons margarine or butter

FILLING
1 cup sugar
½ teaspoon baking powder
¼ teaspoon salt
½ cup lime or Key lime juice
3 egg whites
1 egg

MERINGUE
3 egg whites
¼ teaspoon cream of tartar
¼ teaspoon vanilla
¼ cup sugar
⅓ cup coconut

1. Heat oven to 350°F. Spray 9-inch square pan with nonstick cooking spray. In medium bowl, combine flour and powdered sugar; mix well. With fork or pastry blender, cut in margarine until mixture is crumbly. Firmly press mixture in bottom of sprayed pan.

2. Bake at 350°F. for 13 to 18 minutes or until golden brown.

3. Meanwhile, in small bowl, combine all filling ingredients; beat 1 minute at medium speed.

4. Pour filling over partially baked crust. Bake at 350°F. for 12 to 17 minutes or until filling is set.

5. Meanwhile, in small bowl, beat egg whites, cream of tartar and vanilla at medium speed until soft peaks form, about 1 minute. Beating at high speed, gradually add ¼ cup sugar, 1 tablespoon at a time, until stiff peaks form and sugar is dissolved; fold in coconut.

6. Carefully spread meringue over filling, spreading around outer edges first and filling in center last. Be sure meringue touches sides of pan.

7. Bake at 350°F. for 10 to 15 minutes or until deep golden brown. Cool 2 hours.

8. To serve, cut into squares. Store in refrigerator.

High Altitude (Above 3,500 feet): No change.

Nutrition per Serving: Serving Size: ⅑ of Recipe. Calories 260; Calories from Fat 70; Total Fat 8g; Saturated Fat 2g; Cholesterol 25mg; Sodium 210mg; Dietary Fiber 0g

Dietary Exchange: 1 Starch, 2 Fruit, 1½ Fat OR 3 Carbohydrate, 1½ Fat

SWEDISH BAKED APPLE DESSERT

Yield: 10 servings; **Prep Time:** 25 minutes
(Ready in 55 minutes)

Crushed cookies go into a quick topping for spiced apple slices baked with lemon and nuts.

½ cup margarine or butter
1 (10-oz.) pkg. shortbread or oatmeal cookies, crushed
½ cup sugar
2 teaspoons cinnamon
8 cups (8 medium) sliced peeled apples
1 tablespoon sugar
1 tablespoon lemon juice
⅓ cup chopped almonds, if desired

1. In large skillet, melt 6 tablespoons of the margarine over medium heat. Add cookie crumbs, ½ cup sugar and cinnamon; cook and stir over heat for 3 minutes. Place crumbs in bowl; set aside.

2. In same skillet, combine remaining 2 tablespoons margarine, sliced apples, 1 tablespoon sugar and lemon juice; mix well. Cover; cook over medium heat for about 10 minutes or until apples are tender, stirring frequently.

3. Heat oven to 375°F. In ungreased 2-quart casserole, layer half of apples and half of crumbs. Repeat layers. Sprinkle with almonds.

Swedish Baked Apple Dessert

4. Bake at 375°F. for 25 to 30 minutes or until golden brown. If desired, serve warm with cream.

Nutrition per Serving: Serving Size: $1/10$ of Recipe. Calories 350; Calories from Fat 160; Total Fat 18g; Saturated Fat 4g; Cholesterol 5mg; Sodium 240mg; Dietary Fiber 3g

Dietary Exchange: 1 Starch, 2 Fruit, 3 $1/2$ Fat OR 3 Carbohydrate, 3 $1/2$ Fat

MOM'S APPLE DUMPLINGS

✦

Yield: 6 servings; **Prep Time:** 25 minutes
(Ready in 1 hour 15 minutes)

Apples bake to perfection inside the pastry crust surrounded by spiced syrup. For a whimsical touch, before baking, decorate with pastry cut into the shape of apple leaves.

SAUCE
1 ½ cups sugar
1 ½ cups water
¼ cup red cinnamon candies
¼ teaspoon cinnamon
¼ teaspoon nutmeg

DUMPLINGS
2 cups all-purpose flour
2 teaspoons baking powder
1 teaspoon salt
⅔ cup shortening

½ to ⅔ cup cold milk
6 small (2 ½-inch diameter) baking
    apples, peeled and cored
3 tablespoons margarine or butter
1 egg white, beaten
1 tablespoon sugar

1. In medium saucepan, combine all sauce ingredients. Bring to a full rolling boil, stirring occasionally. Set aside.

Mom's Apple Dumplings

2. Heat oven to 375°F. In large bowl, combine flour, baking powder and salt. With pastry blender or fork, cut in shortening until mixture resembles coarse crumbs. Sprinkle flour mixture with milk while tossing and mixing lightly with fork, adding enough milk to form a soft dough. Shape dough into ball.

3. On lightly floured surface, roll dough into 18 × 12-inch rectangle. Cut rectangle into 6 squares. Place 1 apple in center of each pastry square; dot with margarine. Bring corners of pastry squares up to tops of apples; press edges to seal. Place in ungreased 13 × 9-inch pan. Pour sauce in pan evenly around dumplings. Brush dumplings with egg white; sprinkle with 1 tablespoon sugar.

4. Bake at 375°F. for 40 to 50 minutes or until dumplings are light golden brown and apples are tender. Serve dumplings warm or cool with sauce and, if desired, half-and-half.

Tip: If desired, prepare 5 dumplings, omitting 1 apple and reserving remaining pastry square for decorative cutouts. Garnish sealed dumplings with cutouts before baking.

High Altitude (Above 3,500 feet): No change.

Nutrition per Serving: Serving Size: 1 Dumpling. Calories 730; Calories from Fat 260; Total Fat 29g; Saturated Fat 7g; Cholesterol 2mg; Sodium 610mg; Dietary Fiber 3g

Dietary Exchange: 2 Starch, 5 1/2 Fruit, 5 1/2 Fat OR 7 1/2 Carbohydrate, 5 1/2 Fat

PEACH DUMPLINGS WITH RASPBERRY SAUCE

Yield: 4 servings; **Prep Time:** 20 minutes (Ready in 1 hour 15 minutes)

Golden peaches plus red raspberries: the combination is as pretty as it is delectable.

DUMPLINGS
1 refrigerated pie crust (from 15-oz. pkg.)
1 (16-oz.) can peach halves in light syrup, drained, reserving liquid
1 egg white, slightly beaten
1 tablespoon sugar

SAUCE
1/2 cup red raspberry preserves
1/4 teaspoon almond extract

1. Allow crust pouch to stand at room temperature for 15 to 20 minutes.

2. Heat oven to 425°F. Remove crust from pouch; unfold. Peel off plastic sheets; cut crust into quarters.

3. Divide peaches evenly onto crust quarters; brush crust edges lightly with reserved peach liquid. Bring sides of each crust quarter up to tops of peaches; press edges to seal, making 3 seams. Place, seam side up, in ungreased 8-inch square or 12 × 8-inch (2-quart) baking dish. Brush with egg white; sprinkle with sugar.

4. Bake at 425°F. for 22 to 32 minutes or until golden brown.

5. Meanwhile, in small saucepan, combine sauce ingredients. Heat over low heat until warm, stirring occasionally.

6. Immediately remove dumplings from baking dish; place in individual dessert dishes. Serve warm sauce with warm dumplings.

Nutrition per Serving: Serving Size: 1/4 of Recipe. Calories 410; Calories from Fat 140; Total Fat 15g; Saturated Fat 6g; Cholesterol 15mg; Sodium 300mg; Dietary Fiber 2g

Dietary Exchange: 1 Starch, 3 1/2 Fruit, 2 1/2 Fat OR 4 1/2 Carbohydrate, 2 1/2 Fat

STRAWBERRY SHORTCAKE

Yield: 8 servings; **Prep Time:** 15 minutes
(Ready in 45 minutes)

Savor this spring classic: flaky baking powder biscuits piled high with sliced berries and real whipped cream.

SHORTCAKE
2 cups all-purpose flour
1/2 cup sugar
3 teaspoons baking powder
1/2 teaspoon salt
1/2 cup margarine or butter
3/4 cup milk
2 eggs, slightly beaten

FRUIT
2 pints (4 cups) fresh strawberries, sliced
1/2 cup sugar

TOPPING
1 cup whipping cream
2 tablespoons powdered sugar
1/2 teaspoon vanilla

1. Heat oven to 375°F. Grease and flour 8 or 9-inch round cake pan. In large bowl, combine flour, 1/2 cup sugar, baking powder and salt; mix well. With pastry blender or fork, cut in margarine until mixture resembles coarse crumbs. Add milk and eggs, stirring just until dry ingredients are moistened. Spoon into greased and floured pan.

2. Bake at 375°F. for 25 to 30 minutes or until toothpick inserted in center comes out clean. Cool 10 minutes.

3. Meanwhile, in medium bowl, combine strawberries and 1/2 cup sugar; mix well. Refrigerate 30 minutes or until serving time.

4. Just before serving, in small bowl, beat whipping cream until soft peaks form. Add powdered sugar and vanilla; beat until stiff peaks form.

5. Invert shortcake onto serving platter. If desired, split shortcake into 2 layers. Serve shortcake topped with strawberries and whipped cream. Store in refrigerator.

High Altitude (Above 3,500 feet): Increase flour to 2 cups plus 2 tablespoons; decrease baking powder to 2 1/2 teaspoons. Bake at 375°F. for 30 to 35 minutes.

Nutrition per Serving: Serving Size: 1/8 of Recipe. Calories 490; Calories from Fat 230; Total Fat 25g; Saturated Fat 10g; Cholesterol 95mg; Sodium 490mg; Dietary Fiber 3g

Dietary Exchange: 2 Starch, 2 Fruit, 4 1/2 Fat OR 4 Carbohydrate, 4 1/2 Fat

LEMON-GINGER-BLUEBERRY SHORTCAKES

Yield: 8 servings; **Prep Time:** 35 minutes

For a change from strawberry shortcake, ginger-scented biscuits form a lovely shortcake base for the refreshing filling of blueberries layered with whipped topping blended with lemon yogurt.

SHORTCAKES
1 cup all-purpose flour
1/4 cup sugar
2 teaspoons baking powder
1 teaspoon grated lemon peel
1/2 teaspoon ginger
3 tablespoons margarine or butter, cut into 4 pieces
7 to 9 tablespoons skim milk

FILLING
1 (5-oz.) container (1/2 cup) nonfat lemon yogurt
1/3 cup frozen light whipped topping, thawed
1 teaspoon grated lemon peel
1 1/2 cups fresh blueberries
1 to 2 teaspoons powdered sugar

1. Heat oven to 450°F. Spray cookie sheet with nonstick cooking spray. In medium bowl, combine flour, sugar, baking powder, 1 teaspoon lemon peel and ginger. With pastry blender or fork, cut in margarine until mixture resembles coarse crumbs. Add milk; stir

Lemon-Ginger-Blueberry Shortcakes

until dough is moistened and clings together. Drop dough by heaping tablespoons onto sprayed cookie sheet, making 8 short-cakes.

2. Bake at 450° F. for 6 to 10 minutes or until toothpick inserted in center comes out clean. Remove from cookie sheet; place on plate. Cool in refrigerator 5 to 10 minutes.

3. Meanwhile, in small bowl, combine yogurt, whipped topping and 1 teaspoon lemon peel; mix well.

4. To serve, split shortcakes; fill with blueberries and yogurt mixture. Sprinkle with powdered sugar. Store filling in refrigerator.

High Altitude (Above 3,500 feet): Decrease milk in shortcakes to 5 to 7 tablespoons. Bake as directed in step 2.

Nutrition per Serving: Serving Size: $\frac{1}{8}$ of Recipe. Calories 170; Calories from Fat 45; Total Fat 5g; Saturated Fat 1g; Cholesterol 0mg; Sodium 190mg; Dietary Fiber 1g

Dietary Exchange: 1 Starch, 1 Fruit, $\frac{1}{2}$ Fat OR 2 Carbohydrate, $\frac{1}{2}$ Fat

NONFAT CREME CARAMEL

◆

Yield: 8 servings; **Prep Time:** 15 minutes
(Ready in 4 hours 15 minutes)

Nonfat ingredient choices give this baked custard the silken texture and syrupy topping of a traditional flan, but with no fat.

1 cup sugar

1¾ cups skim milk

1 cup refrigerated or frozen
  fat-free egg product, thawed,
  or 4 eggs

¼ teaspoon salt

1 teaspoon vanilla

1 teaspoon grated orange peel

1 cup fresh berries (blackberries,
  blueberries, raspberries and/or
  sliced strawberries)

1. Heat oven to 325°F. In medium nonstick skillet, heat ½ cup of the sugar over medium heat for 7 to 10 minutes or until sugar melts and turns a light caramel color, stirring frequently. Immediately pour sugar into 8-inch round cake pan. MIXTURE WILL BE VERY HOT. Turn pan to coat bottom with sugar. Place on wire rack.

2. In large bowl, combine remaining ½ cup sugar, milk, egg product, salt, vanilla and orange peel; mix well. Pour into sugar-coated pan. Place pan in 13 × 9-inch pan; place in oven. Pour very hot water around cake pan to within ½ inch of top of pan.

3. Bake at 325°F. for 50 to 60 minutes or until knife inserted in center comes out clean. Remove cake pan from hot water. Cover; refrigerate 3 hours or overnight until thoroughly chilled.

4. To unmold, run knife around edge of custard to loosen; invert onto serving platter. Top with fruit. Garnish as desired.

Nutrition per Serving: Serving Size: ⅛ of Recipe. Calories 140; Calories from Fat 0; Total Fat 0g; Saturated Fat 0g; Cholesterol 0mg; Sodium 140mg; Dietary Fiber 1g

Dietary Exchange: 1 Starch, 1 Fruit OR 2 Carbohydrate

Nonfat Creme Caramel

BAKED CUSTARD

Yield: 6 servings; **Prep Time:** 10 minutes
(Ready in 1 hour 5 minutes)

Simple and old-fashioned, baked custard is smoothly sweet and satisfying.

3 eggs, slightly beaten
¼ cup sugar
⅛ teaspoon salt
1 teaspoon vanilla
2½ cups milk
Dash nutmeg

1. Heat oven to 350°F. In large bowl, combine eggs, sugar, salt and vanilla; blend well. Gradually stir in milk. Pour into 6 ungreased 6-oz. custard cups. Sprinkle with nutmeg. Place custard cups in 13 × 9-inch pan; place in oven. Pour boiling water into pan around custard cups to a depth of 1 inch.

2. Bake at 350°F. for 45 to 55 minutes or until knife inserted near center comes out clean. Serve warm or cold. Store in refrigerator.

Tip: If desired, pour mixture into 1 or 1½-quart casserole. Place in 13 × 9-inch pan; pour boiling water into pan around casserole to a depth of 1 inch. Bake at 350°F. for 50 to 60 minutes.

Nutrition per Serving: Serving Size: ⅙ of Recipe. Calories 120; Calories from Fat 35; Total Fat 4g; Saturated Fat 2g; Cholesterol 115mg; Sodium 125mg; Dietary Fiber 0g

Dietary Exchange: 1 Starch, ½ Medium-Fat Meat OR 1 Carbohydrate, ½ Medium-Fat Meat

CARAMEL FLAN

Yield: 8 servings; **Prep Time:** 15 minutes
(Ready in 5 hours 45 minutes)

Flan (caramel custard) is the national dessert of Spain, served in every restaurant from the most inauspicious local "dive" to the finest five-star eatery.

1 cup sugar
5 eggs
2½ cups milk
1 teaspoon vanilla
3 cups fresh fruit (sliced strawberries or kiwi fruit, seedless grapes and/or pineapple cubes)

1. Heat oven to 325°F. In small, heavy skillet, heat ½ cup of the sugar over medium heat until sugar melts and turns a rich golden brown color, stirring constantly. Immediately pour sugar into 8-inch ring mold. Holding ring mold with pot holders, swirl so sugar coats bottom and sides.

2. In large bowl, slightly beat eggs. Stir in milk, remaining ½ cup sugar and vanilla. Place sugar-coated ring mold in shallow baking pan; place in oven. Pour egg mixture over sugar in mold. Pour very hot water into pan around mold to a depth of 1 inch.

3. Bake at 325°F. for 55 to 60 minutes or until knife inserted halfway between center and edge

comes out clean. Remove mold from hot water; place on wire rack. Cool 1 hour or until completely cooled. Refrigerate at least 3½ hours.

4. To unmold, run knife around edge of custard to loosen; invert onto serving platter. Spoon any caramel that remains in mold over custard. Serve with fruit. Store in refrigerator.

Nutrition per Serving: Serving Size: ⅛ of Recipe. Calories 210; Calories from Fat 45; Total Fat 5g; Saturated Fat 2g; Cholesterol 140mg; Sodium 80mg; Dietary Fiber 1g

Dietary Exchange: 2 Starch, 1 Fat OR 2 Carbohydrate, 1 Fat

CARAMEL-TOPPED CHOCOLATE FLAN

Yield: 6 servings; **Prep Time:** 20 minutes
(Ready in 1 hour 10 minutes)

The caramel topping, made from melted sugar, hardens after it's poured into custard cups, only to soften into a dark, sweet sauce after the custard mixture is poured in. Enjoy it warm or cold.

CARAMEL
⅓ cup sugar
2 tablespoons water
⅛ teaspoon cream of tartar

FLAN

1 1/3 cups half-and-half
3 oz. sweet cooking chocolate, chopped
2 tablespoons sugar
3 eggs
1/2 teaspoon vanilla

1. In small, heavy saucepan, heat 1/3 cup sugar, water and cream of tartar over medium heat until mixture comes to a boil, stirring constantly. Let boil without stirring until mixture begins to caramelize, about 10 to 12 minutes. If mixture darkens in one spot, swirl pan around gently. Stir until mixture is a medium caramel color. Immediately pour caramel into bottom of 6 ungreased 6-oz. custard cups. Set aside.

2. Heat oven to 325°F. In small saucepan, combine half-and-half, chocolate and 2 tablespoons sugar; cook over low heat, stirring constantly until chocolate is melted and mixture is smooth. Remove from heat.

3. In small bowl, beat eggs and vanilla until light and lemon colored. Gradually add chocolate mixture; blend well. Carefully pour custard over caramel in custard cups. Place cups in 13 × 9-inch pan; place in oven. Pour very hot water into pan to within 1/2 inch of tops of custard cups.

4. Bake at 325°F. for 50 minutes or until knife inserted in center comes out clean. Remove custard cups from hot water. Serve warm or refrigerate in custard cups and serve cold.

5. To unmold, run knife around edge of cups to loosen; invert onto individual dessert plates. If desired, garnish with whipped cream and fresh fruit. Store in refrigerator.

Nutrition per Serving: Serving Size: 1/6 of Recipe. Calories 250; Calories from Fat 130; Total Fat 14g; Saturated Fat 7g; Cholesterol 125mg; Sodium 55mg; Dietary Fiber 1g

Dietary Exchange: 2 Starch, 2 Fat OR 2 Carbohydrate, 2 Fat

APRICOT SOUFFLÉ

Yield: 8 servings; Prep Time: 20 minutes
(Ready in 1 hour 45 minutes)

Ethereal and elegant, this soufflé boasts another plus: it has no fat. As with any soufflé, timing is critical. Serve it as soon as it's out of the oven.

SOUFFLÉ

2 tablespoons cornstarch
2 tablespoons sugar
3/4 cup lite evaporated skimmed milk
1/4 cup apricot preserves
3 tablespoons apricot nectar
1 teaspoon vanilla
6 egg whites
1/2 teaspoon cream of tartar

SAUCE

1/3 cup apricot preserves
2 tablespoons apricot nectar

1. Spray 2 1/2-quart soufflé dish with nonstick cooking spray. In small saucepan, combine cornstarch and sugar. Add milk, 1/4 cup preserves and 3 tablespoons apricot nectar; mix well. Cook over medium heat until mixture boils and thickens, stirring constantly. Pour into large bowl; stir in vanilla. Cover surface with plastic wrap. Refrigerate about 1 hour or until completely cooled.

2. Heat oven to 425°F. In large bowl, beat egg whites and cream of tartar until stiff peaks form, about 2 to 3 minutes. Gently fold egg white mixture into cooled apricot mixture. Spoon into sprayed soufflé dish. Place soufflé dish in 13 × 9-inch pan; pour boiling water into pan around soufflé dish to a depth of 1 inch.

3. Place in 425°F. oven. Immediately reduce heat to 350°F.; bake 25 minutes or until puffy, set and golden brown.

4. Meanwhile, in small saucepan, combine sauce ingredients; cook over medium heat until thoroughly heated. Serve soufflé immediately with sauce.

Nutrition per Serving: Serving Size: 1/8 of Recipe. Calories 120; Calories from Fat 0; Total Fat 0g; Saturated Fat 0g; Cholesterol 0mg; Sodium 80mg; Dietary Fiber 0g

Dietary Exchange: 1 1/2 Starch OR 1 1/2 Carbohydrate

CHOCOLATE SOUFFLÉ

◆

Yield: 10 servings; **Prep Time:** 15 minutes
(Ready in 1 hour 5 minutes)

A soufflé depends on beaten egg whites to attain its lofty height. If any trace of yolk or other grease touches the egg whites, they will not whip properly, so make sure your bowl and beaters are scrupulously clean and dry.

¹/₂ cup sugar
2 tablespoons cornstarch
¹/₄ teaspoon salt
³/₄ cup milk
2 oz. unsweetened chocolate or
    2 envelopes premelted
    unsweetened chocolate
3 tablespoons margarine or butter
1 teaspoon vanilla
4 eggs, separated
¹/₄ teaspoon cream of tartar
Whipped cream or topping, if
    desired

1. Heat oven to 350°F. Prepare 4 to 5-cup soufflé dish or casserole with foil band by cutting 3-inch strip of foil to go around top of dish. Lightly grease dish and strip of foil. With greased side toward inside of dish, secure foil band around top of dish, letting it extend 2 inches above edge of dish.

2. In medium saucepan, combine sugar, cornstarch and salt. Stir in milk. Cook over medium heat until mixture boils and thickens, stirring constantly. Remove from heat; stir in chocolate and margarine until melted. Stir in vanilla. Add egg yolks 1 at a time, beating well after each addition.

3. In large bowl, beat egg whites with cream of tartar until soft peaks form. Gently fold in chocolate mixture. Pour into greased soufflé dish.*

4. Bake at 350°F. for 45 to 50 minutes or until knife inserted near center comes out clean. Remove foil band. Immediately serve soufflé with whipped cream or topping.

Tip: Soufflé can stand at room temperature, loosely covered, up to 1 hour before baking.

Nutrition per Serving: Serving Size: ¹/₁₀ of Recipe. Calories 190; Calories from Fat 120; Total Fat 13g; Saturated Fat 6g; Cholesterol 100mg; Sodium 135mg; Dietary Fiber 1g

Dietary Exchange: 1 Starch, 2¹/₂ Fat OR 1 Carbohydrate, 2¹/₂ Fat

VARIATION

Chocolate Mocha Soufflé: Add 1 teaspoon instant coffee granules or crystals with cornstarch.

Chocolate Soufflé

MOCHA BREAD PUDDING WITH CARAMEL AND VANILLA SAUCES

Yield: 16 servings; **Prep Time:** 25 minutes
(Ready in 1 hour 15 minutes)

Two sauces transform a family-style bread pudding into a decadent treat. If you're pressed for time, use either sauce alone with the nutty coffee pudding.

PUDDING
10 oz. day-old Italian or French
    bread, torn into pieces (about
    8 cups)
1 cup chopped dates
1 cup flaked coconut
1 cup chopped nuts
1 teaspoon cinnamon
3/4 cup sugar
2 cups half-and-half
1 cup milk
1/2 cup coffee-flavored liqueur or
    coffee
1/2 cup butter, melted
3 eggs

CARAMEL SAUCE
3/4 cup firmly packed brown sugar
1/4 cup butter
1 tablespoon light corn syrup
1/4 cup half-and-half
2 tablespoons coffee-flavored
    liqueur or coffee

VANILLA SAUCE
3/4 cup sugar
1 tablespoon all-purpose flour
2/3 cup half-and-half
2 tablespoons butter
1 teaspoon vanilla

1. Heat oven to 325°F. Grease 13×9-inch pan. Place bread in greased pan. Add dates, coconut, nuts and cinnamon; toss to mix. In medium bowl, combine all remaining pudding ingredients; beat until well blended. Pour over bread mixture; toss to mix well. Let stand 15 minutes or until most of liquid is absorbed.

2. Bake at 325°F. for 1 hour or until set.

3. Meanwhile, prepare sauces. In medium saucepan, combine brown sugar, 1/4 cup butter and corn syrup; cook over low heat until mixture boils, stirring constantly. Cook 1 minute. Stir in 1/4 cup half-and-half and 2 tablespoons liqueur. Remove from heat; keep warm.

4. In separate medium saucepan, combine 3/4 sugar and flour; mix well. Stir in 2/3 cup half-and-half; cook over medium heat until mixture boils, stirring constantly. Stir in 2 tablespoons butter and vanilla. Remove from heat; keep warm.

5. To serve, top each serving of warm bread pudding with 1 tablespoon of each of the warm sauces.

Tip: To reheat bread pudding, heat at 250°F. for 15 minutes or until warm. Reheat sauces in small saucepans over low heat.

Nutrition per Serving: Serving Size: 1/16 of Recipe. Calories 480; Calories from Fat 210; Total Fat 23g; Saturated Fat 12g; Cholesterol 85mg; Sodium 270mg; Dietary Fiber 2g

Dietary Exchange: 2 Starch, 2 Fruit, 4 1/2 Fat OR 4 Carbohydrate, 4 1/2 Fat

**Mocha Bread Pudding with Caramel
and Vanilla Sauces**

CUSTARD NOODLE PUDDING

Yield: 12 servings; **Prep Time**: 15 minutes
(Ready in 1 hour 15 minutes)

A cousin of rice pudding that's also known as "kugel," this old-fashioned baked dessert consists of noodles and raisins in sweet custard. In some households, it's served as a sweet side dish rather than a dessert. Also include it in a buffet menu for a change of pace.

11 oz. (4 cups) uncooked fine egg
   noodles
3 eggs
1 cup sugar
¼ cup raisins
2 cups milk
1½ teaspoons vanilla
1 teaspoon nutmeg

1. Heat oven to 350°F. Grease 13 × 9-inch (3-quart) baking dish. Cook noodles to desired doneness as directed on package. Drain.

2. Beat eggs in large bowl. Stir in sugar, raisins, milk, vanilla and cooked noodles. Spoon mixture into greased baking dish. Sprinkle with nutmeg. Cover with foil.

3. Bake at 350°F. for 55 to 60 minutes or until knife inserted near center comes out clean. If desired, serve with light whipped topping. Store in refrigerator.

Nutrition per Serving: Serving Size: ¹⁄₁₂ of Recipe. Calories 220; Calories from Fat 25; Total Fat 3g; Saturated Fat 1g; Cholesterol 80mg; Sodium 40mg; Dietary Fiber 1g

Dietary Exchange: 2 ½ Starch, ½ Fat OR 2 ½ Carbohydrate, ½ Fat

BANANA EGGNOG BREAD PUDDING WITH RUM SAUCE

Yield: 12 servings; **Prep Time**: 25 minutes
(Ready in 1 hour 5 minutes)

Translate eggnog's holiday spirit into a rich baked pudding flavored with banana and nutmeg.

PUDDING
1 (1-lb.) loaf raisin bread, cut into
   cubes
2 medium bananas, sliced
3½ cups eggnog
4 eggs
¼ cup sugar
¼ teaspoon nutmeg

SAUCE
1 cup firmly packed brown sugar
½ cup whipping cream
¼ cup dark corn syrup
2 tablespoons butter
½ teaspoon rum extract

1. Heat oven to 350°F. Butter 13 × 9-inch (3-quart) baking dish. Place half of bread cubes in buttered baking dish. Top with banana slices and remaining bread cubes. In large bowl, combine eggnog, eggs, sugar and nutmeg; blend well. Pour over bread cubes. Let stand 5 minutes.

2. Bake at 350°F. for 40 to 50 minutes or until knife inserted in center comes out clean.

3. Meanwhile, in small saucepan, combine all sauce ingredients except rum extract. Cook over medium heat, stirring constantly, until mixture boils and thickens. Reduce heat to low; simmer 5 minutes, stirring constantly. Stir in rum extract. Serve warm sauce over pudding.

Nutrition per Serving: Serving Size: ¹⁄₁₂ of Recipe. Calories 420; Calories from Fat 140; Total Fat 15g; Saturated Fat 8g; Cholesterol 135mg; Sodium 250mg; Dietary Fiber 2g

Dietary Exchange: 3 Starch, 1 Fruit, 2 ½ Fat OR 4 Carbohydrate, 2 ½ Fat

**Banana Eggnog Bread Pudding
with Rum Sauce**

OLD-FASHIONED BREAD PUDDING WITH BRANDY HARD SAUCE

Yield: 10 servings; **Prep Time:** 15 minutes
(Ready in 1 hour 10 minutes)

Bread pudding, originally a thrifty way to transform stale bread into a family dessert, is especially good on a cold winter night.

PUDDING

5 cups cubed white and whole
    wheat bread*
2 1/2 cups warm milk
1/2 cup sugar
1 teaspoon cinnamon
3/4 teaspoon nutmeg
1 teaspoon vanilla
2 eggs, beaten
1 cup raisins
1/4 cup chopped nuts

HARD SAUCE

2 cups powdered sugar
1/2 cup butter, softened
1 tablespoon hot water
2 tablespoons brandy or
    2 teaspoons brandy extract

1. Heat oven to 350°F. Grease 2-quart casserole. In greased casserole, combine bread cubes and milk. In medium bowl, combine sugar, cinnamon, nutmeg, vanilla and eggs; mix well. Stir in raisins and nuts. Add egg mixture to soaked bread cubes; blend well.

2. Bake at 350°F. for 50 to 60 minutes or until pudding is set.

3. Meanwhile, in small bowl, combine all hard sauce ingredients. Beat at high speed until well blended. Cover; refrigerate until serving time. Serve hard sauce over warm pudding.

Tip: Four slices white bread and four slices whole wheat bread yield about 5 cups bread cubes.

Nutrition per Serving: Serving Size: 1/10 of Recipe. Calories 390; Calories from Fat 130; Total Fat 14g; Saturated Fat 7g; Cholesterol 70mg; Sodium 250mg; Dietary Fiber 2g

Dietary Exchange: 2 Starch, 2 Fruit, 2 1/2 Fat OR 4 Carbohydrate, 2 1/2 Fat

BLACK FOREST BREAD PUDDING

Yield: 12 servings; **Prep Time:** 30 minutes
(Ready in 1 hour 20 minutes)

A moist baked pudding puts a new spin on the classic Black Forest partners: chocolate and cherries.

PUDDING

1 1/2 cups firmly packed brown
    sugar
1/3 cup unsweetened cocoa
1 1/4 cups refrigerated or frozen
    fat-free egg product, thawed, or
    5 eggs
3 (12-oz.) cans lite evaporated
    skimmed milk
2 (1-oz.) envelopes premelted
    unsweetened chocolate

2 teaspoons vanilla
1 teaspoon almond extract
12 cups (1 lb.) French bread cubes
    (1-inch)

SAUCE

1 (21-oz.) can cherry pie filling
3 tablespoons cherry-flavored
    liqueur or 3/4 teaspoon brandy
    extract

1. Heat oven to 375°F. Spray 13×9-inch (3-quart) baking dish with nonstick cooking spray.

2. In large bowl, combine brown sugar, cocoa, egg product, milk, chocolate, vanilla and almond extract. With wire whisk, blend until smooth. Fold in bread cubes. Let stand 10 minutes, stirring occasionally.

3. Pour bread mixture into sprayed baking dish; cover loosely with foil. Set dish in larger pan (a roasting pan works well); place in oven. Pour 1 inch boiling water into larger pan.

4. Bake at 375°F. for 40 minutes. Remove foil; bake an additional 10 to 15 minutes or until knife inserted in center comes out clean.

5. In small saucepan, heat pie filling over medium heat for 4 to 5 minutes or until warm. Stir in liqueur. Serve sauce with warm bread pudding.

Nutrition per Serving: Serving Size: 1/12 of Recipe. Calories 400; Calories from Fat 35; Total Fat 4g; Saturated Fat 2g; Cholesterol 3mg; Sodium 390mg; Dietary Fiber 3g

Dietary Exchange: 5 Starch OR 5 Carbohydrate

APPLE STREUSEL BREAD PUDDING

◆

Yield: 8 servings; **Prep Time:** 25 minutes
(Ready in 1 hour 35 minutes)

French bread (especially day-old) works well in this old-style recipe because it retains some integrity as it bakes in the custard. Slightly stale raisin bread may be substituted.

PUDDING
4 cups French bread cubes (1-inch)
1 cup chunky applesauce
1/4 cup raisins
1/4 teaspoon cinnamon
1/8 teaspoon nutmeg
2 eggs
2 cups milk
1/3 cup sugar
1/2 teaspoon cinnamon
1/2 teaspoon vanilla

TOPPING
1/4 cup all-purpose flour
1/4 cup firmly packed brown sugar
2 tablespoons margarine or butter

1. Heat oven to 350°F. Grease 8-inch square (2-quart) baking dish or 2-quart casserole. Place 3 cups of the bread cubes in greased baking dish. In small bowl, combine applesauce, raisins, 1/4 teaspoon cinnamon and nutmeg; blend well. Spoon by scant teaspoonfuls evenly over bread cubes. Top with remaining 1 cup bread cubes.

2. Beat eggs in medium bowl. Add milk, sugar, 1/2 teaspoon cinnamon and vanilla; blend well. Pour over bread cubes; let stand 10 minutes.

3. Meanwhile, in small bowl, combine flour and brown sugar; mix well. With fork or pastry blender, cut in margarine until mixture is crumbly. Sprinkle over top of bread cube mixture.

4. Bake at 350°F. for 50 to 60 minutes or until knife inserted in center comes out clean. Let stand 10 minutes before serving. If desired, serve warm with half-and-half. Store in refrigerator.

Nutrition per Serving: Serving Size: 1/8 of Recipe. Calories 250; Calories from Fat 50; Total Fat 6g; Saturated Fat 2g; Cholesterol 60mg; Sodium 210mg; Dietary Fiber 1g

Dietary Exchange: 2 Starch, 1 Fruit, 1/2 Fat OR 3 Carbohydrate, 1/2 Fat

FESTIVE RICE PUDDING

Yield: 7 (1/2-cup) servings;
Prep Time: 25 minutes
(Ready in 1 hour 15 minutes)

Rice pudding seems to be a staple on the menu of nearly every diner in the country, but have you ever had it made with dried cranberries? They add color and a special burst of flavor.

1 1/2 cups cooked rice (cooked as directed on package)
2 cups half-and-half
1/2 cup sugar
1 teaspoon vanilla
4 eggs
1/2 cup sweetened dried cranberries or raisins
1/8 teaspoon nutmeg
1/8 teaspoon cinnamon

1. Heat oven to 350°F. While rice is cooking, in medium saucepan, heat half-and-half over low heat until very warm. DO NOT BOIL. Remove from heat.

2. In large bowl, combine sugar, vanilla and eggs; beat well. Gradually add half-and-half; blend well. Stir in cooked rice and cranberries. Pour into ungreased 2-quart casserole. Place casserole in 13 × 9-inch pan; place in oven. Pour hot water into pan around casserole to a depth of 1 inch.

3. Bake at 350°F. for 30 minutes. Stir pudding; bake an additional 15 to 20 minutes or until knife inserted in center comes out clean. Sprinkle with nutmeg and cinnamon. Serve warm or cold. Store in refrigerator.

Nutrition per Serving: Serving Size: 1/2 Cup. Calories 280; Calories from Fat 100; Total Fat 11g; Saturated Fat 6g; Cholesterol 145mg; Sodium 65mg; Dietary Fiber 1g

Dietary Exchange: 2 Starch, 1/2 Fruit, 2 Fat OR 2 1/2 Carbohydrate, 2 Fat

SWEDISH BAKED RICE PUDDING

Yield: 9 servings; **Prep Time:** 35 minutes
(Ready in 1 hour 45 minutes)

Based on a Swedish family recipe, this baked rice pudding separates into a rich custard layer, followed by a rice layer and crowned with a golden brown topping.

RICE MIXTURE
½ cup uncooked regular long-grain white rice
2 tablespoons sugar
2 cups milk
1 tablespoon margarine or butter

PUDDING
6 eggs
1 cup sugar
½ teaspoon cinnamon
¼ teaspoon salt
¼ teaspoon nutmeg
½ cup raisins
2 cups milk

1. In medium saucepan, combine all rice mixture ingredients. Bring to a boil. Reduce heat to low; cook uncovered 20 to 25 minutes or until creamy, stirring occasionally. Remove from heat; cool 10 minutes.

2. Heat oven to 350°F. Lightly grease 8-inch square (2-quart) baking dish. In large bowl, beat eggs; stir in remaining pudding ingredients and rice mixture. Pour into greased baking dish.

3. Bake at 350°F. for 55 to 60 minutes or until set. Serve warm or cold. If desired, serve with cream or whipped cream. Store in refrigerator.

Nutrition per Serving: Serving Size: ⅑ of Recipe. Calories 280; Calories from Fat 60; Total Fat 7g; Saturated Fat 3g; Cholesterol 150mg; Sodium 170mg; Dietary Fiber 1g

Dietary Exchange: 3 Starch, 1 Fat OR 3 Carbohydrate, 1 Fat

FRUIT AND RICE PUDDING

Yield: 6 servings; **Prep Time:** 45 minutes
(Ready in 1 hour 50 minutes)

This is a lower-fat version of a soothing favorite, speckled with dried fruit bits that plump up in the oven.

2 cups cooked brown rice (cooked as directed on package)
1 ½ cups skim milk
½ cup dried fruit bits
¼ cup firmly packed brown sugar
¼ teaspoon cinnamon
½ cup refrigerated or frozen fat-free egg product, thawed, or 2 eggs
1 teaspoon vanilla

1. Heat oven to 350°F. While rice is cooking, in small saucepan, heat milk over low heat until very warm. DO NOT BOIL. Remove from heat.

2. In ungreased 1½-quart casserole, combine warm milk and all remaining ingredients. Stir in cooked rice. Place casserole in 13×9-inch pan; place in oven. Pour boiling water into pan around casserole to a depth of 1 inch.

3. Bake at 350°F. for 40 minutes. Carefully stir pudding; bake an additional 15 to 25 minutes or until knife inserted in center comes out clean. Serve warm.

Nutrition per Serving: Serving Size: ⅙ of Recipe. Calories 170; Calories from Fat 10; Total Fat 1g; Saturated Fat 0g; Cholesterol 0mg; Sodium 70mg; Dietary Fiber 2g

Dietary Exchange: 2 Starch OR 2 Carbohydrate

Swedish Baked Rice Pudding

STEAMED PLUM PUDDING

Yield: 8 servings; **Prep Time:** 20 minutes
(Ready in 2 hours 20 minutes)

*England's traditional holiday "pudd"
is a hearty mixture of spices, nuts
and dried fruits sweetened with molasses and brown sugar. Slow steam-
ing on the top of the stove produces a
dessert that is incredibly moist and
aromatic. Hard sauce flavored with
rum or brandy is the traditional
topping.*

PUDDING
1 cup all-purpose flour
3 tablespoons brown sugar
1 teaspoon cinnamon
1/2 teaspoon baking powder
1/2 teaspoon allspice
1/2 teaspoon cloves
1/4 teaspoon baking soda
1/2 cup milk
3 tablespoons oil
2 tablespoons molasses
1 egg
1 cup mixed candied fruit
1/2 cup raisins
1/2 cup chopped nuts

HARD SAUCE
1 cup powdered sugar
Dash salt
1/4 cup butter, softened
1 tablespoon rum or brandy, or 1
    teaspoon rum or brandy extract
1/2 teaspoon vanilla

1. Using solid shortening, generously grease 1-quart mold or
casserole. In medium bowl, combine all pudding ingredients except fruit, raisins and nuts; mix
until dry ingredients are moistened. Fold in fruit, raisins and
nuts. Spoon into greased mold;
cover with lid or foil.

2. Place mold on wire rack in
large steamer or kettle. Add
enough boiling water to steamer
to come halfway up side of mold;
cover. Keep water boiling gently
over low heat. If necessary, add
water to maintain steam. Steam
1 1/2 to 2 hours or until pudding
springs back when touched lightly
in center.

3. Meanwhile, in small bowl,
combine all hard sauce ingredients; beat at high speed until well
blended. Refrigerate until serving
time.

4. To serve, cut warm pudding
into slices; top with hard sauce.

*Tip: To reheat, wrap in foil. Bake
at 350°F. for 20 to 25 minutes or
until warm.*

High Altitude (Above 3,500 feet): No change.

Nutrition per Serving: Serving Size: 1/8 of Recipe.
Calories 430; Calories from Fat 150; Total Fat 17g;
Saturated Fat 5g; Cholesterol 45mg; Sodium 230mg;
Dietary Fiber 2g

Dietary Exchange: 2 Starch, 2 Fruit, 3 1/2 Fat OR 4 Carbohydrate, 3 1/2 Fat

APPLE STRUDEL SQUARES

Yield: 12 servings; **Prep Time:** 35 minutes
(Ready in 1 hour 10 minutes)

*A Viennese specialty, classic apple
strudel consists of a raisin- and nut-
studded apple filling wrapped in a
roll of flaky pastry. Our version is
easier, taking advantage of frozen
phyllo and stacking the layers in a
13×9-inch pan.*

STRUDEL
Butter-flavored nonstick cooking
    spray
4 large baking apples, peeled,
    sliced
1/2 cup dried currants
1/3 cup firmly packed brown sugar
1/4 cup slivered almonds
2 tablespoons all-purpose flour
1/2 teaspoon cinnamon
1/4 teaspoon nutmeg
18 (17×12-inch) sheets frozen
    phyllo (filo) pastry, thawed

TOPPING
1/2 cup nonfat sour cream
1 tablespoon brown sugar
1/4 teaspoon cinnamon
1/8 teaspoon nutmeg

1. Heat oven to 425°F. Lightly
spray 13×9-inch pan with nonstick cooking spray. In large bowl,
combine all strudel ingredients
except pastry sheets; mix well.

2. Unroll pastry sheets; cover with plastic wrap or towel. On work surface, quickly layer 6 pastry sheets, spraying each with nonstick cooking spray after stacking. Fold stack in half to form $12 \times 8\frac{1}{2}$-inch rectangle. Place in sprayed pan. Top with half of apple mixture.

3. Stack 4 pastry sheets, again spraying each sheet. Fold in half to form $12 \times 8\frac{1}{2}$-inch rectangle. Place on top of apples in pan. Top with remaining apples.

4. Stack remaining 8 pastry sheets, spraying each sheet. Fold in half; place on top of apples. Spray top with cooking spray. If desired, sprinkle with $\frac{1}{2}$ teaspoon sugar.

5. Bake at 425°F. for 5 minutes. Reduce heat to 350°F.; bake an additional 25 to 35 minutes or until deep golden brown. Cool slightly.

6. In small bowl, combine all topping ingredients; blend well. Refrigerate until serving time.

7. To serve, cut strudel into squares. Serve warm or at room temperature with topping.

Nutrition per Serving: Serving Size: $\frac{1}{12}$ of Recipe. Calories 270; Calories from Fat 100; Total Fat 11g; Saturated Fat 1g; Cholesterol 0mg; Sodium 160mg; Dietary Fiber 3g

Dietary Exchange: $1\frac{1}{2}$ Starch, 1 Fruit, 2 Fat OR $2\frac{1}{2}$ Carbohydrate, 2 Fat

FLAKY PLUM PIES

Yield: 6 servings; **Prep Time:** 25 minutes (Ready in 45 minutes)

Italian prune plums, with their firm texture, work well in baked recipes. Frozen sheets of phyllo pastry offer a quick route to a super-flaky crust.

3 tablespoons butter
9 plums, seeded, thinly sliced
$\frac{1}{3}$ cup firmly packed brown sugar
$\frac{1}{4}$ teaspoon cinnamon
6 (17×12-inch) sheets frozen phyllo (filo) pastry, thawed
Nonstick cooking spray

1. Heat oven to 400°F. Place 6 ungreased 10-oz. ovenproof custard cups or ramekins in $15 \times 10 \times 1$-inch baking pan.

2. In large skillet, melt butter over medium-high heat. Add plums, brown sugar and cinnamon; cook and stir 5 to 7 minutes or until plums are tender and sauce is thickened. Remove from heat.

3. Unroll pastry sheets; cover with plastic wrap or towel. On work surface, quickly layer all 6 pastry sheets, spraying each with nonstick cooking spray after stacking. With sharp knife or kitchen scissors and rim of custard cup as guide, cut 6 rounds from pastry, $\frac{1}{2}$ inch larger than custard cup, cutting through all layers.

4. Ladle hot plum mixture into custard cups. Place 1 stack of pastry rounds on top of each filled cup. Gently press down pastry $\frac{1}{2}$ inch to form a slightly fluted edge that fits within rim of custard cup. Using sharp knife or kitchen scissors, cut 2-inch "X" in center of each. Pull back corners to expose filling. Lightly spray pastry with nonstick cooking spray.

5. Bake at 400°F. for 15 to 18 minutes or until filling is bubbly and pastry is crisp and golden brown. Serve warm.

Nutrition per Serving: Serving Size: $\frac{1}{6}$ of Recipe. Calories 230; Calories from Fat 80; Total Fat 9g; Saturated Fat 4g; Cholesterol 15mg; Sodium 160mg; Dietary Fiber 2g

Dietary Exchange: 1 Starch, $1\frac{1}{2}$ Fruit, $1\frac{1}{2}$ Fat OR $2\frac{1}{2}$ Carbohydrate, $1\frac{1}{2}$ Fat

CREAM CHEESE AND BERRY NAPOLEONS

◆

Yield: 4 servings; Prep Time: 35 minutes

This recipe is easily doubled if you're serving more people. The pastry will remain at its crispest if the Napoleons are assembled just before they're served.

3 (17 × 12-inch) sheets frozen
    phyllo (filo) pastry, thawed
Butter-flavored nonstick cooking
    spray
2 teaspoons sugar
4 oz. fat-free cream cheese (from
    8-oz. pkg.), softened
2 tablespoons sugar
1/4 teaspoon almond extract
2 cups frozen light whipped
    topping, thawed
2 cups fresh berries (sliced
    strawberries, blueberries,
    raspberries and/or blackberries)
Mint leaves, if desired

1. Heat oven to 350°F. Unroll pastry sheets; cover with plastic wrap or towel. On work surface, quickly layer 3 pastry sheets, spraying each with nonstick cooking spray after stacking. After spraying top sheet, sprinkle with 2 teaspoons sugar. Using pizza cutter or sharp knife, cut pastry into 12 (4-inch) squares. Place on ungreased cookie sheets.

2. Bake at 350°F. for 5 to 10 minutes or until crisp and light golden brown. Cool.

3. Meanwhile, in small bowl, beat cream cheese, 2 tablespoons sugar and almond extract until smooth. Fold in whipped topping.

4. To serve, place 1 pastry square on each of 4 individual dessert plates. Spread each with scant 1/4 cup whipped topping mixture; top each with 1/4 cup berries. Repeat layers; top each with third pastry square. Garnish with small dollops of whipped topping mixture, additional berries if desired, and mint leaves.

Nutrition per Serving: Serving Size: 1/4 of Recipe. Calories 250; Calories from Fat 50; Total Fat 6g; Saturated Fat 4g; Cholesterol 4mg; Sodium 250mg; Dietary Fiber 4g

Dietary Exchange: 2 Starch, 1 Fruit, 1/2 Fat OR 3 Carbohydrate, 1/2 Fat

Cream Cheese and Berry Napoleons

STRAWBERRY CREAM PUFF

✦

Yield: 10 servings; **Prep Time:** 40 minutes
(Ready in 2 hours 30 minutes)

A heart-shaped dessert slathered with whipped cream and berries is a sweet tribute for your Valentine or an anniversary celebration.

CRUST
⅔ cup all-purpose flour
⅓ cup margarine or butter
2 to 5 teaspoons ice water

PUFF
½ cup water
¼ cup margarine or butter
½ cup all-purpose flour
2 eggs

FILLING
1 cup whipping cream
⅓ cup powdered sugar
¼ cup sour cream
1 pint (2 cups) fresh strawberries, sliced*

GLAZE
2 tablespoons semi-sweet chocolate chips
1 tablespoon margarine or butter

1. Heat oven to 375°F. Cut heart-shaped pattern about 10 inches long and 9 inches wide from waxed paper or foil.

2. Place ⅔ cup flour in small bowl. With fork or pastry blender, cut ⅓ cup margarine into flour until mixture resembles fine crumbs. Sprinkle with ice water, 1 teaspoon at a time, tossing lightly with fork until mixture is moistened and soft dough forms.

3. Place dough on ungreased cookie sheet. Place pattern over dough. Using pattern as a guide, press dough evenly into heart shape; remove pattern.

4. In medium saucepan, combine ½ cup water and ¼ cup margarine. Bring to a boil over medium heat. Stir in ½ cup flour. Cook until mixture leaves sides of pan in smooth ball, stirring constantly. Remove from heat.

5. Add eggs 1 at a time, beating vigorously after each addition until mixture is smooth and glossy. With back of spoon, spread puff mixture over crust to within ¾ inch of edge of crust, building up sides and shaping into heart.

6. Bake at 375°F. for 20 minutes. Remove from oven; prick center of puff once with fork. Return to oven; bake an additional 20 to 30 minutes or until deep golden brown and puffed. Cool on cookie sheet for 1 hour or until completely cooled.

7. To assemble, slide cooled puff shell onto serving plate. In small bowl, beat whipping cream and powdered sugar until stiff peaks form. Fold in sour cream. Spoon into puff shell. Arrange strawberries in heart shape, overlapping slightly, over whipped cream mixture.

8. In small saucepan over low heat, melt glaze ingredients; stir until smooth. Drizzle over strawberries. Serve immediately. Store in refrigerator.

Tip: Sliced peaches, nectarines, grapes or raspberries can be substituted for the strawberries.

High Altitude (Above 3,500 feet): No change.

Nutrition per Serving: Serving Size: ⅒ of Recipe. Calories 310; Calories from Fat 220; Total Fat 24g; Saturated Fat 9g; Cholesterol 80mg; Sodium 160mg; Dietary Fiber 1g

Dietary Exchange: 1½ Starch, 4 Fat OR 1½ Carbohydrate, 4 Fat

Strawberry Cream Puff

CREAM PUFFS

◆

Yield: 6 cream puffs; **Prep Time:** 15 minutes
(Ready in 1 hour 55 minutes)

The French call the light but rich cooked dough that's used for cream puffs and eclairs "choux" pastry (pronounced "shoe"). Choux is French for "cabbage" and refers here to the many flaky layers that are reminiscent of cabbage leaves.

½ cup water
¼ cup margarine or butter
½ cup all-purpose flour
¼ teaspoon salt
2 eggs

1. Heat oven to 425°F. Grease cookie sheet. In medium saucepan, combine water and margarine. Bring to a boil over medium heat. Stir in flour and salt; cook, stirring vigorously until mixture leaves sides of pan in smooth ball. Remove from heat.

2. Add eggs 1 at a time, beating vigorously after each addition until mixture is smooth and glossy.* Spoon 6 mounds of dough (about ¼ cup each) 3 inches apart onto greased cookie sheet.

3. Bake at 425°F. for 30 to 40 minutes or until golden brown. Remove from oven; prick puffs with sharp knife to allow steam to escape. Remove from cookie sheet; cool 1 hour or until completely cooled.

4. Split cream puffs; if desired, remove any filaments of soft dough. Fill with ice cream, whipped cream or pudding. If desired, top with chocolate sauce.

Tip: An electric mixer at medium speed can be used to beat in eggs. Beat for 1 minute after each addition until smooth and glossy. DO NOT OVERBEAT.

Nutrition per Serving: Serving Size: ⅙ of Recipe. Calories 130; Calories from Fat 80; Total Fat 9g; Saturated Fat 2g; Cholesterol 70mg; Sodium 200mg; Dietary Fiber 0g

Dietary Exchange: ½ Starch, 2 Fat OR ½ Carbohydrate, 2 Fat

VARIATIONS

Eclairs: Drop cream puff dough into 12 long ovals about 1 inch wide. Bake at 425°F. for 20 to 25 minutes. When cool, fill with prepared vanilla pudding and glaze with Chocolate Glaze (page 61).

Snack Cream Puffs: Drop dough by tablespoons, making 20 small cream puffs. Bake at 425°F. for 15 to 20 minutes.

Praline Cream Puffs: Prepare and bake 6 cream puffs as directed above. When cool, fill with vanilla ice cream. Drizzle with warm caramel ice cream topping; sprinkle with chopped pecans.

EASY-METHOD PUFF PASTRY

◆

Yield: TK; **Prep Time:** 35 minutes
(Ready in 1 hour 35 minutes)

Puff pastry's claim to fame is its many, many crisp, flaky layers. To achieve the desired result, it's important that you use cold butter so that it remains in distinct layers. Steam rising as moisture evaporates between the layers during baking causes the characteristic flakiness.

4 cups all-purpose flour
½ teaspoon salt
2 cups cold butter
1¼ cups ice water
1 teaspoon lemon juice

1. In large bowl, combine flour and salt. Cut butter into ½-inch slices; add to flour mixture. Toss until butter is thoroughly coated with flour and slices are separated. In small bowl, combine ice water and lemon juice. Pour over flour mixture. Using large spoon, quickly stir together. (Butter will remain in slices and flour will not be completely moistened.)

2. On lightly floured surface, knead dough about 10 times or until a very rough looking ball forms. Shape dough into rectangle. (Dough will have dry-looking areas.) Flatten dough slightly, making corners square.

3. On well-floured surface, roll dough to 15 × 12-inch rectangle, keeping corners square. Fold dough crosswise into thirds, forming 12 × 5-inch rectangle. Give dough quarter turn and repeat folding crosswise into thirds, forming 5 × 4-inch rectangle. Cover tightly with plastic wrap; refrigerate 20 minutes.

4. Repeat the rolling, folding, turning and folding steps, form-

ing 5×4-inch rectangle. Cover tightly with plastic wrap; refrigerate 20 minutes.

5. Repeat the rolling, folding, turning and folding steps forming 5×4-inch rectangle. Cover tightly with plastic wrap; refrigerate at least 20 minutes.

6. Shape and bake puff pastry as directed in following recipes: Palmiers and Patty Shells below.

Nutrition Information: Not possible to calculate because of recipe variables.

PALMIERS

◆

Yield: 56 palmiers; Prep Time: 30 minutes
(Ready in 1 hour 10 minutes)

Thanks to Easy-Method Puff Pastry (page 150), this bakery-style specialty is simple to make at home. The cinnamon-sugar mixture provides just the right touch of sticky sweetness for the flaky pastry.

**1 recipe Easy-Method Puff Pastry
  (page 150)**
¹⁄₂ cup sugar
1 teaspoon cinnamon

1. Line cookie sheets with parchment paper. With sharp knife, cut dough crosswise in half. Cover half of dough with plastic wrap; return to refrigerator.

2. Heat oven to 375°F. In small bowl, combine sugar and cinnamon; mix well. On lightly floured surface, roll half of dough into 14×10-inch rectangle. Sprinkle with half of sugar-cinnamon mixture; press lightly into dough. Starting from 2 shortest sides, roll sides to meet in center. With sharp knife, cut into about ³⁄₈-inch slices. Place 2 inches apart on paper-lined cookie sheets.

3. Bake at 375°F. for 15 to 20 minutes or until golden brown. Remove from paper; cool on wire rack. Repeat with remaining half of dough and sugar-cinnamon mixture.

Nutrition per Serving: Serving Size: 1 Palmier. Calories 100; Calories from Fat 60; Total Fat 7g; Saturated Fat 4g; Cholesterol 20mg; Sodium 85mg; Dietary Fiber 0g

Dietary Exchange: ¹⁄₂ Starch, 1 ¹⁄₂ Fat OR ¹⁄₂ Carbohydrate, 1 ¹⁄₂ Fat

PATTY SHELLS

Yield: 18 patty shells;
Prep Time: 30 minutes
(Ready in 1 hour 10 minutes)

Almost anything goes when it comes to filling these versatile pastry shells: sliced fresh strawberries and whipped cream, chocolate pudding, frozen yogurt and Fruity Salsa Topping (page 326)—whatever creamy, nutty or fruity concoction you can dream up. Fill them just before serving.

**1 recipe Easy-Method Puff Pastry
  (page 150)**

1. Line cookie sheets with parchment paper. With sharp knife, cut dough crosswise in half. Cover half of dough with plastic wrap; return to refrigerator.

2. Heat oven to 425°F. On lightly floured surface, roll dough into 12-inch square. Cut dough with floured 3¹⁄₂-inch round cookie cutter. Do not twist cutter. Dip cutter in flour between cuts. With floured 2¹⁄₂-inch round cutter, cut into centers of 3¹⁄₂-inch rounds by cutting to but not completely through pastry. (This will create center portion to be removed after baking.) Place 2 inches apart on paper-lined cookie sheets.

3. Bake at 425°F. for 15 to 20 minutes or until golden brown. Remove from paper. Using fork, remove centers from patty shells; cool on wire rack. Repeat with remaining half of dough. Fill with favorite pudding or fruit filling.

Nutrition per Serving: Serving Size: 1 Patty Shell. Calories 290; Calories from Fat 190; Total Fat 21g; Saturated Fat 13g; Cholesterol 55mg; Sodium 270mg; Dietary Fiber 1g

Dietary Exchange: 1 ¹⁄₂ Starch, 4 Fat OR 1 ¹⁄₂ Carbohydrate, 4 Fat

AMARETTO NAPOLEONS ON CHERRY SAUCE

◆

Yield: 12 servings; **Prep Time:** 30 minutes
(Ready in 1 hour 50 minutes)

Streamline preparation of this showy dessert by using pudding mix enriched with amaretto and cherry pie filling mixed with cranberry juice concentrate. If you wish, garnish each serving with a few toasted slivered almonds.

PASTRY
1 sheet frozen puff pastry (from 17¼-oz. pkg.)

FILLING
1 (3-oz.) pkg. vanilla pudding and pie filling mix (not instant)
1½ cups milk
2 tablespoons amaretto

SAUCE
1 (21-oz.) can cherry pie filling
½ cup frozen cranberry juice concentrate, thawed
1 tablespoon powdered sugar

1. Thaw pastry sheet 20 minutes. Heat oven to 400°F. Unfold pastry; cut into 3 strips along fold lines. Cut each strip crosswise into 4 equal pieces. Arrange on ungreased cookie sheet.

Amaretto Napoleons on Cherry Sauce

2. Bake at 400°F. for 12 to 15 minutes or until puffed and golden brown. Remove from cookie sheet; place on wire rack. While still warm, split each pastry into 2 layers. Cool 1 hour or until completely cooled. Store loosely covered.

3. Meanwhile, in large saucepan, combine pudding mix and milk; mix well. Cook over medium heat until mixture boils, stirring constantly. Remove saucepan from heat; stir in amaretto. To prevent skin from forming, place plastic wrap directly on surface of pudding. Cool 1 hour or until completely cooled. Store in refrigerator.

4. In medium bowl, combine pie filling and juice concentrate; blend well. Refrigerate.

5. Just before serving, place bottom half of each pastry on dessert plate. Spoon 2 tablespoons pudding evenly over pastry; cover with top half of pastry. Dust with powdered sugar. Spoon 3 tablespoons cherry sauce onto plate around pastry. Store in refrigerator.

Nutrition per Serving: Serving Size: 1/12 of Recipe. Calories 250; Calories from Fat 80; Total Fat 9g; Saturated Fat 2g; Cholesterol 2mg; Sodium 125mg; Dietary Fiber 1g.

Dietary Exchange: 1 Starch, 1 1/2 Fruit, 2 Fat OR 2 1/2 Carbohydrate, 2 Fat

FRUIT-FILLED CHOCOLATE MERINGUES

Yield: 6 servings; **Prep Time:** 15 minutes
(Ready in 3 hours 30 minutes)

*Don't peek! For the crispest, melt-in-your-mouth meringues, follow the directions for baking then turning off the oven and leaving the meringues in the oven **with the door closed** for 1 1/2 hours.*

MERINGUES
2 egg whites
1/4 teaspoon salt
1/4 teaspoon vinegar
1/2 cup sugar
1/2 teaspoon vanilla
1 tablespoon unsweetened cocoa

FILLING
1 to 1 1/2 cups fresh fruit (sliced peaches, kiwi fruit, or strawberries, blueberries, seedless grapes and/or raspberries)
1/2 cup fudge ice cream topping, if desired

1. Heat oven to 275°F. Line cookie sheet with parchment paper. In small bowl, beat egg whites, salt and vinegar until foamy. Gradually add sugar and vanilla, beating until stiff peaks form.

2. Sift cocoa over beaten egg whites; fold into mixture. Drop 6 heaping tablespoons meringue onto parchment-lined cookie sheet. Make deep well in center of each, spreading meringue to form 3-inch rounds.*

3. Bake at 275°F. for 45 minutes or until crisp. Turn oven off; leave meringues in oven with door closed for 1 1/2 hours. Remove meringues from oven; cool 1 hour or until completely cooled.

4. To serve, remove meringues from parchment paper. Fill with fresh fruit. Serve with ice cream topping.

Tip: Meringue can be spooned into decorating bag with large star tip. Pipe six 3-inch circles; pipe meringue to fill in bottoms.

Nutrition per Serving: Serving Size: 1/6 of Recipe. Calories 200; Calories from Fat 35; Total Fat 4g; Saturated Fat 1g; Cholesterol 3mg; Sodium 140mg; Dietary Fiber 2g

Dietary Exchange: 1 Starch, 1 1/2 Fruit, 1/2 Fat OR 2 1/2 Carbohydrate, 1/2 Fat

PAVLOVA

Yield: 8 servings; **Prep Time:** 20 minutes
(Ready in 2 hours 20 minutes)

Every baker from New Zealand worth her or his salt can turn out a beautiful pavlova—a baked meringue circle filled with whipped cream and fruit. Named in honor of the famous Russian ballerina Anna Pavlova, the dessert is as light and fluffy as a tutu.

MERINGUE
4 egg whites
¼ teaspoon cream of tartar
1 cup sugar
1 teaspoon vanilla

FILLING
1 cup whipping cream, whipped*
Sliced fresh fruit (kiwi fruit,
    peaches, pineapple and/or
    strawberries)

1. Heat oven to 300°F. Line large cookie sheet with parchment paper. Draw 10-inch circle on paper. In large bowl, beat egg whites and cream of tartar at medium speed until foamy. Gradually add sugar 1 tablespoon at a time, beating at high speed until stiff glossy peaks form and sugar is almost dissolved, about 6 minutes. Beat in vanilla.

2. Spoon meringue onto circle on paper-lined cookie sheet. Shape to 10-inch round, building up sides with back of spoon.

3. Place in 300°F. oven. Immediately reduce oven temperature to 250°F.; bake 50 to 60 minutes or until firm and dry to the touch. (Inside of meringue will still be soft.) Remove from oven; cool on wire rack for 1 hour or until completely cooled. Carefully remove meringue from paper.

4. To serve, place cooled meringue on serving plate. Fill center with whipped cream; arrange sliced fruit over whipped cream. Store in refrigerator.**

Tips: *One pint (2 cups) lemon sorbet can be substituted for the whipping cream.

**Pavlova can be assembled, lightly covered and stored in refrigerator for up to 4 hours before serving.

Nutrition per Serving: Serving Size: ⅛ of Recipe. Calories 250; Calories from Fat 100; Total Fat 11g; Saturated Fat 7g; Cholesterol 40mg; Sodium 40mg; Dietary Fiber 2g

Dietary Exchange: 1 Starch, 1½ Fruit, 2 Fat OR 2½ Carbohydrate, 2 Fat

Pavlova

CHEESE-CAKES

♦ ♦ ♦

Cheesecake seems so luxurious

that it surprises many bakers to

learn how easy it is to make.

This chapter contains twenty-five

versions, from the simply classic

Cheesecake to the luscious Creamy

Chocolate Lace Cheesecake or the

delicate Key Lime Cheesecake with

Raspberry Sauce. You'll find

no-bake delights plus cheesecakes

flavored with pumpkin, vanilla,

strawberry, amaretto and more.

PRALINE CHEESECAKE, PAGE 177

*Bakery cheesecakes
demand high prices;
easy homemade versions
command high praise!*

EQUIPMENT FOR CHEESECAKES

SPRINGFORM PAN. Most of the recipes in this chapter specify a 9 or 10-inch springform pan, which has a clip that holds the sides of the pan together tightly for baking. After the cheesecake bakes and is completely cooled, unbuckle the clip to loosen and remove the sides.

ELECTRIC MIXER. While many cakes and cookies can be mixed by hand, cheesecakes made with cream cheese are best prepared with an electric mixer to blend the cream cheese evenly and smooth out the many little lumps.

CHEESECAKE BASICS

Cheesecakes, which are nearly always made with a crumb crust, come in two basic styles: creamy cakes made with cream cheese and fluffy cakes made in the Italian style with ricotta cheese.

For recipes that call for cream cheese, you can choose regular cream cheese or ⅓-less-fat cream cheese (sometimes labeled as "Neufchatel"). In the absence of side-by-side taste tests of cheesecakes made with regular or ⅓-less-fat cream cheese, this is one type of dessert in which most

people are not likely to notice the difference between the higher- and lower-fat versions. If you want to use fat-free cream cheese, it's best to select a recipe specifically formulated for it. Whichever version you choose, it's critical to let the cream cheese soften at room temperature for about an hour. Or speed things up by microwaving each 8-ounce package on HIGH for 30 to 60 seconds—be sure to remove foil wrapper first.

Many recipes use plain unflavored gelatin to give stability to the cake. Follow the directions carefully to make sure the gelatin dissolves thoroughly, or you may end up with an unappealing stringy texture.

AVOIDING CRACKS. If you plan to cover the baked cheesecake with fruit, chocolate sauce or another topping, it may not matter if the top cracks during baking. If you prefer a smoother top, try these tips:

• Bring the eggs and cream cheese to room temperature before mixing the batter.

• Use an electric mixer or food processor to beat the filling. Beat at medium speed just until smooth. Overbeating or mixing at high speed can cause cracks to form during baking.

• Place a shallow pan half full of water on the lower rack in the oven. The water will help minimize cracking.

• Let the cheesecake "rest" after baking. Unless other directions are specified in the recipe, when the cheesecake is done, turn off the oven and open the door. Allow the cheesecake to rest for 30 minutes, then transfer it to a cooling rack in a draft-free spot until it reaches room temperature. When completely cool, remove the sides of the pan and refrigerate the cheesecake.

• Don't jar the cheesecake while it is baking or cooling.

TESTING FOR DONENESS. Most of the recipes in this chapter specify cooking the cheesecake until the center is set. The fully cooked cheesecake will have a thin "skin" on top, and a knife inserted into the center will come out clean. Other recipes consider the cheesecake done when the edges are set (a knife inserted into the edge should come out clean) and the center is still soft.

SLICING CHEESECAKE. While the thought of freshly baked cheesecake is tantalizing, cheesecake usually needs to cool for several hours (overnight is better) to firm up properly for neat slicing. Make sure you refrigerate it.

❖   ❖   ❖

CHEESECAKE

Yield: 16 servings; Prep Time: 15 minutes
(Ready in 3 hours 40 minutes)

Sometimes the basics are the best. Here's a delicious, straightforward cheesecake, with sweet and tang perfectly balanced in a creamy, rich filling. Top it as you like, with fresh fruit, purchased pie filling or even chocolate sauce.

CRUST
2 cups graham cracker crumbs (32 squares)
½ cup margarine or butter, melted

FILLING
3 eggs
2 (8-oz.) pkg. cream cheese, softened
1 cup sugar
¼ teaspoon salt
2 teaspoons vanilla
3 cups sour cream

1. Heat oven to 350°F. In medium bowl, combine crust ingredients; mix well. Press mixture in bottom and 1½ inches up sides of ungreased 10-inch springform pan.*

2. In large bowl, beat eggs. Add cream cheese, sugar, salt and vanilla; beat until smooth. Add sour cream; blend well. Pour into crust-lined pan.

3. Bake at 350°F. for 60 to 70 minutes or until edges are set; center of cheesecake will be soft. Cool in pan 15 minutes. Carefully remove sides of pan. Cool 2 hours or until completely cooled. Store in refrigerator.

Tip: If desired, cheesecake can be baked in two ungreased 8-inch round cake pans. Bake at 375°F. for 25 to 30 minutes or until set.

Nutrition per Serving: Serving Size: ¹⁄₁₆ of Recipe. Calories 360; Calories from Fat 240; Total Fat 27g; Saturated Fat 14g; Cholesterol 90mg; Sodium 280mg; Dietary Fiber 0g

Dietary Exchange: 1 ½ Starch, 5 ½ Fat OR 1 ½ Carbohydrate, 5 ½ Fat

TRIPLE VANILLA CHEESECAKE

Yield: 8 servings; Prep Time: 15 minutes
(Ready in 3 hours 20 minutes)

Vanilla wafers, vanilla chips and vanilla extract give extraordinary savor to an "ordinary" flavor. As cheesecakes go, this creamy-textured dessert is leaner than most, with only 190 calories and 5 grams of fat per serving.

CRUST
¾ cup vanilla wafer crumbs (15 wafers)
1 tablespoon margarine or butter, melted

FILLING
2 (8-oz.) pkg. fat-free cream cheese, softened
½ cup sugar
1 teaspoon vanilla
2 eggs

TOPPING
2 tablespoons white vanilla chips

1. Heat oven to 375°F. In small bowl, combine crust ingredients; mix well. Press in bottom of ungreased 8-inch springform pan.

2. In medium bowl, combine cream cheese, sugar and vanilla; beat until smooth. Add eggs; beat well. Pour into crust-lined pan.

3. Bake at 375°F. for 27 to 33 minutes or until center is soft set.

4. Meanwhile, place vanilla chips in small, resealable, heavy-duty plastic bag; seal tightly.* Place in bowl under running hot water until chips are melted. Cut small hole in corner of bag; drizzle over warm cheesecake. Cool 30 minutes. Refrigerate at least 2 hours or until set. Store in refrigerator.

Tip: To melt chips in microwave, place in small microwave-safe bowl. Microwave on HIGH for 40 to 60 seconds or until chips can be stirred until smooth. With small spoon, drizzle over warm cheesecake.

Nutrition per Serving: Serving Size: ⅛ of Recipe. Calories 190; Calories from Fat 45; Total Fat 5g; Saturated Fat 2g; Cholesterol 60mg; Sodium 420mg; Dietary Fiber 0g

Dietary Exchange: 1 Starch, ½ Fruit, 1 Very Lean Meat, 1 Fat OR 1 ½ Carbohydrate, 1 Very Lean Meat, 1 Fat

CHOCOLATE CHEESECAKE

Yield: 16 servings; **Prep Time:** 15 minutes
(Ready in 7 hours 20 minutes)

Chocolate plus cheesecake equals a super-rich dessert guaranteed to evoke praise (and recipe requests).

CRUST
1 (9-oz.) pkg. chocolate wafer cookies, crushed (1 3/4 cups)
6 tablespoons margarine or butter, melted

FILLING
2 (8-oz.) pkg. cream cheese, softened
2/3 cup sugar
3 eggs
1 (12-oz.) pkg. (2 cups) semi-sweet chocolate chips, melted
1 cup whipping cream
2 tablespoons margarine or butter, melted
1 teaspoon vanilla

1. Heat oven to 325°F. In medium bowl, combine crust ingredients; reserve 1 tablespoon crumbs for garnish. Press remaining crumbs in bottom and 2 inches up sides of ungreased 10-inch springform pan. Refrigerate.

2. Meanwhile, in large bowl, combine cream cheese and sugar; beat until smooth. Add eggs 1 at a time, beating well after each addition. Add melted chocolate; beat well. Add all remaining filling ingredients; beat until smooth. Pour into crust-lined pan.

3. Bake at 325°F. for 55 to 65 minutes or until edges are set; center of cheesecake will be soft. (To minimize cracking, place shallow pan half full of hot water on lower oven rack during baking.) Cool in pan 5 minutes.

4. Carefully remove sides of pan. Cool 2 hours or until completely cooled. Garnish with reserved crumbs. Refrigerate at least 4 hours or overnight. Store in refrigerator.

Nutrition per Serving: Serving Size: 1/16 of Recipe. Calories 440; Calories from Fat 280; Total Fat 31g; Saturated Fat 15g; Cholesterol 90mg; Sodium 260mg; Dietary Fiber 2g

Dietary Exchange: 2 Starch, 6 Fat OR 2 Carbohydrate, 6 Fat

CREAMY CHOCOLATE LACE CHEESECAKE

Yield: 16 servings; **Prep Time:** 20 minutes
(Ready in 7 hours 20 minutes)

A tangy sour cream crown makes a delightful contrast to the sweet chocolate filling. The lace garnish contributes an intensely chocolate accent.

CRUST
1 1/2 cups chocolate wafer cookie crumbs (24 cookies)
1/2 cup finely chopped almonds
1/4 cup margarine or butter, melted

FILLING
2 (8-oz.) pkg. cream cheese, softened
2/3 cup sugar
3 eggs
1 (12-oz.) pkg. (2 cups) semi-sweet chocolate chips, melted, cooled
1 cup whipping cream
2 tablespoons margarine or butter, melted
1 teaspoon vanilla

TOPPING
1 cup sour cream
1 1/2 teaspoons vanilla
1 teaspoon sugar
1/2 oz. unsweetened chocolate, melted

1. Heat oven to 325°F. Butter 9-inch springform pan. In large bowl, combine all crust ingredients; mix well. Press mixture in bottom and up sides of buttered pan. Refrigerate.

2. In large bowl, combine cream cheese and 2/3 cup sugar; beat at medium speed until smooth and creamy. At low speed, add eggs 1 at a time, beating just until blended. Add melted chocolate chips; beat well. Add all remaining filling ingredients; beat until smooth. Pour into crust-lined pan.

Creamy Chocolate Lace Cheesecake

3. Bake at 325°F. for 55 to 65 minutes or until edges are set; center of cheesecake will be soft. Cool in pan 5 minutes. Carefully remove sides of pan. Cool 2 hours or until completely cooled.

4. In small bowl, combine sour cream, 1 ½ teaspoons vanilla and 1 teaspoon sugar; stir until smooth. Spread over cooled cheesecake. Drizzle with melted unsweetened chocolate in lace pattern. Refrigerate at least 4 hours or over-night. Garnish as desired. Store in refrigerator.

Nutrition per Serving: Serving Size: ¹/₁₆ of Recipe. Calories 470; Calories from Fat 310; Total Fat 34g; Saturated Fat 17g; Cholesterol 100mg; Sodium 220mg; Dietary Fiber 2g

Dietary Exchange: 2 Starch, 7 Fat OR 2 Carbohydrate, 7 Fat

BLACK BOTTOM WHITE CHOCOLATE CHEESECAKE

◆

Yield: 16 servings; **Prep Time:** 25 minutes
(Ready in 7 hours)

Melted vanilla chips boost the richness of the filling. To add a touch of tartness and color, top each luscious wedge with fresh raspberries.

CRUST
1 (9-oz.) pkg. chocolate wafer
   cookies, crushed (1 ¾ cups)
¼ cup margarine or butter, melted

FILLING
2 (8-oz.) pkg. cream cheese,
   softened
½ cup sugar
3 eggs
1 (12-oz.) pkg. (2 cups) white
   vanilla chips or vanilla-flavored
   candy coating, cut into pieces,
   melted*
1 cup whipping cream
2 tablespoons margarine or butter,
   melted
1 teaspoon vanilla

1. Heat oven to 325°F. In medium bowl, combine crust ingredients; mix well. Press in bottom and up sides of ungreased 10-inch springform pan. Refrigerate.

2. In large bowl, beat cream cheese until smooth. Gradually add sugar, beating until smooth. Add eggs 1 at a time, beating well after each addition. Add all remaining filling ingredients; beat until smooth. Pour into crust-lined pan.

3. Bake at 325°F. for 55 to 65 minutes or until edges are set; center of cheesecake will be soft. (To minimize cracking, place shallow pan half full of hot water on lower oven rack during baking.) Turn oven off; open oven door at least 4 inches. Let cheesecake sit in oven for 30 minutes or until center is set.

4. Remove cheesecake from oven. Cool in pan on wire rack for 1 hour or until completely cooled. Carefully remove sides of pan. Refrigerate at least 4 hours or overnight. Store in refrigerator.

*Tip: To melt chips, place 1 cup at a time in medium microwave-safe bowl. Microwave on MEDIUM for 3 to 4 minutes or until melted, stirring once halfway through cooking. Stir until smooth.

Nutrition per Serving: Serving Size: ¹⁄₁₆ of Recipe. Calories 420; Calories from Fat 270; Total Fat 30g; Saturated Fat 15g; Cholesterol 95mg; Sodium 260mg; Dietary Fiber 1g

Dietary Exchange: 2 Starch, 6 Fat OR 2 Carbohydrate, 6 Fat

FUDGE-GLAZED CHEESECAKE WITH PRALINE SAUCE

◆

Yield: 16 servings; **Prep Time:** 30 minutes
(Ready in 6 hours 15 minutes)

This luscious cheesecake with chocolate, caramel and pecans was inspired by the popular "turtle" candies.

CRUST
1 cup crushed creme-filled
   chocolate sandwich cookies
   (10 cookies)
¼ cup chopped pecans
1 tablespoon margarine or butter,
   melted

FILLING
2 (8-oz.) pkg. cream cheese,
   softened
½ cup sugar
¼ cup whipping cream
2 eggs

GLAZE
2 oz. semi-sweet chocolate, cut up
2 tablespoons whipping cream

SAUCE
1 cup caramel ice cream topping
½ cup pecan halves, toasted*

1. Heat oven to 325°F. Line 8 or 9-inch round cake pan with foil. In large bowl, combine all crust ingredients; mix well. Press in bottom of foil-lined pan. Bake at 325°F. for 8 minutes.

2. Meanwhile, in large bowl, beat cream cheese until smooth and creamy. Gradually beat in sugar and cream. Add eggs 1 at a time, beating well after each addition. Pour into partially baked crust.

3. Bake at 325°F. for 35 to 45 minutes or until center is set. Cool in pan on wire rack for 1 hour or until completely cooled.

4. In small saucepan, combine glaze ingredients; cook over very low heat until chocolate is melted, stirring constantly. Spread over cheesecake. Cover; refrigerate at least 4 hours or overnight.

5. Just before serving, in small bowl, combine sauce ingredients; mix well. To serve, lift foil-lined cheesecake from pan; remove foil. Place cheesecake on serving plate; cut into wedges. Serve with sauce. Store in refrigerator.

*Tip: To toast pecans, spread on cookie sheet; bake at 350°F. for 5 to 7 minutes or until golden brown, stirring occasionally.

Nutrition per Serving: Serving Size: 1/16 of Recipe. Calories 300; Calories from Fat 170; Total Fat 19g; Saturated Fat 9g; Cholesterol 65mg; Sodium 210mg; Dietary Fiber 1g

Dietary Exchange: 1 Starch, 1 Fruit, 3 1/2 Fat OR 2 Carbohydrate, 3 1/2 Fat

Fudge-Glazed Cheesecake with Praline Sauce

COOKIES 'N CREAM CHEESECAKE

Yield: 16 servings; **Prep Time:** 15 minutes
(Ready in 10 hours 45 minutes)

Crushed cookies, a favorite ice-cream mix-in, enliven cheesecake, too. The crust and topping both use crushed chocolate sandwich cookies; bigger cookie chunks give texture to the filling.

CRUST
1 ½ cups crushed creme-filled
    chocolate sandwich cookies
    (15 cookies)
2 tablespoons margarine or butter,
    softened

FILLING
3 (8-oz.) pkg. cream cheese,
    softened
1 cup sugar
3 eggs
1 cup whipping cream
2 tablespoons margarine or butter,
    melted
2 teaspoons vanilla
1 cup coarsely chopped creme-
    filled chocolate sandwich
    cookies (about 10 cookies)

TOPPING
Whipped cream
Crushed creme-filled chocolate
    sandwich cookies

1. Heat oven to 325°F. In medium bowl, combine crust ingredients; mix well. Press in bottom and up sides of ungreased 10-inch springform pan. Refrigerate.

2. In large bowl, beat cream cheese at medium speed until smooth and creamy. Gradually add sugar, beating until smooth. At low speed, add eggs 1 at a time, beating just until blended. Add whipping cream, 2 tablespoons margarine and vanilla; beat until smooth. Stir in 1 cup chopped cookies. Pour into crust-lined pan.

3. Bake at 325°F. for 50 to 60 minutes or until edges are set; center of cheesecake will be soft. Turn oven off; open oven door at least 4 inches. Let cheesecake sit in oven for 30 minutes or until center is set.

4. Remove cheesecake from oven. Cool in pan on wire rack for 1 hour or until completely cooled. Carefully remove sides of pan. Refrigerate 8 hours.

5. Just before serving, top cheesecake with whipped cream; sprinkle with crushed cookies. Store in refrigerator.

Nutrition per Serving: Serving Size: 1/16 of Recipe. Calories 450; Calories from Fat 310; Total Fat 34g; Saturated Fat 18g; Cholesterol 125mg; Sodium 310mg; Dietary Fiber 1g

Dietary Exchange: 2 Starch, 6½ Fat OR 2 Carbohydrate, 6½ Fat

KEY LIME CHEESECAKE WITH RASPBERRY SAUCE

Yield: 16 servings; **Prep Time:** 25 minutes
(Ready in 7 hours 10 minutes)

Key lime pie, a classic from the Florida Keys, gets a rich new interpretation as cheesecake.

CRUST
1 cup shortbread cookie crumbs
    (15 cookies) or vanilla wafer
    crumbs (20 wafers)
2 tablespoons margarine or butter,
    melted

FILLING
3 (8-oz.) pkg. cream cheese,
    softened
1 cup sugar
3 eggs
1 tablespoon grated lime peel
¼ cup Key lime juice

SAUCE
1 (10-oz.) pkg. frozen raspberries
    in light syrup, thawed
1 tablespoon cornstarch
⅓ cup red currant jelly

1. Heat oven to 325°F. In medium bowl, combine crust ingredients; mix well. Press mixture in bottom of ungreased 9-inch springform pan. Refrigerate.

2. In large bowl, beat cream cheese until smooth. Gradually beat in sugar. At low speed, beat in eggs 1 at a time, blending just until smooth. Add lime peel and juice; beat until smooth. Pour into crust-lined pan.

3. Bake at 325°F. for 55 to 65 minutes or until set. (To minimize cracking, place shallow pan half full of hot water on lower oven rack during baking.) Turn oven off; open oven door at least 4 inches. Let cheesecake sit in oven for 30 minutes. Remove from oven; let stand 10 minutes. Carefully remove sides of pan. Cool in pan on wire rack for 1 hour or until completely cooled. Refrigerate at least 4 hours or overnight.

4. To prepare sauce, drain raspberries, reserving syrup. Add water to syrup to make ³⁄₄ cup. In small saucepan, combine syrup mixture and cornstarch; mix well. Add jelly; cook and stir over medium heat until thickened and clear. Stir in raspberries. Refrigerate until cold. Serve sauce with cheesecake. Store in refrigerator.

Nutrition per Serving: Serving Size: ¹⁄₁₆ of Recipe. Calories 280; Calories from Fat 170; Total Fat 19g; Saturated Fat 10g; Cholesterol 90mg; Sodium 190mg; Dietary Fiber 1g

Dietary Exchange: 1 Starch, ½ Fruit, 3½ Fat OR 1½ Carbohydrate, 3½ Fat

BANANA SPLIT CHEESECAKE

Yield: 16 servings; **Prep Time:** 25 minutes (Ready in 11 hours)

This fabulously rich cheesecake is a take-off on the popular soda fountain favorite, right down to the cherry on the top.

CRUST
1½ cups crushed creme-filled chocolate sandwich cookies (15 cookies)
2 tablespoons margarine or butter, softened

FILLING
3 (8-oz.) pkg. cream cheese, softened
1 cup sugar
3 eggs
½ cup mashed banana
½ cup whipping cream
1 tablespoon lemon juice
2 teaspoons vanilla

TOPPING
1 cup whipped cream
⅓ cup chopped peanuts
16 maraschino cherries
½ cup hot fudge ice cream topping, warmed

1. Heat oven to 350°F. In medium bowl, combine crust ingredients; mix well. Press mixture in bottom and up sides of ungreased 9-inch springform pan. Refrigerate.

2. In large bowl, beat cream cheese until smooth. Gradually add sugar, beating until smooth. Add eggs 1 at a time, beating well after each addition. Add remaining filling ingredients; beat until smooth. Pour into crust-lined pan.

3. Bake at 350°F. for 55 to 65 minutes or until center is set. (To minimize cracking, place shallow pan half full of hot water on lower oven rack during baking.) Turn oven off; open oven door at least 4 inches. Let cheesecake sit in oven for 30 minutes.

4. Remove cheesecake from oven. Carefully remove sides of pan. Cool on wire rack for 1 hour or until completely cooled. Refrigerate 8 hours.

5. Just before serving, top cheesecake with whipped cream, peanuts, cherries and fudge sauce. Store in refrigerator.

Nutrition per Serving: Serving Size: ¹⁄₁₆ of Recipe. Calories 430; Calories from Fat 260; Total Fat 29g; Saturated Fat 15g; Cholesterol 110mg; Sodium 280mg; Dietary Fiber 1g

Dietary Exchange: 2½ Starch, 5 Fat OR 2½ Carbohydrate, 5 Fat

APPLESAUCE CHEESECAKE

◆

Yield: 16 servings; Prep Time: 15 minutes
(Ready in 7 hours 15 minutes)

Applesauce, with a hint of cinnamon and nutmeg, lends delicate apple flavor to a creamy, smooth cheesecake.

CRUST

1 ¼ cups graham cracker crumbs
   (20 squares)
½ cup chopped pecans, toasted*
¼ cup firmly packed brown sugar
¼ cup margarine or butter, melted

FILLING

3 (8-oz.) pkg. cream cheese,
   softened
1 cup sugar
2 tablespoons all-purpose flour
3 eggs
1 cup applesauce
½ teaspoon cinnamon
⅛ teaspoon nutmeg

1. Heat oven to 350°F. In medium bowl, combine all crust ingredients; mix well. Press mixture in bottom of ungreased 10-inch springform pan.

2. In large bowl, combine cream cheese and sugar; beat at medium speed until smooth and creamy. Add flour; blend well. At low speed, add eggs 1 at a time, beating just until blended. Add remaining ingredients; blend well. Pour into crust-lined pan.

3. Bake at 350°F. for 50 to 60 minutes or until center is set. Cool 2 hours or until completely cooled. Refrigerate at least 4 hours or overnight.

4. Just before serving, carefully remove sides of pan. Store in refrigerator.

Tip: To toast pecans, spread on cookie sheet; bake at 350°F. for 5 to 7 minutes or until golden brown, stirring occasionally.

Nutrition per Serving: Serving Size: ¹⁄₁₆ of Recipe. Calories 330; Calories from Fat 200; Total Fat 22g; Saturated Fat 11g; Cholesterol 85mg; Sodium 210mg; Dietary Fiber 1g

Dietary Exchange: 1 ½ Starch, ½ Fruit, 4 Fat OR 2 Carbohydrate, 4 Fat

CHERRIES JUBILEE CHEESECAKE

◆

Yield: 16 servings; Prep Time: 20 minutes
(Ready in 7 hours 20 minutes)

Flaming cherry topping makes a dramatic finale to a formal meal.

CRUST

2 cups crushed creme-filled
   chocolate sandwich cookies
   (20 cookies)
2 tablespoons margarine or butter,
   melted

FILLING

3 (8-oz.) pkg. cream cheese,
   softened
1 cup sugar
4 eggs
1 ½ cups sour cream
1 teaspoon grated lemon peel
1 teaspoon vanilla

SAUCE

3 tablespoons cornstarch
2 (16-oz.) cans (4 cups) pitted dark
   sweet cherries, undrained
½ cup brandy

1. Heat oven to 350°F. In medium bowl, combine crust ingredients; mix well. Press mixture in bottom and ½ to 1 inch up sides of ungreased 10-inch springform pan.

2. In large bowl, combine cream cheese and sugar; beat until light and fluffy. Add eggs 1 at a time, beating well after each addition. Add sour cream, lemon peel and vanilla; blend well. Pour into crust-lined pan.

3. Bake at 350°F. for 50 to 60 minutes or until center is set. (To minimize cracking, place shallow pan half full of hot water on lower oven rack during baking.) Cool 2 hours or until completely cooled. Refrigerate at least 4 hours or overnight.

Cherries Jubilee Cheesecake

4. Just before serving, carefully remove sides of pan. In chafing dish or skillet, combine cornstarch and cherries. Cook over medium heat until mixture boils and thickens, stirring occasionally. In small saucepan over low heat, heat brandy just until vapors are visible. DO NOT OVERHEAT. Using long-handled match, carefully ignite brandy in saucepan. Pour ignited brandy carefully over cherries; stir gently. Spoon cherry mixture over each serving.

Nutrition per Serving: Serving Size: 1/16 of Recipe. Calories 430; Calories from Fat 230; Total Fat 26g; Saturated Fat 14g; Cholesterol 110mg; Sodium 290mg; Dietary Fiber 1g

Dietary Exchange: 2 1/2 Starch, 5 Fat OR 2 1/2 Carbohydrate, 5 Fat

CRANBERRY RIBBON CHEESECAKE

✦

Yield: 16 servings; Prep Time: 30 minutes
(Ready in 7 hours 40 minutes)

A beautiful, marbleized dessert under a mantle of glistening berries.

CRUST
1½ cups finely crushed chocolate creme-filled sandwich cookies (15 cookies)
2 tablespoons margarine or butter, melted

CRANBERRY SAUCE
1 cup sugar
2 tablespoons cornstarch
1½ cups fresh or frozen cranberries
1 cup cranberry juice cocktail

FILLING
1 cup sugar
3 (8-oz.) pkg. cream cheese, softened
4 eggs
1½ cups sour cream
2 teaspoons grated orange peel

1. Heat oven to 350°F. Grease 9-inch springform pan. In small bowl, combine crust ingredients; mix well. Press mixture in bottom of greased pan. Set aside.

2. In medium saucepan, combine 1 cup sugar and cornstarch; blend well. Add cranberries and cranberry juice. Cook over medium heat until mixture is bubbly and thickened, stirring constantly. Cook an additional 2 minutes, stirring constantly. In food processor bowl with metal blade or blender container, process cranberry sauce until smooth. Set aside to cool.

3. Meanwhile, in large bowl, combine 1 cup sugar and cream cheese; beat until light and fluffy. Add eggs 1 at a time, beating well after each addition. Add sour cream and orange peel; blend well.

4. Pour half of filling (3 cups) into crust-lined pan. Drizzle with half of cranberry sauce (¾ cup). Cover and refrigerate remaining cranberry sauce for topping. Carefully spoon remaining filling over cranberry sauce in pan.

5. Bake at 350°F. for 60 to 70 minutes or until center is set. (To minimize cracking, place shallow pan half full of hot water on lower oven rack during baking.) Cool 2 hours or until completely cooled. Refrigerate at least 4 hours or overnight.

6. Just before serving, run knife around edge of pan; carefully remove sides of pan. Spread reserved cranberry sauce over cheesecake. Store in refrigerator.

Nutrition per Serving: Serving Size: ¹⁄₁₆ of Recipe. Calories 390; Calories from Fat 220; Total Fat 24g; Saturated Fat 13g; Cholesterol 110mg; Sodium 230mg; Dietary Fiber 1g

Dietary Exchange: 2 Starch, ½ Fruit, 4½ Fat OR 2½ Carbohydrate, 4½ Fat

Cranberry Ribbon Cheesecake

PEPPERMINT PARTY CHEESECAKE

Yield: 16 servings; **Prep Time**: 30 minutes
(Ready in 6 hours 30 minutes)

Charlie Brown's friend would certainly approve of this pepperminty, pink-tinted dessert. It's a fun choice for a birthday celebration.

CRUST

1 ½ cups graham cracker crumbs
   (24 squares)
¼ cup margarine or butter, melted

FILLING

3 (8-oz.) pkg. cream cheese,
   softened
1 cup sugar
4 eggs
1 ½ cups sour cream
1 teaspoon vanilla
½ teaspoon peppermint extract
2 to 3 drops red food color

1. Heat oven to 350°F. In medium bowl, combine crust ingredients; mix well. Press in bottom of ungreased 10-inch springform pan.

2. In large bowl, combine cream cheese and sugar; beat until light and fluffy. Add eggs 1 at a time, beating well after each addition. Add sour cream and vanilla; blend well. Place 1 cup mixture in small bowl; stir in peppermint extract and food color.

3. Pour remaining cream cheese mixture into crust-lined pan. Drop spoonfuls of peppermint mixture over cream cheese mixture. Pull knife randomly through batter in wide curves; turn pan and repeat for swirl effect.

4. Bake at 350°F. for 50 to 60 minutes or until center is set. (To minimize cracking, place shallow pan half full of hot water on lower oven rack during baking.) Cool in pan on wire rack for 1 hour or until completely cooled. Refrigerate at least 4 hours or overnight.

5. Just before serving, carefully remove sides of pan. Garnish as desired. Store in refrigerator.

Nutrition per Serving: Serving Size: ¹/₁₆ of Recipe. Calories 320; Calories from Fat 220; Total Fat 24g; Saturated Fat 13g; Cholesterol 110mg; Sodium 230mg; Dietary Fiber 0g

Dietary Exchange: 1 ½ Starch, 4 ½ Fat OR 1 ½ Carbohydrate, 4 ½ Fat

Peppermint Party Cheesecake

LEMON YOGURT CHEESECAKE

◆

Yield: 16 servings; **Prep Time:** 30 minutes
(Ready in 6 hours 50 minutes)

Made with Neufchatel (reduced-fat cream cheese), egg substitute and low-fat yogurt, this lemony cheesecake retains plenty of richness while reducing the fat.

CRUST
⅓ cup vanilla wafer crumbs
 (7 wafers)
2 teaspoons sugar
¼ teaspoon grated lemon peel

FILLING
3 (8-oz.) pkg. ⅓-less-fat cream
 cheese (Neufchatel), softened
1 cup sugar
1 cup refrigerated or frozen
 fat-free egg product, thawed
1 (8-oz.) container low-fat lemon
 yogurt
2 teaspoons vanilla
1 teaspoon grated lemon peel

TOPPING
1 (11¼-oz.) jar lemon curd (about
 1 cup)
4 cups fresh fruit (sliced
 strawberries, sliced kiwi fruit
 and/or raspberries)

1. Heat oven to 350°F. Spray 9-inch springform pan with non-stick cooking spray. In small bowl, combine all crust ingredients; mix well. Sprinkle crust mixture into bottom and halfway up sides of sprayed pan.

2. In large bowl, beat cream cheese until smooth. Gradually add 1 cup sugar, beating until smooth. Add all remaining filling ingredients; beat until smooth. Pour into crust-lined pan.

3. Bake at 350°F. for 50 to 60 minutes or until center is almost set. (To minimize cracking, place shallow pan half full of hot water on lower oven rack during baking.) Cool in pan on wire rack for 1½ hours or until completely cooled.

4. In small bowl, stir lemon curd to soften. Spread evenly over top of cheesecake. Refrigerate 4 hours or overnight.

5. Just before serving, carefully remove sides of pan. Top each serving with fresh fruit. Store in refrigerator.

Nutrition per Serving: Serving Size: ¹⁄₁₆ of Recipe. Calories 280; Calories from Fat 110; Total Fat 12g; Saturated Fat 7g; Cholesterol 35mg; Sodium 230mg; Dietary Fiber 1g

Dietary Exchange: 2 Starch, ½ Fruit, 2 Fat OR 2½ Carbohydrate, 2 Fat

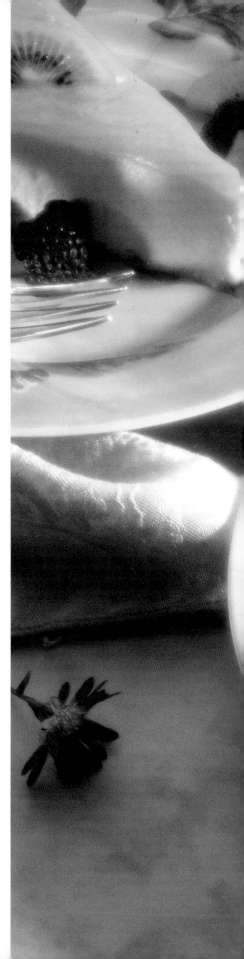

Lemon Yogurt Cheesecake

GRASSHOPPER CHEESECAKE

◆

Yield: 16 servings; **Prep Time:** 20 minutes
(Ready in 7 hours 40 minutes)

"Grasshopper" is the whimsical name given to the delectable combination of mint (usually tinted green) and chocolate.

CRUST
1 (9-oz.) pkg. chocolate wafer
  cookies, crushed (1 ¾ cups)
¼ cup margarine or butter, melted

FILLING
4 eggs
3 (8-oz.) pkg. cream cheese,
  softened
1 cup sugar
2 cups sour cream
3 oz. semi-sweet chocolate,
  melted
¼ cup creme de cacao
¼ cup green creme de menthe

TOPPING
3 oz. semi-sweet chocolate,
  melted
½ cup sour cream

1. Heat oven to 325°F. In medium bowl, combine crust ingredients; mix well. Press mixture in bottom and 2 inches up sides of ungreased 10-inch springform pan.

2. In large bowl, beat eggs. Add cream cheese and sugar; beat until smooth. Add 2 cups sour cream; blend well. Divide mixture in half. Stir 3 oz. melted chocolate and creme de cacao into half of mixture; pour into crust-lined pan. Stir creme de menthe into remaining mixture. Carefully spoon over chocolate mixture.

3. Bake at 325°F. for 65 to 80 minutes or until center is set. (To minimize cracking, place shallow pan half full of hot water on lower oven rack during baking.) Cool 2 hours or until completely cooled.

4. In small bowl, combine topping ingredients; mix well. Spread over top of cooled cheesecake. If desired, make spiral design with frosting comb or fork. Refrigerate at least 4 hours or overnight.

5. Just before serving, carefully remove sides of pan. Store in refrigerator.

Nutrition per Serving: Serving Size: ¹⁄₁₆ of Recipe. Calories 470; Calories from Fat 290; Total Fat 32g; Saturated Fat 18g; Cholesterol 115mg; Sodium 280mg; Dietary Fiber 1g

Dietary Exchange: 2 Starch, ½ Fruit, 6 Fat OR 2 ½ Carbohydrate, 6 Fat

GLAZED ALMOND AMARETTO CHEESECAKE

Yield: 16 servings; **Prep Time:** 30 minutes
(Ready in 8 hours)

Amaretto (Italian almond liqueur) underscores the nutty flavor in a cheesecake distinguished by an almond crumb crust and glazed almond topping.

TOPPING
½ cup sugar
¼ cup water
1 cup sliced almonds
1 teaspoon amaretto

CRUST
2 cups graham cracker crumbs
  (32 squares)
¼ cup finely chopped almonds
⅓ cup margarine or butter, melted

FILLING
2 (8-oz.) pkg. cream cheese,
  softened
1 cup sugar
3 eggs
1 cup sour cream
½ cup whipping cream
¼ cup amaretto
½ teaspoon almond extract

1. In small saucepan, combine ½ cup sugar and water. Bring to a boil; boil 2 minutes. Remove from heat. Stir in sliced almonds and 1 teaspoon amaretto. With slotted spoon, remove almonds and place on waxed paper; separate with fork. Cool.

2. Heat oven to 350°F. In medium bowl, combine all crust ingredients; mix well. Press mixture in bottom and 1 1/2 inches up sides of ungreased 10-inch springform pan.

3. In large bowl, combine cream cheese and 1 cup sugar; beat at medium speed until smooth and creamy. At low speed, add eggs 1 at a time, beating just until blended. Add all remaining filling ingredients; blend well. Pour into crust-lined pan.

4. Bake at 350°F. for 60 to 75 minutes or until center is set, arranging sliced almonds in 2-inch-wide circle around outer edge of cheesecake during last 15 minutes of baking time. Cool 15 minutes. Run knife around edge of pan; carefully remove sides of pan. Cool 2 hours or until completely cooled. Refrigerate at least 4 hours or overnight. Store in refrigerator.

Nutrition per Serving: Serving Size: 1/16 of Recipe. Calories 390; Calories from Fat 230; Total Fat 26g; Saturated Fat 12g; Cholesterol 90mg; Sodium 220mg; Dietary Fiber 1g

Dietary Exchange: 2 Starch, 5 Fat OR 2 Carbohydrate, 5 Fat

ITALIAN ALMOND CHEESECAKE

Yield: 16 servings; Prep Time: 15 minutes
(Ready in 7 hours 30 minutes)

Italian-style cheesecakes, typically made with ricotta, have a fluffier, somewhat drier texture than cheesecakes made with cream cheese.

CRUST
1 cup unseasoned dry bread crumbs
1/2 cup finely chopped sliced almonds
1/3 cup sugar
1 teaspoon grated orange peel
6 tablespoons butter, melted

FILLING
2 (15-oz.) containers (3 1/2 cups) ricotta cheese
1/2 cup sugar
1 tablespoon cornstarch
4 eggs, beaten
1 cup whipping cream
1 teaspoon almond extract

TOPPING
1/4 cup sliced almonds
2 teaspoons sugar
1/8 teaspoon cinnamon

1. Heat oven to 325°F. Grease 9-inch springform pan. In medium bowl, combine all crust ingredients; mix well. Press in bottom and halfway up sides of greased pan.

Bake at 325°F. for 12 to 14 minutes or until lightly browned around edges. Cool 15 minutes or until completely cooled.

2. Meanwhile, in large bowl, combine ricotta cheese, 1/2 cup sugar and cornstarch; beat until fluffy. Add eggs; beat until smooth. Add whipping cream and extract; beat until smooth. Pour into partially baked crust. Arrange sliced almonds over filling. In small bowl, combine 2 teaspoons sugar and cinnamon; sprinkle over almonds.

3. Bake at 325°F. for 65 to 75 minutes or until center is almost set and knife inserted 2 inches from edge comes out clean. Cool 2 hours or until completely cooled. Refrigerate at least 4 hours or overnight.

4. Just before serving, remove sides of pan. Store in refrigerator.

Nutrition per Serving: Serving Size: 1/16 of Recipe. Calories 290; Calories from Fat 160; Total Fat 18g; Saturated Fat 9g; Cholesterol 100mg; Sodium 190mg; Dietary Fiber 1g

Dietary Exchange: 1 Starch, 1/2 Fruit, 1 Medium-Fat Meat, 2 1/2 Fat OR 1 1/2 Carbohydrate, 1 Medium-Fat Meat, 2 1/2 Fat

PUMPKIN CHEESECAKE WITH PRALINE SAUCE

Yield: 16 servings; **Prep Time:** 30 minutes
(Ready in 7 hours 30 minutes)

Here's a wonderful change of pace from pumpkin pie. Be sure to purchase plain canned pumpkin, not "pumpkin pie filling," for this recipe.

CRUST

1 tablespoon butter, softened
1 ¼ cups finely chopped pecans
¼ cup unseasoned dry bread crumbs
2 tablespoons sugar
2 tablespoons butter, melted

FILLING

4 (8-oz.) pkg. cream cheese, softened
1 cup firmly packed brown sugar
⅔ cup sugar
5 eggs
¼ cup all-purpose flour
2 teaspoons pumpkin pie spice
2 tablespoons brandy, if desired
1 (16-oz.) can (2 cups) pumpkin

SAUCE

½ cup firmly packed brown sugar
¼ cup water
¼ cup butter
1 egg, beaten
¼ cup chopped pecans
½ teaspoon vanilla

Pumpkin Cheesecake with Praline Sauce

1. Heat oven to 350°F. Butter 9-inch springform pan using 1 tablespoon butter. In medium bowl, combine 1 1/4 cups pecans, bread crumbs and 2 tablespoons sugar. Drizzle melted butter over pecan mixture; toss to combine. Press in bottom and up sides of buttered pan. Refrigerate.

2. In large bowl, beat cream cheese at medium speed until smooth and creamy. Gradually beat in 1 cup brown sugar and 2/3 cup sugar until smooth. At low speed, add 5 eggs 1 at a time, beating just until blended.

3. In small bowl, combine flour, pumpkin pie spice, brandy and pumpkin; mix well. Gradually add to cream cheese mixture; beat until smooth. Pour into crust-lined pan.

4. Bake at 350°F. for 1 hour 20 minutes to 1 hour 30 minutes or until center is set. Turn oven off; open oven door at least 4 inches. Let cheesecake sit in oven for 30 minutes. Remove cheesecake from oven. Run knife around sides of pan. Cool in pan on wire rack for 1 hour or until completely cooled. Refrigerate at least 4 hours or overnight.

5. Just before serving, in small saucepan, combine 1/2 cup brown sugar, water and 1/4 cup butter. Bring to a boil over medium heat. Boil 2 minutes. Gradually blend small amount of hot syrup into beaten egg. Add egg mixture to saucepan; cook over low heat for 1 minute, stirring constantly. Remove from heat; stir in 1/4 cup pecans and vanilla. Carefully remove sides of pan. Serve slightly warm sauce over each serving. Store in refrigerator.

High Altitude (Above 3,500 feet): Increase flour in filling to 1/4 cup plus 1 tablespoon. Bake at 350°F. for 1 hour 15 minutes to 1 hour 25 minutes.

Nutrition per Serving: Serving Size: 1/16 of Recipe. Calories 500; Calories from Fat 310; Total Fat 34g; Saturated Fat 17g; Cholesterol 155mg; Sodium 270mg; Dietary Fiber 2g

Dietary Exchange: 2 1/2 Starch, 6 1/2 Fat OR 2 1/2 Carbohydrate, 6 1/2 Fat

PRALINE CHEESECAKE

PICTURED ON PAGE 157.

Yield: 16 servings; Prep Time: 30 minutes (Ready in 6 hours)

Exquisite contrast: a crunchy pecan crust and brown sugar topping encase a creamy-textured filling.

CRUST
1 cup graham cracker crumbs (16 squares)
1/4 cup chopped pecans
1/4 cup butter, melted

FILLING
3 (8-oz.) pkg. cream cheese, softened
1 cup firmly packed brown sugar
3 eggs
1 cup whipping cream
2 teaspoons vanilla

TOPPING
1/2 cup firmly packed brown sugar
1/4 cup butter

GARNISH
Pecan halves, if desired

1. Heat oven to 450°F. In small bowl, combine all crust ingredients; mix well. Press firmly in bottom of ungreased 9-inch springform pan.

2. In large bowl, beat cream cheese at medium speed until smooth and creamy. Gradually beat in 1 cup brown sugar. At low speed, add eggs 1 at a time, beating just until blended. Add whipping cream and vanilla; beat until smooth. Pour into crust-lined pan.

3. Bake at 450°F. for 10 minutes. Reduce oven temperature to 250°F.; bake an additional 65 to 75 minutes or until center is set. Cool 10 minutes. Carefully remove sides of pan. Cool 2 hours or until completely cooled.

4. In small saucepan, combine topping ingredients. Cook over medium heat until thick and well blended, stirring constantly. Spread evenly over top of cooled cheesecake. Garnish with pecan halves. Refrigerate at least 2 hours or overnight. Store in refrigerator.

Nutrition per Serving: Serving Size: 1/16 of Recipe. Calories 390; Calories from Fat 260; Total Fat 29g; Saturated Fat 17g; Cholesterol 120mg; Sodium 240mg; Dietary Fiber 0g

Dietary Exchange: 1 1/2 Starch, 6 Fat OR 1 1/2 Carbohydrate, 6 Fat

RINGS OF PRALINE CHEESECAKE

✦

Yield: 16 servings; **Prep Time:** 15 minutes
(Ready in 6 hours)

Arranged in concentric rings atop the cheesecake mixture, the praline sauce gives the cheesecake an attractive presentation on the dessert platter and an equally enticing look when cut into slices.

CRUST
1 cup crushed creme-filled chocolate sandwich cookies (10 cookies)
1 tablespoon margarine or butter, melted

CHEESECAKE
2 (8-oz.) pkg. cream cheese, softened
2/3 cup sugar
2 eggs
1/2 cup caramel ice cream topping
1/4 cup finely chopped pecans

SAUCE
1 1/2 cups chocolate or hot fudge ice cream topping, warmed, if desired

1. Heat oven to 325°F. Line 9-inch round cake pan with foil. In small bowl, combine crust ingredients; mix well. Press in bottom of foil-lined pan.

2. In large bowl, beat cream cheese until smooth and creamy. Gradually beat in sugar. Add eggs 1 at a time, beating well after each addition. Pour into crust-lined pan.

3. In small bowl, combine caramel ice cream topping and pecans. Spoon part of topping mixture into 3-inch ring in center of cheesecake. Then, using remaining topping mixture, spoon another ring of topping 1 1/2 inches from first ring.

4. Bake at 325°F. for 35 to 45 minutes or until center is set. Cool in pan on wire rack for 1 hour or until completely cooled. Refrigerate at least 4 hours or overnight.

5. Just before serving, lift foil-lined cheesecake from pan; remove foil. Serve chocolate topping over each serving. Store in refrigerator.

Nutrition per Serving: Serving Size: 1/16 of Recipe. Calories 340; Calories from Fat 160; Total Fat 18g; Saturated Fat 9g; Cholesterol 60mg; Sodium 210mg; Dietary Fiber 1g

Dietary Exchange: 1 1/2 Starch, 1 Fruit, 3 1/2 Fat OR 2 1/2 Carbohydrate, 3 1/2 Fat

SWIRLS OF STRAWBERRY-LEMON CHEESECAKE

✦

Yield: 12 servings; **Prep Time:** 30 minutes
(Ready in 4 hours 30 minutes)

Cutting into the pie reveals a beautifully marbled gold and crimson interior. If you wish, garnish each portion with sliced fresh strawberries.

CREAM CHEESE FILLING
1 envelope unflavored gelatin
2/3 cup cold water
1/3 cup fresh lemon juice
12 oz. cream cheese, softened
1/2 cup sour cream
1/2 cup sugar
1 teaspoon grated lemon peel

STRAWBERRY FILLING
1 envelope unflavored gelatin
1/4 cup cold water
1 (10-oz.) pkg. frozen strawberries in syrup, thawed

CRUST
1 (9-oz.) or 2 (6-oz.) graham cracker crumb crusts

1. In small saucepan, sprinkle 1 envelope gelatin over 2/3 cup cold water; let stand 1 minute. Place over low heat; cook and stir about 2 minutes or until gelatin is dissolved. Remove from heat; stir in lemon juice.

Swirls of Strawberry-Lemon Cheesecake

2. In large bowl, combine cream cheese, sour cream, sugar and lemon peel; blend well. Stir in gelatin mixture; mix well. Refrigerate 1 hour or until cream cheese filling is the consistency of egg whites, stirring occasionally.

3. Meanwhile, in another small saucepan, sprinkle 1 envelope gelatin over ¼ cup cold water; let stand 1 minute. Place over low heat; cook and stir about 2 minutes or until gelatin is dissolved. Remove from heat. Stir in strawberries with syrup; mix well. Refrigerate 10 to 15 minutes or until filling is the consistency of egg whites.

4. To assemble cheesecake, pour half of cream cheese filling into crumb crust. Pour strawberry filling over cream cheese filling. Top with remaining cream cheese filling. Pull knife through all layers to swirl strawberry filling. Refrigerate at least 3 hours or overnight. Store in refrigerator.

Nutrition per Serving: Serving Size: ¹⁄₁₂ of Recipe. Calories 290; Calories from Fat 150; Total Fat 17g; Saturated Fat 9g; Cholesterol 35mg; Sodium 210mg; Dietary Fiber 1g

Dietary Exchange: 1½ Starch, ½ Fruit, 3 Fat OR 2 Carbohydrate, 3 Fat

NO-BAKE PINEAPPLE CHEESECAKE WITH STRAWBERRY-RHUBARB SAUCE

Yield: 20 servings; **Prep Time:** 25 minutes
(Ready in 2 hours 25 minutes)

Angel food cake, processed into crumbs, makes a unique no-fat crust. Choose pineapple yogurt for a sweeter filling; lemon for a pie that's slightly tarter.

CHEESECAKE
½ (10-inch-round) angel food cake
2 (6-oz.) cans (1½ cups) pineapple juice
2 envelopes unflavored gelatin
1⅓ cups sugar
3 (8-oz.) pkg. ⅓-less-fat cream cheese (Neufchatel), softened
2 (8-oz.) containers pineapple or lemon yogurt

SAUCE
3 cups sliced fresh or frozen rhubarb, thawed
½ cup sugar
1 (10-oz.) pkg. frozen strawberries in syrup
¼ teaspoon cinnamon
1 tablespoon water
1 tablespoon cornstarch

1. Generously spray 13 × 9-inch (3-quart) baking dish with nonstick cooking spray.

2. Break cake into 1½-inch pieces; place in food processor bowl with metal blade. Cover; process until crumbs form, making about 2½ cups crumbs. Press crumbs in bottom of sprayed dish. Set aside.

3. Place 3 tablespoons of the pineapple juice in small saucepan. Sprinkle gelatin over top; let stand 1 minute to soften.

4. Meanwhile, in medium saucepan, combine remaining pineapple juice and 1⅓ cups sugar; cook and stir over medium heat until sugar is dissolved.

5. Heat softened gelatin over low heat until dissolved, stirring frequently. Add to pineapple juice mixture; blend well.

6. In large bowl with electric mixer, beat cream cheese until fluffy. Gradually add gelatin mixture, beating until smooth. Beat in yogurt. Pour mixture into crumb-lined dish. Cover with plastic wrap; refrigerate at least 2 hours or until set.

7. Meanwhile, in medium saucepan; combine all sauce ingredients except water and cornstarch; mix well. Bring to a boil. Reduce heat; simmer 20 minutes or until rhubarb is tender.

8. In small bowl, combine water and cornstarch; blend well. Add to rhubarb mixture; cook and stir until bubbly and thickened. Remove from heat; cool 1 hour or until completely cooled. Serve sauce over cheesecake squares. Store in refrigerator.

Nutrition per Serving: Serving Size: ⅟₂₀ of Recipe. Calories 240; Calories from Fat 70; Total Fat 8g; Saturated Fat 5g; Cholesterol 25mg; Sodium 230mg; Dietary Fiber 1g

Dietary Exchange: 2 Starch, ½ Fruit, 1 Fat OR 2½ Carbohydrate, 1 Fat

NO-BAKE FRUIT-TOPPED CHEESECAKE

Yield: 10 servings; **Prep Time:** 30 minutes
(Ready in 3 hours)

Lemon-flavored gelatin helps to set a delectable no-bake cheesecake mixture made with ricotta cheese and lemon yogurt.

CRUST
¾ cup graham cracker crumbs (12 squares)
2 tablespoons margarine or butter, melted

FILLING
1 cup boiling water
1 (3-oz.) pkg. lemon flavor gelatin
¼ cup orange juice
2 cups low-fat ricotta cheese
1 (8-oz.) container low-fat lemon yogurt
3 tablespoons sugar

TOPPING
2 tablespoons orange marmalade

½ teaspoon lemon juice

1 cup fresh fruit (blueberries, raspberries and/or strawberries)

1. Spray bottom of 8 or 9-inch springform pan with nonstick cooking spray. In small bowl, combine crust ingredients; mix well. Press in bottom of sprayed pan. Refrigerate.

2. In medium bowl, combine boiling water and gelatin; stir until dissolved. Stir in orange juice. Refrigerate 20 to 30 minutes or until lukewarm.

3. In food processor bowl with metal blade or blender container, combine ricotta cheese, yogurt and sugar; process until smooth. Gradually add to gelatin mixture in bowl, folding together until completely mixed. Pour into crust-lined pan. Refrigerate 2 to 2½ hours or until firm.

4. Just before serving, carefully remove sides of pan. In small bowl, combine orange marmalade and lemon juice; spread over top of cheesecake. Arrange fruit on top. Store in refrigerator.

Nutrition per Serving: Serving Size: ¹⁄₁₀ of Recipe. Calories 210; Calories from Fat 60; Total Fat 7g; Saturated Fat 3g; Cholesterol 15mg; Sodium 160mg; Dietary Fiber 1g

Dietary Exchange: ½ Starch, 1½ Fruit, 1 Medium-Fat Meat OR 2 Carbohydrate, 1 Medium-Fat Meat

ORANGE CHEESECAKE

◆

Yield: 12 servings; **Prep Time:** 30 minutes
(Ready in 4 hours 30 minutes)

Citrus flavors work particularly well with cheesecake, as the tang balances the rich sweetness. Stir a teaspoon of grated orange peel into the cheese mixture for even more intense orange flavor.

CRUST
1 cup vanilla wafer crumbs (20 wafers)

2 tablespoons margarine or butter, melted

FILLING
⅓ cup sugar

¾ cup orange juice

2 envelopes unflavored gelatin

1 (15-oz.) container (1¾ cups) light ricotta cheese

1 (16-oz.) container nonfat vanilla yogurt

2 tablespoons orange-flavored liqueur or orange juice, if desired

1 (11-oz.) can mandarin orange segments, well drained

1. Heat oven to 375°F. In small bowl, combine crust ingredients; mix well. Press in bottom of ungreased 9 or 10-inch springform pan. Bake at 375°F. for 8 to 10 minutes or until light golden brown. Cool.

2. Meanwhile, in small saucepan, combine sugar, orange juice and gelatin; mix well. Let stand 1 minute. Stir over medium heat until dissolved.

3. In blender container or food processor bowl with metal blade, process ricotta cheese until smooth. Add yogurt, liqueur and gelatin mixture; blend well. Stir in orange segments. Pour into partially baked crust. Cover; refrigerate at least 4 hours or until firm.

4. Just before serving, carefully remove sides of pan. Store in refrigerator.

Nutrition per Serving: Serving Size: ¹⁄₁₂ of Recipe. Calories 180; Calories from Fat 50; Total Fat 6g; Saturated Fat 3g; Cholesterol 10mg; Sodium 115mg; Dietary Fiber 1g

Dietary Exchange: 1 Starch, ½ Fruit, ½ Medium-Fat Meat, ½ Fat OR 1½ Carbohydrate, ½ Medium-Fat Meat, ½ Fat

APRICOT-YOGURT CHEESECAKE

♦

Yield: 10 servings; **Prep Time:** 30 minutes
(Ready in 8 hours 30 minutes)

Chopped almonds make the crust crunchy good. Peanuts can be substituted.

CRUST
½ cup margarine or butter
1 cup all-purpose flour
½ cup chopped almonds
¼ cup sugar

FILLING
1 envelope unflavored gelatin
1 (16-oz.) can apricot halves,
    drained, reserving ⅓ cup liquid
½ cup sugar
2 (8-oz.) pkg. cream cheese,
    softened
1 (8-oz.) container plain yogurt
1 teaspoon grated lemon peel

TOPPING
¾ cup apricot preserves
1 to 2 tablespoons amaretto*

1. Melt margarine in large skillet over low heat. Stir in all remaining crust ingredients. Cook over medium heat until mixture is golden brown and crumbly, stirring constantly. Cool slightly. Press in bottom of ungreased 9-inch springform pan. Refrigerate 30 minutes or until firm.

2. Meanwhile, in small saucepan, combine gelatin and reserved ⅓ cup apricot liquid; let stand 1 minute. Cook over low heat until dissolved, stirring constantly. Cool slightly.

3. In food processor bowl with metal blade or blender container, puree apricots. Add all remaining filling ingredients; process until smooth. Carefully stir in gelatin mixture. Pour cream cheese mixture into crust-lined pan. Refrigerate 8 hours or until set.

4. Just before serving, in small saucepan over low heat, heat preserves until melted. Stir in amaretto. Carefully remove sides of springform pan. Drizzle about 1 tablespoon preserves mixture over each serving.

*Tip: One to 2 tablespoons water and ¼ teaspoon almond extract can be substituted for the amaretto.

Nutrition per Serving: Serving Size: ¹⁄₁₀ of Recipe. Calories 510; Calories from Fat 250; Total Fat 28g; Saturated Fat 12g; Cholesterol 50mg; Sodium 270mg; Dietary Fiber 2g

Dietary Exchange: 2 ½ Starch, 1 Fruit, 5 ½ Fat OR 3 ½ Carbohydrate, 5 ½ Fat

Apricot-Yogurt Cheesecake

REFRIG-ERATED DESSERTS

✦ ✦ ✦

While warm-from-the-oven desserts have their devotees, there are those who like nothing better than a chilled confection. Refrigerated desserts run the gamut from puddings and custards to creamy and crunchy layered concoctions. Plain or fancy, the recipes in this chapter share a common theme: all are great make-ahead treats that are amony the easiest of any desserts to assemble.

LEMON BERRY TIRAMISÙ, PAGE 208

*Refrigerated desserts
are many and varied.
Some of the most common
types are explained below.*

DEFINING DESSERTS

Refrigerated desserts are many and varied. Some are a suitable finale for an elegant dinner, while others are the kind of unpretentious treat to share in the kitchen at the end of a weeknight supper. Plain or fancy, the recipes in this chapter share a common theme: all are great make-ahead treats that are among the easiest of any desserts to assemble. The more common types include:

CHIFFON. Chiffon fabric is characterized by its filmy billowiness; chiffon desserts have a light, billowy texture. As with a mousse, the light texture may be deceptive if it's due to whipped cream or another rich ingredient.

COMPOTES. Compotes, supremely homey desserts, are made of fresh or dried fruit (or a combination), sometimes gently sweetened or spiced, then simmered slowly. The finished dessert has a soft texture with richly mingled flavors.

DESSERT SQUARES. There are no hard and fast rules about "dessert squares." Even the shape into which they are cut for serving is likely not to be a true square. Most of these desserts, however, consist of layered ingredients in a square or oblong pan. There may be a cake or crumb crust and a filling of fruit or whipped cream. They're typically luscious, fairly easy to assemble in advance and ideal for potlucks and buffets because they're easy to serve.

MOUSSE. Mousse is a variant of pudding that is absolutely heavenly, at once light textured and meltingly rich. It's usually made with whipped cream and eggs, so it's easy to see why the description "light" may be misleading. Mousses are either cold (and stored in the refrigerator) or frozen.

PUDDING. Puddings fall into two general categories. The first type, made on the stove-top, is thickened with cornstarch. Custard-style puddings, in contrast, can be made in the oven or on the stove and gain their rich, smooth texture from a blend of egg and milk (or cream). They can be light, silken preparations, or hearty mixtures made with bread, noodles, rice or fruit. Most are equally good warm or cold; all should be stored in the refrigerator. Packaged mixes are usually cornstarch based and have streamlined pudding preparation.

TRIFLE. English in origin, a trifle usually refers to slices of cake, sometimes soaked in liquor or fruit juice, layered in a bowl with pudding, custard and/or whipped cream and fruit. Served in a showy clear glass serving dish, a trifle converts leftover cake into an elegant company dessert.

DRESS IT UP

From simple to showy, these presentation tips offer ideas for dressing up desserts.

+ Serve dessert in wide-mouthed champagne saucers with ribbon tied around the stems, china teacups, water goblets or sturdy coffee mugs.

+ Kids love almost anything scooped into an ice cream cone.

+ Whipped cream dresses up dessert in a snap, whether you prefer homemade, frozen whipped topping or a swirl from a pressurized can. Dollop the cream on top of each serving or make a "moat" to surround the dessert.

+ Dress up whipped cream with a few berries, a maraschino cherry, sifted cocoa, chopped nuts, sprinkles or candy-colored chocolates.

+ Serve fruit desserts with a scoop of ice cream or sorbet garnished with a mint sprig.

ORANGE-PISTACHIO CHIFFON

Yield: 4 servings; **Prep Time:** 20 minutes
(Ready in 35 minutes)

With its slightly sweet flavor, the pistachio has a natural affinity for orange, such as in this cloud of chilled chiffon-style pudding.

1 envelope unflavored gelatin
½ cup orange juice
½ cup nonfat vanilla yogurt
2 tablespoons orange-flavored
   liqueur or orange juice
1 tablespoon lemon juice
⅓ cup sugar
1½ teaspoons grated orange peel
4 ice cubes
1½ cups frozen light whipped
   topping, thawed
1 tablespoon chopped shelled
   pistachios

1. In small saucepan, sprinkle gelatin over ¼ cup of the orange juice; let stand 2 minutes to soften. Cook and stir over low heat until gelatin is dissolved. Cool 10 minutes or until slightly cooled.

2. In blender container, combine remaining ¼ cup orange juice, yogurt, liqueur, lemon juice, sugar and orange peel. Blend at high speed for 20 to 30 seconds or until combined. With blender running, add gelatin mixture and ice cubes, blending at high speed for 1 minute or until ice cubes are crushed and mixture is thoroughly combined.

3. Pour into medium bowl; gently stir in whipped topping. Pour into individual stemmed glasses. Sprinkle with pistachios. Place in refrigerator or freezer for 15 minutes to chill quickly. If desired, garnish with orange slices and fresh mint leaves. Store in refrigerator.

Nutrition per Serving: Serving Size: ¼ of Recipe. Calories 200; Calories from Fat 35; Total Fat 4g; Saturated Fat 3g; Cholesterol 0mg; Sodium 20mg; Dietary Fiber 0g

Dietary Exchange: 1 Starch, 1½ Fruit, ½ Fat OR 2½ Carbohydrate, ½ Fat

INDIVIDUAL CREME DE MENTHE MOUSSE

Yield: 6 servings; **Prep Time:** 30 minutes

A "mint condition" dessert furnishes an exclamation point for a fine meal.

1 envelope unflavored gelatin
1 cup skim milk
⅓ cup sugar
2 tablespoons green creme de
   menthe liqueur*
2 cups frozen light whipped
   topping, thawed
2 oz. white chocolate baking bar,
   grated or chopped, or ⅓ cup
   white vanilla chips, chopped

1. In small saucepan, sprinkle gelatin over ¼ cup of the milk; let stand 5 minutes to soften.

2. Place saucepan over low heat; stir until gelatin is dissolved. Add sugar; stir until dissolved.

3. In medium bowl, combine gelatin mixture, remaining ¾ cup milk and creme de menthe; blend well. If necessary, refrigerate 5 to 10 minutes or until soft-set.

4. Fold whipped topping into gelatin mixture. Divide mixture evenly into six 6-oz. custard cups or dessert dishes. Serve immediately, or cover and refrigerate until serving time.

5. Just before serving, sprinkle each serving with grated baking bar.

Tip: To substitute for liqueur, use ¼ teaspoon peppermint extract plus 2 tablespoons water. Add 2 drops green food color with whipped topping.

Nutrition per Serving: Serving Size: ⅙ of Recipe. Calories 190; Calories from Fat 50; Total Fat 6g; Saturated Fat 5g; Cholesterol 3mg; Sodium 30mg; Dietary Fiber 0g

Dietary Exchange: 1 Starch, 1 Fruit, 1 Fat OR 2 Carbohydrate, 1 Fat

TANGERINE MOUSSE

Yield: 9 (½-cup) servings;
Prep Time: 25 minutes
(Ready in 1 hour 40 minutes)

Mandarin orange segments dipped into melted chocolate make an elegant garnish for a light-textured mousse flavored with tangerine concentrate.

¼ cup sugar
2 envelopes unflavored gelatin
2 eggs or ½ cup refrigerated or frozen fat-free egg product, thawed
1 ½ cups skim milk
2 cups crushed ice
1 (6-oz.) can frozen tangerine juice concentrate*
1 (11-oz.) can mandarin orange segments, drained
2 tablespoons semi-sweet chocolate chips, melted, if desired

1. In medium saucepan, combine sugar, gelatin and eggs; beat until smooth. Stir in milk; cook over medium heat until mixture coats a spoon, stirring constantly. DO NOT BOIL. Cool slightly.

2. Pour mixture into large blender container or food processor bowl with metal blade; blend at medium speed. While blender is running, add ice and spoonfuls of tangerine concentrate, blending until ice is melted. Pour into 1 ½-quart bowl; refrigerate 10 to 15 minutes or until partially set.

3. Reserve 9 mandarin orange segments for garnish; place on paper towel. Fold remaining orange segments into mixture. Refrigerate 1 to 2 hours or until set. (If desired, mixture can be poured into individual dessert dishes before refrigerating.)

4. Dip each orange segment halfway into melted chocolate; place on waxed paper. Let stand until set. Garnish each serving with chocolate-dipped orange segment.

Tip: Frozen orange juice concentrate can be substituted for the tangerine juice concentrate.

Nutrition per Serving: Serving Size: ½ Cup. Calories 120; Calories from Fat 20; Total Fat 2g; Saturated Fat 1g; Cholesterol 50mg; Sodium 40mg; Dietary Fiber 1g

Dietary Exchange: 1 ½ Starch OR 1 ½ Carbohydrate

GINGER MOUSSE WITH STRAWBERRY SAUCE

Yield: 12 servings; **Prep Time:** 25 minutes
(Ready in 2 hours 25 minutes)

An enticing dessert, this cool mousse gets gingery zing three times over from crystallized ginger, ginger liqueur and gingersnaps.

MOUSSE
2 cups whipping cream
¼ cup sugar
3 tablespoons brandy or ginger-flavored liqueur
1 ½ cups shredded coconut
3 tablespoons chopped crystallized ginger
7 oz. (32 to 50) gingersnaps

SAUCE
2 (10-oz.) pkg. frozen sliced strawberries in syrup, thawed

1. In large bowl, combine whipping cream, sugar and brandy; beat at high speed until stiff peaks form. Fold in coconut and ginger.

2. In 1 ½-quart soufflé dish or bowl, layer cream mixture and gingersnaps, beginning and ending with cream mixture. (Cookies should be in single layer, not overlapped.) Cover; refrigerate at least 2 hours or up to 8 hours.

Ginger Mousse with Strawberry Sauce

3. Just before serving, place strawberries in blender container or food processor bowl with metal blade; blend until pureed.

4. To serve, spoon mousse into individual dessert dishes. Top each with sauce. Store in refrigerator.

Nutrition per Serving: Serving Size: $^1/_{12}$ of Recipe. Calories 340; Calories from Fat 170; Total Fat 19g; Saturated Fat 12g; Cholesterol 55mg; Sodium 150mg; Dietary Fiber 2g

Dietary Exchange: $^1/_2$ Starch, 2 Fruit, 4 Fat OR 2 $^1/_2$ Carbohydrate, 4 Fat

MARBLED CHOCOLATE TERRINE

Yield: 8 servings; **Prep Time:** 30 minutes
(Ready in 3 hours 45 minutes)

"Terrine" usually refers to a savory, layered loaf; here, chocolate and vanilla pudding gain body from gelatin and are swirled together to make a sweet dessert loaf.

VANILLA PUDDING
1 ¼ teaspoons unflavored gelatin
2 ½ cups milk
1 (4.6-oz.) pkg. (6-serving size) vanilla pudding and pie filling mix (not instant)
2 oz. white chocolate baking bar, chopped

CHOCOLATE PUDDING
1 ¼ teaspoons unflavored gelatin
2 ½ cups milk
1 (5-oz.) pkg. (6-serving size) chocolate fudge pudding and pie filling mix (not instant)
2 oz. semi-sweet chocolate, chopped

GARNISH
½ cup whipping cream, whipped
Chocolate curls, if desired

1. Line 8 × 4-inch loaf pan with plastic wrap; smooth out all wrinkles. Set aside.

2. To prepare vanilla pudding, in medium saucepan, sprinkle 1 ¼ teaspoons gelatin over 1 cup of the milk; let stand 2 minutes to soften. Add remaining 1 ½ cups milk and vanilla pudding mix. Cook over medium heat until mixture comes to a boil, stirring constantly.

3. Remove saucepan from heat; add white chocolate baking bar and stir until melted. Place plastic wrap over surface of pudding; let stand 15 minutes to cool. Meanwhile, repeat process to prepare chocolate pudding.

4. To assemble, randomly spoon each mixture into lined pan. Using narrow spatula or knife, gently swirl through mixture to marble. Cover with plastic wrap; refrigerate at least 3 hours before serving.

5. Just before serving, unmold onto serving platter. Garnish with whipped cream and chocolate curls. Cut into slices or spoon mixture to serve. Store in refrigerator.

Nutrition per Serving: Serving Size: ⅛ of Recipe. Calories 350; Calories from Fat 130; Total Fat 14g; Saturated Fat 9g; Cholesterol 35mg; Sodium 280mg; Dietary Fiber 1g

Dietary Exchange: 2 ½ Starch, 1 Fruit, 2 Fat OR 3 ½ Carbohydrate, 2 Fat

Marbled Chocolate Terrine

CHERRY SUNDAES IN CHOCOLATE MOUSSE SHELLS

✦

Yield: 4 servings; **Prep Time:** 30 minutes

Luxury on a dessert plate! Vanilla ice cream nestles inside edible cups made of frozen chocolate mousse; cherry topping and toasted almonds complete the sundae.

1 (2.8-oz.) pkg. dark chocolate mousse mix
2/3 cup cold skim milk
2 tablespoons sliced almonds
3/4 cup cherry pie filling (from 21-oz. can)
1/8 teaspoon vanilla
1 cup fat-free vanilla frozen yogurt or low-fat vanilla ice cream

1. Prepare mousse mix as directed on package, using the 2/3 cup skim milk. Spoon about 1/3 cup mousse onto center of each of 4 dessert plates. Using back of spoon, shape each into shell about 3 1/2 inches in diameter, building up edges slightly. Place mousse shells in freezer for 15 minutes to chill.

2. Meanwhile, place almonds in small nonstick skillet; toast over medium heat for 5 to 7 minutes or until lightly browned, stirring occasionally. Remove from skillet; cool.

Cherry Sundaes in Chocolate Mousse Shells

3. For topping, in small bowl, combine pie filling and vanilla.

4. Just before serving, fill each mousse shell with ¼ cup frozen yogurt. Spoon cherry topping over yogurt and mousse. Sprinkle with almonds. Serve immediately.

Nutrition per Serving: Serving Size: ¼ of Recipe. Calories 250; Calories from Fat 35; Total Fat 4g; Saturated Fat 2g; Cholesterol 3mg; Sodium 65mg; Dietary Fiber 4g

Dietary Exchange: 3 Starch OR 3 Carbohydrate

RASPBERRY-CINNAMON BREAD PUDDING

◆

Yield: 8 servings; **Prep Time:** 25 minutes
(Ready in 8 hours 25 minutes)

This recipe also works well with white, whole wheat or raisin bread.

½ cup sugar

3 tablespoons cornstarch

2 (10-oz.) pkg. frozen raspberries in syrup, thawed

12 to 14 slices cinnamon bread, crusts removed, cubed

1 cup whipping cream, whipped

1. In medium saucepan, combine sugar and cornstarch; blend well. Stir in raspberries. Cook over medium heat until mixture boils and thickens, stirring constantly. Remove from heat; cool 1 hour or until completely cooled.

2. Line 1½-quart round bowl with plastic wrap. Place 1 layer bread cubes over bottom and halfway up sides of bowl. Pour small amount of raspberry sauce over bread. Repeat, alternating layers of bread and raspberry sauce, ending with bread on top. Place plastic wrap over top of pudding. Cover with plate that fits tightly inside bowl; place heavy object on top of plate to mold pudding. Refrigerate at least 8 hours or overnight.

3. Just before serving, remove plate and plastic wrap; unmold onto serving plate. Remove plastic wrap. Frost sides of pudding with swirls of whipped cream.

Nutrition per Serving: Serving Size: ⅛ of Recipe. Calories 380; Calories from Fat 140; Total Fat 15g; Saturated Fat 7g; Cholesterol 40mg; Sodium 270mg; Dietary Fiber 3g

Dietary Exchange: 2 Starch, 2 Fruit, 2 Fat OR 4 Carbohydrate, 2 Fat

RICE CUSTARD WITH PINEAPPLE-APRICOT SAUCE

◆

Yield: 10 servings; **Prep Time:** 45 minutes

When you don't have time for an oven-baked rice pudding, try this sweet stove-top version instead.

CUSTARD

3 cups warm cooked rice (cooked as directed on package)

½ cup sugar

½ teaspoon salt

3 cups milk

2 eggs, slightly beaten

½ teaspoon almond extract

½ teaspoon vanilla

SAUCE

1 (8-oz.) can apricots, drained, reserving liquid

⅓ cup firmly packed brown sugar

1 tablespoon cornstarch

2 tablespoons lemon juice

1 (8-oz.) can crushed pineapple, undrained

1. In large saucepan, combine cooked rice, sugar, salt, milk and eggs; mix well. Cook over medium-low heat for 20 to 25 minutes or until slightly thickened, stirring frequently. DO NOT BOIL. Stir in almond extract and vanilla.

2. Meanwhile, to prepare sauce, chop apricots; place in small saucepan. Add reserved apricot liquid and remaining sauce ingredients; blend well. Cook over medium heat for about 7 minutes or until mixture boils, stirring frequently. Reduce heat; simmer 2 to 3 minutes or until thickened, stirring occasionally. Serve custard and sauce warm or cold. Store in refrigerator.

Nutrition per Serving: Serving Size: 1/10 of Recipe. Calories 240; Calories from Fat 25; Total Fat 3g; Saturated Fat 1g; Cholesterol 50mg; Sodium 160mg; Dietary Fiber 1g

Dietary Exchange: 2 Starch, 1 Fruit, ½ Fat OR 3 Carbohydrate, ½ Fat

COOKIES AND MINT CHOCOLATE PUDDING

Yield: 4 (¾-cup) servings;
Prep Time: 25 minutes

For a finishing touch, mint-flavored chocolate chips or mint candies.

¾ cup sugar
½ cup unsweetened cocoa
¼ cup cornstarch
3 cups milk
½ teaspoon mint extract
4 chocolate fudge mint cookies, coarsely chopped

1. In medium saucepan, combine sugar, cocoa and cornstarch; mix well. With wire whisk, slowly stir in milk until smooth. Bring to a boil, stirring constantly.

2. Reduce heat to medium; cook and stir with wire whisk for 8 to 12 minutes or until thickened. Remove from heat; stir in mint extract. Spoon pudding into individual dessert dishes. Cool slightly.

3. Just before serving, sprinkle with chopped cookies. Serve warm or cool.

Nutrition per Serving: Serving Size: ¾ Cup. Calories 360; Calories from Fat 60; Total Fat 7g; Saturated Fat 3g; Cholesterol 15mg; Sodium 160mg; Dietary Fiber 4g

Dietary Exchange: 3 Starch, 1½ Fruit, ½ Fat OR 4½ Carbohydrate, ½ Fat

TRIPLE CHOCOLATE PUDDING

Yield: 6 (½-cup) servings;
Prep Time: 25 minutes
(Ready in 2 hours 40 minutes)

If you judge the quality of a dessert by the intensity of the chocolate flavor, try this. Cocoa, semi-sweet chocolate and chopped-up chocolate-covered peanut butter candy add up to a rich treat.

PUDDING
2 ¼ cups milk
2 oz. semi-sweet chocolate, finely chopped
½ cup sugar*
2 tablespoons cornstarch
¼ cup unsweetened cocoa
2 eggs
2 tablespoons margarine or butter
1 teaspoon vanilla

TOPPING
½ cup whipping cream
2 tablespoons powdered sugar
1 (2.1-oz.) chocolate-covered peanut butter candy bar, chopped

1. In medium heavy saucepan, bring 2 cups of the milk to a boil. Remove from heat; stir in semi-sweet chocolate. Set aside.

2. In small bowl, combine sugar, cornstarch and cocoa; mix well. Stir in remaining ¼ cup milk.

3. With wire whisk, beat chocolate milk mixture until all chocolate is melted. Add cocoa mixture, beating until well blended. Bring to a boil over medium heat, beating constantly. Reduce heat; simmer 1 minute. Remove saucepan from heat.

4. In small bowl, beat eggs. Slowly beat in about 1 cup chocolate mixture. Add egg mixture to saucepan; cook over medium heat until mixture thickens and just begins to boil, beating constantly. Remove from heat; beat in margarine and vanilla. Place waxed paper or plastic wrap over surface of pudding. Cool 15 minutes. Refrigerate 2 hours or until cold.

5. In small bowl, beat whipping cream and powdered sugar until stiff peaks form. Fold in half of candy pieces.

6. To serve, spoon pudding into parfait glasses or dessert dishes. Top each with whipped cream mixture; sprinkle with remaining half of candy pieces. Store in refrigerator.

Tip: For a sweeter pudding, increase sugar to ⅔ cup.

Nutrition per Serving: Serving Size: ½ Cup. Calories 380; Calories from Fat 190; Total Fat 21g; Saturated Fat 10g; Cholesterol 105mg; Sodium 150mg; Dietary Fiber 2g

Dietary Exchange: 2½ Starch, 4 Fat OR 2½ Carbohydrate, 4 Fat

Triple Chocolate Pudding

2 eggs, separated
2 tablespoons sugar
¼ cup sugar
2 tablespoons quick-cooking tapioca
Dash salt
2 cups milk
1 teaspoon vanilla

1. In small bowl, beat egg whites until foamy. Gradually add 2 tablespoons sugar, beating until stiff peaks form. Set aside.

2. In medium saucepan, combine ¼ cup sugar, tapioca and salt; mix well. Stir in milk and egg yolks. Cook over medium heat for 10 to 15 minutes or until mixture comes to a full boil, stirring constantly. Remove saucepan from heat; stir in vanilla. Fold in egg white mixture. Spoon into individual dessert dishes. Cool at least 30 minutes before serving.

Tip: If desired, ½ cup finely chopped dates, peaches, apricots, strawberries, raspberries or other fruit can be folded into pudding before spooning into dishes.

Nutrition per Serving: Serving Size: ½ Cup. Calories 90; Calories from Fat 20; Total Fat 2g; Saturated Fat 1g; Cholesterol 60mg; Sodium 65mg; Dietary Fiber 0g

Dietary Exchange: 1 Starch OR 1 Carbohydrate

FLOATING ISLANDS IN LIGHT CUSTARD SAUCE

Yield: 4 servings; Prep Time: 35 minutes

The "islands" are actually ovals of soft meringue, swimming in a sea of nonfat custard. Shredded orange peel can substitute for the cocoa garnish.

SAUCE
¼ cup sugar
3 tablespoons cornstarch
2 cups skim milk
1 (8-oz.) carton (1 cup) refrigerated or frozen fat-free egg product, thawed, or 4 eggs, beaten
2 teaspoons all-natural butter-flavor granules, if desired
1 tablespoon vanilla

MERINGUES
2 egg whites
2 tablespoons sugar

GARNISH
2 teaspoons unsweetened cocoa

1. In medium saucepan, combine ¼ cup sugar and cornstarch; mix well. Slowly blend in milk. Cook over medium heat for 7 to 10 minutes or until thickened, stirring constantly. Remove from heat.

2. Place egg product in medium bowl. Slowly blend half of milk mixture into egg product. Gradually stir egg mixture into milk mixture remaining in saucepan. Cook over medium-low heat for 1 minute, stirring constantly. Remove from heat. Stir in butter-flavor granules and vanilla until smooth. Spoon sauce into 4 dessert dishes.

3. In large skillet, heat about 1 inch water over medium heat until very hot, but not boiling. In large bowl, beat egg whites at medium speed until foamy. Gradually add 2 tablespoons sugar, beating at high speed until stiff glossy peaks form. Using 2 large spoons, form meringue mixture into 4 oval shapes and drop into hot water. Cook 2 minutes, turning once.

4. With slotted spoon, remove meringues from water; place over sauce in dessert dishes. Lightly sprinkle meringues with cocoa. Store in refrigerator.

Nutrition per Serving: Serving Size: ¼ of Recipe. Calories 180; Calories from Fat 0; Total Fat 0g; Saturated Fat 0g; Cholesterol 2mg; Sodium 280mg; Dietary Fiber 0g

Dietary Exchange: 1 Starch, 1 Fruit, 1 Very Lean Meat OR 2 Carbohydrate, 1 Very Lean Meat

CHOCOLATE RICE MOLD

◆

Yield: 12 servings; 2 cups custard;
Prep Time: 1 hour 35 minutes
(Ready in 3 hours 50 minutes)

Europe's answer to America's oven-baked rice pudding, Chocolate Rice Mold sets up with gelatin. A vanilla custard sauce, prepared separately on the stove-top, graces the chilled dessert.

RICE MOLD
Sugar
2 ½ cups milk
½ cup uncooked regular long-grain white rice
½ cup sugar
2 envelopes unflavored gelatin
7 oz. semi-sweet chocolate, cut up
2 tablespoons margarine or butter
1 teaspoon vanilla
1 cup whipping cream, whipped

CUSTARD
3 eggs, well beaten
¼ cup sugar
Dash salt
1 ¼ cups half-and-half or milk
1 teaspoon vanilla

1. Spray 5-cup mold with non-stick cooking spray; sprinkle with sugar. In medium saucepan, bring milk to a boil over medium heat.

Stir in rice. Reduce heat; simmer about 5 minutes, stirring constantly. Cover; cook about 45 minutes or until milk is almost absorbed and rice is tender and creamy, stirring occasionally.

2. In small bowl, combine ½ cup sugar and gelatin; stir into rice mixture until dissolved. Stir in chocolate, margarine and 1 teaspoon vanilla. Cool 30 minutes or until completely cooled, stirring occasionally.

3. Reserve 2 to 3 tablespoons whipped cream for garnish. Fold remaining whipped cream into rice mixture. Pour into sprayed mold. Cover; refrigerate at least 2 hours. Place serving platter in refrigerator to chill.

4. Meanwhile, to prepare custard, in heavy saucepan or in top of double boiler, combine eggs, ¼ cup sugar and salt. Gradually stir in half-and-half. Cook over low heat, stirring constantly, until mixture coats spoon, about 10 minutes. DO NOT BOIL. Remove from heat; stir in 1 teaspoon vanilla. Cover; refrigerate until cool.

5. Just before serving, dip mold into hot water. Invert and shake onto chilled serving platter. Garnish with reserved whipped cream and, if desired, chocolate curls. Serve with custard. Store any re-

maining dessert and custard in refrigerator.

Nutrition per Serving: Serving Size: ¹⁄₁₂ of Recipe. Calories 340; Calories from Fat 170; Total Fat 19g; Saturated Fat 11g; Cholesterol 95mg; Sodium 95mg; Dietary Fiber 1g

Dietary Exchange: 2 Starch, 4 Fat OR 2 Carbohydrate, 4 Fat

ORANGE CRUNCH PARFAITS

Yield: 8 (½-cup) servings;
Prep Time: 15 minutes

While you might wish to make and chill the pudding in advance, save the actual layering of parfait ingredients until just before serving to retain crispness of the nut–cookie crumb mixture.

1 tablespoon margarine or butter
¼ cup chopped nuts
12 vanilla wafers, coarsely crushed (½ cup)
½ teaspoon cinnamon
1 (3.4-oz.) pkg. instant vanilla pudding and pie filling mix
2 cups cold milk
1 (16-oz.) container vanilla yogurt
¼ cup orange spreadable fruit or orange marmalade

1. Melt margarine in small skillet over low heat. Add nuts; cook 3 minutes or until toasted, stirring frequently. Remove from heat; stir in wafer crumbs and cinnamon. Set aside.

2. In large bowl, combine pudding mix and milk; beat with wire whisk for 1 to 2 minutes or until well blended. In small bowl, combine yogurt and spreadable fruit; blend well.

3. Just before serving, spoon 2 tablespoons pudding into each of 8 small parfait glasses or dessert dishes. Top each with 2 tablespoons yogurt mixture and 2 teaspoons crumb mixture. Repeat layers. Serve immediately.

Nutrition per Serving: Serving Size: ½ Cup. Calories 230; Calories from Fat 60; Total Fat 7g; Saturated Fat 2g; Cholesterol 5mg; Sodium 290mg; Dietary Fiber 1g

Dietary Exchange: 2 Starch, ½ Fruit, 1 Fat OR 2 ½ Carbohydrate, 1 Fat

CRANBERRY-RASPBERRY TRIFLE SQUARES

Yield: 10 servings; Prep Time: 25 minutes
(Ready in 4 hours 25 minutes)

For a racier dessert, replace 2 tablespoons of the juice concentrate with 2 tablespoons of rum, brandy or orange or raspberry liqueur.

BASE
1 (12-oz.) pkg. frozen raspberries, thawed
1 (10.75-oz.) frozen pound cake
6 tablespoons frozen raspberry-cranberry juice concentrate, thawed

FILLING
1 (5.1-oz.) pkg. (6-serving size) instant vanilla pudding and pie filling mix
2 cups milk
¾ cup purchased eggnog

TOPPING
1 cup whipping cream
1 tablespoon sugar

GARNISH
Fresh raspberries, if desired
Tiny mint sprigs, if desired

1. Drain raspberries on several layers of paper towels. Set aside.

2. Cut pound cake crosswise into 10 slices. Arrange in 2 rows in ungreased 12 × 8-inch (2-quart) baking dish. Spoon juice concentrate over cake; top with drained raspberries.

3. In medium bowl, combine all filling ingredients; beat at low speed for 2 minutes. Pour over raspberries. Let stand 5 minutes to set.

4. Meanwhile, in small bowl, combine topping ingredients; beat until soft peaks form. DO NOT OVERBEAT. Carefully spread over pudding. Cover; refrigerate at least 4 hours or overnight.

5. To serve, cut into squares. Garnish each serving with fresh raspberries and mint sprig. Store in refrigerator.

Nutrition per Serving: Serving Size: ⅟₁₀ of Recipe. Calories 380; Calories from Fat 150; Total Fat 17g; Saturated Fat 8g; Cholesterol 65mg; Sodium 370mg; Dietary Fiber 2g

Dietary Exchange: 1 ½ Starch, 2 Fruit, 3 Fat OR 3 ½ Carbohydrate, 3 Fat

FRESH FRUIT TRIFLE

◆

Yield: 10 servings; **Prep Time:** 15 minutes
(Ready in 2 hours 15 minutes)

If you prefer, substitute regular instant pudding mix for the sugar-free version. Sponge cake or any other leftover cake can be used, too.

1 ¼ cups skim milk
½ cup low-fat plain yogurt
1 teaspoon grated orange peel
1 (1-oz.) pkg. instant sugar-free vanilla pudding and pie filling mix
8 cups angel food cake cubes
4 cups sliced fresh fruit (grapes, nectarines, oranges, pineapple and/or strawberries)

1. In medium bowl, combine milk, yogurt and orange peel; blend well. Add pudding mix; beat until well blended. Let stand 5 minutes.

2. In large serving bowl, layer half of cake cubes, ⅓ of fruit and half of pudding mixture. Repeat layers. Arrange remaining fruit over top. Cover; refrigerate at least 2 hours or up to 6 hours.

Nutrition per Serving: Serving Size: ¹⁄₁₀ of Recipe. Calories 150; Calories from Fat 10; Total Fat 1g; Saturated Fat 0g; Cholesterol 0mg; Sodium 390mg; Dietary Fiber 2g

Dietary Exchange: 1 Starch, 1 Fruit OR 2 Carbohydrate

Fresh Fruit Trifle

FRESH FRUIT CHOCOLATE TRIFLE

◆

Yield: 16 servings; **Prep Time:** 15 minutes
(Ready in 1 hour 15 minutes)

Trifle, which probably came about as a way for the British to use up leftover cake by mixing it with custard, is less exact than many other recipes. As long as you measure the milk for the pudding mix, a little more or a little less of the ingredients specified won't matter.

1 loaf angel food or sponge cake (about 9 × 5 inches)
1 (3.9-oz.) pkg. instant chocolate fudge pudding and pie filling mix
2 cups skim milk
1 teaspoon vanilla
2 cups cut-up fresh fruit (apricots, bananas, mangoes, nectarines, peaches, pineapple and/or strawberries)*
1 cup frozen light whipped topping, thawed
1 tablespoon grated chocolate or 1 teaspoon chocolate sprinkles
1 tablespoon sliced almonds

1. Cut cake into ¾-inch cubes. Place half of cake cubes in bottom of 2 to 2 ½-quart clear glass bowl or soufflé dish.

2. Prepare pudding as directed on package using the 2 cups skim milk. Stir in vanilla. Top cake with half of pudding. Arrange half of fruit over pudding. Repeat layers, ending with fruit. Top with whipped topping. Cover; refrigerate about 1 hour or until thoroughly chilled.

3. Just before serving, sprinkle with grated chocolate and sliced almonds. Store in refrigerator.

Tip: Sprinkle fruits that darken, such as bananas, nectarines and peaches, with lemon juice before assembling trifle.

Nutrition per Serving: Serving Size: ¹⁄₁₆ of Recipe. Calories 110; Calories from Fat 10; Total Fat 1g; Saturated Fat 1g; Cholesterol 0mg; Sodium 260mg; Dietary Fiber 1g

Dietary Exchange: 1 Starch, ½ Fruit OR 1 ½ Carbohydrate

TROPICAL TRIFLE SQUARES

✦

Yield: 10 servings; **Prep Time:** 45 minutes
(Ready in 4 hours 45 minutes)

Winter got you down? Take a culinary trip to somewhere exotic with this easy dessert, bursting with the tropical flavors of mango, pineapple, kiwi fruit, coconut and rum.

2 (3-oz.) pkg. vanilla pudding and
  pie filling mix (not instant)
3 ½ cups milk
½ cup coconut
1 (10.75-oz.) frozen pound cake,
  cut into ½-inch slices
¼ cup light rum
¼ cup pineapple juice
2 ripe mangoes, peeled, seeded
  and sliced
2 ripe kiwi fruit, peeled, halved
  lengthwise and sliced
1 ½ cups whipping cream
3 tablespoons powdered sugar

1. In medium saucepan, combine pudding mix and milk. Cook over medium heat until mixture boils, stirring constantly. Remove from heat. Stir in coconut. Cover surface of pudding with plastic wrap; cool 15 minutes.

2. Meanwhile, arrange cake slices in bottom of ungreased 13 × 9-inch (3-quart) baking dish, cutting pieces as necessary to fit.

3. In glass measuring cup, combine rum and pineapple juice;

Tropical Trifle Squares

drizzle over cake slices. Arrange mangoes and kiwi fruit over cake. Spoon pudding evenly over fruit. Cover; refrigerate 4 hours or overnight.

4. In small bowl, combine whipping cream and powdered sugar; beat until soft peaks form. Carefully spread over pudding.

5. To serve, cut into squares. Store in refrigerator.

Nutrition per Serving: Serving Size: $\frac{1}{10}$ of Recipe. Calories 440; Calories from Fat 200; Total Fat 22g; Saturated Fat 12g; Cholesterol 75mg; Sodium 320mg; Dietary Fiber 2g

Dietary Exchange: 2 Starch, 1 $\frac{1}{2}$ Fruit, 4 Fat OR 3 $\frac{1}{2}$ Carbohydrate, 4 Fat

FRESH LEMON AND CREAM CHEESE TRIFLE

◆

Yield: 12 servings; **Prep Time:** 30 minutes
(Ready in 4 hours 30 minutes)

Layers of luscious lemon and ladyfingers—lovely!

2 (8-oz.) pkg. fat-free cream cheese
2 (3.4-oz.) pkg. instant lemon pudding and pie filling mix
2 cups skim milk
1 tablespoon grated lemon peel
1 cup lemon juice (4 to 5 lemons)
1 (8-oz.) container frozen light whipped topping, thawed
3 (3-oz.) pkg. ladyfingers, split

1. In food processor bowl with metal blade, combine cream cheese, pudding mixes, milk, lemon peel and lemon juice; process until smooth.* Gently fold in whipped topping until well blended.

2. Arrange $\frac{1}{3}$ of split ladyfingers in bottom of 13 × 9-inch (3-quart) baking dish. Spoon $\frac{1}{3}$ of pudding mixture evenly over ladyfingers. Repeat layers 2 more times. Cover with plastic wrap; refrigerate at least 4 hours or overnight.

3. To serve, cut into squares. If desired, garnish each serving with thin lemon twists and fresh mint leaves. Store in refrigerator.

Tip: If food processor is unavailable, beat cream cheese in large bowl with electric mixer until fluffy. Add milk; beat well. Gradually add 1 package pudding mix and lemon juice; beat until blended. Add remaining pudding mix and lemon peel; beat until well combined.

Nutrition per Serving: Serving Size: $\frac{1}{12}$ of Recipe. Calories 210; Calories from Fat 25; Total Fat 3g; Saturated Fat 3g; Cholesterol 35mg; Sodium 510mg; Dietary Fiber 0g

Dietary Exchange: 2 $\frac{1}{2}$ Starch OR 2 $\frac{1}{2}$ Carbohydrate

BERRY DELIGHT

Yield: 8 servings; **Prep Time:** 15 minutes

Whipped topping folded into chocolate pudding makes a heavenly topping for an angel food base.

8 ($\frac{1}{2}$-inch) slices angel food cake
1 (3.9-oz.) pkg. instant chocolate pudding and pie filling mix
1 cup skim milk
1 $\frac{1}{2}$ cups frozen light whipped topping, thawed
3 cups quartered fresh strawberries

1. Line bottom of 12 × 8-inch (2-quart) baking dish with cake slices, overlapping slightly. Prepare pudding mix as directed on package using *only* the 1 cup skim milk.

2. When pudding mixture is slightly thickened, fold in 1 cup of the whipped topping. Spread pudding mixture evenly over cake layer in dish. Top with strawberries. Serve immediately, or cover and refrigerate until serving time.

3. Just before serving, cut into squares. Top each serving with 1 tablespoon of the remaining whipped topping. If desired, garnish with fresh mint sprigs. Store in refrigerator.

Nutrition per Serving: Serving Size: $\frac{1}{8}$ of Recipe. Calories 170; Calories from Fat 20; Total Fat 2g; Saturated Fat 2g; Cholesterol 0mg; Sodium 400mg; Dietary Fiber 2g

Dietary Exchange: 1 Starch, 1 $\frac{1}{2}$ Fruit OR 2 $\frac{1}{2}$ Carbohydrate

BLUEBERRY, PEACHES 'N CREAM ANGEL FOOD DESSERT

Yield: 24 servings; **Prep Time:** 15 minutes
(Ready in 3 hours 30 minutes)

Since the angel food cubes soften up when folded into the creamy filling, day-old cake is ideal as it will hold its shape better. If you want to substitute fresh peaches for the canned, toss the slices with a little orange juice to keep the color bright.

1 (14-oz.) can sweetened condensed milk (not evaporated)
1 cup water
1 (3.4-oz.) pkg. instant banana cream or vanilla pudding and pie filling mix
1 cup whipping cream, whipped
10 cups cubed angel food cake
1 (29-oz.) can sliced peaches in heavy syrup, well drained
½ cup fresh or frozen blueberries

1. In large bowl, combine condensed milk and water. Add pudding mix; beat at low speed for 1 to 2 minutes or until smooth. Refrigerate 15 minutes or until thickened.

2. Fold in whipped cream. Add angel food cake cubes; fold gently to combine. Spoon into ungreased 13×9-inch pan. Top evenly with peach slices. Refrigerate at least 3 hours before serving.

3. Just before serving, sprinkle blueberries over top. Cut into squares. Store in refrigerator.

Nutrition per Serving: Serving Size: ¹⁄₂₄ of Recipe. Calories 170; Calories from Fat 45; Total Fat 5g; Saturated Fat 3g; Cholesterol 20mg; Sodium 260mg; Dietary Fiber 1g

Dietary Exchange: 1 Starch, 1 Fruit, ½ Fat OR 2 Carbohydrate, ½ Fat

RASPBERRY PRETZEL DELIGHT

Yield: 16 servings; **Prep Time:** 30 minutes
(Ready in 2 hours 30 minutes)

As anyone who loves a margarita or salted nuts atop an ice cream sundae will tell you, a little bit of salt can bring out the flavor of sweet ingredients. Here, a salty pretzel crust offsets a sweet filling.

CRUST
1 ½ cups crushed pretzels
¼ cup sugar
½ cup margarine or butter, melted

FILLING
1 (12-oz.) can sweetened condensed milk (not evaporated)
½ cup water
1 (3.4-oz.) pkg. instant vanilla pudding and pie filling mix
1 (4-oz.) container (1 ½ cups) frozen whipped topping, thawed

TOPPING
1 (21-oz.) can raspberry pie filling

1. Heat oven to 350°F. In large bowl, combine all crust ingredients; mix well. Press in bottom of ungreased 13×9-inch pan. Bake at 350°F. for 8 minutes. Cool 10 minutes.

2. Meanwhile, in same large bowl, combine condensed milk and water; blend well. Add pudding mix; beat 2 minutes. Refrigerate 5 minutes. Fold in whipped topping. Spread over cooled baked crust. Refrigerate about 1 hour or until filling is firm.

3. Spoon raspberry pie filling over filling. Cover; refrigerate at least 1 hour or until serving time.

4. To serve, cut into squares. If desired, garnish with additional whipped topping, fresh raspberries and mint leaves. Store in refrigerator.

Nutrition per Serving: Serving Size: ¹⁄₁₆ of Recipe. Calories 250; Calories from Fat 90; Total Fat 10g; Saturated Fat 4g; Cholesterol 5mg; Sodium 280mg; Dietary Fiber 1g

Dietary Exchange: 1 Starch, 1 ½ Fruit, 2 Fat OR 2 ½ Carbohydrate, 2 Fat

VARIATIONS

Blueberry Pretzel Delight: Substitute 21-oz. can blueberry pie filling for raspberry pie filling.
Cherry Pretzel Delight: Substitute 21-oz. can cherry pie filling for raspberry pie filling.

Raspberry Pretzel Delight

LIGHT TIRAMISÙ

✦

Yield: 12 servings; Prep Time: 25 minutes
(Ready in 4 hours 25 minutes)

"Pick me up," the rough translation of the Italian tiramisù, *refers to the indisputable restorative properties of this tasty dessert made from coffee-dipped cake layered with chocolate and cream cheese blended with whipped cream. In Italy,* tiramisù *is made with mascarpone, a rich spreadable cheese with a slight tang that's pleasing in combination with the flavors of the strong coffee and the sweet cream.*

8 oz. semi-sweet chocolate
¼ cup refrigerated or frozen fat-
    free egg product, thawed
1 cup sugar
1½ teaspoons vanilla
1 (8-oz.) pkg. fat-free cream
    cheese, cut into pieces, room
    temperature
1 tablespoon instant espresso
    powder
¼ cup hot water
1 cup cold water
1 (13.5-oz.) fat-free pound cake or
    1 (10.75-oz.) frozen reduced-fat
    pound cake, thawed, cut into
    ½-inch slices
1 (8-oz.) container frozen light
    whipped topping, thawed

1. In food processor bowl with metal blade, finely chop chocolate. Set aside.

2. In food processor bowl with metal blade, process egg product and sugar for 30 seconds. Add vanilla; process 1 minute or until pale yellow. Add cream cheese pieces, a few at a time, processing until smooth. Spoon mixture into medium bowl. Cover; refrigerate 1 hour.

3. In shallow dish, dissolve espresso powder in ¼ cup hot water; add 1 cup cold water. Quickly dip cake slices into espresso, turning to coat all sides. Arrange slices in bottom of ungreased 13 × 9-inch (3-quart) baking dish or 12-cup shallow dish, smoothing with fingers to mold cake slices together. Sprinkle with half of the chopped chocolate.

4. Fold whipped topping into cream cheese mixture. Spoon and spread over chocolate. Sprinkle with remaining chocolate. Cover; refrigerate at least 3 hours or overnight.

5. To serve, cut into squares. Store in refrigerator.

Nutrition per Serving: Serving Size: ¹⁄₁₂ of Recipe. Calories 310; Calories from Fat 70; Total Fat 8g; Saturated Fat 6g; Cholesterol 3mg; Sodium 240mg; Dietary Fiber 1g

Dietary Exchange: 2 Starch, 1½ Fruit, 1½ Fat OR 3½ Carbohydrate, 1½ Fat

Light Tiramisù

LEMON BERRY TIRAMISÙ

✦

Yield: 12 servings; **Prep Time:** 25 minutes
(Ready in 55 minutes)

*The technique of layering ladyfingers
with a cheesy filling translates very
well to this new version using lemon,
orange and berries.*

1/3 cup frozen pineapple-orange-
   strawberry juice concentrate,
   thawed
3 tablespoons orange-flavored
   liqueur or orange juice
1 cup light ricotta cheese
4 oz. 1/3-less-fat cream cheese
   (Neufchatel), softened
1 (15.75-oz.) can lemon pie filling
2 (3-oz.) pkg. ladyfingers, split
1 pint (2 cups) fresh strawberries,
   sliced
1/2 pint (1 cup) fresh raspberries

1. In small bowl, combine juice
concentrate and liqueur; blend
well. Set aside.

2. In large bowl, combine ricotta cheese and cream cheese;
beat at medium speed until
smooth. Add pie filling; beat until
well blended and fluffy, scraping
sides of bowl occasionally.

3. Line bottom of 12 × 8-inch
(2-quart) baking dish with half of
ladyfingers, cut side up. Brush
ladyfingers with half of juice concentrate mixture. Spread half of
lemon filling evenly over lady-

fingers. Top with half each of
strawberries and raspberries. Repeat layers. Cover; refrigerate
30 minutes or until serving time.
To serve, cut into squares. Store in
refrigerator.

Nutrition per Serving: Serving Size: 1/12 of Recipe.
Calories 210; Calories from Fat 50; Total Fat 6g; Saturated Fat 3g; Cholesterol 65mg; Sodium 130mg; Dietary Fiber 2g

Dietary Exchange: 1 1/2 Starch, 1/2 Fruit, 1/2 Medium-
Fat Meat, 1/2 Fat OR 2 Carbohydrate, 1/2 Medium-Fat
Meat, 1/2 Fat

CHERRY-BLUEBERRY DESSERT SQUARES

Yield: 15 servings; **Prep Time:** 30 minutes
(Ready in 2 hours 15 minutes)

*Tote this beautiful layered dessert
along to your next gathering.*

CRUST
1 1/2 cups finely crushed pretzels*
2 tablespoons sugar
3/4 cup margarine or butter, melted

FILLING
1 (8-oz.) pkg. cream cheese,
   softened
1/2 cup sugar
1 (4-oz.) container (1 1/2 cups)
   frozen whipped topping,
   thawed
1 (3-oz.) pkg. black raspberry
   flavor gelatin
1 cup boiling water
1/2 cup cold water

1 (16-oz.) pkg. frozen blueberries
1 (21-oz.) can cherry pie filling

GARNISH
15 miniature pretzel twists,
   if desired

1. Heat oven to 350°F. In
medium bowl, combine all crust
ingredients; mix well. Press in bottom of ungreased 13 × 9-inch pan.
Bake at 350°F. for 10 minutes.
Cool 15 minutes.

2. In large bowl, combine
cream cheese and 1/2 cup sugar;
beat until well blended. Fold in
whipped topping. Spread evenly
over cooled crust. Cover; refrigerate 30 minutes.

3. In medium bowl, dissolve
gelatin in boiling water. Stir in
cold water and frozen blueberries
until mixture is partially set. (If
necessary, chill until partially set.)
Spoon gelatin mixture over cream
cheese filling. Cover; refrigerate
about 1 hour or until set.

4. Just before serving, carefully
spoon pie filling evenly over blueberry mixture. Cut into squares.
Garnish each serving with pretzel
twist. Store in refrigerator.

*Tip: To crush pretzels, place in
plastic bag and seal; crush with
rolling pin. Or crush in food processor bowl with metal blade.*

Nutrition per Serving: Serving Size: 1/15 of Recipe.
Calories 330; Calories from Fat 150; Total Fat 17g;
Saturated Fat 7g; Cholesterol 15mg; Sodium 370mg;
Dietary Fiber 1g

Dietary Exchange: 1 Starch, 1 1/2 Fruit, 3 1/2 Fat OR 2 1/2
Carbohydrate, 3 1/2 Fat

Lime-Kiwi Cloud with Strawberry Sauce

LIME-KIWI CLOUD WITH STRAWBERRY SAUCE

◆

Yield: 15 servings; **Prep Time**: 30 minutes
(Ready in 3 hours 30 minutes)

Serve this attractive dessert to coordinate with a Christmas color scheme or try it as a make-ahead treat to beat the summer heat.

DESSERT
1 large angel food cake, cut into
    1-inch cubes (about 12 cups)
2 (6-oz.) containers custard-style
    vanilla yogurt

2 teaspoons grated lime peel
¼ cup lime juice
1 (8-oz.) container frozen light
    whipped topping, thawed
6 kiwi fruit, peeled, sliced

SAUCE
2 (10-oz.) pkg. frozen strawberries
    in syrup, thawed
2 teaspoons cornstarch

1. Arrange half of cake cubes in ungreased 13 × 9-inch (3-quart) baking dish.

2. In large bowl, combine yogurt, lime peel and lime juice; blend well. Fold in whipped topping. Spoon half of mixture over cake cubes in dish; press down to smooth layer. Arrange sliced kiwi fruit over mixture. Repeat cake and yogurt layers; press down. Cover; refrigerate 3 hours or until set.

3. Meanwhile, drain strawberries, reserving liquid in medium saucepan. Stir in cornstarch; blend well. Bring to a boil over medium heat, stirring constantly. Remove from heat; cool 15 minutes. Stir in strawberries. Refrigerate 30 minutes or until chilled.

4. To serve, cut into squares. Spoon sauce over each serving. Store in refrigerator.

Nutrition per Serving: Serving Size: ¹⁄₁₅ of Recipe. Calories 190; Calories from Fat 35; Total Fat 4g; Saturated Fat 4g; Cholesterol 0mg; Sodium 190mg; Dietary Fiber 2g

Dietary Exchange: 1 Starch, 1 ½ Fruit, ½ Fat OR 2 ½ Carbohydrate, ½ Fat

CHERRY CREAM TORTE

Yield: 9 servings; **Prep Time:** 15 minutes
(Ready in 1 hour 15 minutes)

Pleasantly tangy owing to the inclusion of buttermilk and sour cream, the no-bake filling requires no cooking at all. To vary the presentation, try blueberry pie filling instead of cherry.

CRUST
½ cup finely crushed pretzels*
2 tablespoons sugar
2 tablespoons margarine or butter, melted

FILLING
1 (5.1-oz.) pkg. (6-serving size) instant vanilla pudding and pie filling mix
1 (8-oz.) container light sour cream
1 cup nonfat buttermilk**

TOPPING
1 cup light cherry pie filling (from 20-oz. can), chilled

1. In small bowl, combine all crust ingredients; mix well. Press in bottom of ungreased 8-inch square pan.

2. In medium bowl, combine all filling ingredients; beat at low speed until smooth and thickened. (Mixture will be of frosting consistency.) Spread evenly over crust. Cover; refrigerate at least 1 hour or until set.

3. Just before serving, cut into squares. Top each serving with dollop of pie filling.

*Tips: *To crush pretzels, place in plastic bag and seal; crush with rolling pin. Or crush in food processor bowl with metal blade.*

**To substitute for buttermilk, use 1 tablespoon vinegar or lemon juice plus skim milk to make 1 cup.

Nutrition per Serving: Serving Size: ⅑ of Recipe. Calories 190; Calories from Fat 45; Total Fat 5g; Saturated Fat 2g; Cholesterol 10mg; Sodium 370mg; Dietary Fiber 0g

Dietary Exchange: 1 Starch, 1 Fruit, 1 Fat OR 2 Carbohydrate, 1 Fat

LEMON BAVARIAN DESSERT

Yield: 20 servings; **Prep Time:** 35 minutes
(Ready in 1 hour 5 minutes)

Bavarian cream is a custard-style filling lightened with whipped cream and set with gelatin.

2 envelopes unflavored gelatin
¼ cup cold water
4 eggs
1 ¼ cups sugar
½ cup lemon juice
32 ice cubes
4 teaspoons grated lemon peel
18 ladyfingers (from two 3-oz. pkg.), split

⅓ cup frozen raspberry juice concentrate, thawed, or raspberry-flavored liqueur
1 (8-oz.) container frozen light whipped topping, thawed
½ pint (1 cup) fresh raspberries

1. In small bowl, sprinkle gelatin over cold water; let stand 5 minutes to soften. In another small bowl, beat eggs slightly; set aside.

2. In medium saucepan, combine sugar and lemon juice; cook and stir over medium-high heat for about 4 minutes or until mixture is very hot and sugar is dissolved. Add softened gelatin; stir until dissolved.

3. Slowly blend half of hot lemon mixture into beaten eggs. Reduce heat to low; gradually stir egg mixture into remaining hot lemon mixture. Cook 1 minute, stirring constantly. (Mixture will not thicken.) Remove from heat.

4. Pour half of lemon mixture into blender container. Add half of ice cubes. Cover; blend until smooth. Pour into medium bowl. Repeat with remaining lemon mixture and remaining ice cubes. Add to bowl. Stir in lemon peel. Freeze 5 to 10 minutes or until mixture is partially set.

5. Meanwhile, line bottom of ungreased 13×9-inch (3-quart) baking dish with 24 ladyfinger halves, cut side up. Cut remaining 12 ladyfinger halves in half crosswise; arrange around inside edges

Lemon Bavarian Dessert

of dish, cut side facing in. Brush ladyfingers with raspberry juice concentrate.

6. Place whipped topping in large bowl. Fold partially set lemon mixture into whipped topping.

Spoon mixture into ladyfinger-lined dish. Sprinkle raspberries over top. Cover; refrigerate 20 to 30 minutes or until mixture is set.

7. To serve, cut into squares. Store in refrigerator.

Nutrition per Serving: Serving Size: 1/20 of Recipe. Calories 130; Calories from Fat 25; Total Fat 3g; Saturated Fat 2g; Cholesterol 50mg; Sodium 35mg; Dietary Fiber 1g

Dietary Exchange: 1 Starch, 1/2 Fruit, 1/2 Fat OR 1 1/2 Carbohydrate, 1/2 Fat

STRAWBERRY CELEBRATION DESSERT

◆

Yield: 16 servings; Prep Time: 25 minutes
(Ready in 2 hours 55 minutes)

Here's an alternative to a strawberry pie, perfect for a family gathering.

CRUST
1 ½ cups graham cracker crumbs
(24 squares)
¼ cup sugar
⅓ cup margarine or butter, melted

FILLING
3 cups miniature marshmallows
½ cup orange juice
2 cups whipping cream, whipped
¼ teaspoon almond extract
2 pints (4 cups) fresh strawberries, sliced

1. In small bowl, combine all crust ingredients; mix well. Press in bottom of ungreased 13×9-inch pan. Refrigerate to cool.

2. Meanwhile, in medium saucepan, combine marshmallows and orange juice; cook over low heat until marshmallows are melted, stirring constantly. Cool 30 minutes.

3. Fold whipped cream and almond extract into marshmallow mixture. Spoon half of whipped cream mixture over crust. Arrange strawberries evenly over whipped cream mixture. Top with remaining whipped cream mixture. Refrigerate 2 to 3 hours to blend flavors.

4. To serve, cut into squares. If desired, garnish each serving with additional strawberries. Store in refrigerator.

Nutrition per Serving: Serving Size: ¹⁄₁₆ of Recipe. Calories 240; Calories from Fat 140; Total Fat 16g; Saturated Fat 8g; Cholesterol 40mg; Sodium 105mg; Dietary Fiber 1g

Dietary Exchange: ½ Starch, 1 Fruit, 3 Fat OR 1 ½ Carbohydrate, 3 Fat

STRAWBERRY-VANILLA LAYERED DESSERT

◆

Yield: 20 servings; Prep Time: 30 minutes

Thanks to the coldness of the frozen strawberries, the gelatin mixture sets up quickly. Unlike many gelatin-based concoctions, this dessert can be served as soon as it's assembled.

⅓ cup graham cracker crumbs
(6 squares)
5 (8-oz.) containers low-fat plain yogurt
2 (5.1-oz.) or 3 (3.4-oz.) pkg. instant vanilla pudding and pie filling mix
2 envelopes unflavored gelatin
⅔ cup water
¼ cup sugar
2 (10-oz.) pkg. frozen strawberries in syrup
1 (8-oz.) container frozen light whipped topping, thawed
20 fresh strawberries

1. Generously spray 13×9-inch (3-quart) baking dish with nonstick cooking spray. Add graham cracker crumbs; tilt dish to coat bottom evenly.

2. In large bowl, combine yogurt and pudding mix; beat at low speed for 2 minutes or until mixture thickens. Carefully spoon small mounds into crumb-coated dish; gently spread into even layer. Cover; refrigerate while preparing strawberry topping.

3. In small saucepan, sprinkle gelatin over water. Let stand 1 minute to soften. Heat over low heat until dissolved, stirring frequently. Add sugar; cook and stir until dissolved. Pour mixture into blender container.

4. Break up frozen strawberries and syrup into chunks. Add to gelatin mixture all at once; blend until smooth. Scrape down sides of blender container as necessary during blending. (Mixture will set up quickly.)

5. In large bowl, combine strawberry mixture and whipped topping; stir gently until well blended. Spoon small mounds onto pudding mixture; gently spread into even layer. Serve immediately, or cover and refrigerate until serving time.

6. Just before serving, top with fresh strawberries. Cut into squares. Store in refrigerator.

Nutrition per Serving: Serving Size: 1/20 of Recipe. Calories 170; Calories from Fat 25; Total Fat 3g; Saturated Fat 2g; Cholesterol 3mg; Sodium 260mg; Dietary Fiber 1g

Dietary Exchange: 1 Starch, 1 Fruit, 1/2 Fat OR 2 Carbohydrate, 1/2 Fat

STRAWBERRY-RHUBARB ANGEL SQUARES

✦

Yield: 12 servings; **Prep Time**: 15 minutes
(Ready in 5 hours 15 minutes)

Celebrate spring with this pretty pink-and-white dessert, rich with layers of whipped cream, strawberry-rhubarb filling and angel cake cubes.

2 cups chopped fresh or frozen rhubarb
2 cups water
2 (3-oz.) pkg. strawberry flavor gelatin
1 (10-oz.) pkg. frozen strawberries in syrup
1 1/2 cups whipping cream
1 (14-oz.) loaf angel food cake, cut into 1-inch cubes

1. In medium saucepan, combine rhubarb and water. Cook over high heat for 8 to 10 minutes or until mixture comes to a boil. Stir in gelatin; cook an additional 2 minutes, stirring frequently.

2. Add frozen strawberries; stir until strawberries break apart. Refrigerate 2 to 3 hours or until mixture begins to thicken.

3. In small deep bowl, beat whipping cream at high speed until stiff peaks form.

4. In ungreased 12 × 8-inch (2-quart) baking dish, layer half each of cake cubes, rhubarb mixture and whipped cream. Repeat layers. Refrigerate at least 3 hours or until set.

5. To serve, cut into squares. Store in refrigerator.

Nutrition per Serving: Serving Size: 1/12 of Recipe. Calories 280; Calories from Fat 100; Total Fat 11g; Saturated Fat 7g; Cholesterol 40mg; Sodium 300mg; Dietary Fiber 1g

Dietary Exchange: 1 1/2 Starch, 1 Fruit, 2 Fat OR 2 1/2 Carbohydrate, 2 Fat

FRESH FRUIT YOGURT DESSERT

✦

Yield: 9 servings; **Prep Time**: 25 minutes
(Ready in 2 hours 25 minutes)

Vanilla wafer crumbs and chopped walnuts make a tasty crust for a cool and lofty raspberry filling.

CRUST
1 cup vanilla wafer crumbs (20 wafers)
1/4 cup finely chopped walnuts
2 tablespoons margarine or butter, melted

FILLING
1 (3-oz.) pkg. raspberry flavor gelatin
1 1/4 cups boiling water
1 (8-oz.) container vanilla yogurt
1 1/2 cups fresh raspberries

GARNISH
1/2 cup frozen whipped topping, thawed
Fresh raspberries, if desired

1. In small bowl, combine all crust ingredients; mix well. Press mixture firmly in bottom of ungreased 8-inch square pan. Refrigerate while preparing filling.

2. In large bowl, dissolve gelatin in boiling water. Stir in yogurt until well blended. Cover; refrigerate until thickened but not set, about 1 hour.

3. Beat gelatin mixture at high speed until doubled in volume, about 5 minutes. Fold in 1 1/2 cups raspberries; pour over crust. Cover; refrigerate 1 hour or until firm.

4. Just before serving, cut into squares. Garnish each serving with whipped topping and fresh raspberries. Store in refrigerator.

Nutrition per Serving: Serving Size: 1/9 of Recipe. Calories 170; Calories from Fat 60; Total Fat 7g; Saturated Fat 2g; Cholesterol 0mg; Sodium 100mg; Dietary Fiber 2g

Dietary Exchange: 1 Starch, 1/2 Fruit, 1 1/2 Fat OR 1 1/2 Carbohydrate, 1 1/2 Fat

CHOCOLATE-MINT COOKIE CAKE

◆

Yield: 12 servings; **Prep Time:** 25 minutes
(Ready in 5 hours 25 minutes)

Here's a dessert easy enough for the children to assemble, tasty enough for all ages to enjoy.

2 cups whipping cream
2 tablespoons powdered sugar
1 teaspoon vanilla
1 cup crushed pastel party mint candies
1 (9-oz.) pkg. chocolate wafer cookies (40 cookies)

1. In large bowl, combine whipping cream, powdered sugar and vanilla; beat until stiff peaks form. Fold in crushed candies.

2. On one side of each of 7 chocolate wafers, spread about 2 teaspoons whipped cream mixture. Stack wafers on top of each other. Top stack with plain wafer. Repeat until all wafers are used, making 5 stacks of 8 wafers each.

3. Turn each stack on its side; place stacks side by side on serving platter, forming 11 1/2 x 3-inch rectangle. Frost rectangle with remaining whipped cream mixture. Cover; refrigerate at least 5 hours or until wafers have softened.

4. To serve, cut cake crosswise into slices. Store in refrigerator.

Nutrition per Serving: Serving Size: 1/12 of Recipe. Calories 270; Calories from Fat 160; Total Fat 18g; Saturated Fat 10g; Cholesterol 55mg; Sodium 150mg; Dietary Fiber 1g

Dietary Exchange: 1 Starch, 1/2 Fruit, 3 1/2 Fat OR 1 1/2 Carbohydrate, 3 1/2 Fat

CHILLED STRAWBERRY-RASPBERRY SOUP

◆

Yield: 8 (1/2-cup) servings;
Prep Time: 15 minutes

Fruit soups, a Scandinavian tradition, offer a refreshing respite on a hot day.

1 1/2 cups raspberry-cranberry drink, chilled
1 (10-oz.) pkg. frozen strawberries in syrup, thawed
1 (10-oz.) pkg. frozen raspberries in syrup, thawed
1/2 teaspoon cinnamon
1/2 cup vanilla yogurt
1 tablespoon grated orange peel

1. In food processor bowl with metal blade, combine raspberry-cranberry drink, strawberries, raspberries and cinnamon. Process until smooth.

2. Place strainer over medium bowl; pour berry mixture into strainer. Press mixture through strainer with back of spoon to remove seeds; discard seeds.

3. Add yogurt and orange peel to pureed mixture; mix until well blended. Serve immediately, or cover and refrigerate until serving time.

4. To serve, spoon soup into individual small bowls. Garnish as desired.

Nutrition per Serving: Serving Size: 1/2 Cup. Calories 120; Calories from Fat 0; Total Fat 0g; Saturated Fat 0g; Cholesterol 0mg; Sodium 15mg; Dietary Fiber 2g

Dietary Exchange: 2 Fruit OR 2 Carbohydrate

Chocolate-Mint Cookie Cake

CRANBERRY-RASPBERRY PEARS

◆

Yield: 4 servings; **Prep Time:** 25 minutes
(Ready in 6 hours 25 minutes)

Bosc pears, with their firm texture, are a good choice for this poached dessert. The fruit takes on a rosy tinge from the raspberry-cranberry juice poaching liquid.

2 large pears, peeled, halved and cored
1 cinnamon stick
2 cups raspberry-cranberry drink
1 tablespoon cornstarch
2 tablespoons white vanilla chips
1 teaspoon oil
¼ cup fresh raspberries, if desired

1. In medium saucepan, combine pear halves, cinnamon stick and raspberry-cranberry drink. Cook over medium heat for 5 to 10 minutes or until pears are slightly tender. Cool slightly. Cover; refrigerate at least 2 hours or until pears are pink.

2. Remove pears from saucepan. Reserve 1 cup liquid in saucepan; stir in cornstarch. Cook over medium heat until mixture boils, thickens and becomes clear. Boil 1 minute, stirring constantly.

Cranberry-Raspberry Pears

Return pears to saucepan; cover and refrigerate at least 4 hours or until cold.

3. Just before serving, in small saucepan, combine chips and oil. Melt chips over very low heat, stirring occasionally.

4. To serve, place pear halves on individual dessert plates. Spoon sauce over and around pears. Drizzle each with melted chips. Top with raspberries.

Nutrition per Serving: Serving Size: ¼ of Recipe. Calories 210; Calories from Fat 35; Total Fat 4g; Saturated Fat 1g; Cholesterol 0mg; Sodium 10mg; Dietary Fiber 4g

Dietary Exchange: 3 Fruit, ½ Fat OR 3 Carbohydrate, ½ Fat

ORANGE MARINATED FRUIT

◆

Yield: 12 (½-cup) servings;
Prep Time: 20 minutes
(Ready in 4 hours 20 minutes)

If you're a mint lover, add a tablespoon or two of shredded mint leaves to the fruit mixture in addition to the garnish. Serve the fruit solo, over plain cake or topped with a scoop of sorbet.

¼ cup sugar
2 tablespoons thin orange peel strips or grated orange peel
¼ cup orange juice
2 tablespoons orange-flavored liqueur, if desired
2 cups pineapple cubes
2 cups cantaloupe balls
1 pint (2 cups) fresh strawberries

1. In resealable plastic bag or large nonmetal bowl, combine sugar, orange peel, orange juice and liqueur; blend well. Add pineapple and cantaloupe. Seal bag or cover bowl; refrigerate 4 hours or overnight, turning or stirring once or twice.

2. Just before serving, add strawberries to fruit mixture. If desired, garnish serving bowl or individual servings with mint leaves and additional orange peel strips.

Nutrition per Serving: Serving Size: ½ Cup. Calories 60; Calories from Fat 0; Total Fat 0g; Saturated Fat 0g; Cholesterol 0mg; Sodium 0mg; Dietary Fiber 1g

Dietary Exchange: 1 Fruit OR 1 Carbohydrate

MARINATED FRUIT COMPOTE

◆

Yield: 8 (½-cup) servings;
Prep Time: 15 minutes
(Ready in 2 hours 15 minutes)

Tequila adds some kick to a sunset-colored combo of pineapple, mango and papaya in a citrus-honey marinade.

MARINADE
3 tablespoons orange juice
2 tablespoons lime juice
2 tablespoons honey
1 cinnamon stick
2 tablespoons tequila, if desired

FRUIT
1 cup fresh or canned pineapple chunks
1 papaya, peeled, seeded and cubed
1 mango, peeled, seeded and cubed

1. In small saucepan, combine orange juice, lime juice, honey and cinnamon stick; blend well. Bring to a boil over medium heat. Reduce heat; simmer 2 minutes. Cool 1 hour.

2. Meanwhile, in medium bowl or large resealable plastic bag, combine fruit.

3. Remove cinnamon stick from marinade; stir in tequila. Pour marinade over fruit; stir gently to coat. Cover bowl or seal plastic bag; refrigerate at least 1 hour to blend flavors, stirring or turning once.

Nutrition per Serving: Serving Size: ½ Cup. Calories 70; Calories from Fat 0; Total Fat 0g; Saturated Fat 0g; Cholesterol 0mg; Sodium 0mg; Dietary Fiber 1g

Dietary Exchange: 1 ½ Fruit OR 1 ½ Carbohydrate

FRESH NECTARINE AND RASPBERRY COMPOTE

Yield: 4 servings; **Prep Time:** 20 minutes
(Ready in 2 hours 20 minutes)

Sliced nectarines, soaked in a sweet port sauce and topped with raspberries, epitomize the beauty of simplicity.

1 cup sugar
1 cup port wine
4 medium nectarines, sliced
  (3 cups)
½ cup fresh raspberries

1. In medium saucepan, combine sugar and wine. Cook and stir over medium-high heat for 3 to 4 minutes or until mixture comes to a rolling boil and sugar is dissolved. Remove from heat; cool 15 minutes.

2. Place nectarines in single layer in 12 × 8-inch (2-quart) baking dish. Pour cooled wine mixture over nectarines; stir gently until well coated. Refrigerate at least 2 hours to blend flavors, stirring occasionally.

3. Just before serving, spoon nectarine mixture into individual stemmed glasses. Top with raspberries. If desired, garnish each with sugar wafer cookie.

Nutrition per Serving: Serving Size: ¼ of Recipe. Calories 330; Calories from Fat 10; Total Fat 1g; Saturated Fat 0g; Cholesterol 0mg; Sodium 0mg; Dietary Fiber 3g

Dietary Exchange: 4½ Fruit, 1½ Fat OR 4½ Carbohydrate, 1½ Fat

---

GREEN FRUIT COMPOTE

Yield: 4 (¾-cup) servings;
Prep Time: 10 minutes
(Ready in 40 minutes)

While "green" often conjures up an image of vegetables, here's proof that the color has its sweet side, too. Green grapes, kiwi fruit and pears bask in honey and lime.

2 tablespoons lime juice
2 tablespoons honey
1 cup seedless green grapes
2 kiwi fruit, peeled, cut into bite-sized pieces
2 pears, cut into ½-inch pieces

1. In medium bowl, combine lime juice and honey; blend well.

2. Add all remaining ingredients; toss gently. Spoon into individual dessert dishes. Refrigerate at least 30 minutes or until serving time.

Nutrition per Serving: Serving Size: ¾ Cup. Calories 150; Calories from Fat 10; Total Fat 1g; Saturated Fat 0g; Cholesterol 0mg; Sodium 0mg; Dietary Fiber 4g

Dietary Exchange: 2½ Fruit OR 2½ Carbohydrate

SPARKLING MELON MEDLEY

Yield: 6 (½-cup) servings;
Prep Time: 25 minutes
(Ready in 2 hours 25 minutes)

An effervescent innovation in fruit desserts, this cool mélange bathes colorful assorted melon balls with sparkling cider. For an extra-special celebration, try substituting champagne.

1 cup seeded watermelon balls or cubes
1 cup cantaloupe balls or cubes
1 cup honeydew melon balls or cubes
6 mint sprigs
1½ cups sparkling apple cider, chilled

1. In medium bowl, combine watermelon, cantaloupe and honeydew melon. Cover; refrigerate 2 hours or until chilled.

2. To serve, spoon fruit into 6 individual dessert dishes. Top each serving with mint sprig. Pour ¼ cup cider over each serving.

Nutrition per Serving: Serving Size: ½ Cup. Calories 60; Calories from Fat 0; Total Fat 0g; Saturated Fat 0g; Cholesterol 0mg; Sodium 10mg; Dietary Fiber 1g

Dietary Exchange: 1 Fruit OR 1 Carbohydrate

Fresh Nectarine and Raspberry Compote

WHITE CHOCOLATE DESSERT CUPS WITH RASPBERRY FOOL

Yield: 8 servings; **Prep Time:** 30 minutes
(Ready in 1 hour 30 minutes)

A child's balloon (washed and dried) becomes an innovative mold for making an edible cup of white chocolate. Once the melted chocolate has solidified around the balloon form, carefully remove the balloon and leave your guests to wonder how you got those cups so nicely rounded. Pale pink and creamy, raspberry filling looks pretty in the cups.

DESSERT CUPS
10 oz. vanilla-flavored candy
  coating, cut into pieces
8 small round balloons
8 spring clips*

RASPBERRY FOOL
3 cups chopped fresh raspberries
¾ cup sugar
1 tablespoon cornstarch
1 cup whipping cream, whipped

1. In small saucepan, melt candy coating over low heat, stirring constantly. Pour onto 12-inch square of foil. Cool until lukewarm but still melted.**

2. Meanwhile, line cookie sheet with foil. Thoroughly wash and dry balloons. Inflate each balloon to 3½ inches, twisting top and securing with spring clip. DO NOT TIE INTO KNOT.

3. Roll bottom of each balloon in candy coating, rocking back and forth across bottom and ⅓ up sides to form bottom and sides of cup. Stand each coated balloon on foil-lined cookie sheet. Refrigerate about 10 minutes or until set.

4. Meanwhile, place half of chopped raspberries in food processor bowl with metal blade or blender container; process until smooth.

5. In small saucepan, combine sugar and cornstarch; mix well. Add raspberry puree. Bring to a boil over medium heat, stirring constantly until thickened. Boil 1 minute. Pour into medium bowl. Add remaining chopped raspberries; mix well. Refrigerate about 1 hour or until thoroughly chilled. (Raspberry mixture can be cooled quickly by placing bowl in a larger bowl or pan filled with ice water.)

6. To remove balloons from candy coating cups, hold opening of one balloon with one hand and remove clip, slowly letting out air; carefully remove balloon. Repeat with remaining balloons.***

7. Just before serving, gently fold whipped cream into chilled raspberry mixture. To serve, place cups on individual serving plates; spoon raspberry mixture into cups.

*Tips: *Twist ties used for plastic storage bags can be used in place of spring clips. Be sure sharp ends of twist ties do not puncture balloons.*

* **Candy coating must be cooled to lukewarm to prevent balloons from bursting.*

* ***If desired, at this point, chocolate can be drizzled over outside or inside of cups. In small saucepan, combine 2 tablespoons semi-sweet chocolate chips and 1 teaspoon shortening; cook over low heat, stirring constantly until smooth. Drizzle over cups.*

Nutrition per Serving: Serving Size: ⅛ of Recipe. Calories 410; Calories from Fat 210; Total Fat 23g; Saturated Fat 14g; Cholesterol 50mg; Sodium 45mg; Dietary Fiber 3g

Dietary Exchange: 1 Starch, 2 Fruit, 4½ Fat OR 3 Carbohydrate, 4½ Fat

White Chocolate Dessert Cups with Raspberry Fool

STRAWBERRY-ORANGE FOOL

Yield: 4 servings; **Prep Time:** 15 minutes

The orange filling is sweetly tangy, a great foil for the fresh strawberries.

½ cup nonfat sour cream
1 tablespoon powdered sugar
1 teaspoon grated orange peel
1 tablespoon orange-flavored
   liqueur
1½ cups frozen fat-free whipped
   topping, thawed
3 cups sliced fresh strawberries

1. In medium bowl, combine sour cream, powdered sugar, orange peel and liqueur; blend well. Fold in whipped topping.

2. For each serving, use ⅓ cup orange cream and ¾ cup strawberries. In each dessert dish, layer 2 tablespoons of the cream and half of the berries. Repeat layers. Top with remaining cream. Serve immediately or refrigerate until serving time. If desired, garnish each serving with additional sliced strawberries. Store in refrigerator.

Nutrition per Serving: Serving Size: ¼ of Recipe. Calories 110; Calories from Fat 0; Total Fat 0g; Saturated Fat 0g; Cholesterol 0mg; Sodium 75mg; Dietary Fiber 3g

Dietary Exchange: 1 Starch, ½ Fruit OR 1½ Carbohydrate

RHUBARB CREAM DESSERT

Yield: 10 (½-cup) servings;
Prep Time: 25 minutes
(Ready in 2 hours 25 minutes)

Two springtime best friends, rhubarb and strawberries, join forces with vanilla ice cream in a cool, refrigerated dessert. Flavored gelatin underscores the fruit nuances and firms up the blend.

4 cups chopped fresh or frozen
   rhubarb
¼ cup water
1 (3-oz.) pkg. strawberry or
   raspberry flavor gelatin
¾ cup sugar
1 (10-oz.) pkg. frozen strawberries
   or raspberries in syrup,
   undrained
1 pint (2 cups) vanilla ice cream

1. In large saucepan, combine rhubarb and water; bring to a boil. Cover; simmer over medium heat until rhubarb is tender, about 15 minutes.

2. Remove saucepan from heat. Stir in gelatin and sugar until dissolved. Add frozen strawberries and ice cream; let stand until thawed, stirring occasionally. Pour into individual dessert dishes. Refrigerate 2 to 3 hours or until firm.

Nutrition per Serving: Serving Size: ½ Cup. Calories 190; Calories from Fat 25; Total Fat 3g; Saturated Fat 2g; Cholesterol 10mg; Sodium 45mg; Dietary Fiber 1g

Dietary Exchange: 1 Starch, 1½ Fruit, ½ Fat OR 2½ Carbohydrate, ½ Fat

Strawberry-Orange Fool

FROZEN DESSERTS

❖ ❖ ❖

Ice cream must have seemed like a miracle in the days before refrigeration, its sweet frostiness a treat in the midst of summer heat. Today, ice cream and other frozen treats enjoy year-round popularity —and they're so much easier to make. Frozen desserts are a great choice for dinner parties because they can be made ahead with no last-minute fussing, and many yield crowd-sized quantities.

FROZEN KEY LIME TORTE, PAGE 250

At one end of the frozen desserts spectrum, super-rich ice creams hold court; the other end boasts frosty no-fat treats.

FROZEN DEFINITIONS

The difference between one frozen dessert and another may not always be definitive, but here are some general descriptions:

FROZEN YOGURT. Frozen yogurt has a creamy texture similar to that of ice cream. Depending on whether low-fat, nonfat or regular yogurt is used, the dessert may have a lower fat content than ice cream, but it may have more sugar.

ICE. Also called granita or Italian ice, it's made from water (or juice) processed with sugar and flavoring, yielding a nonfat frozen treat with a fine crystalline texture.

ICE CREAM. Ice cream can be made in two basic ways. The simplest method freezes a combination of cream, sugar and flavorings. A richer, smoother-textured ice cream is made from egg, sugar and milk or cream cooked into a thick custard on the stove-top, then chilled and frozen. Egg-based ice creams are richer and smoother textured than ice creams made without egg.

SHERBET. Sherbet is similar to sorbet, with the addition of egg white or a small amount of milk or cream to yield a dessert that's creamier than sorbet or ice but less rich than ice cream.

SORBET. Sorbet adds pureed fruit to the basic recipe for granita or ice; sorbets are typically smoother than ices or granitas, though not creamy like ice cream.

TIPS FOR MAKING FROZEN DESSERTS

◆ Since freezing mutes flavors somewhat, use more intense flavorings than those used for warm desserts.

◆ Chill all ingredients before you begin processing or freezing.

◆ Desserts not made in an ice cream machine will usually require stirring several times as they freeze, to prevent them from becoming a solid block of ice and to make the texture consistent throughout. A metal pan will hasten freezing. For best results, stir with a metal fork every 30 minutes or so, breaking up crystals that form on the edge of the pan.

◆ Ice cream makers can be noisy. If yours is too loud, try secluding it in a pantry or hallway, perhaps muffled with a couple of thick towels.

◆   ◆   ◆

BANANA SORBET WITH KIWI FRUIT SAUCE

◆

Yield: 6 servings (½-cup); **Prep Time:** 15 minutes (Ready in 5 hours 15 minutes)

The refreshing bright green color of the kiwi sauce contrasts beautifully with the banana sorbet.

SORBET
⅔ cup sugar
⅔ cup water
2 ripe large bananas
1 cup orange juice
1 tablespoon lemon juice

SAUCE AND GARNISH
1 kiwi fruit, peeled
2 teaspoons sugar
Kiwi fruit slices

1. In small saucepan, combine ⅔ cup sugar and water. Bring to a boil, stirring until sugar is dissolved. Cool 30 minutes. Refrigerate 30 minutes or until chilled.

2. In blender container or food processor bowl with metal blade, puree bananas. Add orange juice, lemon juice and sugar-water mixture; blend until smooth. Pour into ungreased 9-inch square pan; cover with foil. Freeze 4 to 6 hours or until firm, stirring several times.*

3. To prepare sauce, in blender container or food processor bowl with metal blade, puree 1 kiwi fruit and 2 teaspoons sugar. Serve over sorbet. Garnish with kiwi fruit slices.

Tip: If sorbet has been frozen overnight, let stand 5 to 10 minutes at room temperature before serving.

Nutrition per Serving: Serving Size: 1/6 of Recipe. Calories 170; Calories from Fat 0; Total Fat 0g; Saturated Fat 0g; Cholesterol 0mg; Sodium 0mg; Dietary Fiber 2g

Dietary Exchange: 3 Fruit OR 3 Carbohydrate

FRESH STRAWBERRY-BANANA SORBET

◆

Yield: 6 (1/2-cup) servings;
Prep Time: 30 minutes
(Ready in 4 hours)

Strawberries and bananas have naturally complementary flavors that are particularly good in frozen desserts such as this sorbet.

1/3 cup sugar
2/3 cup water
2 tablespoons light corn syrup
1 ripe banana, cut up
1 pint (2 cups) fresh strawberries

1. In small saucepan, combine sugar, water and corn syrup; mix well. Bring to a boil. Boil 1 minute. Cool slightly; refrigerate 30 to 45 minutes or until chilled.

2. In food processor bowl with metal blade or blender container, combine banana and strawberries; process until blended. Gradually add chilled sugar syrup; blend until smooth.* Pour into ungreased 8-inch square (2-quart) baking dish; cover with foil. Freeze 3 to 4 hours or until firm, stirring once.

Tip: To prepare sorbet in small ice cream maker, prepare recipe to this point. Freeze mixture in ice cream maker according to manufacturer's directions.

Nutrition per Serving: Serving Size: 1/2 Cup. Calories 100; Calories from Fat 0; Total Fat 0g; Saturated Fat 0g; Cholesterol 0mg; Sodium 10mg; Dietary Fiber 2g

Dietary Exchange: 1 1/2 Fruit OR 1 1/2 Carbohydrate

SPICED CRANBERRY-RASPBERRY SORBET

◆

Yield: 8 (1/2-cup) servings;
Prep Time: 30 minutes
(Ready in 4 hours 30 minutes)

Try this as a summer cool-down or at Thanksgiving as a reinterpretation of the fall holiday's well-loved red berry.

1 1/2 cups fresh or frozen
    cranberries
3/4 cup sugar
1/8 teaspoon allspice

2 1/2 cups water
1 1/2 cups frozen raspberries
    without syrup

1. In medium saucepan, combine cranberries, sugar, allspice and water. Bring to a boil. Boil 10 minutes, stirring occasionally. Remove from heat; stir in raspberries. Cool 10 minutes.

2. Place half of mixture in food processor bowl with metal blade or blender container; process until smooth. Press pureed mixture through strainer into bowl to remove seeds; discard seeds. Repeat with remaining mixture.*

3. Pour into ungreased 8 or 9-inch pan. Cover with foil; freeze 2 hours, stirring occasionally. Without stirring, freeze an additional 2 hours or until firm.

4. To serve, let stand at room temperature for 15 to 20 minutes. Scoop into individual dessert dishes.

Tip: To prepare sorbet in small ice cream maker, prepare recipe to this point. Freeze mixture in ice cream maker according to manufacturer's directions.

Nutrition per Serving: Serving Size: 1/2 Cup. Calories 110; Calories from Fat 0; Total Fat 0g; Saturated Fat 0g; Cholesterol 0mg; Sodium 0mg; Dietary Fiber 4g

Dietary Exchange: 2 Fruit OR 2 Carbohydrate

RASPBERRY SORBET

Yield: 4 (½-cup) servings;
Prep Time: 30 minutes
(Ready in 7 hours 30 minutes)

To make a good thing even better, offer a sampler dish of two or more sorbet flavors. Raspberry Sorbet would go especially well with Cool and Refreshing Lemon-Lime Ice (page 230) or Mango Sorbet (page 228).

1 ½ teaspoons unflavored gelatin
½ cup water
1 (10-oz.) pkg. frozen raspberries
    in syrup, partially thawed
⅓ cup raspberry-flavored liqueur*
2 tablespoons lemon juice

1. In small saucepan, combine gelatin and water; let stand 1 minute to soften. Cook over medium heat until gelatin is dissolved, stirring constantly. Set aside to cool.

2. Place partially thawed raspberries in food processor bowl with metal blade or blender container; process until smooth. Add liqueur, lemon juice and gelatin mixture; process until smooth. Pour into ungreased 9-inch square pan; cover with foil. Freeze 3 to 5 hours or until almost firm, stirring occasionally.

3. Spoon partially frozen mixture into food processor bowl with metal blade or large bowl; process or beat at medium speed until mixture is smooth and fluffy, but not thawed. Pour into nonmetal freezer container; cover. Freeze 4 to 6 hours or until firm. If desired, serve with papaya, kiwi fruit and fresh raspberries.

*Tip: Raspberry-cranberry drink can be substituted for the liqueur. Mixture will freeze until almost firm in 1 ½ to 3 hours.

Nutrition per Serving: Serving Size: ½ Cup. Calories 150; Calories from Fat 0; Total Fat 0g; Saturated Fat 0g; Cholesterol 0mg; Sodium 0mg; Dietary Fiber 3g

Dietary Exchange: 2 Fruit, ½ Fat OR 2 Carbohydrate, ½ Fat

MANGO SORBET

◆

Yield: 12 servings (½-cup);
Prep Time: 15 minutes
(Ready in 5 hours 30 minutes)

Be patient with mangoes: they're at their sweetest when absolutely ripe (slightly soft to the touch and red-tinged yellow skin instead of solid green). If you buy them hard, ripen them in a brown paper bag at room temperature for a few days.

1 cup water
½ cup powdered sugar
2 teaspoons lime juice
1 teaspoon grated lime peel
2 ripe mangoes, peeled, seeded
    and cut up (about 4 cups)
Mint leaves

1. In food processor bowl with metal blade or blender container, combine all ingredients except mint leaves; process until smooth. Pour into nonmetal freezer container. Cover; freeze 4 to 5 hours or until almost firm, stirring occasionally.

2. Line 12 muffin cups with foil baking cups. Spoon mixture into foil cups. Freeze at least 1 hour or until firm.

3. To serve, let stand at room temperature for 15 to 20 minutes. Garnish with mint leaves.

Nutrition per Serving: Serving Size: ½₂ of Recipe. Calories 45; Calories from Fat 0; Total Fat 0g; Saturated Fat 0g; Cholesterol 0mg; Sodium 0mg; Dietary Fiber 1g

Dietary Exchange: 1 Fruit OR 1 Carbohydrate

Mango Sorbet

CANTALOUPE SNOW

♦

Yield: 10 (½-cup) servings;
Prep Time: 15 minutes
(Ready in 3 hours 45 minutes)

This summer refresher is a little sweet (melon and sherbet), a little tangy (buttermilk is the secret ingredient), a little spicy (a hint of ginger) and a lot frosty and fabulous.

2 cups cubed cantaloupe
¼ cup sugar
1 pint (2 cups) orange sherbet
2 cups buttermilk
¼ teaspoon ground ginger

1. In food processor bowl with metal blade or blender container, combine cantaloupe and sugar; process with on/off pulses until smooth. Spoon sherbet into processor bowl; process with on/off pulses just until combined. Add buttermilk and ginger; process just until blended.

2. Pour into 1½-quart freezer container; cover. Freeze 3 to 4 hours or until firm.

3. To serve, let stand at room temperature for 20 to 30 minutes. Spoon into chilled individual dessert dishes.

Nutrition per Serving: Serving Size: ½ Cup. Calories 110; Calories from Fat 10; Total Fat 1g; Saturated Fat 1g; Cholesterol 4mg; Sodium 70mg; Dietary Fiber 0g

Dietary Exchange: ½ Starch, 1 Fruit OR 1½ Carbohydrate

VARIATION

Frosty Refresher: Prepare recipe as directed. Spoon ½ cup into each serving glass. Gently stir in ¼ cup sparkling mineral water or ginger ale.

Yield: 10 (¾-cup) servings

COOL AND REFRESHING LEMON-LIME ICE

Yield: 12 (½-cup) servings;
Prep Time: 30 minutes
(Ready in 2 hours)

Mixing in a little lime puts a twist on a hot-weather classic.

1½ cups sugar
5 cups cold water
1 teaspoon grated lemon peel
1 teaspoon grated lime peel
⅓ cup fresh lemon juice
¼ cup fresh lime juice

1. In small saucepan, combine sugar and 1 cup of the water; mix well. Bring to a boil over high heat. Cook until sugar is dissolved, stirring constantly. Pour into medium bowl; cover. Refrigerate 1 hour or until thoroughly chilled.

2. When ready to freeze, add remaining 4 cups cold water and all remaining ingredients; mix well. Freeze mixture in ice cream

---

maker according to manufacturer's directions.*

Tip: To prepare without ice cream maker, pour mixture into 13 × 9-inch pan. Freeze 1 to 2 hours or until partially firm, stirring occasionally. Chill food processor bowl with metal blade or large bowl and beaters. Spoon partially frozen lemon mixture into chilled bowl; process at medium speed until mixture is light and fluffy but not thawed. Spoon into same pan; cover with foil. Freeze 3 to 4 hours or until firm. If necessary, let stand at room temperature for 30 minutes before serving.

Nutrition per Serving: Serving Size: ½ Cup. Calories 100; Calories from Fat 0; Total Fat 0g; Saturated Fat 0g; Cholesterol 0mg; Sodium 0mg; Dietary Fiber 0g

Dietary Exchange: 1½ Fruit OR 1½ Carbohydrate

KIWI ICE

Yield: 10 (½-cup) servings;
Prep Time: 15 minutes
(Ready in 5 hours 45 minutes)

If you prefer, don't bother straining out the kiwi seeds—they add an interesting bit of color and texture.

12 kiwi fruit, peeled, cubed
2 cups orange juice
1⅓ cups corn syrup

1. In food processor bowl with metal blade or blender container, combine kiwi fruit and orange juice. Cover; process or blend until

smooth. Press mixture through strainer into nonmetal container to remove seeds; discard seeds. Stir in corn syrup. Freeze about 3 hours or until almost firm.

2. Place kiwi fruit mixture in food processor bowl with metal blade or large bowl. Process or beat with electric mixer until fluffy. Pour into same nonmetal container. Return to freezer; freeze 2 hours or until firm.

3. To serve, let stand at room temperature for about 30 minutes. Scoop into individual dessert dishes.

Nutrition per Serving: Serving Size: ½ Cup. Calories 210; Calories from Fat 0; Total Fat 0g; Saturated Fat 0g; Cholesterol 0mg; Sodium 60mg; Dietary Fiber 3g

Dietary Exchange: 3 ½ Fruit OR 3 ½ Carbohydrate

Kiwi Ice

CAPPUCCINO GRANITA

✦

Yield: 7 (1-cup) servings;
Prep Time: 10 minutes
(Ready in 3 hours 10 minutes)

For a pretty presentation, scoop the granita into champagne glasses or wine goblets.

½ cup sugar
2 tablespoons unsweetened cocoa
3 cups hot strong coffee
1 cup milk

1. Place 13×9-inch metal pan in freezer to chill. Meanwhile, in medium bowl, combine all ingredients; blend well. Cool 30 minutes or until completely cooled.

2. Pour cooled mixture into chilled pan. Freeze 30 minutes.

3. When ice crystals begin to form at edges of pan, stir mixture with fork. Return to freezer; freeze about 2 hours or until completely frozen, stirring every 30 minutes.

4. To serve, scoop into individual dessert dishes.

Nutrition per Serving: Serving Size: 1 Cup. Calories 90; Calories from Fat 10; Total Fat 1g; Saturated Fat 1g; Cholesterol 3mg; Sodium 20mg; Dietary Fiber 1g

Dietary Exchange: 1 Starch OR 1 Carbohydrate

LEMON GRANITA

✦

Yield: 7 (1-cup) servings;
Prep Time: 10 minutes
(Ready in 2 hours 40 minutes)

Granita is just perfect as a light conclusion to a no-holds-barred summer barbecue. Decorate each serving with a fresh mint sprig or a couple of fresh Bing cherries.

¾ cup sugar
1 teaspoon grated lemon peel
3 cups water
½ cup fresh lemon juice

1. Place 13×9-inch metal pan in freezer to chill. Meanwhile, in medium bowl, combine ingredients; blend well. Pour mixture into chilled pan. Freeze 30 minutes.

2. When ice crystals begin to form at edges of pan, stir mixture with fork. Return to freezer; freeze about 2 hours or until completely frozen, stirring every 30 minutes.

3. To serve, scoop into individual dessert dishes.

Nutrition per Serving: Serving Size: 1 Cup. Calories 90; Calories from Fat 0; Total Fat 0g; Saturated Fat 0g; Cholesterol 0mg; Sodium 0mg; Dietary Fiber 0g

Dietary Exchange: 1 ½ Fruit OR 1 ½ Carbohydrate

Cappuccino Granita, Lemon Granita, Dried Cherry Biscotti, page 308

MISTY MELON FREEZE

◆

Yield: 8 (½-cup) servings;
Prep Time: 30 minutes
(Ready in 5 hours 30 minutes)

Melon-flavored Midori liqueur intensifies the honeydew flavor. If you can't find it, you can substitute Alize (passionfruit liqueur) or an orange liqueur such as Grand Marnier, Cointreau or Triple Sec.

1 envelope unflavored gelatin
¼ cup lemon juice
¼ cup water
2 cups honeydew melon cubes
¼ cup melon-flavored liqueur
2 tablespoons honey
2 cups frozen light whipped topping, thawed
1 (6-oz.) container low-fat lemon yogurt

1. In small saucepan, combine gelatin and lemon juice; let stand 1 minute to soften. Add water; cook over medium heat until gelatin is dissolved, stirring constantly. Set aside to cool.

2. In blender container or food processor bowl with metal blade, combine melon, liqueur and honey; blend until smooth. Add cooled gelatin mixture; blend until mixed. Pour into shallow nonmetal freezer container; refrigerate about 10 minutes or until mixture is thick and syrupy, stirring occasionally.

3. Meanwhile, in medium bowl, combine whipped topping and yogurt; blend well. Fold in chilled melon mixture. Pour into same freezer container. Freeze 3 to 4 hours or until almost firm, stirring occasionally.

4. Place mixture in large bowl; beat with electric mixer until smooth and creamy. Freeze 2 to 3 hours or until firm.

5. To serve, let stand at room temperature for 10 minutes.

Nutrition per Serving: Serving Size: ½ Cup. Calories 110; Calories from Fat 20; Total Fat 2g; Saturated Fat 2g; Cholesterol 0mg; Sodium 20mg; Dietary Fiber 0g

Dietary Exchange: ½ Starch, 1 Fruit OR 1½ Carbohydrate

FROZEN STRAWBERRY YOGURT

Yield: 8 (½-cup) servings;
Prep Time: 30 minutes
(Ready in 5 hours 45 minutes)

Delicious enough for dessert, yet light enough for a snack.

2 cups chopped fresh strawberries
⅔ cup sugar
1 envelope unflavored gelatin
1 (8-oz.) container low-fat strawberry yogurt
½ cup buttermilk
2 tablespoons lemon juice

1. In medium bowl, combine strawberries and sugar. Let stand at room temperature for 15 minutes.

2. Drain strawberry mixture over small saucepan. Set strawberries aside. Add gelatin to liquid in saucepan; stir to combine. Let stand 1 minute. Stir over medium heat until gelatin is dissolved. Pour over strawberries; mix well. Stir in remaining ingredients; mix well.* Cover tightly with foil. Freeze 1 to 2 hours or until almost firm.

3. Break mixture apart with spoon. Beat at medium speed until smooth. Cover tightly. Return to freezer; freeze 4 to 5 hours or until firm.

4. To serve, let stand at room temperature for 15 to 20 minutes.

Tip: To prepare frozen yogurt in ice cream maker, prepare to this point. Freeze mixture in ice cream maker according to manufacturer's directions.

Nutrition per Serving: Serving Size: ½ Cup. Calories 130; Calories from Fat 10; Total Fat 1g; Saturated Fat 0g; Cholesterol 0mg; Sodium 35mg; Dietary Fiber 1g

Dietary Exchange: 1 Starch, 1 Fruit OR 2 Carbohydrate

Frozen Strawberry Yogurt

MAPLE NUT ICE CREAM

◆

Yield: 10 (½-cup) servings;
Prep Time: 30 minutes
(Ready in 3 hours)

Walnuts are a traditional partner for maple sugar or maple syrup; pecans or hazelnuts would taste good in this ice cream, too. For best results, make sure the custard mixture is thoroughly chilled before pouring it into the ice cream machine.

¾ cup firmly packed brown sugar
2 cups milk
2 eggs, slightly beaten
1 pint (2 cups) whipping cream
2 to 3 teaspoons maple flavor
¾ cup chopped nuts

1. In medium saucepan, combine brown sugar, milk and eggs; mix well. Cook over medium heat for about 12 minutes or until mixture is slightly thickened and coats a metal spoon, stirring constantly. DO NOT BOIL. Cool 30 minutes.*

2. Add whipping cream and maple flavor; blend well. Stir in nuts. Refrigerate until ready to freeze.

3. When ready to freeze, freeze mixture in ice cream maker according to the manufacturer's directions.

*Tip: Recipe can be prepared ahead to this point. Cover; refrigerate up to 24 hours. When ready to freeze, continue from this point.

Nutrition per Serving: Serving Size: ½ Cup. Calories 330; Calories from Fat 230; Total Fat 25g; Saturated Fat 12g; Cholesterol 110mg; Sodium 60mg; Dietary Fiber 0g

Dietary Exchange: 1 ½ Starch, 4 ½ Fat OR 1 ½ Carbohydrate, 4 ½ Fat

CHAMPAGNE ICE CREAM WITH STRAWBERRY SAUCE

◆

Yield: 12 servings; **Prep Time:** 2 hours

Looking for an extraordinary dessert for an engagement party, anniversary celebration or milestone birthday? Chocolate "cups," easy to make with milk chocolate, offer an elegant and delightful edible container for sumptuous Champagne Ice Cream topped with bright red Strawberry Sauce.

ICE CREAM
3 ¼ cups whipping cream
¾ cup sugar
½ cup light corn syrup
3 eggs
¾ cup champagne
1 tablespoon vanilla

CHOCOLATE CUPS
1 (12-oz.) pkg. milk chocolate chips
3 tablespoons shortening

SAUCE
1 (10-oz.) pkg. frozen strawberries in syrup, thawed
1 teaspoon cornstarch

1. In medium saucepan, combine 2 cups of the whipping cream, sugar, corn syrup and eggs; mix well. Cook over medium heat for 12 to 14 minutes or until slightly thickened, stirring constantly. Remove from heat.* Cool 1 hour or until completely cooled.

2. Meanwhile, to make chocolate cups, line 12 muffin cups with foil or paper baking cups. In small saucepan over low heat, melt chocolate chips and shortening, stirring until smooth. Remove from heat. With small pastry brush or back of teaspoon, brush thin layer of chocolate evenly over bottom and up sides of each cup. Freeze 10 to 20 minutes or until firm.

3. When ready to freeze ice cream, stir in remaining 1 ¼ cups whipping cream, champagne and vanilla. Freeze mixture in ice cream maker according to manufacturer's directions.

4. Brush sides of chocolate cups with another thin layer of chocolate. Freeze an additional 10 minutes or until firm. Carefully peel foil cups away from chocolate cups. Store in refrigerator.

5. In food processor bowl with metal blade or blender container, process strawberries until smooth. If desired, press pureed strawberries through strainer into small saucepan to remove seeds; discard seeds. Add cornstarch to strawberries; blend well. Cook over medium heat for 5 to 8 minutes or until slightly thickened. Cool slightly. Cover; store in refrigerator.

6. Just before serving, place chocolate cups on individual dessert plates. Place 1 scoop of ice cream in each cup. Drizzle with strawberry sauce. Garnish as desired.

*Tips: Ice cream can be prepared ahead to this point. Cover; refrigerate up to 2 days. When ready to freeze, continue from this point.

To prepare without ice cream maker, prepare to *. Pour into 13× 9-inch pan. Freeze until edges are set. In small bowl, beat 1 1/4 cups whipping cream and vanilla until thickened. In large bowl, beat partially frozen mixture until smooth and light. Fold whipped cream into mixture. Gently fold in champagne. Spoon into same pan; cover with foil. Freeze 4 to 6 hours or until firm.

Nutrition per Serving: Serving Size: 1/12 of Recipe. Calories 560; Calories from Fat 330; Total Fat 37g; Saturated Fat 21g; Cholesterol 150mg; Sodium 80mg; Dietary Fiber 1g

Dietary Exchange: 2 Starch, 1 1/2 Fruit, 7 Fat OR 3 1/2 Carbohydrate, 7 Fat

Champagne Ice Cream with Strawberry Sauce

GOURMET CHOCOLATE CHIP ICE CREAM

Yield: 12 (¹/₂-cup) servings;
Prep Time: 30 minutes
(Ready in 3 hours)

This gloriously rich custard-based ice cream reverses the usual combination by mixing vanilla chips into chocolate ice cream. Chopped macadamias impart a touch of luxury.

1 cup sugar
1 pint (2 cups) half-and-half
4 oz. unsweetened chocolate, cut into pieces, melted
2 eggs, slightly beaten
1 pint (2 cups) whipping cream
2 teaspoons vanilla
¹/₂ cup white vanilla chips, finely chopped
¹/₂ cup macadamia nuts, finely chopped, if desired

1. In medium saucepan, combine sugar, half-and-half, melted chocolate and eggs; mix well. Cook over medium heat for about 12 minutes or until mixture is slightly thickened and coats a metal spoon, stirring constantly. DO NOT BOIL. Cool 30 minutes.*

2. Add whipping cream and vanilla; blend well. Refrigerate until ready to freeze.

3. When ready to freeze, freeze mixture in ice cream maker according to manufacturer's directions. Add vanilla chips and macadamia nuts during last 5 minutes of freezing process.

*Tip: Recipe can be prepared ahead to this point. Cover; refrigerate up to 24 hours. When ready to freeze, continue from this point.

Nutrition per Serving: Serving Size: ¹/₂ Cup. Calories 420; Calories from Fat 290; Total Fat 32g; Saturated Fat 17g; Cholesterol 105mg; Sodium 50mg; Dietary Fiber 2g

Dietary Exchange: 2 Starch, 6 Fat OR 2 Carbohydrate, 6 Fat

VANILLA CUSTARD ICE CREAM

Yield: 10 (¹/₂-cup) servings;
Prep Time: 30 minutes
(Ready in 3 hours)

This just may be the very best basic vanilla ice cream ever, ready to be topped with hot fudge or fresh fruit— or savored exactly as is.

³/₄ cup sugar
2 cups milk
2 eggs, slightly beaten
1 pint (2 cups) whipping cream
2 to 3 teaspoons vanilla

1. In medium saucepan, combine sugar, milk and eggs; mix well. Cook over medium heat for about 12 minutes or until mixture is slightly thickened and coats a metal spoon, stirring constantly. DO NOT BOIL. Cool 30 minutes.*

2. Add whipping cream and vanilla; blend well. Refrigerate until ready to freeze.

3. When ready to freeze, freeze mixture in ice cream maker according to the manufacturer's directions.

*Tip: Recipe can be prepared ahead to this point. Cover; refrigerate up to 24 hours. When ready to freeze, continue from this point.

Nutrition per Serving: Serving Size: ¹/₂ Cup. Calories 270; Calories from Fat 180; Total Fat 20g; Saturated Fat 12g; Cholesterol 110mg; Sodium 55mg; Dietary Fiber 0g

Dietary Exchange: 1 Starch, 4 Fat OR 1 Carbohydrate, 4 Fat

VARIATION

Rum Raisin Ice Cream: In small bowl, combine ³/₄ cup raisins and 3 tablespoons dark rum; soak overnight. Add to ice cream in middle of freezing process.

CHOCOLATE TORTONI

◆

Yield: 12 servings; **Prep Time:** 15 minutes
(Ready in 2 hours 15 minutes)

Chances are good you've enjoyed vanilla tortoni at a local Italian restaurant. The classic features a rounded scoop of ice cream that's been mixed with a combination of candied fruit, nuts and chocolate, sometimes rolled in chopped nuts. Here, chocolate ice cream makes the dessert even richer.

- 12 whole maraschino cherries
- 2 tablespoons brandy, if desired
- 1 quart (4 cups) chocolate ice cream, softened
- ½ cup coarsely chopped almonds
- 6 soft coconut macaroon cookies, coarsely crumbled
- ½ cup chopped maraschino cherries, drained
- 1 teaspoon brandy extract
- 1 teaspoon grated orange peel
- 1 teaspoon grated lemon peel
- 2 (1.55-oz.) bars milk chocolate candy, coarsely chopped

1. In small bowl, combine whole cherries and brandy. Set aside to marinate.

2. Line 12 muffin cups with paper or foil baking cups. In large bowl, combine all remaining ingredients; mix lightly to blend. Immediately spoon into lined muffin cups, mounding slightly. Top each with marinated cherry.

Cover loosely with plastic wrap or foil. Freeze at least 2 hours or until firm.

3. To serve, if desired, remove baking cups from desserts. Let stand at room temperature for 10 minutes before serving.

Nutrition per Serving: Serving Size: ¹⁄₁₂ of Recipe. Calories 230; Calories from Fat 100; Total Fat 11g; Saturated Fat 6g; Cholesterol 20mg; Sodium 70mg; Dietary Fiber 1g

Dietary Exchange: 1 Starch, 1 Fruit, 2 Fat OR 2 Carbohydrate, 2 Fat

BANANA BROWNIE SPLIT SUNDAES

◆

Yield: 10 servings; **Prep Time:** 25 minutes
(Ready in 1 hour 45 minutes)

If you're looking for a dessert worthy of a "splurge," try this rich combination of brownies, ice cream, berries, hot fudge and whipped cream.

- 1 (1 lb. 3.5-oz.) pkg. fudge brownie mix
- ½ cup oil
- ¼ cup water
- 2 eggs
- 1 quart (4 cups) strawberry ice cream
- 2 bananas, sliced
- 1 cup sliced fresh strawberries
- ⅔ to 1 cup hot fudge ice cream topping, warmed
- ⅔ cup frozen whipped topping, thawed

1. Heat oven to 350°F. Line 15 × 10 × 1-inch baking pan with foil, leaving 2 inches of foil extending over each end. Lightly grease foil.

2. Prepare brownie mix as directed on package using oil, water, and eggs. Spread batter evenly in greased foil-lined pan. Bake at 350°F. for 15 to 20 minutes. Cool 1 hour.

3. To remove brownies from pan, lift foil ends; place on flat surface. Cut brownies using 2 ½ to 3-inch star-shaped or round cookie cutter. Remove from foil with pancake turner. (Save scraps from cutouts for another use.)

4. Just before serving, scoop ice cream into bowl; top with banana slices and strawberries. Drizzle with ice cream topping; top with whipped topping. Garnish with brownie stars.

High Altitude (Above 3,500 feet): Add ½ cup flour to dry brownie mix; decrease oil to ⅓ cup; increase water to ⅓ cup. Bake at 375° F. for 15 to 20 minutes.

Nutrition per Serving: Serving Size: ¹⁄₁₀ of Recipe. Calories 620; Calories from Fat 250; Total Fat 28g; Saturated Fat 9g; Cholesterol 70mg; Sodium 250mg; Dietary Fiber 3g

Dietary Exchange: 2 Starch, 3 ½ Fruit, 5 ½ Fat OR 5 ½ Carbohydrate, 5 ½ Fat

FROZEN CHOCOLATE CHIP DESSERT

◆

Yield: 20 servings; **Prep Time:** 20 minutes
(Ready in 5 hours 10 minutes)

Think of this decadent layered dessert as frozen sundae squares—great for a crowd!

CRUST

2 1/2 cups finely crushed crisp chocolate chip cookies (25 to 28 cookies)

3 tablespoons margarine or butter, melted

FILLING

1 1/4 cups chocolate fudge ice cream topping, slightly softened

1/2 gallon (8 cups) chocolate chip ice cream, slightly softened

2 cups miniature marshmallows

1/2 cup caramel ice cream topping

1. Line 13 × 9-inch pan with foil. In medium bowl, combine crust ingredients; mix well. Press in bottom of foil-lined pan. Freeze 20 minutes or until chilled.

2. Spread 1 cup of the fudge ice cream topping over crust. Freeze 30 minutes or until firm.

3. In large bowl, combine ice cream and marshmallows; spoon and spread over fudge topping. Cover; freeze at least 4 hours or overnight until firm.

4. Place remaining 1/4 cup fudge topping in decorating bag with writing tip or in small resealable plastic bag with one tiny corner cut off. Pipe desired message on ice cream. Return to freezer.

5. To serve, drizzle or serve with caramel ice cream topping.

Nutrition per Serving: Serving Size: 1/20 of Recipe. Calories 320; Calories from Fat 130; Total Fat 14g; Saturated Fat 6g; Cholesterol 25mg; Sodium 170mg; Dietary Fiber 1g

Dietary Exchange: 1 Starch, 2 Fruit, 2 1/2 Fat OR 3 Carbohydrate, 2 1/2 Fat

CREAMY MOCHA FROZEN DESSERT

◆

Yield: 16 servings; **Prep Time:** 20 minutes
(Ready in 8 hours 20 minutes)

So rich, so good! Coffee's slight bitterness balances the sweetness of chocolate, bringing out the best of both flavors. Serve with espresso or your favorite style of brewed coffee.

CRUST

1 cup chocolate wafer cookie crumbs (16 cookies)

1/2 cup finely chopped pecans

1/4 cup margarine or butter, melted

FILLING

2 (8-oz.) pkg. cream cheese, softened

1 (14-oz.) can sweetened condensed milk (not evaporated)

1/2 cup chocolate-flavored syrup

2 teaspoons instant coffee granules or crystals

1 tablespoon water

1 (8-oz.) container frozen whipped topping, thawed

1/4 cup chopped pecans

1. In medium bowl, combine all crust ingredients; mix well. Press firmly in bottom of ungreased 13 × 9-inch pan or 10-inch springform pan.

2. In large bowl, beat cream cheese until fluffy. Add condensed milk and syrup; beat until smooth. In small bowl, combine instant coffee and water; stir until dissolved. Stir into cream cheese mixture. Fold in whipped topping; spoon into crust-lined pan. Sprinkle evenly with 1/4 cup pecans. Freeze 8 hours or until firm.

3. To serve, let stand at room temperature for 5 to 10 minutes.

Nutrition per Serving: Serving Size: 1/16 of Recipe. Calories 340; Calories from Fat 210; Total Fat 23g; Saturated Fat 12g; Cholesterol 40mg; Sodium 250mg; Dietary Fiber 1g

Dietary Exchange: 2 Starch, 4 Fat OR 2 Carbohydrate, 4 Fat

Creamy Mocha Frozen Dessert

FUDGE SUNDAE CAKE

◆

Yield: 8 servings; Prep Time: 30 minutes
(Ready in 4 hours 30 minutes)

The simplest components imaginable —purchased pound cake, fudge topping and ice cream—become a fancy dessert when presented as a layered ensemble.

1 (10.75-oz.) frozen pound cake
¾ cup thick fudge ice cream topping
1 quart (4 cups) cherry nut ice cream, slightly softened

1. Cut frozen cake horizontally into 4 thin slices. Place bottom layer in center of 20 × 18-inch sheet of heavy-duty foil.

2. Spread ¼ cup of the ice cream topping over bottom cake layer. Spoon ⅓ of the ice cream over topping; smooth top. Repeat layers twice; top with remaining cake slice. Press cake firmly. Wrap tightly in foil. Freeze 4 hours or until firm.

3. To serve, let stand at room temperature for 5 to 10 minutes. Cut into slices.

Nutrition per Serving: Serving Size: ⅛ of Recipe. Calories 400; Calories from Fat 160; Total Fat 18g; Saturated Fat 8g; Cholesterol 55mg; Sodium 250mg; Dietary Fiber 1g

Dietary Exchange: 2 Starch, 1½ Fruit, 3½ Fat OR 3½ Carbohydrate, 3½ Fat

Fudge Sundae Cake

MINT CHOCOLATE MOUSSE DESSERT

Yield: 18 servings; Prep Time: 45 minutes
(Ready in 5 hours 45 minutes)

Requiring just four ingredients, the mousse filling remains delightfully creamy even when frozen and can also be made separately and served in bowls for a simpler dessert.

CRUST
2 cups vanilla wafer crumbs (40 wafers)
⅓ cup margarine or butter, melted

FILLING
1 (8-oz.) pkg. cream cheese, softened
2 cups powdered sugar
3 oz. unsweetened chocolate, melted
3 eggs
½ gallon (8 cups) pink peppermint or green mint ice cream, slightly softened

SAUCE
4 oz. semi-sweet chocolate, chopped
⅓ cup margarine or butter
1½ cups powdered sugar
1 (5-oz.) can (⅔ cup) evaporated milk
1 teaspoon vanilla

1. Heat oven to 350°F. In small bowl, combine crust ingredients; mix well. Press in bottom of ungreased 13 × 9-inch pan. Bake at 350°F. for 10 minutes or until light golden brown.

2. Meanwhile, in small bowl, beat cream cheese until fluffy. Add 2 cups powdered sugar; beat until smooth. Add melted chocolate; beat well. Add eggs 1 at a time, beating well after each addition. Pour over partially baked crust.

3. Bake at 350°F. for 12 to 15 minutes or until filling is set. Cool 1 hour or until completely cooled.

4. Spread ice cream over chocolate layer. Cover with foil; freeze 4 hours or until firm.

5. Just before serving, in heavy medium saucepan, combine all sauce ingredients except vanilla; mix well. Bring to a boil over medium heat, stirring constantly. Reduce heat to low; cook 5 minutes, stirring constantly. Remove from heat; stir in vanilla.

6. To serve, let stand at room temperature for 10 minutes. Cut into squares; place on individual dessert plates. Drizzle warm sauce over each serving.

Nutrition per Serving: Serving Size: 1/18 of Recipe. Calories 470; Calories from Fat 230; Total Fat 26g; Saturated Fat 15g; Cholesterol 95mg; Sodium 220mg; Dietary Fiber 1g

Dietary Exchange: 2 Starch, 1½ Fruit, 5 Fat OR 3½ Carbohydrate, 5 Fat

WHITE CHOCOLATE FROZEN YOGURT CUPS

Yield: 8 servings; **Prep Time:** 30 minutes
(Ready in 1 hour)

The white chocolate cups resemble little baskets. Serve to conclude a sophisticated warm-weather luncheon.

6 oz. vanilla-flavored candy
    coating, cut into pieces
2 teaspoons shortening
1 1/2 pints (3 cups) raspberry frozen
    yogurt
Fresh raspberries
Fresh mint leaves
1 oz. vanilla-flavored candy
    coating, grated

1. Invert 8 foil baking cups on cookie sheet. Place in freezer. In small saucepan over low heat, melt 6 oz. candy coating and shortening, stirring constantly. Cool slightly.

2. Pour coating into small squeeze bottle or decorating bag with small writing tip. Drizzle coating randomly over bottom and sides of cups, carefully connecting drizzled lines to prevent weak spots. Freeze 30 minutes.

3. Unmold by carefully peeling foil cups from candy coating.* To serve, place cups on individual dessert plates. Fill each with about 1/3 cup frozen yogurt. Garnish with raspberries, mint leaves and grated candy coating.

*Tip: If cup breaks, mend with melted candy coating.

Nutrition per Serving: Serving Size: 1/8 of Recipe. Calories 220; Calories from Fat 80; Total Fat 9g; Saturated Fat 5g; Cholesterol 5mg; Sodium 65mg; Dietary Fiber 0g

Dietary Exchange: 1 1/2 Starch, 1/2 Fruit, 1 1/2 Fat OR 2 Carbohydrate, 1 1/2 Fat

MINT CHOCOLATE CHIP TORTE

♦

Yield: 12 servings; **Prep Time:** 30 minutes
(Ready in 6 hours 30 minutes)

Homemade whipped cream, folded into softened mint chocolate chip ice cream, gives this dessert simultaneous rich flavor and light texture.

TORTE
1 1/2 cups chocolate wafer cookie
    crumbs (24 cookies)
1/4 cup margarine or butter, melted
1 quart (4 cups) mint chocolate
    chip ice cream, softened*
1 cup whipping cream, whipped

SAUCE
3 tablespoons margarine or butter
1/3 cup unsweetened cocoa
1 cup powdered sugar
1/2 cup lite evaporated skimmed
    milk
1/2 teaspoon mint extract

1. In medium bowl, combine cookie crumbs and 1/4 cup margarine; mix well. Reserve 1/4 cup crumbs for topping. Press remaining crumbs in bottom and 1/2 inch up sides of ungreased 9-inch springform pan. Freeze 1 hour.

2. Place ice cream in large bowl; gently fold in whipped cream. Spoon mixture into crust-lined pan. Sprinkle with reserved crumbs. Cover with foil; freeze 5 hours or overnight until firm.

3. Melt 3 tablespoons margarine in small saucepan over medium heat. Remove from heat. Stir in cocoa; blend well. Gradually stir in powdered sugar and milk. Return to heat; cook until powdered sugar is dissolved and sauce boils and thickens, stirring constantly. Stir in extract. Serve warm sauce over torte.

*Tip: If mint chocolate chip ice cream is unavailable, use chocolate chip ice cream and fold 1/4 teaspoon mint extract into whipped cream before folding it into ice cream.

Nutrition per Serving: Serving Size: 1/12 of Recipe. Calories 340; Calories from Fat 190; Total Fat 21g; Saturated Fat 10g; Cholesterol 45mg; Sodium 210mg; Dietary Fiber 1g

Dietary Exchange: 1 1/2 Starch, 1 Fruit, 3 1/2 Fat OR 2 1/2 Carbohydrate, 3 1/2 Fat

Mint Chocolate Chip Torte

S'MORE ICE CREAM SQUARES

◆

Yield: 15 servings; **Prep Time:** 30 minutes
(Ready in 2 hours 30 minutes)

A Girl Scout favorite, traditionally served warm from the campfire, gets a cool reinterpretation.

15 graham cracker cookie squares
½ gallon (8 cups) cookies 'n cream ice cream, slightly softened
1 (3.9-oz.) pkg. instant chocolate fudge pudding and pie filling mix
1 ¾ cups milk
½ cup chocolate fudge ice cream topping

1. Place graham crackers in bottom of ungreased 13 × 9-inch pan to form crust. Spoon and spread ice cream evenly over graham crackers. Place in freezer.

2. In small bowl, combine pudding mix and milk; beat 1 minute or until thickened and smooth. Add ice cream topping; beat until smooth. Spread over ice cream layer. Cover with foil; freeze at least 2 hours or until firm.

3. To serve, let stand at room temperature for 5 to 10 minutes. Cut into squares.

Nutrition per Serving: Serving Size: ⅟₁₅ of Recipe. Calories 270; Calories from Fat 100; Total Fat 11g; Saturated Fat 6g; Cholesterol 35mg; Sodium 230mg; Dietary Fiber 1g

Dietary Exchange: 1 ½ Starch, 1 Fruit, 2 Fat OR 2 ½ Carbohydrate, 2 Fat

PEANUT ICE CREAM BALLS WITH HOT FUDGE SAUCE

◆

Yield: 8 servings; **Prep Time:** 30 minutes
(Ready in 2 hours)

This is an attractive variation on a hot fudge sundae. For a change of pace, try this dessert with coffee ice cream.

ICE CREAM BALLS
1 quart (4 cups) vanilla ice cream
1 ½ cups chopped peanuts

SAUCE
1 cup sugar
½ cup unsweetened cocoa
2 tablespoons all-purpose flour
¼ teaspoon salt
1 cup water
3 tablespoons margarine or butter
1 teaspoon vanilla

1. Line cookie sheet with foil or waxed paper. Using ice cream scoop or ½ cup measuring cup, scoop 4 mounds ice cream onto sheet of waxed paper. Quickly shape into balls; transfer to foil-lined cookie sheet. Place in freezer. Repeat to make 4 additional ice cream balls. Freeze 30 minutes or until firm.

2. Roll ice cream balls in peanuts until well coated. Cover; freeze 1 hour or until firm.*

3. In medium saucepan, combine sugar, cocoa, flour and salt; mix well. Stir in water. Bring to a boil over medium heat, stirring occasionally. Cook until mixture thickens, stirring constantly. Remove from heat; stir in margarine and vanilla. Serve warm fudge sauce over ice cream balls.

*Tip: Recipe can be prepared ahead to this point. Freeze ice cream balls for up to 24 hours.

Nutrition per Serving: Serving Size: ⅛ of Recipe. Calories 500; Calories from Fat 240; Total Fat 27g; Saturated Fat 8g; Cholesterol 30mg; Sodium 300mg; Dietary Fiber 5g

Dietary Exchange: 3 ½ Starch, 5 Fat OR 3 ½ Carbohydrate, 5 Fat

EASY STRAWBERRY MARGARITA DESSERT

Yield: 10 servings; **Prep Time:** 15 minutes
(Ready in 4 hours 30 minutes)

Planning a fiesta? This sweet-yet-slightly-salty dessert can be made and frozen up to a week in advance. Prepare it with or without real tequila according to your preference.

CRUST
1 ¼ cups crushed pretzels
¼ cup sugar
½ cup margarine or butter, melted

Easy Strawberry Margarita Dessert

FILLING

1 (14-oz.) can sweetened
  condensed milk (not
  evaporated)
½ cup frozen concentrated
  margarita mix, thawed*
1 (10-oz.) pkg. frozen strawberries
  in syrup, thawed
1 cup whipping cream, whipped

1. In small bowl, combine all crust ingredients; mix well. Press firmly in bottom of ungreased 8 or 9-inch springform pan. Refrigerate while preparing filling.

2. In large bowl, combine condensed milk and margarita mix; beat until smooth. Add strawberries; beat at low speed until well blended. Fold in whipped cream. Pour over crust-lined pan. Freeze 4 to 6 hours or until firm.

3. To serve, let stand at room temperature for 15 minutes. Garnish as desired.

Tip: For alcoholic version, substitute ¼ cup lime juice, 2 tablespoons tequila and 2 tablespoons orange-flavored liqueur for margarita mix.

Nutrition per Serving: Serving Size: ¹⁄₁₀ of Recipe. Calories 400; Calories from Fat 200; Total Fat 22g; Saturated Fat 9g; Cholesterol 45mg; Sodium 290mg; Dietary Fiber 1g

Dietary Exchange: 2 Starch, 1 Fruit, 4 Fat OR 3 Carbohydrate, 4 Fat

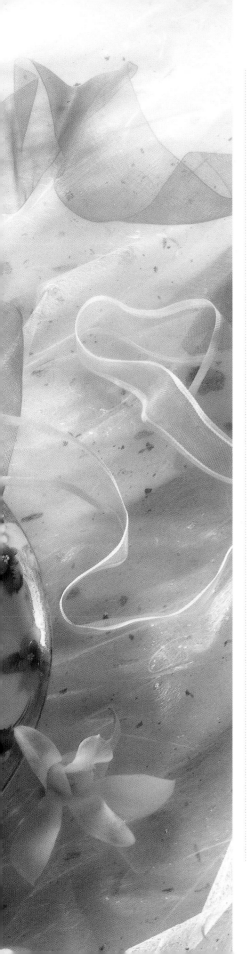

BLUEBERRY-LEMON FROZEN ANGEL DESSERT

Yield: 8 servings; **Prep Time:** 10 minutes
(Ready in 1 hour 10 minutes)

As showy as it is simple, this lovely dessert is easily assembled from purchased ingredients.

1 (14-oz.) loaf angel food cake
1 pint (2 cups) lemon sherbet,
   slightly softened
1 (21-oz.) can blueberry pie filling
1 tablespoon amaretto

1. Slice cake in half horizontally. Spread sherbet over bottom half of cake; replace top. Wrap and freeze 1 hour or until firm.

2. Just before serving, in small bowl, combine pie filling and amaretto; blend well. Cut frozen cake crosswise into slices. Top each serving with pie filling mixture.

Nutrition per Serving: Serving Size: ⅛ of Recipe. Calories 310; Calories from Fat 25; Total Fat 3g; Saturated Fat 1g; Cholesterol 2mg; Sodium 390mg; Dietary Fiber 2g

Dietary Exchange: 1 Starch, 3½ Fruit, ½ Fat OR 4½ Carbohydrate, ½ Fat

Blueberry-Lemon Frozen Angel Dessert

FROZEN FRUIT POINSETTIA CUPS

Yield: 10 servings; **Prep Time:** 15 minutes
(Ready in 2 hours 45 minutes)

Catch the holiday spirit! Cleverly arranged strawberry, kiwi and lemon peel resemble the season's trademark flower.

2 (8-oz.) containers low-fat strawberry or any fruit-flavored yogurt
1 (8¼-oz.) can crushed pineapple
   in heavy syrup, undrained
Red food color, if desired
10 strawberries, thinly sliced
   lengthwise
1 kiwi fruit, peeled, sliced and
   quartered
Grated lemon peel

1. Line 10 muffin cups with foil baking cups. In food processor bowl with metal blade or blender container, combine yogurt, pineapple and food color; process until smooth. Spoon mixture into muffin cups until ¾ full. Freeze 2 hours or until firm.

2. To serve, arrange strawberries and kiwi fruit on top of each cup; place lemon peel in center to resemble poinsettia. Let stand at room temperature for 30 minutes before serving.

Nutrition per Serving: Serving Size: ¹⁄₁₀ of Recipe. Calories 80; Calories from Fat 10; Total Fat 1g; Saturated Fat 0g; Cholesterol 0mg; Sodium 25mg; Dietary Fiber 1g

Dietary Exchange: 1 Starch OR 1 Carbohydrate

CRANBERRY-ORANGE ANGEL LOAF

Yield: 4 servings; **Prep Time:** 15 minutes
(Ready in 4 hours 15 minutes)

The unassuming angel food cake exterior conceals a gorgeous pink filling, and the light, refreshing flavor is especially welcome after a huge holiday meal.

½ (14-oz.) loaf angel food cake
1 (¼-inch-thick) unpeeled orange slice
¼ cup fresh or frozen cranberries
1 tablespoon sugar
½ pint (1 cup) raspberry sherbet, slightly softened

1. Cut ½-inch-thick horizontal slice from top of cake. Make a cavity in loaf by removing cake from center, leaving ½-inch-thick shell on 4 sides and bottom. (Save cake pieces for a later use.)

2. In food processor bowl with metal blade, combine orange slice, cranberries and sugar; process just until finely chopped. Do not puree.

3. Spoon sherbet into medium bowl. Fold in cranberry-orange mixture until well blended. Spoon sherbet mixture into cake cavity. Replace top slice of cake. Wrap cake in foil; freeze about 4 hours or until firm.

4. To serve, let stand at room temperature for 20 minutes. Cut loaf into slices.

Nutrition per Serving: Serving Size: ¼ of Recipe. Calories 200; Calories from Fat 10; Total Fat 1g; Saturated Fat 1g; Cholesterol 2mg; Sodium 340mg; Dietary Fiber 1g

Dietary Exchange: 1 Starch, 2 Fruit OR 3 Carbohydrate

FROZEN KEY LIME TORTE

PICTURED ON PAGE 225.

Yield: 10 servings; **Prep Time:** 15 minutes
(Ready in 4 hours 30 minutes)

Here's a treat for citrus lovers, with Key lime juice intensifying the tang of lime sherbet and lemon sorbet. Garnish each slice with a thin twist of lemon or lime.

1 pint (2 cups) lime sherbet
1 pint (2 cups) lemon sorbet
1 pint (2 cups) vanilla frozen yogurt
1¼ cups graham cracker crumbs (20 squares)
2 tablespoons sugar
¼ cup margarine or butter, melted
1 tablespoon Key lime juice
¼ cup coconut, toasted*

1. Place sherbet, sorbet and frozen yogurt in refrigerator to soften while preparing crust.

2. In small bowl, combine graham cracker crumbs, sugar and margarine; mix well. Press mixture in bottom of ungreased 9-inch springform pan. Freeze 15 minutes.

3. Spoon or scoop softened sherbet, sorbet and frozen yogurt into large bowl. Add lime juice; stir gently to mix. Spoon mixture over crust in pan, spreading evenly. Sprinkle with coconut; press lightly. Freeze at least 4 hours or until firm.

4. To serve, let stand at room temperature for 15 minutes. Cut into wedges.

*Tip: To toast coconut, spread on cookie sheet; bake at 350°F. for 7 to 8 minutes or until light golden brown, stirring occasionally.

Nutrition per Serving: Serving Size: ¹⁄₁₀ of Recipe. Calories 270; Calories from Fat 60; Total Fat 7g; Saturated Fat 2g; Cholesterol 3mg; Sodium 160mg; Dietary Fiber 1g

Dietary Exchange: 1 Starch, 2 Fruit, 1½ Fat OR 3 Carbohydrate, 1½ Fat

MANDARIN FREEZE

Yield: 9 servings; **Prep Time:** 30 minutes
(Ready in 4 hours 40 minutes)

A famous ice cream truck duo, orange and vanilla, gets a grown-up twist when sherbet and ice cream are swirled together in a coconut crust. Another time, fill the crust with chocolate and vanilla ice cream.

CRUST

½ cup margarine or butter
1 cup all-purpose flour
¼ cup sugar
½ cup coconut

FILLING

1½ pints (3 cups) orange sherbet, softened
1½ pints (3 cups) vanilla ice cream, softened
Mandarin orange segments

1. Melt margarine in large skillet over medium-high heat. Add flour, sugar and coconut; cook 3 to 4 minutes or until mixture is golden brown and crumbly, stirring constantly.

2. Reserve ¼ cup crumb mixture for topping, if desired. Using spoon, press remaining mixture firmly in bottom of ungreased 9-inch square pan.

3. In large bowl, combine sherbet and ice cream, swirling to marble. Spread filling over crust. Sprinkle with reserved crumb mixture. Cover; freeze 4 hours or until firm.

4. To serve, let stand at room temperature for about 10 minutes. Cut into squares; place on individual dessert plates. Garnish each square with mandarin orange segment.

Nutrition per Serving: Serving Size: ⅑ of Recipe. Calories 370; Calories from Fat 160; Total Fat 18g; Saturated Fat 7g; Cholesterol 25mg; Sodium 190mg; Dietary Fiber 1g

Dietary Exchange: 1½ Starch, 2 Fruit, 3 Fat OR 3½ Carbohydrate, 3 Fat

FROZEN PISTACHIO CREAM DESSERT WITH RUBY RASPBERRY SAUCE

Yield: 9 servings; **Prep Time:** 30 minutes
(Ready in 6 hours 30 minutes)

With its festive pairing of red and green, this frozen pie looks very pretty in a holiday dessert buffet.

CRUST

1 cup vanilla wafer crumbs (20 wafers)
½ cup finely chopped shelled red pistachios
¼ cup margarine or butter, melted

FILLING

2 (3-oz.) pkg. cream cheese, softened
1 (3.4-oz.) pkg. instant pistachio pudding and pie filling mix
1¼ cups milk
1 (8-oz.) container frozen whipped topping, thawed, reserving ¾ cup

SAUCE

1 (10-oz.) pkg. frozen raspberries in syrup, partially thawed
2 tablespoons sugar
2 tablespoons orange-flavored liqueur

GARNISH

Reserved ¾ cup whipped topping
2 tablespoons chopped shelled red pistachios

1. In medium bowl, combine all crust ingredients; mix well. Press firmly in bottom of ungreased 8-inch springform or 8-inch square pan.

2. In small bowl, beat cream cheese until light and fluffy. Add pudding mix and milk; beat until smooth. Reserve ¾ cup of the whipped topping; cover and refrigerate. Fold 2¼ cups whipped topping into cream cheese mixture; spoon into crust-lined pan. Freeze 5 hours or overnight until firm.

3. Meanwhile, in blender container or food processor bowl with metal blade, combine raspberries, sugar and liqueur. Cover; blend until smooth. Press raspberry mixture through strainer into bowl to remove seeds; discard seeds.

4. Before serving, let dessert thaw in refrigerator for about 1 hour. Top with reserved whipped topping, sauce and 2 tablespoons chopped pistachios.

Nutrition per Serving: Serving Size: ⅑ of Recipe. Calories 410; Calories from Fat 230; Total Fat 25g; Saturated Fat 12g; Cholesterol 25mg; Sodium 320mg; Dietary Fiber 3g

Dietary Exchange: 1½ Starch, 1 Fruit, 5 Fat OR 2½ Carbohydrate, 5 Fat

FROZEN RASPBERRY DELIGHT

Yield: 20 servings; **Prep Time:** 30 minutes
(Ready in 6 hours 45 minutes)

File this crowd-sized dessert in the "elegant and easy" section of your recipe file.

CRUST

2 cups chocolate wafer cookie crumbs (32 cookies)

⅓ cup margarine or butter, melted

¼ cup sugar

FILLING

1 cup chocolate fudge ice cream topping, slightly softened

1 quart (4 cups) vanilla ice cream, slightly softened

1 pint (2 cups) raspberry sherbet, slightly softened

1 (12-oz.) pkg. frozen raspberries without syrup

TOPPING

1 (8-oz.) container frozen whipped topping, thawed

1. In medium bowl, combine all crust ingredients; mix well. Reserve ¼ cup for topping. Press remaining crumb mixture in bottom of ungreased 13 × 9-inch pan. Refrigerate 15 minutes.

2. Spread ice cream topping over crust. Spoon ice cream over topping. Place spoonfuls of sherbet randomly over ice cream; swirl gently into ice cream. Top with raspberries; press gently into sherbet.

3. Spread whipped topping over ice cream–sherbet mixture; top with reserved crumb mixture. Cover tightly with foil. Freeze 6 hours or overnight until firm.

4. To serve, let stand at room temperature for 10 to 15 minutes. Cut into squares.

Nutrition per Serving: Serving Size: ¹⁄₂₀ of Recipe. Calories 280; Calories from Fat 120; Total Fat 13g; Saturated Fat 6g; Cholesterol 15mg; Sodium 160mg; Dietary Fiber 2g

Dietary Exchange: 1 Starch, 1 ½ Fruit, 2 ½ Fat OR 2 ½ Carbohydrate, 2 ½ Fat

Frozen Raspberry Delight

FROZEN STRAWBERRY PARFAITS

Yield: 10 servings; **Prep Time:** 30 minutes
(Ready in 3 hours)

Think of a parfait as a well-planned sundae. Careful layering of ingredients enhances its presentation.

CRUMBS

1 cup all-purpose flour

½ cup chopped pecans

¼ cup firmly packed brown sugar

½ cup margarine or butter

FILLING

1 (14-oz.) can sweetened condensed milk (not evaporated)

3 tablespoons lemon juice

3 tablespoons orange juice

1 pint (2 cups) fresh strawberries, halved

1 cup whipping cream, whipped

1. Heat oven to 350°F. In medium bowl, combine flour, pecans and brown sugar; mix well. With pastry blender or fork, cut in margarine until mixture resembles coarse crumbs. Spread in ungreased 15 × 10 × 1-inch baking pan. Bake at 350°F. for 15 to 20 minutes or until light golden brown, stirring occasionally. Cool 30 minutes or until completely cooled.

2. In large bowl, combine condensed milk, lemon juice and orange juice; beat until smooth. Add 2 cups strawberries; beat at low speed until broken up. Fold in whipped cream. In ten 4-oz. parfait glasses, alternate layers of strawberry mixture with crumbs, ending with crumbs. Freeze 2 hours or until firm.

3. To serve, let stand at room temperature for 15 to 30 minutes. If desired, garnish with additional whipped cream, strawberries and mint leaves.

Nutrition per Serving: Serving Size: ¹⁄₁₀ of Recipe. Calories 410; Calories from Fat 230; Total Fat 25g; Saturated Fat 10g; Cholesterol 45mg; Sodium 170mg; Dietary Fiber 2g

Dietary Exchange: 1 ½ Starch, 1 Fruit, 5 Fat OR 2 ½ Carbohydrate, 5 Fat

RASPBERRY RAZZLE DAZZLE

✦

Yield: 15 servings; **Prep Time:** 30 minutes
(Ready in 7 hours 15 minutes)

Cassis, a specialty of France's Dijon area, is a sweet, pungent liqueur made from black currants. It adds depth of flavor to a beautiful red-purple sauce for a frozen raspberry-vanilla dessert.

DESSERT
30 chocolate-covered graham cracker cookies, finely crushed (about 2 cups crumbs)
1 quart (4 cups) vanilla ice cream, slightly softened
1 pint (2 cups) raspberry sherbet, slightly softened
1 (4-oz.) container (1 ½ cups) frozen whipped topping, thawed

SAUCE
½ cup cranberry juice cocktail
2 tablespoons sugar
2 teaspoons cornstarch
¼ cup creme de cassis or cranberry juice cocktail
1 (12-oz.) pkg. frozen raspberries without syrup, thawed

1. Heat oven to 375°F. Spray 13 × 9-inch pan with nonstick cooking spray. Press cookie crumbs in bottom of sprayed pan. Bake at 375°F. for 7 minutes. Place in refrigerator or freezer until cool.

2. Spoon ice cream over cooled crust. Place spoonfuls of sherbet randomly over ice cream; swirl gently into ice cream. If necessary, smooth top with knife. If ice cream is very soft, freeze 20 minutes. Spread whipped topping over top. Cover with foil or plastic wrap; freeze 6 hours or overnight.

3. In medium saucepan, combine cranberry juice cocktail, sugar and cornstarch; blend well. Cook over medium heat until mixture boils and thickens, stirring constantly. Remove from heat; cool 15 minutes. Stir in creme de cassis and raspberries. Cool 30 minutes or until completely cooled.

4. Just before serving, let stand at room temperature for 10 to 15 minutes. Cut into squares; place on individual plates. Spoon sauce over each serving. If desired, garnish each with additional frozen whipped topping and chocolate filigree.*

Tip: To make chocolate filigrees, draw desired 1 ½-inch design on a square of white paper. Place pattern on cookie sheet; place square of waxed paper (cut one for each filigree) over pattern. Place 2 to 3 tablespoons of chocolate chips in small resealable plastic bag. Seal bag tightly; place in bowl of hot water until chips are melted. Wipe bag; cut off tiny corner to create small opening. Pipe chocolate onto waxed paper, tracing pattern. (Chocolate lines should be about ¼ inch wide.) Care-fully remove pattern piece. Make additional filigrees on separate squares of waxed paper. Refrigerate 30 minutes or until serving time. Carefully remove waxed paper.

Nutrition per Serving: Serving Size: ¹/₁₅ of Recipe. Calories 290; Calories from Fat 110; Total Fat 12g; Saturated Fat 7g; Cholesterol 15mg; Sodium 105mg; Dietary Fiber 2g

Dietary Exchange: 1 Starch, 2 Fruit, 2 Fat OR 3 Carbohydrate, 2 Fat

CARAMEL-BANANA ICE CREAM DESSERT

✦

Yield: 12 servings; **Prep Time:** 15 minutes
(Ready in 2 hours 15 minutes)

Think of this as a banana split disguised as an ice-cream pie.

½ cup coarsely chopped pecans
1 ½ quarts (6 cups) fat-free vanilla ice cream, slightly softened
4 ripe medium bananas, sliced
25 vanilla wafers, coarsely crushed
¼ cup fat-free caramel ice cream topping
¼ cup chocolate-flavored syrup

1. Heat oven to 375°F. Line cookie sheet with foil; place pecans in single layer on sheet. Bake at 375°F. for 3 to 5 minutes or until golden brown. Remove pecans from sheet; set aside to cool.*

2. Scoop ice cream into 13 × 9-inch (3-quart) baking dish; gently spread over bottom of dish.** Top with banana slices. Sprinkle evenly with crushed wafers.

3. Heat caramel topping in microwave on HIGH for about 10 seconds or until warmed to pourable consistency but not hot. Repeat to warm chocolate-flavored syrup. Drizzle caramel and chocolate over crushed wafers. Sprinkle evenly with pecans. Cover tightly with sprayed plastic wrap; freeze at least 2 hours before serving. To serve, cut into squares.

*Tips: *If desired, pecans can be broiled instead of baked. Line broiler pan with foil; place pecans in single layer on pan. Broil 4 to 6 inches from heat for about 1 minute or just until they begin to brown, being careful not to burn them.*

***If desired, spray sheet of plastic wrap with nonstick cooking spray; place over scoops of ice cream. With hand, spread ice cream evenly; remove plastic wrap.*

Nutrition per Serving: Serving Size: 1/12 of Recipe. Calories 290; Calories from Fat 70; Total Fat 8g; Saturated Fat 1g; Cholesterol 0mg; Sodium 130mg; Dietary Fiber 2g

Dietary Exchange: 2 Starch, 1 1/2 Fruit, 1 Fat OR 3 1/2 Carbohydrate, 1 Fat

CINNAMON-HONEY "FRIED" ICE CREAM

Yield: 12 servings; **Prep Time:** 25 minutes
(Ready in 1 hour)

A much simpler alternative to restaurant-style deep-fried ice cream.

1 1/2 quarts (6 cups) chocolate or vanilla ice cream
3 cups finely crushed cinnamon-toast-flavored sweetened cereal
1/3 cup honey
1/4 cup honey, warmed

1. Scoop 12 (1/2-cup) balls of ice cream onto cookie sheet. Freeze 15 minutes.

2. Meanwhile, place cereal in shallow pan. Drizzle 1/3 cup honey evenly over cereal; mix well with fork until crumbly.

3. Quickly roll 1 ball of ice cream at a time in cereal mixture to coat; return to cookie sheet. Freeze ice cream balls about 20 minutes or until firm. (If desired, cover and freeze until serving time.)

4. Just before serving, place ice cream balls in individual dessert dishes. Drizzle each with 1 teaspoon warm honey.

Nutrition per Serving: Serving Size: 1/12 of Recipe. Calories 290; Calories from Fat 90; Total Fat 10g; Saturated Fat 5g; Cholesterol 30mg; Sodium 210mg; Dietary Fiber 1g

Dietary Exchange: 1 Starch, 2 Fruit, 2 Fat OR 3 Carbohydrate, 2 Fat

SPUMONI LOAF

Yield: 8 servings; **Prep Time:** 20 minutes
(Ready in 9 hours 30 minutes)

Made in a loaf pan, spumoni is just as pretty but simpler to make at home than the roll configuration on many Italian restaurant menus. If you wish, make it with the colors of the Italian flag: red (raspberry sherbet), white (vanilla ice cream) and green (pistachio ice cream), which frequently turns up in commercial spumoni.

1 pint (2 cups) raspberry or orange sherbet, softened
1 pint (2 cups) low-fat vanilla ice cream
1/2 cup diced mixed candied fruit

1. Line 8 × 4-inch loaf pan with foil. With back of spoon, spread sherbet evenly in bottom and 2 inches up sides of foil-lined pan. Cover with foil; freeze about 1 hour or until firm.

2. Soften ice cream; stir in candied fruit. Spoon into sherbet-lined pan; spread evenly. Freeze 8 hours or overnight until firm.

3. To serve, invert onto chilled platter; remove foil. Let stand at room temperature for 10 minutes. Cut into slices.

Nutrition per Serving: Serving Size: 1/8 of Recipe. Calories 150; Calories from Fat 20; Total Fat 2g; Saturated Fat 1g; Cholesterol 5mg; Sodium 80mg; Dietary Fiber 0g

Dietary Exchange: 1 Starch, 1 Fruit OR 2 Carbohydrate

FROZEN PUMPKIN PRALINE SQUARES

✦

Yield: 16 servings; **Prep Time:** 1 hour
(Ready in 5 hours 45 minutes)

Looking for something a little more glamorous than pumpkin pie this Thanksgiving? Folding pumpkin filling with whipped topping gives a lighter texture and more subtle flavor; a sweet pecan mixture brings the crunch of Southern pralines to the top.

PRALINE CRUNCH
1 cup sugar
2 tablespoons butter
1 cup chopped pecans

CRUST
1 cup all-purpose flour
1/2 cup chopped pecans
1/4 cup firmly packed brown sugar
1/2 cup butter

FILLING
1 (16-oz.) can (2 cups) pumpkin
1/2 cup firmly packed brown sugar
2 teaspoons pumpkin pie spice
1 quart (4 cups) vanilla ice cream, softened
1 (8-oz.) container frozen whipped topping, thawed

1. Line cookie sheet with foil; lightly butter foil. In large, heavy skillet, combine sugar and 2 tablespoons butter; cook over medium-high heat for about 5 minutes or until sugar is melted and turns golden brown, stirring constantly. Add 1 cup pecans; cook and stir about 1 minute or until pecans are lightly toasted and well coated with sugar mixture. Quickly spread evenly onto foil-lined cookie sheet. Cool 1 hour or until completely cooled. Break or chop into bite-sized pieces.

2. Meanwhile, heat oven to 350°F. In medium bowl, combine flour, 1/2 cup pecans and 1/4 cup brown sugar; mix well. With pastry blender or fork, cut in 1/2 cup butter until mixture resembles coarse crumbs. Press in bottom of ungreased 13 × 9-inch pan. Bake at 350°F. for 10 to 14 minutes or until light golden brown. Cool 30 minutes.

3. In large bowl, combine pumpkin, 1/2 cup brown sugar and pumpkin pie spice; mix well. Fold in ice cream, 2 cups of the whipped topping and 1 cup of the praline crunch. Spread over cooled crust. Reserve remaining whipped topping and praline crunch for garnish. Cover tightly with foil. Freeze 4 hours or until firm.

4. To serve, let stand at room temperature for 15 minutes. Cut into squares; place on individual dessert plates. Garnish each square with reserved whipped topping and praline crunch.

Nutrition per Serving: Serving Size: 1/16 of Recipe. Calories 330; Calories from Fat 170; Total Fat 19g; Saturated Fat 10g; Cholesterol 30mg; Sodium 160mg; Dietary Fiber 2g

Dietary Exchange: 1 Starch, 1 1/2 Fruit, 3 1/2 Fat OR 2 1/2 Carbohydrate, 3 1/2 Fat

Frozen Pumpkin Praline Squares

ITALIAN ICE CREAM BOMBE

◆

Yield: 14 servings; **Prep Time:** 30 minutes
(Ready in 9 hours 30 minutes)

Unmolded onto the serving platter, the bombe resembles an igloo; cutting the dessert into wedges reveals the beautifully layered vanilla, chocolate and raspberry interior.

- 1 1/2 pints (3 cups) French vanilla ice cream, slightly softened
- 6 candied or well-drained maraschino cherries
- 1/3 cup chopped slivered almonds, toasted*
- 1 1/2 pints (3 cups) chocolate ice cream, slightly softened
- 1/2 pint (1 cup) raspberry sherbet, slightly softened
- 1/2 cup whipping cream
- 1 tablespoon powdered sugar
- Red or green food color, if desired
- 1/2 cup fresh or frozen raspberries, thawed

1. Line 1 1/2-quart bowl with plastic wrap. Place in freezer for 15 minutes.

2. Spread softened French vanilla ice cream evenly over bottom and up sides of chilled bowl. Place cherries in circle on ice cream in bottom of bowl. Freeze 30 minutes.

3. In medium bowl, stir almonds into chocolate ice cream; spread evenly over frozen vanilla layer. Freeze 30 minutes.

4. Spoon sherbet into center of mold; smooth top. Cover with plastic wrap; freeze at least 8 hours.

5. Just before serving, uncover bowl; invert onto chilled plate. Remove bowl and plastic wrap. In small bowl, combine whipping cream, powdered sugar and food color; beat until stiff peaks form. Garnish bombe with whipped cream and raspberries. To serve, cut into wedges.**

*Tips: *To toast almonds, spread on cookie sheet; bake at 350°F. for 5 to 7 minutes or until golden brown, stirring occasionally. Or spread in thin layer in microwave-safe pie pan. Microwave on HIGH for 3 to 4 minutes or until light golden brown, stirring frequently.*

***For easier slicing, cut with long, sharp knife dipped in hot water.*

Nutrition per Serving: Serving Size: 1/14 of Recipe. Calories 200; Calories from Fat 100; Total Fat 11g; Saturated Fat 6g; Cholesterol 35mg; Sodium 60mg; Dietary Fiber 1g

Dietary Exchange: 1 Starch, 1/2 Fruit, 2 Fat OR 1 1/2 Carbohydrate, 2 Fat

ICE CREAM ROLL

◆

Yield: 10 servings; **Prep Time:** 30 minutes
(Ready in 8 hours 30 minutes)

The technique for combining two flavors of ice cream into a spiral roll is extremely simple, yet very clever as it lends itself to multiple variations.

Embellish each slice with hot fudge or another dessert sauce, whipped cream, chopped nuts or berries.

- 1 quart (4 cups) chocolate ice cream, softened
- 1 quart (4 cups) mint ice cream, softened

1. Line 15 × 10 × 1-inch baking pan with waxed paper, leaving 2 inches extending over each end. Chill in freezer. Spread chocolate ice cream evenly in chilled waxed paper–lined pan. Freeze about 3 hours or until firm.

2. Spread mint ice cream evenly over chocolate ice cream. Freeze 3 hours or until firm but not solid. (If ice cream freezes solid it will crack when rolled.)

3. To remove ice cream from pan, lift paper ends; place on flat surface. To roll, loosen long sides of ice cream from paper. Working quickly, lift short end of paper and turn over end of ice cream, pressing with fingers to start roll. Roll up jelly-roll fashion, peeling paper back and continuing to lift paper and roll ice cream to end. Discard paper. Place ice cream roll, seam side down, on freezerproof platter. Freeze 2 hours or until firm. To serve, cut into slices.

Nutrition per Serving: Serving Size: 1/10 of Recipe. Calories 220; Calories from Fat 110; Total Fat 12g; Saturated Fat 7g; Cholesterol 45mg; Sodium 85mg; Dietary Fiber 0g

Dietary Exchange: 1 1/2 Starch, 2 Fat OR 1 1/2 Carbohydrate, 2 Fat

Ice Cream Roll

PEANUT BUTTER CANDY ICE CREAM DESSERT

◆

Yield: 16 servings; **Prep Time:** 30 minutes
(Ready in 9 hours)

Here's an absolute sensation for your taste buds, with the contrast of slightly salty peanut butter and sweet fudge sauce; crunchy crumbled candy and smooth vanilla ice cream, all slathered with homemade whipped cream.

³⁄₄ cup peanut butter
¹⁄₄ cup half-and-half
¹⁄₄ cup light corn syrup
2 tablespoons margarine or butter
¹⁄₄ cup powdered sugar
¹⁄₂ gallon (8 cups) vanilla ice cream, slightly softened
1 (12-oz.) jar (1 cup) hot fudge ice cream topping
2 (3.8-oz.) Butterfinger® candy bars, crumbled (1 ¹⁄₄ cups)
1 cup whipping cream, whipped

1. In small saucepan, combine peanut butter, half-and-half, corn syrup and margarine; mix well. Cook over medium heat just until margarine melts and mixture is smooth, stirring occasionally. Remove from heat. Add powdered sugar; beat until smooth and creamy. Cool 30 minutes or until completely cooled.

2. Line 9-inch springform pan with foil. Spread ¹⁄₃ of ice cream in bottom of pan. Spread ice cream topping over ice cream. Spread ¹⁄₃ of ice cream over topping.

3. Stir 1 cup of the crumbled candy into peanut butter mixture; spoon and spread over ice cream. Top with remaining ¹⁄₃ of ice cream. (If ice cream softens too much, freeze between additions of layers.) Cover with foil; freeze at least 8 hours or overnight until firm.

4. Just before serving, remove sides of pan; remove foil. Spread whipped cream over dessert. Sprinkle with remaining candy.

Nutrition per Serving: Serving Size: ¹⁄₁₆ of Recipe. Calories 450; Calories from Fat 230; Total Fat 26g; Saturated Fat 12g; Cholesterol 55mg; Sodium 190mg; Dietary Fiber 1g

Dietary Exchange: 3 Starch, 4¹⁄₂ Fat OR 3 Carbohydrate, 4¹⁄₂ Fat

Butterfinger® is a registered trademark of Nestlé Foods Corporation, Purchase, N.Y.

Peanut Butter Candy Ice Cream Dessert

BAKE-OFF®
DESSERTS

❖ ❖ ❖

To see the great "kitchen" where the Bake-Off® Contest takes place is truly amazing! One hundred individual cooking stations, set up side-by-side, are abuzz with activity as cooks from all over the United States set to work to prepare their special recipes for the judges. Never mind winning the Grand Prize; just getting to the Bake-Off® Contest is a grand achievement.

CHOCOLATE PRALINE LAYER CAKE, PAGE 268

American ingenuity and fabulous flavors shine brightly in Bake-Off® desserts submitted over the years.

SINCE IT BEGAN, the Bake-Off® Contest has enjoyed enduring and unwavering enthusiasm from the legions of home cooks who have entered each contest. Submissions are carefully researched for originality and evaluated for appeal, attractiveness and ease of preparation; recipes undergo a further screening—a literal "trial by fire"—in the Pillsbury test kitchens. Those that make the final cut to compete at the Bake-Off® contest are truly exceptional. And we all end up winners, as many of the recipes go on to become classics interwoven into our national culinary heritage. Bake-Off recipes eventually are adopted as "signature" dishes by cooks around the country who are asked time and time again to bring "their" specialty to the next family celebration.

Topsy Turvy Apple Pie (recipe, page 278), for example, has stood the test of time since it was an entry in 1951; in 1996, Macadamia Fudge Torte (recipe, page 266) earned Kurt Wait two firsts: the distinction of being the first man to win top honors and the good fortune of being the first million-dollar winner. These recipes plus 24 other competition entries—some updated to take advantage of convenience products unavailable when the recipes were first submitted or to address food-safety concerns that have come to light in the intervening years—will brighten your dessert table.

❖   ❖   ❖

BANANA CRUNCH CAKE

❖

Yield: 16 servings; **Prep Time:** 25 minutes
(Ready in 2 hours 40 minutes)

A penny saved by inventing a cake to use overripe bananas was $25,000 earned for Bonnie Brooks, the Grand Prize winner in 1973. She doctored up a packaged cake mix with bananas and sour cream, embellished with a layer of crunchy streusel.

½ cup all-purpose flour
1 cup coconut
1 cup rolled oats
¾ cup firmly packed brown sugar
½ cup chopped pecans
½ cup margarine or butter
1 ½ cups (2 large) sliced *very ripe* bananas
½ cup sour cream
4 eggs
1 (1 lb. 2.5-oz.) pkg. pudding-included yellow cake mix

1. Heat oven to 350°F. Grease and flour 10-inch tube pan. In medium bowl, combine flour, coconut, rolled oats, brown sugar and pecans; mix well. With fork or pastry blender, cut in margarine until mixture is crumbly. Set aside.

2. In large bowl, combine bananas, sour cream and eggs; beat at low speed until smooth. Add cake mix; beat 2 minutes at high speed. Spread ⅓ of batter in greased and floured pan; sprinkle with ⅓ of coconut mixture. Repeat layers 2 more times using remaining batter and coconut mixture, ending with coconut mixture.

3. Bake at 350°F. for 50 to 60 minutes or until toothpick inserted near center comes out clean. Cool upright in pan 15 minutes. Remove cake from pan; place on serving plate, coconut side up. Cool 1 hour or until completely cooled.

High Altitude (Above 3,500 feet): Add 3 tablespoons flour to dry cake mix. Bake at 375°F. for 45 to 55 minutes.

Nutrition per Serving: Serving Size: ¹⁄₁₆ of Recipe. Calories 360; Calories from Fat 140; Total Fat 16g; Saturated Fat 5g; Cholesterol 55mg; Sodium 300mg; Dietary Fiber 2g

Dietary Exchange: 1 ½ Starch, 2 Fruit, 3 Fat OR 3 ½ Carbohydrate, 3 Fat

FUDGY ORANGE CAPPUCCINO TORTE

PICTURED ON COVER.

Yield: 16 servings; **Prep Time:** 30 minutes
(Ready in 3 hours 45 minutes)

This rich, indulgent torte is simple to make with brownie mix and is finished off with a delectable filling and topping. It's a real showstopper!

BROWNIE
1 (1 lb. 3.5-oz.) pkg. fudge
   brownie mix
½ cup oil
¼ cup water
¼ cup orange-flavored liqueur or
   orange juice
2 eggs
1 teaspoon grated orange peel
4 oz. sweet dark chocolate or
   semi-sweet baking chocolate,
   coarsely chopped

FILLING
1 cup sweetened condensed milk
   (not evaporated)
6 oz. sweet dark chocolate or
   semi-sweet baking chocolate,
   chopped
2 egg yolks, slightly beaten
2 tablespoons orange-flavored
   liqueur or orange juice
¾ cup finely chopped nuts

TOPPING
1 ½ cups whipping cream
¾ cup powdered sugar
⅓ cup unsweetened cocoa
2 tablespoons orange-flavored
   liqueur or orange juice
1 teaspoon grated orange peel
⅛ teaspoon salt

GARNISH
Orange slices, twisted, if desired
Orange leaves, if desired

1. Heat oven to 350°F. Grease bottom only of 9 or 10-inch springform pan. In large bowl, combine all brownie ingredients except 4 oz. chocolate; beat 50 strokes with spoon. Stir in chocolate. Spread in greased pan.

2. Bake at 350°F. for 35 to 45 minutes or until center is set. Cool on wire rack for 1 ½ hours or until completely cooled.

3. In medium saucepan, combine consensed milk and 6 oz. chocolate. Cook over low heat, stirring constantly, until chocolate is melted and mixture is smooth. Remove from heat. Stir 2 tablespoons hot mixture into egg yolks. Gradually stir yolk mixture into hot mixture in saucepan. Cook over medium heat 3 minutes, stirring constantly. Remove from heat. Stir in 2 tablespoons liqueur and nuts. Refrigerate just until cool, about 25 minutes.

4. Spread cooled filling mixture over top of cooled brownie. Refrigerate at least 1 hour or until filling is set.

5. To serve, run knife around sides of pan to loosen; remove sides of pan. Place brownie on serving plate. In large bowl, combine all topping ingredients; beat at low speed until blended. Beat at high speed until stiff peaks form. Pipe or spoon topping mixture evenly over chilled filling. Garnish with orange slices and leaves. Store in refrigerator.

High Altitude (Above 3,500 feet): Add ½ cup flour to dry brownie mix; decrease oil to ⅓ cup. Bake at 375°F. for 35 to 45 minutes.

Nutrition per Serving: Serving Size: ¹⁄₁₆ of Recipe. Calories 550; Calories from Fat 270; Total Fat 30g; Saturated Fat 12g; Cholesterol 90mg; Sodium 160mg; Dietary Fiber 3g

Dietary Exchanges: 2 Starch, 2 Fruit, 6 Fat OR 4 Carbohydrate, 6 Fat

MACADAMIA FUDGE TORTE

◆

Yield: 12 servings; **Prep Time:** 30 minutes
(Ready in 3 hours)

Kurt Wait of Redwood City, California, went straight to the top in 1996 when he became the first man to win the Bake-Off® Grand Prize. His creation won $1 million—the largest prize ever awarded in a cooking contest.

FILLING
⅓ cup low-fat sweetened
    condensed milk (not
    evaporated)
½ cup semi-sweet chocolate chips

CAKE
1 (1 lb. 2.25-oz.) pkg. pudding-
    included devil's food cake mix
1 ½ teaspoons cinnamon
⅓ cup oil
1 (16-oz.) can sliced pears in light
    syrup, drained
2 eggs
⅓ cup chopped macadamia nuts
    or pecans
2 teaspoons water

SAUCE
1 (17-oz.) jar butterscotch caramel
    fudge ice cream topping
⅓ cup milk

1. Heat oven to 350°F. Spray 9 or 10-inch springform pan with nonstick cooking spray. In small saucepan, combine filling ingredients. Cook over medium-low heat until chocolate is melted, stirring occasionally.

2. In large bowl, combine cake mix, cinnamon and oil; blend at low speed for 20 to 30 seconds or until crumbly. (Mixture will be dry.)

3. Place pears in blender container or food processor bowl with metal blade; cover and blend until smooth.

4. In another large bowl, combine 2 ½ cups of the cake mix mixture, pureed pears and eggs; beat at low speed until moistened. Beat 2 minutes at medium speed. Spread batter evenly in sprayed pan. Drop filling by spoonfuls over batter. Stir nuts and water into remaining cake mix mixture. Sprinkle over filling.

5. Bake at 350°F. for 45 to 50 minutes or until top springs back when touched lightly in center. Cool 10 minutes. Remove sides of pan. Cool 1 ½ hours or until completely cooled.

6. In small saucepan, combine sauce ingredients. Cook over medium-low heat for 3 to 4 minutes or until well blended, stirring occasionally. Just before serving, spoon 2 tablespoons warm sauce onto each serving plate; top with wedge of torte. If desired, serve with vanilla ice cream or frozen yogurt and garnish with chocolate curls.

High Altitude (Above 3,500 feet): Add ⅓ cup flour to dry cake mix. Bake as directed above.

Nutrition per Serving: Serving Size: ¹/₁₂ of Recipe. Calories 460; Calories from Fat 140; Total Fat 16g; Saturated Fat 4g; Cholesterol 35mg; Sodium 490mg; Dietary Fiber 3g

Dietary Exchange: 1 ½ Starch, 3 ½ Fruit, 3 Fat OR 5 Carbohydrate, 3 Fat

BROWNIE SOUFFLÉ CAKE WITH MINT CREAM

Yield: 12 servings; **Prep Time:** 15 minutes
(Ready in 1 hour 25 minutes)

This dessert earned Edwina Gadsby of Great Falls, Montana, $10,000 at the 1998 Bake-Off® contest.

MINT CREAM
2 ⅔ cup whipping cream
3 oz. white chocolate baking bar,
    finely chopped
¼ to ½ teaspoon mint extract

CAKE
1 (1 lb. 3.5 oz.) pkg. fudge
    brownie mix
½ cup water
½ cup oil
½ to 1 teaspoon mint extract,
    if desired
4 eggs, separated
Powdered sugar
Mint sprigs, if desired

Brownie Soufflé Cake with Mint Cream

1. Heat oven to 375°F. Spray 9 or 10-inch springform pan with nonstick cooking spray. In medium microwave-safe bowl, microwave whipping cream on HIGH for 45 to 60 seconds or until warm. Add white chocolate and $1/4$ to $1/2$ teaspoon mint extract; stir until chocolate is melted. Refrigerate for at least 1 hour or until well chilled.

2. Meanwhile, in large bowl, combine brownie mix, water, oil, $1/2$ to 1 teaspoon mint extract and egg yolks; beat 50 strokes with spoon. In small bowl, beat egg whites until soft peaks form. Gradually fold into brownie mixture. Pour batter into sprayed pan.

3. Bake at 375°F. for 32 to 38 minutes or until center is almost set. Cool 30 minutes. (Center will sink slightly.) Carefully remove sides of pan. Sprinkle top of cake with powdered sugar.

4. Just before serving, beat chilled mint cream until soft peaks form. Cut cake into wedges; top each wedge with mint cream. Garnish with mint sprigs.

High Altitude (Above 3,500 feet): Add $1/2$ cup flour to dry brownie mix. Bake as directed above.

Nutrition per Serving: Serving Size: $1/12$ of Recipe. Calories 420; Calories from Fat 220; Total Fat 24g; Saturated Fat 8g; Cholesterol 95mg; Sodium 180mg; Dietary Fiber 2g

Dietary Exchange: $1^{1}/_{2}$ Starch, $1^{1}/_{2}$ Fruit, $4^{1}/_{2}$ Fat OR 3 Carbohydrate, $4^{1}/_{2}$ Fat

CHOCOLATE PRALINE LAYER CAKE

Yield: 16 servings; **Prep Time:** 25 minutes
(Ready in 2 hours 15 minutes)

Julie Konecne's two-layer chocolate cake, the 1988 Grand Prize winner, is a real showpiece dessert. A rich pecan–brown sugar "upside-down" topping nestles under a mantle of whipped cream frosting, and chocolate curls plus pecans make a professional bakery-style garnish.

CAKE
½ cup butter or margarine
¼ cup whipping cream
1 cup firmly packed brown sugar
¾ cup coarsely chopped pecans
1 (1 lb. 2.25-oz.) pkg. pudding-
    included devil's food cake mix
1¼ cups water
⅓ cup oil
3 eggs

TOPPING
1¾ cups whipping cream
¼ cup powdered sugar
¼ teaspoon vanilla
16 whole pecans, if desired
16 chocolate curls, if desired

1. Heat oven to 325°F. In small, heavy saucepan, combine butter, ¼ cup whipping cream and brown sugar. Cook over low heat just until butter is melted, stirring occasionally. Pour into 2 ungreased 9 or 8-inch round cake pans; sprinkle evenly with chopped pecans.

2. In large bowl, combine cake mix, water, oil and eggs; beat at low speed until moistened. Beat 2 minutes at high speed. Carefully spoon batter over pecan mixture.

3. Bake at 325°F. for 35 to 45 minutes or until cake springs back when touched lightly in center. Cool 5 minutes. Remove from pans. Cool 1 hour or until completely cooled.

4. In small bowl, beat 1¾ cups whipping cream until soft peaks form. Blend in powdered sugar and vanilla; beat until stiff peaks form.

5. To assemble cake, place 1 layer, praline side up, on serving plate. Spread with half of whipped cream. Top with second layer, praline side up. Spread top with remaining whipped cream. Garnish with whole pecans and chocolate curls. Store in refrigerator.

Tip: Cake can be prepared in 13 × 9-inch pan. Bake at 325°F. for 50 to 60 minutes or until cake springs back when touched lightly in center. Cool 5 minutes; invert onto serving platter. Cool completely. Frost cake or pipe with whipped cream. Garnish with pecan halves and chocolate curls. Serve with any remaining whipped cream. Store in refrigerator.

High Altitude (Above 3,500 feet): Add 2 tablespoons flour to dry cake mix; increase water to 1⅓ cups. Bake at 350°F. for 30 to 35 minutes. Immediately remove from pans.

Nutrition per Serving: Serving Size: ⅟₁₆ of Recipe. Calories 460; Calories from Fat 270; Total Fat 30g; Saturated Fat 13g; Cholesterol 95mg; Sodium 330mg; Dietary Fiber 1g

Dietary Exchange: 1 Starch, 2 Fruit, 6 Fat OR 3 Carbohydrate, 6 Fat

STARLIGHT DOUBLE-DELIGHT CAKE

Yield: 12 servings; **Prep Time:** 25 minutes
(Ready in 2 hours 10 minutes)

Helen Weston's 1951 Grand Prize winner uses a unique technique: some of the frosting is blended with the cake batter before it's baked, yielding a superbly moist, rich cake.

FROSTING
2 (3-oz.) pkg. cream cheese,
    softened
½ cup margarine or butter,
    softened
½ teaspoon vanilla
½ teaspoon peppermint extract
6 cups powdered sugar
¼ cup hot water
4 oz. semi-sweet chocolate,
    melted

CAKE
¼ cup margarine or butter,
    softened
3 eggs
2 cups all-purpose flour
1½ teaspoons baking soda
1 teaspoon salt
¾ cup milk

1. Heat oven to 350°F. Grease and flour two 9-inch round cake pans. In large bowl, combine cream cheese, 1/2 cup margarine, vanilla and peppermint extract; blend until smooth. Add powdered sugar alternately with hot water, beating until smooth. Add chocolate; blend well.

2. In another large bowl, combine 2 cups of the frosting mixture and 1/4 cup margarine; blend well. Beat in eggs 1 at a time, beating well after each addition. Add flour, baking soda, salt and milk; beat until smooth. Pour batter evenly into greased and floured pans.

3. Bake at 350°F. for 30 to 40 minutes or until toothpick inserted in center comes out clean. Cool 5 minutes; remove from pans. Cool 1 hour or until completely cooled.

4. To assemble cake, place 1 layer, top side down, on serving plate. Spread with about 1/4 of frosting. Top with second layer, top side up. Spread sides and top of cake with remaining frosting. Store in refrigerator.

High Altitude (Above 3,500 feet): Increase flour to 2 1/2 cups; use 1 1/2 cups of frosting mixture in cake. Bake as directed above.

Nutrition per Serving: Serving Size: 1/12 of Recipe. Calories 550; Calories from Fat 190; Total Fat 21g; Saturated Fat 8g; Cholesterol 70mg; Sodium 540mg; Dietary Fiber 1g

Dietary Exchange: 2 Starch, 3 1/2 Fruit, 4 Fat OR 5 1/2 Carbohydrate, 4 Fat

ALMOND-FILLED COOKIE CAKE

Yield: 24 servings; **Prep Time:** 25 minutes
(Ready in 2 hours 55 minutes)

Elizabeth Meijer of Danbury, Connecticut, took home the Bake-Off® $40,000 Grand Prize for this recipe in 1982. Grated lemon peel brings out the flavor of almonds in a moist filling of a sandwich cookielike cake.

CRUST
2 2/3 cups all-purpose flour
1 1/3 cups sugar
1 1/3 cups butter, softened (do not use margarine)
1/2 teaspoon salt
1 egg

FILLING
1 cup finely chopped almonds
1/2 cup sugar
1 teaspoon grated lemon peel
1 egg, slightly beaten
4 whole blanched almonds

1. Heat oven to 325°F. Place cookie sheet in oven to preheat. Grease 10 or 9-inch springform pan. In large bowl, blend all crust ingredients at low speed until dough forms. If desired, refrigerate dough for easier handling. Divide dough in half. Spread half in bottom of greased pan to form crust.

2. In small bowl, combine all filling ingredients except whole almonds; blend well. Spread over crust to within 1/2 inch of sides of pan.

3. Between 2 sheets of waxed paper, press remaining dough to 10 or 9-inch round. Remove top sheet of waxed paper; place dough over filling. Remove waxed paper; press dough in place. Top with whole almonds.

4. Place cake on preheated cookie sheet. Bake at 325°F. for 65 to 75 minutes or until top is light golden brown. Cool 15 minutes; remove sides of pan. Cool 1 hour or until completely cooled.

High Altitude (Above 3,500 feet): No change.

Nutrition per Serving: Serving Size: 1/24 of Recipe. Calories 250; Calories from Fat 130; Total Fat 14g; Saturated Fat 7g; Cholesterol 45mg; Sodium 50mg; Dietary Fiber 1g

Dietary Exchange: 1 Starch, 1 Fruit, 2 1/2 Fat OR 2 Carbohydrate, 2 1/2 Fat

"MY INSPIRATION" CAKE

Yield: 16 servings; **Prep Time:** 25 minutes
(Ready in 2 hours 10 minutes)

This beautiful cake, layered with pecans and chocolate, looks as if it came straight from the gourmet bakery down the street. Created by Lois Kanago of Webster, South Dakota, it garnered the Grand Prize in 1953.

CAKE
1 cup chopped pecans
2 ¼ cups all-purpose flour
1 ½ cups sugar
4 teaspoons baking powder
½ teaspoon salt
⅔ cup shortening
1 ¼ cups milk
1 teaspoon vanilla
4 egg whites
2 oz. semi-sweet chocolate, grated

FROSTING
½ cup sugar
2 oz. unsweetened chocolate
¼ cup water
½ cup shortening
1 teaspoon vanilla
2 ¼ cups powdered sugar
1 to 2 tablespoons water

1. Heat oven to 350°F. Grease and flour two 9-inch round cake pans. Sprinkle pecans evenly in bottom of greased and floured pans.

2. In large bowl, combine all remaining cake ingredients except egg whites and chocolate; beat 1 ½ minutes at medium speed. Add egg whites; beat 1 ½ minutes. Carefully spoon ¼ of batter into each pecan-lined pan. Sprinkle with grated chocolate. Spoon remaining batter over grated chocolate; spread carefully.

3. Bake at 350°F. for 30 to 40 minutes or until cake is golden brown and top springs back when touched lightly in center. Cool 10 minutes; remove from pans. Cool 1 hour or until completely cooled.

4. Meanwhile, in small saucepan, combine ½ cup sugar, unsweetened chocolate and ¼ cup water; cook over low heat until melted, stirring constantly until smooth. Remove from heat; cool.

5. In small bowl, combine ½ cup shortening and 1 teaspoon vanilla. Gradually beat in 2 cups of the powdered sugar until well blended. Reserve ⅓ cup white frosting. To remaining frosting, add cooled chocolate, remaining ¼ cup powdered sugar and enough water for desired spreading consistency.

6. To assemble cake, place 1 layer, pecan side up, on serving plate. Spread with about ½ cup chocolate frosting. Top with second layer, pecan side up. Frost sides and ½ inch around top edge of cake with remaining chocolate frosting. If necessary, thin reserved white frosting with enough water for desired piping consistency; pipe around edge of nuts on top of cake.

High Altitude (Above 3,500 feet): Increase flour in cake to 2 ½ cups; decrease baking powder in cake to 3 teaspoons. Bake as directed above.

Nutrition per Serving: Serving Size: ⅟₁₆ of Recipe. Calories 470; Calories from Fat 210; Total Fat 23g; Saturated Fat 6g; Cholesterol 0mg; Sodium 210mg; Dietary Fiber 2g

Dietary Exchange: 1 Starch, 3 Fruit, 4 ½ Fat OR 4 Carbohydrate, 4 ½ Fat

"My Inspiration" Cake

FUDGY BONBONS

Yield: 5 dozen cookies;
Prep Time: 1 hour 10 minutes

Chocolate drizzled on top entices, but the real surprise is the candy kiss completely concealed inside the cookie dough of Mary Anne Tyndall's 1994 $50,000 Grand Prize winner.

1 (12-oz.) pkg. (2 cups) semi-sweet chocolate chips
¼ cup margarine or butter
1 (14-oz.) can sweetened condensed milk (not evaporated)
2 cups all-purpose flour
½ cup finely chopped nuts, if desired
1 teaspoon vanilla
60 milk chocolate candy kisses or white and chocolate striped candy kisses, unwrapped
2 oz. white chocolate baking bar or vanilla-flavored candy coating
1 teaspoon shortening or oil

1. Heat oven to 350°F. In medium saucepan, combine chocolate chips and margarine; cook and stir over very low heat until chips are melted and smooth. (Mixture will be stiff.) Add condensed milk; mix well.

2. In large bowl, combine flour, nuts, chocolate mixture and vanilla; mix well. Shape 1 tablespoon dough (use measuring spoon) around each candy kiss, covering completely. Place 1 inch apart on ungreased cookie sheets.

3. Bake at 350°F. for 6 to 8 minutes. DO NOT OVERBAKE. Cookies will be soft and appear shiny but will become firm as they cool. Remove from cookie sheets. Cool 15 minutes or until completely cooled.

4. Meanwhile, in small saucepan, combine baking bar and shortening; cook and stir over low heat until melted and smooth. Drizzle over cooled cookies. Let stand until set. Store in tightly covered container.

High Altitude (Above 3,500 feet): Increase flour to 2 ¼ cups. Bake as directed above.

Nutrition per Serving: Serving Size: 1 Cookie. Calories 120; Calories from Fat 50; Total Fat 6g; Saturated Fat 3g; Cholesterol 5mg; Sodium 20mg; Dietary Fiber 1g

Dietary Exchange: 1 Starch, 1 Fat OR 1 Carbohydrate, 1 Fat

TEXAN-SIZED ALMOND CRUNCH COOKIES

Yield: 4 dozen cookies;
Prep Time: 55 minutes
(Ready in 1 hour 55 minutes)

With the grandness of proportion credited to the Lone Star State, these nut-crunchy cookies are BIG. Barbara Hodgson of Elkhart, Indiana, won $2,000 for this recipe at the 1982 Bake-Off® Contest.

1 cup sugar
1 cup powdered sugar
1 cup margarine or butter, softened
1 cup oil
1 teaspoon almond extract
2 eggs
3 ½ cups all-purpose flour
1 cup whole wheat flour
1 teaspoon baking soda
1 teaspoon salt
1 teaspoon cream of tartar
2 cups coarsely chopped almonds
1 (7.5-oz.) pkg. almond brickle baking chips
Sugar

1. In large bowl, combine 1 cup sugar, powdered sugar, margarine and oil; beat until well blended. Add almond extract and eggs; mix well. Gradually add all-purpose flour, whole wheat flour, baking soda, salt and cream of

Texan-Sized Almond Crunch Cookies

tartar, beating at low speed until well blended. With spoon, stir in almonds and brickle chips. If necessary, cover with plastic wrap; refrigerate 1 hour for easier handling.

2. Heat oven to 350°F. Shape dough into 1 ¾-inch balls; roll in sugar. Place 5 inches apart on un-greased cookie sheets. With fork dipped in sugar, flatten in criss-cross pattern.

3. Bake at 350°F. for 12 to 18 minutes or until edges are light golden brown. Cool 1 minute; re-move from cookie sheets.

High Altitude (Above 3,500 feet): No change.

Nutrition per Serving: Serving Size: 1 Cookie. Calories 210; Calories from Fat 120; Total Fat 13g; Saturated Fat 2g; Cholesterol 10mg; Sodium 140mg; Dietary Fiber 1g

Dietary Exchange: 1 Starch, ½ Fruit, 2 Fat OR 1 ½ Carbohydrate, 2 Fat

CARAMEL LAYER CHOCO-SQUARES

◆

Yield: 36 bars; Prep Time: 40 minutes
(Ready in 2 hours)

This is a surefire winner for a family reunion or school bake sale. Vanilla caramels become a gooey-good filling for a chocolate cake mix that's been spiked with nuts.

1 (5-oz.) can (²/₃ cup) evaporated milk
1 (14-oz.) pkg. vanilla caramels, unwrapped
1 (1 lb. 2.25-oz.) pkg. pudding-included German chocolate cake mix
1 cup chopped nuts
½ cup margarine or butter, softened
1 (6-oz.) pkg. (1 cup) semi-sweet chocolate chips

1. Heat oven to 350°F. Reserve 2 tablespoons evaporated milk for cake mixture. In medium saucepan, combine remaining evaporated milk and caramels. Cook over low heat until caramels are melted and mixture is smooth, stirring frequently. Remove from heat.

2. In large bowl, combine cake mix, nuts, margarine and reserved 2 tablespoons evaporated milk; mix at low speed until crumbly. Press half of dough mixture in bottom of ungreased 13×9-inch pan; reserve remaining dough mixture for topping.

3. Bake at 350°F. for 8 minutes. Remove pan from oven; sprinkle chocolate chips evenly over partially baked crust. Carefully spread caramel mixture over chocolate chips. Crumble reserved dough mixture over caramel mixture.

4. Return to oven; bake an additional 15 to 18 minutes or until filling is set. Cool 1 hour or until completely cooled. Cut into bars.

High Altitude (Above 3,500 feet): No change.

Nutrition per Serving: Serving Size: 1 Bar. Calories 180; Calories from Fat 70; Total Fat 8g; Saturated Fat 3g; Cholesterol 0mg; Sodium 150mg; Dietary Fiber 1g

Dietary Exchange: 1 Starch, ½ Fruit, 1 ½ Fat OR 1 ½ Carbohydrate, 1 ½ Fat

CHOCOLATE CHERRY BARS

◆

Yield: 48 bars; Prep Time: 15 minutes
(Ready in 2 hours)

In the tradition of the famous Black Forest pairing of chocolate and cherries, Frances Jerzak of Porter, Minnesota, enriched a chocolate cake mix with cherry pie filling and almond flavoring, then frosted all with semi-sweet chocolate. She took home the $25,000 Grand Prize in 1974.

BARS
1 (1 lb. 2.25-oz.) pkg. pudding-included devil's food cake mix
1 (21-oz.) can cherry pie filling
1 teaspoon almond extract
2 eggs, beaten

FROSTING
1 cup sugar
⅓ cup milk
5 tablespoons margarine or butter
1 (6-oz.) pkg. (1 cup) semi-sweet chocolate chips

1. Heat oven to 350°F. Grease and flour 15×10×1-inch baking pan or 13×9-inch pan. In large bowl, combine all bar ingredients; stir until well blended. Spread in greased and floured pan.

2. Bake at 350°F. until toothpick inserted in center comes out clean. For 15×10×1-inch pan, bake 20 to 30 minutes; for 13×9-inch pan, bake 25 to 30 minutes.

3. In small saucepan, combine sugar, milk and margarine. Bring to a boil. Boil 1 minute, stirring constantly. Remove from heat; stir in chocolate chips until smooth. Pour and spread over warm bars. Cool 1¼ hours or until completely cooled. Cut into bars.

High Altitude (Above 3,500 feet): Bake at 375°F. as directed above.

Nutrition per Serving: Serving Size: 1 Bar. Calories 110; Calories from Fat 35; Total Fat 4g; Saturated Fat 1g; Cholesterol 10mg; Sodium 100mg; Dietary Fiber 1g

Dietary Exchange: ½ Starch, ½ Fruit, 1 Fat OR 1 Carbohydrate, 1 Fat

FUNFETTI® COOKIES

Yield: 3 dozen cookies;
Prep Time: 40 minutes

Sprinkle-topped cookies are always a favorite with children, and this recipe is easy enough for them to help make. A cake mix simplifies preparation of the cookie dough.

1 (1 lb. 2.9-oz.) pkg. pudding-included white cake mix with candy bits
1/3 cup oil
2 eggs
1/2 (15.6-oz.) can pink vanilla frosting with candy bits

1. Heat oven to 375°F. In large bowl, combine cake mix, oil and eggs; stir with spoon until thoroughly moistened. Shape dough into 1-inch balls; place 2 inches apart on ungreased cookie sheets. With bottom of glass dipped in flour, flatten to 1/4-inch thickness.

2. Bake at 375°F. for 6 to 8 minutes or until edges are light golden brown. Cool 1 minute; remove from cookie sheets.

3. Spread frosting over warm cookies. Immediately sprinkle each with candy bits from frosting. Let stand until set. Store in tightly covered container.

High Altitude (Above 3,500 feet): Add 1/2 cup flour to dry cake mix. Bake as directed above.

Nutrition per Serving: Serving Size: 1 Cookie. Calories 110; Calories from Fat 45; Total Fat 5g; Saturated Fat 1g; Cholesterol 10mg; Sodium 110mg; Dietary Fiber 0g

Dietary Exchange: 1/2 Starch, 1/2 Fruit, 1 Fat OR 1 Carbohydrate, 1 Fat

EASY BAKLAVA BARS

Yield: 48 bars; **Prep Time:** 25 minutes
(Ready in 1 hour 45 minutes)

Inspired by the famous Greek sweet of honey-drenched phyllo layered with nuts, these easy bars shorten prep time by using refrigerated crescent rolls.

CRUST
1 (8-oz.) can refrigerated crescent dinner rolls
2 tablespoons butter or margarine, melted

FILLING
2 cups finely chopped walnuts
1 cup coconut
1 cup quick-cooking rolled oats
2 tablespoons brown sugar
1/2 cup butter or margarine, melted
1/2 teaspoon cinnamon
1/8 teaspoon allspice
1/8 teaspoon cloves

GLAZE
1/2 cup sugar
1/4 cup water
1/4 cup butter or margarine
2 tablespoons honey
1 tablespoon brandy, if desired
1 teaspoon lemon juice
1/4 teaspoon cinnamon
3 whole cloves

1. Heat oven to 350°F. Grease 15 × 10 × 1-inch baking pan. Unroll dough into 2 long rectangles. Place in greased pan; press over bottom to form crust. Firmly press perforations to seal. Brush with 2 tablespoons melted butter. Bake at 350°F. for 5 minutes. Remove from oven.

2. In large bowl, combine all filling ingredients; mix well. Spoon evenly over partially baked crust; gently press down. Return to oven; bake an additional 15 to 20 minutes or until golden brown.

3. In small saucepan, combine all glaze ingredients; mix well. Bring to a boil. Reduce heat; simmer 2 to 3 minutes, stirring constantly. Remove whole cloves. Drizzle glaze evenly over warm bars. Cool 1 hour or until completely cooled. Cut into bars.

Nutrition per Serving: Serving Size: 1 Bar. Calories 110; Calories from Fat 70; Total Fat 8g; Saturated Fat 3g; Cholesterol 10mg; Sodium 75mg; Dietary Fiber 1g

Dietary Exchange: 1/2 Starch, 1 1/2 Fat OR 1/2 Carbohydrate, 1 1/2 Fat

PECAN PIE SURPRISE BARS

◆

Yield: 36 bars; **Prep Time**: 15 minutes
(Ready in 1 hour 55 minutes)

Pearl Hall of Snohomish, Washington, won the $25,000 Grand Prize in 1971 for her innovative transformation of the ever-popular pecan pie into the convenient form of a bar cookie.

BASE

1 (1 lb. 2.25-oz.) pkg. pudding-
  included yellow or butter flavor
  yellow cake mix
⅓ cup margarine or butter,
  softened
1 egg

FILLING

½ cup firmly packed brown sugar
1 ½ cups dark corn syrup
1 teaspoon vanilla
3 eggs
1 cup chopped pecans

1. Heat oven to 350°F. Grease 13 × 9-inch pan. Reserve ⅔ cup of the dry cake mix for filling. In

Apple Nut Lattice Tart

large bowl, combine remaining dry cake mix, margarine and 1 egg; beat at low speed until well blended. Press in bottom of greased pan. Bake at 350°F. for 15 to 20 minutes or until light golden brown.

2. Meanwhile, in large bowl, combine reserved ⅔ cup dry cake mix, brown sugar, corn syrup, vanilla and 3 eggs; beat at low speed until moistened. Beat 1 minute at medium speed or until well blended. Pour filling mixture over warm base; sprinkle with pecans.

3. Return to oven; bake an additional 30 to 35 minutes or until filling is set. Cool 45 minutes or until completely cooled. Cut into bars. Store in refrigerator.

High Altitude (Above 3,500 feet): Decrease brown sugar by 1 tablespoon. Bake base at 375°F. for 15 to 20 minutes; bake filling for 30 to 35 minutes.

Nutrition per Serving: Serving Size: ½ Bar. Calories 160; Calories from Fat 50; Total Fat 6g; Saturated Fat 1g; Cholesterol 25mg; Sodium 140mg; Dietary Fiber 1g

Dietary Exchange: ½ Starch, 1 Fruit, 1½ Fat OR 1½ Carbohydrate, 1½ Fat

APPLE NUT LATTICE TART

Yield: 8 servings; Prep Time: 30 minutes
(Ready in 2 hours 30 minutes)

Mary Lou Warren of Colorado Springs used raisins and pecans and a glazed lattice top to transform a simple apple pie into a top prize winner—$40,000—in 1986.

CRUST
1 (15-oz.) pkg. refrigerated pie crusts

FILLING
3 to 3½ cups (3 to 4 medium) thinly sliced peeled apples
½ cup sugar
3 tablespoons golden raisins
3 tablespoons chopped walnuts or pecans
½ teaspoon cinnamon
¼ to ½ teaspoon grated lemon peel
2 teaspoons lemon juice

TOPPING
1 egg yolk, beaten
1 teaspoon water

GLAZE
¼ cup powdered sugar
1 to 2 teaspoons lemon juice

1. Prepare pie crust as directed on package for *two-crust pie* using 10-inch tart pan with removable bottom or 9-inch pie pan. Place 1 prepared crust in pan; press in bottom and up sides of pan. Trim edges if necessary.

2. Heat oven to 400°F. Place cookie sheet in oven to preheat. In large bowl, combine all filling ingredients; toss lightly to coat. Spoon into crust-lined pan.

3. To make lattice top, cut second crust into ½-inch-wide strips. Arrange strips in lattice design over filling. Trim and seal edges. In small bowl, combine egg yolk and water; gently brush over lattice.

4. Place tart on preheated cookie sheet. Bake at 400°F. for 40 to 60 minutes or until apples are tender and crust is golden brown. Cover edge of crust with strips of foil after 15 to 20 minutes of baking to prevent excessive browning. Cool 1 hour.

5. In small bowl, combine glaze ingredients, adding enough lemon juice for desired drizzling consistency. Drizzle over slightly warm tart. Cool; remove sides of pan.

Nutrition per Serving: Serving Size: ⅛ of Recipe. Calories 370; Calories from Fat 150; Total Fat 17g; Saturated Fat 6g; Cholesterol 40mg; Sodium 280mg; Dietary Fiber 2g

Dietary Exchange: 1 Starch, 2½ Fruit, 3 Fat OR 3½ Carbohydrate, 3 Fat

PINEAPPLE-BLUEBERRY CREAM TART

◆

Yield: 8 servings; **Prep Time:** 35 minutes
(Ready in 1 hour 35 minutes)

Lemon and pineapple filling have enough tartness to balance the sweet blueberry topping, and the two colors look beautiful together, too.

CRUST
1 refrigerated pie crust (from 15-oz. pkg.)

FILLING
1 (2.9-oz.) pkg. lemon pudding and pie filling mix (not instant)
1/2 cup sugar
1/4 cup water
2 egg yolks
2/3 cup canned crushed pineapple with juice
1 1/3 cups water
1 teaspoon grated lemon peel
2 cups fresh or frozen blueberries, thawed, drained on paper towels
1/2 cup blueberry preserves, warmed

TOPPING
1 1/2 cups whipping cream
1/3 cup powdered sugar
1/2 teaspoon vanilla
1 1/2 teaspoons grated lemon peel

1. Heat oven to 450°F. Prepare pie crust as directed on package for *one-crust baked shell* using 10-inch tart pan with removable bottom or 9-inch pie pan. Place prepared crust in pan; press in bottom and up sides of pan. Trim edges if necessary. DO NOT PRICK CRUST. Bake at 450°F. for 9 to 11 minutes or until light golden brown. (If crust puffs up during baking, gently press crust down with back of wooden spoon.) Cool 30 minutes or until completely cooled.

2. In medium saucepan, combine pudding mix, sugar, 1/4 cup water and egg yolks; mix until smooth. Stir in pineapple, 1 1/3 cups water and 1 teaspoon lemon peel. Bring to a boil over medium heat, stirring constantly. Remove from heat; cool at least 15 minutes.

3. In small bowl, combine blueberries and preserves. Spread in cooled baked shell. Spoon pudding mixture over blueberry mixture. Refrigerate 30 minutes or until set.

4. In small bowl, combine whipping cream, powdered sugar and vanilla; beat until stiff peaks form. Spoon or spread over pudding mixture; sprinkle with 1 1/2 teaspoons lemon peel. Serve immediately. Store in refrigerator.

Nutrition per Serving: Serving Size: 1/8 of Recipe. Calories 490; Calories from Fat 230; Total Fat 25g; Saturated Fat 14g; Cholesterol 120mg; Sodium 220mg; Dietary Fiber 2g

Dietary Exchange: 1 Starch, 3 Fruit, 5 Fat OR 4 Carbohydrate, 5 Fat

TOPSY TURVY APPLE PIE

◆

Yield: 8 servings; **Prep Time:** 25 minutes
(Ready in 1 hour 10 minutes)

Brown sugar and pecans make the crust special. After baking, the pie gets a twist: it's inverted onto the serving plate, transforming the sticky bottom crust into a moist, nutty topping.

GLAZE AND CRUST
1/4 cup firmly packed brown sugar
1 tablespoon margarine or butter, melted
1 tablespoon corn syrup
1/4 cup pecan halves
1 (15-oz.) pkg. refrigerated pie crusts

FILLING
2/3 cup sugar
2 tablespoons all-purpose flour
1/2 teaspoon cinnamon
4 cups sliced peeled apples

GARNISH
Whipped cream, if desired

1. In 9-inch pie pan, combine brown sugar, margarine and corn syrup; mix well. Spread evenly in bottom of pan. Arrange pecans over mixture in pan. Prepare pie crust as directed on package for *two-crust pie*; place bottom crust over mixture in pan. Heat oven to 425°F.

Topsy Turvy Apple Pie

2. In small bowl, combine sugar, flour and cinnamon; mix well. Arrange half of apple slices in crust-lined pan. Sprinkle with half of sugar mixture. Repeat with remaining apple slices and sugar mixture. Top with second crust; seal edges and flute. Cut slits in several places in top crust.

3. Bake at 425°F. for 8 minutes. Reduce oven temperature to 325°F.; bake an additional 25 to 35 minutes or until apples are tender and crust is golden brown. (Place pan on foil or cookie sheet during baking to catch any spills.)

4. Loosen edge of pie; carefully invert onto serving plate. Serve warm or cool with whipped cream.

Nutrition per Serving: Serving Size: ⅛ of Recipe. Calories 460; Calories from Fat 220; Total Fat 24g; Saturated Fat 10g; Cholesterol 35mg; Sodium 300mg; Dietary Fiber 2g

Dietary Exchange: 1 Starch, 3 Fruit, 4½ Fat OR 4 Carbohydrate, 4½ Fat

FRENCH SILK CHOCOLATE PIE

Yield: 10 servings; **Prep Time:** 30 minutes
(Ready in 3 hours)

For true chocolate lovers, here's an absolutely heavenly pie, Mrs. Kendall E. Cooper's 1951 prize winner.

CRUST
1 refrigerated pie crust (from 15-oz. pkg.)

FILLING
3 oz. unsweetened chocolate, cut into pieces
¾ cup butter, softened (do not use margarine)
1 cup sugar
½ teaspoon vanilla
¾ cup refrigerated or frozen fat-free egg product, thawed

TOPPING
½ cup sweetened whipped cream
Chocolate curls, if desired

1. Heat oven to 450°F. Prepare pie crust as directed on package for *one-crust baked shell* using 9-inch pie pan. Bake at 450°F. for 9 to 11 minutes or until light golden brown. Cool 30 minutes or until completely cooled.

2. Melt chocolate in small saucepan over low heat; cool. In small bowl, beat butter until fluffy. Gradually add sugar, beating until light and fluffy. Add cooled chocolate and vanilla; blend well.

3. Add egg product ¼ cup at a time, beating at high speed 2 minutes after each addition. Beat until mixture is smooth and fluffy. Pour into cooled baked shell. Refrigerate at least 2 hours before serving. Top with whipped cream and chocolate curls. Store in refrigerator.

Nutrition per Serving: Serving Size: ¹⁄₁₀ of Recipe. Calories 410; Calories from Fat 260; Total Fat 29g; Saturated Fat 17g; Cholesterol 60mg; Sodium 290mg; Dietary Fiber 2g

Dietary Exchange: 1 Starch, 1 Fruit, 6 Fat OR 2 Carbohydrate, 6 Fat

PEACHEESY PIE

Yield: 8 servings; **Prep Time:** 30 minutes
(Ready in 2 hours 20 minutes)

Janis Boykin of Melbourne, Florida, was just a teenager in 1964 when she won the Grand Prize for this peachy pie, scented with pumpkin pie spice and topped with a delectable mixture reminiscent of cheesecake.

CRUST
1 (15-oz.) pkg. refrigerated pie crusts

FILLING
½ cup sugar
2 tablespoons cornstarch
1 to 2 teaspoons pumpkin pie spice
2 tablespoons light corn syrup
2 teaspoons vanilla
1 (28-oz.) can peach slices, drained, reserving 3 tablespoons liquid

TOPPING
3 tablespoons reserved peach liquid
⅓ cup sugar
1 tablespoon lemon juice
2 eggs, slightly beaten
½ cup sour cream
1 (3-oz.) pkg. cream cheese, softened
2 tablespoons margarine or butter

1. Allow crust pouches to stand at room temperature for 15 to 20 minutes.

2. Meanwhile, in medium bowl, combine all filling ingredients except peach liquid; mix well. Set aside.

3. In small saucepan, combine 2 tablespoons of the reserved peach liquid, ⅓ cup sugar, lemon juice and eggs; mix well. Cook over medium heat until mixture boils and thickens, stirring constantly. Boil 1 minute. Remove from heat.

4. In small bowl, combine sour cream and cream cheese; beat until smooth. Gradually beat in hot egg mixture until well blended. Set aside.

5. Heat oven to 425°F. Prepare pie crust as directed on package for *one-crust filled pie* using 9-inch pie pan. Spoon filling into crust-

Peacheesy Pie

lined pan. Dot with margarine. Spoon topping mixture evenly over filling.

6. Unfold second crust. Using floured 3-inch round cutter, cut out 8 rounds from crust. Brush tops of rounds with remaining 1 tablespoon reserved peach liquid. Arrange pie crust rounds over topping.

7. Bake at 425°F. for 10 minutes. Reduce oven temperature to 350°F.; bake an additional 35 to 40 minutes or until crust is golden brown. Cover edge of crust with strips of foil after 15 to 20 minutes of baking to prevent excessive browning. Cool 1 hour or until completely cooled. Store in refrigerator.

Nutrition per Serving: Serving Size: 1/8 of Recipe. Calories 530; Calories from Fat 230; Total Fat 26g; Saturated Fat 11g; Cholesterol 85mg; Sodium 380mg; Dietary Fiber 2g

Dietary Exchange: 1 1/2 Starch, 3 Fruit, 5 Fat OR 4 1/2 Carbohydrate, 5 Fat

SOUR CREAM APPLE SQUARES

Yield: 12 servings; **Prep Time**: 20 minutes
(Ready in 1 hour)

Cinnamon and vanilla lend fragrance to the nutty apple squares that brought the Grand Prize to Luella Maki of Ely, Minnesota, in 1975.

2 cups all-purpose flour
2 cups firmly packed brown sugar
½ cup margarine or butter, softened
1 cup chopped nuts
1 to 2 teaspoons cinnamon
1 teaspoon baking soda
½ teaspoon salt
1 cup sour cream
1 teaspoon vanilla
1 egg
2 cups finely chopped peeled apples

1. Heat oven to 350°F. In large bowl, combine flour, brown sugar and margarine; beat at low speed until crumbly. Stir in nuts. Press 2¾ cups crumb mixture in bottom of ungreased 13 × 9-inch pan.

2. To remaining mixture, add cinnamon, baking soda, salt, sour cream, vanilla and egg; mix well. Stir in apples. Spoon evenly over crumb mixture in pan.

3. Bake at 350°F. for 30 to 40 minutes or until toothpick inserted in center comes out clean. Cut into squares. If desired, serve warm or cool with whipped cream or ice cream.

High Altitude (Above 3,500 feet): Bake at 375°F. for 25 to 35 minutes.

Nutrition per Serving: Serving Size: ¹⁄₁₂ of Recipe. Calories 420; Calories from Fat 170; Total Fat 19g; Saturated Fat 5g; Cholesterol 25mg; Sodium 310mg; Dietary Fiber 2g

Dietary Exchange: 1½ Starch, 2½ Fruit, 3½ Fat OR 4 Carbohydrate, 3½ Fat

APRICOT DESSERT BARS

Yield: 15 servings; **Prep Time**: 30 minutes
(Ready in 1 hour 30 minutes)

The Bake-Off® Contest was in its tenth year when premed student Gregory Patent of San Francisco won $1,000 for these bars in 1958. Sweetened apricots become a spreadable topping that bakes on a coconut-walnut base.

FILLING
2 (6-oz.) pkg. dried apricots, finely cut up (2½ cups)
1½ cups water
¾ cup sugar

BASE
1¾ cups all-purpose flour
1 cup sugar
½ teaspoon salt
½ teaspoon baking soda
¾ cup margarine or butter
1 cup coconut
½ cup chopped walnuts

1. In medium saucepan, combine apricots and water. Cook over medium heat for 10 to 15 minutes or until apricots are very soft, stirring occasionally. Stir in ¾ cup sugar.

2. Heat oven to 400°F. Grease bottom only of 13 × 9-inch pan. In large bowl, combine flour, 1 cup sugar, salt and baking soda; mix well. With fork or pastry blender, cut in margarine until mixture is crumbly. Add coconut and walnuts. Press 3 cups of crumb mixture in bottom of greased pan. Bake at 400°F. for 10 minutes.

3. Remove pan from oven. Spread filling evenly over crust. Sprinkle with remaining crumb mixture.

4. Return to oven; bake an additional 15 to 20 minutes or until golden brown. Cool 30 minutes. Cut into bars.

High Altitude (Above 3,500 feet): No change.

Nutrition per Serving: Serving Size: ¹⁄₁₅ of Recipe. Calories 340; Calories from Fat 120; Total Fat 13g; Saturated Fat 3g; Cholesterol 0mg; Sodium 250mg; Dietary Fiber 3g

Dietary Exchange: 1 Starch, 2½ Fruit, 2½ Fat OR 3½ Carbohydrate, 2½ Fat

Sour Cream Apple Squares

APPLE NUGGET COBBLER

✦

Yield: 10 servings; **Prep Time:** 30 minutes
(Ready in 1 hour 20 minutes)

Refrigerated biscuits update the preparation of this easy version of a traditional pandowdy dessert.

FRUIT MIXTURE
6 cups (6 large) sliced peeled
   apples
½ cup raisins
½ cup chopped nuts, if desired
½ cup sugar
2 tablespoons all-purpose flour
1 teaspoon cinnamon

TOPPING
1 (12-oz.) can refrigerated flaky
   biscuits
¼ cup sugar
½ teaspoon cinnamon
¼ cup margarine or butter, melted

1. Heat oven to 375°F. In ungreased 8-inch square or 12 × 8-inch (2-quart) baking dish, arrange apples, raisins and nuts in layers. In small bowl, combine ½ cup sugar, flour and 1 teaspoon cinnamon; mix well. Sprinkle over fruit. Cover loosely with foil. Bake at 375°F. for 20 to 30 minutes or until apples are almost tender.

2. Remove baking dish from oven. Separate dough into 10 biscuits; cut each into 4 pieces. In resealable plastic bag, combine biscuit pieces, ¼ cup sugar and ½ teaspoon cinnamon; shake to coat. Arrange over hot apple mixture. Sprinkle with any remaining sugar-cinnamon mixture. Drizzle with melted margarine.

3. Return to oven; bake, uncovered, an additional 15 to 20 minutes or until deep golden brown.

Nutrition per Serving: Serving Size: ¹⁄₁₀ of Recipe. Calories 320; Calories from Fat 120; Total Fat 13g; Saturated Fat 2g; Cholesterol 0mg; Sodium 410mg; Dietary Fiber 2g

Dietary Exchange: 1 ½ Starch, 1 ½ Fruit, 2 ½ Fat OR 3 Carbohydrate, 2 ½ Fat

RASPBERRY-MANGO SHORTCAKES

✦

Yield: 8 servings; **Prep Time:** 50 minutes

Nancy Flesch of Kent, Ohio, took the basic idea of shortcake—whipped cream and fruit atop biscuits—and gave it new appeal by spiking the biscuits with coconut and topping them with mango and raspberries. Even her whipped cream has an unexpected accent: it's flavored with brown sugar and ginger. This recipe competed in the 1996 contest.

SHORTCAKES
½ cup coconut
¼ cup sugar
½ teaspoon ginger
1 (17.3-oz.) can large refrigerated
   buttermilk biscuits
2 tablespoons margarine or butter,
   melted

FRUIT
2 cups fresh or frozen raspberries,
   partially thawed
1 ½ cups chopped peeled fresh
   mangoes or 1 (16-oz.) jar or can
   mangoes or peaches, drained,
   chopped
2 tablespoons sugar

TOPPING
1 cup whipping cream
2 tablespoons brown sugar
¼ teaspoon ginger

1. Heat oven to 375°F. In small bowl, combine coconut, ¼ cup sugar and ½ teaspoon ginger; blend well. Separate dough into 8 biscuits. Dip top and sides of each biscuit in margarine; dip in coconut mixture. Place biscuits, coconut side up, 2 inches apart on ungreased cookie sheet. Sprinkle any remaining coconut mixture over tops of biscuits.

2. Bake at 375°F. for 14 to 18 minutes or until biscuits and coconut are light golden brown. Cool 5 minutes.

3. Meanwhile, in medium bowl, combine raspberries, mangoes and 2 tablespoons sugar; stir gently. In small bowl, combine all topping ingredients; beat until stiff peaks form.

4. Just before serving, split biscuits; place bottom halves on 8 individual dessert plates. Spoon generous ⅓ cup fruit mixture over each biscuit half. Top each with ¼ cup topping and biscuit top. Store in refrigerator.

Nutrition per Serving: Serving Size: ⅛ of Recipe. Calories 450; Calories from Fat 230; Total Fat 26g; Saturated Fat 12g; Cholesterol 40mg; Sodium 680mg; Dietary Fiber 4g

Dietary Exchange: 1 ½ Starch, 1 ½ Fruit, 5 Fat OR 3 Carbohydrate, 5 Fat

COUNTRY FRENCH APPLE CRESCENT CASSEROLE

Yield: 8 servings; Prep Time: 25 minutes
(Ready in 1 hour 5 minutes)

Sharon Richardson of Dallas, a 1990 prize winner, combined dumplings and apple slices baked in custard for a wonderful brunch-style sweet.

DUMPLINGS
2 tablespoons sugar
½ to 1 teaspoon cinnamon
1 (8-oz.) can refrigerated crescent dinner rolls
1 large apple, peeled, cut into 8 slices

SAUCE
½ cup sugar
½ cup whipping cream
1 tablespoon almond extract or amaretto
1 egg

TOPPING
½ cup sliced almonds
Cinnamon

1. Heat oven to 375°F. In small bowl, combine 2 tablespoons sugar and ½ to 1 teaspoon cinnamon; blend well. Separate dough into 8 triangles; sprinkle sugar mixture evenly over each. Gently press sugar mixture into each triangle, flattening each slightly.

2. Place apple slice on wide end of each triangle; tuck in edges around apple slice. Roll up, starting at wide end; roll to opposite point. Seal all seams. Place tip side down in ungreased 9-inch round baking dish or pie pan, placing long side of 7 filled crescents around outside edge of dish and 1 in center.

3. Bake at 375°F. for 15 to 20 minutes or until golden brown.

4. Remove baking dish from oven. In small bowl, combine all sauce ingredients; beat with wire whisk until well blended. Spoon sauce evenly over partially baked rolls. Sprinkle with almonds and cinnamon.

5. Return to oven; bake an additional 13 to 18 minutes or until deep golden brown. Cover top of pan with foil during last 5 minutes of baking time if necessary to prevent excessive browning. Serve warm. Store in refrigerator.

Nutrition per Serving: Serving Size: ⅛ of Recipe. Calories 280; Calories from Fat 140; Total Fat 15g; Saturated Fat 5g; Cholesterol 45mg; Sodium 230mg; Dietary Fiber 2g

Dietary Exchange: 1 Starch, 1 Fruit, 3 Fat OR 2 Carbohydrate, 3 Fat

ROYAL MARBLE CHEESECAKE

◆

Yield: 16 servings; **Prep Time:** 35 minutes
(Ready in 12 hours)

Melted chocolate chips add a regal touch to a luxurious cheesecake, lacing it with ribbons of dark chocolate. Dora Feinstein of Atlantic City, New Jersey, entered this creation in the 1964 Bake-Off® Contest.

CRUST

¾ cup all-purpose flour
2 tablespoons sugar
Dash salt
¼ cup margarine or butter
1 (6-oz.) pkg. (1 cup) semi-sweet
   chocolate chips, melted

FILLING

3 (8-oz.) pkg. cream cheese,
   softened
1 cup sugar
¼ cup all-purpose flour

2 teaspoons vanilla
6 eggs
1 cup sour cream

1. Heat oven to 400°F. In small bowl, combine ¾ cup flour, 2 tablespoons sugar and salt; mix well. With pastry blender or fork, cut in margarine until mixture resembles coarse crumbs. Stir in 2 tablespoons of the melted chocolate. Reserve remaining chocolate for filling. Press crumb mixture in

Royal Marble Cheesecake

bottom of ungreased 9-inch springform pan.

2. Bake at 400°F. for 10 minutes or until very light brown. Remove from oven. Reduce oven temperature to 325°F.

3. In large bowl, combine cream cheese and 1 cup sugar; beat until light and fluffy. Add ¼ cup flour and vanilla; blend well. At low speed, add eggs 1 at a time, beating just until blended. Add sour cream; mix well. Place 1 ¾ cups filling mixture in medium bowl; stir in reserved melted chocolate.

4. Pour half of plain filling over crust. Top with spoonfuls of half of the chocolate filling. Cover with remaining plain filling, then with spoonfuls of remaining chocolate filling. Using table knife, swirl chocolate filling through plain filling.

5. Bake at 325°F. for 1 to 1 ¼ hours or until center is almost set. Cool 10 minutes. Remove sides of pan. Cool 2 to 3 hours. Refrigerate 8 hours or overnight before serving. Store in refrigerator.

Nutrition per Serving: Serving Size: ¹⁄₁₆ of Recipe. Calories 380; Calories from Fat 230; Total Fat 26g; Saturated Fat 14g; Cholesterol 135mg; Sodium 200mg; Dietary Fiber 1g

Dietary Exchange: 2 Fruit, 1 Medium-Fat Meat, 4 Fat OR 2 Carbohydrate, 1 Medium-Fat Meat, 4 Fat

CAKE 'N CHEESE CAKE

Yield: 10 servings; Prep Time: 30 minutes
(Ready in 4 hours 50 minutes)

Think of this as two desserts in one, with a dreamy cheesecake topping for a delectable yellow cake. Imogene Noar of Paramount, California, won $1,500 for this invention in 1962.

FILLING
1 (8-oz.) pkg. cream cheese, softened
⅔ cup sugar
½ cup sour cream
1 teaspoon vanilla
2 eggs

CAKE
1 cup all-purpose flour
1 teaspoon baking powder
Dash salt
½ cup margarine or butter, softened
⅔ cup sugar
2 eggs
1 tablespoon milk
1 teaspoon vanilla

TOPPING
1 cup sour cream
2 tablespoons sugar
1 teaspoon vanilla

1. Heat oven to 325°F. Grease and flour bottom only of 10-inch deep dish pie pan or 9-inch square pan. In small bowl, combine cream cheese and ⅔ cup sugar; beat until light and fluffy. Add ½ cup sour cream and 1 teaspoon vanilla; blend well. Add 2 eggs 1 at a time, beating at low speed. Set aside.

2. In medium bowl, combine flour, baking powder and salt; mix well. In large bowl, combine margarine and ⅔ cup sugar; beat until light and fluffy. Add 2 eggs 1 at a time, beating well after each addition. Stir in milk and 1 teaspoon vanilla. Add dry ingredients at low speed until moistened. Beat 1 minute at medium speed. Spread batter in bottom and up sides of greased and floured pan, spreading thinner on sides. Pour cream cheese mixture over batter.

3. Bake at 325°F. for 40 to 45 minutes or until cheesecake is almost set in center and cake is golden brown.

4. Meanwhile, in small bowl, combine all topping ingredients. Remove cake from oven; spread evenly with topping. Bake an additional 5 minutes. Cool 30 minutes. Refrigerate 3 to 4 hours before serving. Store in refrigerator.

High Altitude (Above 3,500 feet): Decrease sugar in filling to ½ cup; decrease sugar in cake to ½ cup. Bake as directed above.

Nutrition per Serving: Serving Size: ¹⁄₁₀ of Recipe. Calories 440; Calories from Fat 240; Total Fat 27g; Saturated Fat 12g; Cholesterol 125mg; Sodium 280mg; Dietary Fiber 0g

Dietary Exchange: 2 Starch, 1 Fruit, 5 Fat OR 3 Carbohydrate, 5 Fat

COOKIES, BARS AND BROWNIES

❖ ❖ ❖

What goes better in a lunch box
than homemade chocolate chip
cookies? What's more delicious
after school than a warm fudge
brownie with a tall glass of milk?
What's more friendly than a plate
of cookies for a new neighbor?
There's a recipe in this chapter for
every baker and every occasion.

LEMON GINGER CREAMS, PAGE 293
SALTED PEANUT-CHOCOLATE-CARAMEL SQUARES, PAGE 318

Follow our tips for cookies, bars and brownies and your success in the kitchen will be all the sweeter.

COOKIE EQUIPMENT

While molds and presses and fancy gizmos are available for elaborate cookies, basic cookie baking requires very little special equipment.

PANCAKE TURNER OR METAL SPATULA. These are efficient for transferring cookies from baking trays to cooling racks.

COOKIE SHEETS. You'll want several so you can bake one sheet while you're preparing another, and a third is cooling. Cookie sheets are available in four basic styles:

◆ SHINY. Shiny, silver-colored aluminum cookie sheets without raised sides are best. The shiny metal reflects heat, so the cookies are less likely to burn.

◆ DOUBLE-LAYER. Cookie sheets with an insulating "cushion of air" between two sheets of metal are designed to improve circulation of hot air around the cookies. The sheets are more expensive and cookies do not brown as much on the bottom, which can make doneness harder to judge. In addition, cooking time increases slightly.

◆ BLACK SURFACE. Cookies bake faster on dark, nonreflective surfaces, which absorb heat, so you must watch more closely to prevent the bottoms from burning.

◆ NONSTICK. These are unnecessary. Many cookies have enough butter that the sheet does not require greasing anyway; others require only a light coating for the first batch.

WOODEN SPOONS. They're traditional, and also more effective (and quieter) than metal kitchen spoons for stirring doughs properly.

TIPS FOR MAKING GREAT COOKIES

CHILLING DOUGH. Some recipes specify chilling the dough for easier handling, especially for cookies that are rolled or shaped. Refrigerate other doughs, if they seem too sticky to work with.

BAKING COOKIES. Place the cookie sheet on a rack set in the center of the oven, leaving space on all sides for air circulation. It's best to bake just one sheet at a time. If you must do two at once, swap shelves and turn the sheets around halfway through baking time.

TESTING FOR DONENESS. Most recipes specify a range of cooking times to compensate for variations in ovens, ingredients, size of cookies and so on. Check at the minimum time, looking for cookies that are firmly set or browned according to recipe directions.

COOLING SHEETS. To prevent the cookies from spreading out too rapidly, always begin with a cool baking sheet.

COOLING COOKIES. Let cookies remain on the tray for a minute or two to firm up for easier handling, then use a spatula to transfer individual cookies from baking sheets to a wire rack. Don't pile warm cookies atop one another.

STORING SOFT COOKIES. Ironically, many decorative cookie jars do not offer airtight storage. Store soft cookies in a tightly closed container between layers of waxed paper to prevent sticking (or in a single layer if frosted or filled). Store different kinds of cookies in separate containers.

STORING CRISP COOKIES. A container with a looser-fitting cover, such as a glass casserole dish or ceramic cookie jar, is best unless the weather is very humid. In that case, crisp cookies will do better in an airtight container. To revive crisp cookies that have gone limp, reheat them on a baking tray in a preheated 300° F. oven for 3 to 5 minutes; cool on a rack.

FREEZING COOKIES. To freeze unfrosted baked cookies, package them in containers with tightfitting lids and freeze for up to 12 months. Freeze frosted cookies uncovered on a baking sheet until hard, then package the frozen cookies between layers of waxed paper in a rigid container for up to 2 months.

THAWING COOKIES. Thaw soft-textured cookies in the container at room temperature or defrost them briefly in the microwave oven. For crisp-textured cookies, remove from the container before thawing.

SHAPING COOKIES

Intricate cookie cutters are fun, but time-consuming to use. Some quicker ideas for shaping rolled dough:

◆ Cut across the entire surface of the dough in two directions to shape rectangles, squares or diamonds; cut across diamonds or squares to make triangles. Use a knife for straight edges or a pastry wheel for ruffled borders.

◆ Use a drinking glass dipped in flour to cut circles. Use your imagination to find everyday kitchen objects to stamp a design in the top. Gently press dough with the bottom of a cut-glass sugar bowl, for example, or a meat mallet.

◆ Crimp the edges with a fork dipped in sugar.

TIPS FOR MAILING COOKIES

◆ Choose moist, firm-textured cookies that will remain fresh and intact during transport. Good choices usually include drop cook-

ies, unfrosted bars, fudgy brownies or other sturdy cookies. Delicate, intricately shaped specialties are best reserved for personal delivery.

◆ Pack the cookies into a firm-sided cardboard, metal or plastic container lined with plastic wrap or foil. Insulate the sides of the container with a "wall" of crumpled waxed paper. Layer the cookies with waxed paper or wrap them in pairs, flat sides together.

◆ For extra protection, place the container into a larger box padded on all sides with crumpled paper or packing material. Wrap securely, mark it "perishable" and send it the speediest way possible, whether by first-class mail or private carrier.

BARS AND BROWNIES

Bar cookies and brownies are made from dough that is spread and baked in a pan. They're convenient when time is short, because once the dough is mixed, there's no fussing with batch after batch of individual cookies.

BAKING PANS FOR BARS. Always use the size specified in the recipe, or your results may be disappointing. As with baking sheets, shiny aluminum is best. Doubled recipes are best baked in two separate pans rather than one pan that is twice as big because the center may still be underbaked while the edges are overdone.

TESTING FOR DONENESS. Cake-like bars and brownies are done when they just begin to pull away from the sides of the pan; when a toothpick inserted into the center comes out clean; or when they are set in the center. It's trickier to tell when fudgy brownies or very moist, dense bars are done. Observe the listed range of baking time. The shorter time will usually produce moist, almost "wet" brownies or bars, while the longer time will cause the dessert to be more set but still moist. In any case, remove the pan from the oven after the maximum suggested baking time, even if the center still looks fairly moist. The brownies or bars will continue to set after removal from the oven.

COOLING BROWNIES AND BARS. Set the pan of brownies or bars on a cooling rack until completely cooled before cutting them, unless otherwise specified. To prevent big cracks in the brownies with a somewhat crisp top over a moist interior, lightly score the cutting lines on the top with a knife while the brownies are still warm; cut them all the way through after they cool.

STORING BARS. To keep bars and brownies fresh, cut only as much as needed. Store the rest in the pan, tightly covered. Brownies freeze well, individually wrapped in plastic wrap, and are quickly thawed in the microwave.

◆　　◆　　◆

SOFT AND CHEWY CHOCOLATE CHIP COOKIES

Yield: 6 dozen cookies;
Prep Time: 55 minutes

Chocolate chip cookies, an American invention, come in many versions, large and small, crisp or soft. Try this version if you're a fan of the large, chewy kind. To keep the cookies from becoming crisp, be careful not to overbake them.

1 ¼ cups sugar
1 ¼ cups firmly packed brown sugar
1 ½ cups margarine or butter, softened
2 teaspoons vanilla
3 eggs
4 ¼ cups all-purpose flour
2 teaspoons baking soda
½ teaspoon salt
1 to 2 (12-oz.) pkg. semi-sweet chocolate chips*

1. Heat oven to 375°F. In large bowl, combine sugar, brown sugar and margarine; beat until light and fluffy. Add vanilla and eggs; blend well. Add flour, baking soda and salt; mix well. Stir in chocolate chips.** Drop dough by rounded tablespoonfuls 2 inches apart onto ungreased cookie sheets.

Soft and Chewy Chocolate Chip Cookies

2. Bake at 375°F. for 8 to 10 minutes or until light golden brown. Cool 1 minute; remove from cookie sheets.

*Tips: *If desired, half of dough can be made with butterscotch, peanut butter, white vanilla or mint chocolate chips instead of semi-sweet chocolate chips.*

**At this point, dough can be frozen. Wrap tightly and freeze up to 2 months. To bake, thaw dough at room temperature for 1 to 2 hours. Bake as directed above.

High Altitude (Above 3,500 feet): Decrease sugar, brown sugar and margarine to 1 cup each. Bake as directed above.

Nutrition per Serving: Serving Size: 1 Cookie. Calories 140; Calories from Fat 60; Total Fat 7g; Saturated Fat 2g; Cholesterol 10mg; Sodium 100mg; Dietary Fiber 1g

Dietary Exchange: ½ Starch, ½ Fruit, 1 ½ Fat OR 1 Carbohydrate, 1 ½ Fat

LEMON GINGER CREAMS

Yield: 4 dozen cookies; **Prep Time:** 1 hour

Old-fashioned spice cookies get a sweet-tangy lift from lemon frosting. If you wish, stir ½ cup of raisins into the dough.

COOKIES
½ cup sugar
¼ cup shortening
½ cup molasses
½ cup hot water
1 egg

2 cups all-purpose flour
1 teaspoon baking soda
½ teaspoon salt
¾ teaspoon ginger
¾ teaspoon cinnamon
¼ teaspoon cloves

FROSTING
2 cups powdered sugar
½ teaspoon grated lemon peel
2 tablespoons margarine or butter, softened
2 tablespoons lemon juice
1 to 2 tablespoons milk

1. Heat oven to 375°F. Spray cookie sheets with nonstick cooking spray. In large bowl, combine sugar, shortening, molasses, water and egg; beat well. Add all remaining cookie ingredients; stir just until blended. Let stand 5 minutes. Drop dough by rounded teaspoonfuls 2 inches apart onto sprayed cookie sheets.

2. Bake at 375°F. for 8 to 12 minutes or until edges are light golden brown. Immediately remove from cookie sheets. Cool 15 minutes or until completely cooled.

3. In small bowl, combine all frosting ingredients, adding enough milk for desired spreading consistency; blend until smooth. Spread frosting over cooled cookies.

High Altitude (Above 3,500 feet): No change.

Nutrition per Serving: Serving Size: 1 Cookie. Calories 80; Calories from Fat 20; Total Fat 2g; Saturated Fat 0g; Cholesterol 4mg; Sodium 55mg; Dietary Fiber 0g

Dietary Exchange: 1 Fruit, ½ Fat OR 1 Carbohydrate, ½ Fat

OATMEAL RAISIN COOKIES

◆

Yield: 3 1/2 dozen cookies;
Prep Time: 45 minutes

These home-style cookie jar favorites make a hearty addition to a lunch box or picnic basket. For a chewier texture, use old-fashioned rolled oats instead of quick-cooking.

3/4 cup sugar
1/4 cup firmly packed brown sugar
1/2 cup margarine or butter, softened
1/2 teaspoon vanilla
1 egg
3/4 cup all-purpose flour
1/2 teaspoon baking soda
1/2 teaspoon cinnamon
1/4 teaspoon salt
1 1/2 cups quick-cooking rolled oats
1/2 cup raisins
1/2 cup chopped nuts

1. Heat oven to 375°F. Grease cookie sheets. In large bowl, combine sugar, brown sugar and margarine; beat until light and fluffy. Add vanilla and egg; blend well. Add flour, baking soda, cinnamon and salt; mix well. Stir in oats, raisins and nuts. Drop dough by rounded teaspoonfuls 2 inches apart onto greased cookie sheets.

2. Bake at 375°F. for 7 to 10 minutes or until edges are light golden brown. Cool 1 minute; remove from cookie sheets.

High Altitude (Above 3,500 feet): Increase flour to 1 cup. Bake as directed above.

Nutrition per Serving: Serving Size: 1 Cookie. Calories 70; Calories from Fat 25; Total Fat 3g; Saturated Fat 0g; Cholesterol 5mg; Sodium 55mg; Dietary Fiber 0g

Dietary Exchange: 1/2 Starch, 1/2 Fat OR 1/2 Carbohydrate, 1/2 Fat

JEWEL TOP JUMBLES

◆

Yield: 3 1/2 dozen cookies;
Prep Time: 1 hour

Mixed-in miniature gumdrops make these a favorite for the kids or any lighthearted occasion.

1/2 cup sugar
1/2 cup firmly packed brown sugar
1 cup margarine or butter, softened
1 teaspoon vanilla
2 eggs
2 3/4 cups all-purpose flour
1/2 teaspoon baking soda
1/2 teaspoon salt
2 1/2 cups miniature gumdrops, halved*

1. Heat oven to 375°F. Lightly grease cookie sheets. In large bowl, combine sugar, brown sugar and margarine; beat until light and fluffy. Add vanilla and eggs; blend well. Add flour, baking soda and salt; mix well. Stir in gumdrops. Drop dough by rounded teaspoonfuls 2 inches apart onto greased cookie sheets.

2. Bake at 375°F. for 10 to 12 minutes or until light golden brown. Immediately remove from cookie sheets.

*Tip: For ease in cutting gumdrops, use kitchen scissors dipped in warm water.

High Altitude (Above 3,500 feet): No change.

Nutrition per Serving: Serving Size: 1 Cookie. Calories 140; Calories from Fat 45; Total Fat 5g; Saturated Fat 1g; Cholesterol 10mg; Sodium 100mg; Dietary Fiber 0g

Dietary Exchange: 1/2 Starch, 1 Fruit, 1 Fat OR 1 1/2 Carbohydrate, 1 Fat

Oatmeal Raisin Cookies

German Chocolate Cake Mix Cookies

GERMAN CHOCOLATE CAKE MIX COOKIES

◆

Yield: 4 dozen cookies;
Prep Time: 50 minutes

When you're pressed for time but longing for the aroma and taste of fresh-baked cookies, take a shortcut by embellishing a box of cake mix to create delicious cookies.

1 (1 lb. 2.25-oz.) pkg. German chocolate cake mix
1 (6-oz.) pkg. (1 cup) semi-sweet chocolate chips
½ cup rolled oats
½ cup raisins
½ cup oil
2 eggs, slightly beaten

1. Heat oven to 350°F. In large bowl, combine all ingredients; blend well. Drop dough by rounded teaspoonfuls 2 inches apart onto ungreased cookie sheets.

2. Bake at 350°F. for 8 to 10 minutes or until set. Cool 1 minute; remove from cookie sheets.

High Altitude (Above 3,500 feet): Add ¼ cup flour to dry cake mix. Bake as directed above.

Nutrition per Serving: Serving Size: 1 Cookie. Calories 100; Calories from Fat 45; Total Fat 5g; Saturated Fat 1g; Cholesterol 10mg; Sodium 70mg; Dietary Fiber 1g

Dietary Exchange: ½ Starch, ½ Fruit, ½ Fat OR 1 Carbohydrate, ½ Fat

COCONUT MACAROONS

Yield: 12 cookies; **Prep Time:** 30 minutes

Coconut macaroons are good anytime. Pair their delightful chewiness with coffee or tea.

2 egg whites
1/3 cup sugar
2 tablespoons all-purpose flour
Dash salt
1/4 teaspoon almond extract
2 cups coconut

1. Heat oven to 325°F. Grease and lightly flour cookie sheet. In medium bowl, beat egg whites until frothy. Add sugar, flour, salt and almond extract; mix well. Stir in coconut. Drop dough by tablespoonfuls 2 inches apart onto greased and floured cookie sheet.

2. Bake at 325°F. for 13 to 17 minutes or until set and light golden brown. Immediately remove from cookie sheet.

High Altitude (Above 3,500 feet): No change.

Nutrition per Serving: Serving Size: 1 Cookie. Calories 90; Calories from Fat 35; Total Fat 4g; Saturated Fat 4g; Cholesterol 0mg; Sodium 50mg; Dietary Fiber 1g

Dietary Exchange: 1/2 Starch, 1/2 Fruit, 1/2 Fat OR 1 Carbohydrate, 1/2 Fat

DATE-FILLED WHOLE WHEAT COOKIES

Yield: 4 1/2 dozen cookies;
Prep Time: 1 hour
(Ready in 2 hours)

These hearty cookies resemble miniature turnovers, with the folded dough concealing a delicious date-almond filling.

COOKIES
1 cup firmly packed brown sugar
3/4 cup margarine or butter, softened
1 teaspoon vanilla
1 egg
1 1/4 cups all-purpose flour
1 cup whole wheat flour
1 1/2 teaspoons baking powder
1 teaspoon cinnamon
1/8 teaspoon salt

FILLING
1/4 cup firmly packed brown sugar
1/4 cup slivered almonds
1/3 cup orange juice
1 (8-oz.) pkg. chopped pitted dates

1. In large bowl, combine 1 cup brown sugar and margarine; beat until light and fluffy. Add vanilla and egg; blend well. Add all-purpose flour, whole wheat flour, baking powder, cinnamon and salt; mix well. Cover with plastic wrap; refrigerate 1 to 2 hours for easier handling.

2. Meanwhile, in food processor bowl with metal blade or blender container, combine all filling ingredients; process 1 to 2 minutes or until thickened.

3. Heat oven to 375°F. On lightly floured surface, roll out 1/3 of dough at a time to 1/8-inch thickness. (Keep remaining dough refrigerated.) Cut with floured 2 1/2-inch round cookie cutter. Place rounds 1/2 inch apart on ungreased cookie sheets. Spoon scant 1 teaspoon filling onto center of each round. Fold half of each round over filling, forming half moon shape. Seal edges with fork.

4. Bake at 375°F. for 5 to 10 minutes or until edges are golden brown. Immediately remove from cookie sheets.

High Altitude (Above 3,500 feet): Increase all-purpose flour to 1 1/2 cups. Bake as directed above.

Nutrition per Serving: Serving Size: 1 Cookie. Calories 80; Calories from Fat 25; Total Fat 3g; Saturated Fat 1g; Cholesterol 4mg; Sodium 50mg; Dietary Fiber 1g

Dietary Exchange: 1/2 Starch, 1/2 Fruit, 1/2 Fat OR 1 Carbohydrate, 1/2 Fat

CREAM CHEESE SUGAR COOKIES

Yield: 6 dozen cookies; **Prep Time:** 1 hour
(Ready in 3 hours)

We prefer butter over margarine for the distinctive flavor and crisp texture it gives this cookie.

1 cup sugar
1 cup butter, softened
1 (3-oz.) pkg. cream cheese, softened
½ teaspoon salt
½ teaspoon almond extract
½ teaspoon vanilla
1 egg yolk
2 cups all-purpose flour
Colored sugar, if desired

1. In large bowl, combine all ingredients except flour and colored sugar; beat until light and fluffy. Add flour; mix well. Cover with plastic wrap; refrigerate 2 hours for easier handling.

2. Heat oven to 375°F. On lightly floured surface, roll out ⅓ of dough at a time to ⅛-inch thickness. (Keep remaining dough refrigerated.) Cut with lightly floured 2½-inch round or desired shape cookie cutters. Place 1 inch apart on ungreased cookie sheets. Leave cookies plain or sprinkle with colored sugar.

3. Bake at 375°F. for 7 to 10 minutes or until light golden brown. Immediately remove from cookie sheets. If desired, frost and decorate plain cookies.

High Altitude (Above 3,500 feet): Increase flour to 2 ¼ cups. Bake as directed above.

Nutrition per Serving: Serving Size: 1 Cookie. Calories 50; Calories from Fat 25; Total Fat 3g; Saturated Fat 2g; Cholesterol 10mg; Sodium 45mg; Dietary Fiber 0g

Dietary Exchange: ½ Starch, ½ Fat OR ½ Carbohydrate, ½ Fat

GINGER COOKIE CUTOUTS

Yield: 5 dozen cookies;
Prep Time: 1 hour 15 minutes
(Ready in 3 hours 15 minutes)

A Christmas classic! Store tightly wrapped for snacktime throughout the season. For cookies intended to be ornaments, use a chopstick to gently make a hole at the top of each cookie before baking. When the cookie is completely cooled, insert a decorative ribbon through the hole. (Note: Unless ornaments are wrapped in plastic, the cookies will probably become too hard and stale to eat.)

¾ cup sugar
½ cup shortening
½ cup molasses
¼ cup warm coffee
1 teaspoon vanilla
1 egg

2 ½ cups all-purpose flour
1 teaspoon baking soda
½ teaspoon ginger
½ teaspoon cinnamon
½ teaspoon allspice
¼ teaspoon salt
Sugar

1. In large bowl, combine sugar and shortening; beat until light and fluffy. Add molasses, coffee, vanilla and egg; blend well. (Mixture may appear curdled.) Add flour, baking soda, ginger, cinnamon, allspice and salt; mix well. Cover with plastic wrap; refrigerate at least 2 hours for easier handling.

2. Heat oven to 350°F. On well-floured surface, roll out dough to ⅛ to ¼-inch thickness.* Cut with floured 2-inch cookie cutter. Place 1 inch apart on ungreased cookie sheets. Sprinkle lightly with sugar.

3. Bake at 350°F. for 8 to 12 minutes or until set. Immediately remove from cookie sheets.

Tip: Rolling dough ⅛ inch thick will yield a thin, crisp cookie; rolling to ¼-inch thickness will yield a more cakelike cookie.

High Altitude (Above 3,500 feet): No change.

Nutrition per Serving: Serving Size: 1 Cookie. Calories 60; Calories from Fat 20; Total Fat 2g; Saturated Fat 0g; Cholesterol 4mg; Sodium 35mg; Dietary Fiber 0g

Dietary Exchange: ½ Starch, ½ Fat OR ½ Carbohydrate, ½ Fat

FESTIVE CHERRY NUT-TOPPED COOKIES

◆

Yield: 4 dozen cookies;
Prep Time: 30 minutes
(Ready in 1 hour 20 minutes)

Ruby-topped sweets make a fine addition to a holiday dessert tray.

²/₃ cup sugar
³/₄ cup margarine or butter, softened
2 teaspoons vanilla
¹/₂ teaspoon almond extract
1 egg
2 cups all-purpose flour
¹/₂ teaspoon baking powder

¹/₃ cup chopped red candied cherries
¹/₄ cup chopped pecans
¹/₄ cup cherry preserves or jelly
Powdered sugar

1. Heat oven to 350°F. In large bowl, combine sugar and margarine; beat until light and fluffy. Add vanilla, almond extract and egg; blend well. Add flour and baking powder; mix well.

2. Divide dough into 4 equal parts. On lightly floured surface, shape each part into 12 × ³/₄-inch roll; place on ungreased cookie sheets. Using handle of wooden spoon or finger, make indentation about ¹/₂ inch wide and ¹/₄ inch deep lengthwise down center of each roll.

Festive Cherry Nut-Topped Cookies

3. In small bowl, combine candied cherries, pecans and preserves; mix well. Fill each dough indentation with 2 tablespoons of the cherry mixture.

4. Bake at 350°F. for 15 to 20 minutes or until light golden brown. Cool 10 minutes. Cut each roll diagonally into 12 equal pieces. Sprinkle lightly with powdered sugar. Remove from cookie sheets; cool on wire racks.

High Altitude (Above 3,500 feet): No change.

Nutrition per Serving: Serving Size: 1 Cookie. Calories 70; Calories from Fat 25; Total Fat 3g; Saturated Fat 1g; Cholesterol 4mg; Sodium 45mg; Dietary Fiber 0g

Dietary Exchange: ¹/₂ Starch, ¹/₂ Fat OR ¹/₂ Carbohydrate, ¹/₂ Fat

PEANUT BUTTER COOKIES

◆

Yield: 4 dozen cookies;
Prep Time: 45 minutes

This American favorite with its characteristic crisscross top pairs beautifully with a tall glass of cold milk. If you like a cookie with a bit more texture, use crunchy peanut butter.

½ cup sugar
½ cup firmly packed brown sugar
½ cup margarine or butter, softened
½ cup peanut butter
1 teaspoon vanilla
1 egg
1 ¼ cups all-purpose flour
1 teaspoon baking soda
½ teaspoon salt
4 teaspoons sugar

1. Heat oven to 375°F. In large bowl, combine ½ cup sugar, brown sugar and margarine; beat until light and fluffy. Add peanut butter, vanilla and egg; blend well. Add flour, baking soda and salt; mix well. Shape dough into 1-inch balls. Place 2 inches apart on ungreased cookie sheets. With fork dipped in sugar, flatten balls in crisscross pattern.

2. Bake at 375°F. for 6 to 9 minutes or until set and golden brown. Immediately remove from cookie sheets.

High Altitude (Above 3,500 feet): Increase flour to 1½ cups. Bake as directed above.

Nutrition per Serving: Serving Size: 1 Cookie. Calories 60; Calories from Fat 25; Total Fat 3g; Saturated Fat 1g; Cholesterol 4mg; Sodium 85mg; Dietary Fiber 0g

Dietary Exchange: ½ Starch, ½ Fat OR ½ Carbohydrate, ½ Fat

VARIATIONS

Chocolate Chip Peanut Butter Cookies: Prepare dough as directed in recipe. Stir in 1 (6-oz.) pkg. (1 cup) semi-sweet chocolate chips.
Yield: 4 ½ dozen cookies

Chocolate Peanut Butter Crunch Bars: Prepare dough as directed in recipe, omitting 4 teaspoons sugar. Stir in ½ cup crisp rice cereal. Press dough in ungreased 15 × 10 × 1-inch baking pan. Bake at 350°F. for 12 to 17 minutes or until golden brown. Cool 15 minutes. In medium saucepan over low heat, melt 1 (6-oz.) pkg. (1 cup) semi-sweet chocolate chips and ½ cup peanut butter. Stir in 1 ½ cups crisp rice cereal. Spoon mixture evenly over slightly cooled bars; spread gently. Cool completely. Cut into bars.
Yield: 48 bars

Giant Peanut Butter Candy Cookies: Prepare dough as directed in recipe, omitting 4 teaspoons sugar. Stir in 1 cup candy-coated chocolate pieces. Using ¼ cup dough per cookie, place cookies 4 inches apart on ungreased cookie sheets. Flatten to 4-inch diameter. Bake at 350°F. for 8 to 12 minutes or until golden brown. Cool 1 minute; remove from cookie sheets.
Yield: 14 cookies

Nutty Peanut Butter Cookies: Prepare dough as directed in recipe. Stir in 1 cup chopped peanuts.
Yield: 4 ½ dozen cookies

Oatmeal Peanut Butter Cookies: Prepare dough as directed in recipe, decreasing flour to ¾ cup and adding ¾ cup rolled oats. Cover dough with plastic wrap; refrigerate 2 hours for easier handling. Shape and flatten balls as directed. Bake at 375°F. for 6 to 10 minutes or until golden brown. Immediately remove from cookie sheets.
Yield: 4 dozen cookies

Peanut Blossoms: Prepare dough and shape into balls as directed in recipe. Increase 4 teaspoons sugar to ¼ cup; roll balls in sugar. Place 1 inch apart on ungreased cookie sheets. Bake as directed. Immediately top each cookie with 1 milk chocolate candy kiss, pressing down firmly so cookie cracks around edge. Remove from cookie sheets.
Yield: 3 ½ dozen cookies

Peanut Butter and Jelly Thumbprints: Prepare dough and shape into balls as directed in recipe. Increase 4 teaspoons sugar to ¼ cup; roll balls in sugar. Place 1 inch apart on ungreased cookie sheets. With thumb or handle of wooden spoon, make deep indentation in center of each cookie. Bake as directed. Remove from cookie sheets. Cool completely. Spoon ½ teaspoon jelly, jam or preserves into center of each cookie.
Yield: 4 dozen cookies

Peanut Butter Brickle Cookies: Prepare dough as directed in recipe. Stir in 1 cup peanut butter chips and ⅔ cup almond brickle baking chips.
Yield: 5 dozen cookies

Peanut Butter Raisin Cookie Pops: Prepare dough as directed in recipe. Stir in 1 cup chocolate-covered raisins. Shape dough into 1 ½-inch balls. Place 4 cookies on each ungreased cookie sheet. With fork dipped in sugar, flatten balls in crisscross pattern. Insert wooden stick into side of each cookie. Bake at 350°F. for 7 to 12 minutes or until golden brown. Cool 1 minute; remove from cookie sheets.
Yield: 22 cookie pops

SNICKERDOODLES

Yield: 4 dozen cookies;
Prep Time: 45 minutes

Despite the amusing name, these are basic, practically foolproof cookies. Gently dusted with cinnamon and sugar, they're nice along with fresh fruit for an informal dessert.

1 ½ cups sugar
½ cup margarine or butter, softened
1 teaspoon vanilla
2 eggs
2 ¾ cups all-purpose flour
1 teaspoon cream of tartar
½ teaspoon baking soda
¼ teaspoon salt
2 tablespoons sugar
2 teaspoons cinnamon

1. Heat oven to 400°F. In large bowl, combine 1 ½ cups sugar and margarine; beat until light and fluffy. Add vanilla and eggs; blend well. Add flour, cream of tartar, baking soda and salt; mix well.

2. In small bowl, combine 2 tablespoons sugar and cinnamon. Shape dough into 1-inch balls; roll in sugar-cinnamon mixture. Place 2 inches apart on ungreased cookie sheets.

3. Bake at 400°F. for 8 to 10 minutes or until set. Immediately remove from cookie sheets.

High Altitude (Above 3,500 feet): No change.

Nutrition per Serving: Serving Size: 1 Cookie. Calories 70; Calories from Fat 20; Total Fat 2g; Saturated Fat 0g; Cholesterol 10mg; Sodium 50mg; Dietary Fiber 0g

Dietary Exchange: ½ Starch, ½ Fat OR ½ Carbohydrate, ½ Fat

VARIATIONS

Chocolate Snickerdoodles: Prepare dough as directed in recipe, substituting ½ cup unsweetened cocoa for ½ cup of the flour. Bake at 400°F. for 6 to 9 minutes or until set. Immediately remove from cookie sheets.

Whole Wheat Snickerdoodles: Prepare dough as directed in recipe, substituting 1 cup whole wheat flour for 1 cup of the all-purpose flour.

HAZELNUT MELTING MOMENTS

PICTURED ON PAGE 312.

Yield: 4 dozen cookies;
Prep Time: 1 hour

Hazelnuts, also called filberts, lend distinctive flavor to this variation on the cookies sometimes known as Russian tea cakes or Mexican wedding cakes. To grind the nuts, process them in a food processor or blender with brief on-and-off turns; overprocessing will result in nut butter.

⅔ cup sugar
1 cup butter, softened
2 teaspoons vanilla
1 teaspoon grated lemon peel
1 egg yolk
2 ¼ cups all-purpose flour
1 ½ cups ground hazelnuts (filberts)*
1 (6-oz.) pkg. (1 cup) semi-sweet chocolate chips
Powdered sugar

1. Heat oven to 325°F. In large bowl, combine sugar and butter; beat until light and fluffy. Add vanilla, lemon peel and egg yolk; blend well. Add flour and hazelnuts; mix well. Shape into 1 ¼-inch balls. Place 2 inches apart on ungreased cookie sheets. With thumb, make indentation in center of each cookie.

2. Bake at 325°F. for 10 to 15 minutes or until light golden brown around edges.

3. In small saucepan over low heat, melt chocolate chips, stirring until smooth. Spoon ½ teaspoon melted chocolate into center of each cookie.** Remove from cookie sheets. Sprinkle lightly with powdered sugar.

*Tips: *If desired, hazelnuts can be toasted before they are ground. To toast hazelnuts, spread on cookie sheet; bake at 325°F. for 9 to 11 minutes or until skins crack, stirring occasionally. If desired, remove skins.*

**If chocolate mixture begins to thicken, warm over low heat.

High Altitude (Above 3,500 feet): No change.

Nutrition per Serving: Serving Size: 1 Cookie. Calories 110; Calories from Fat 60; Total Fat 7g; Saturated Fat 3g; Cholesterol 15mg; Sodium 40mg; Dietary Fiber 1g

Dietary Exchange: ½ Starch, 1 ½ Fat OR ½ Carbohydrate, 1 ½ Fat

MINT MOMENTS

✦

Yield: 3 dozen cookies;
Prep Time: 20 minutes
(Ready in 1 hour 50 minutes)

Powdered sugar and a high proportion of butter give these cookies a melt-in-your-mouth texture. The warm cookies are very delicate; roll them in the sugar–peppermint candy mixture very carefully. The texture will firm up a bit as the cookies cool.

1 cup butter, softened
3/4 cup cornstarch
1/3 cup powdered sugar
1 cup all-purpose flour
3 tablespoons finely crushed
    peppermint candy
3 tablespoons powdered sugar

1. In large bowl, beat butter until light and fluffy. Add cornstarch and 1/3 cup powdered sugar; beat at low speed until moistened. Beat at high speed until light and fluffy. Add flour; mix until dough forms. Cover with plastic wrap; refrigerate 1 hour for easier handling.

2. Heat oven to 350°F. Shape dough into 1-inch balls. Place 1 inch apart on ungreased cookie sheets.

3. Bake at 350°F. for 9 to 15 minutes or until very light golden brown. Cool 1 minute. Remove from cookie sheets; place on wire racks.

Mint Moments, Caramel Nut Thumbprints

4. In small bowl, combine candy and 3 tablespoons powdered sugar; mix well. Carefully roll warm cookies in mixture.

High Altitude (Above 3,500 feet): Increase flour to 1 1/4 cups. Bake as directed above.

Nutrition per Serving: Serving Size: 1 Cookie. Calories 70; Calories from Fat 45; Total Fat 5g; Saturated Fat 3g; Cholesterol 15mg; Sodium 55mg; Dietary Fiber 0g

Dietary Exchange: 1/2 Fruit, 1 Fat OR 1/2 Carbohydrate, 1 Fat

CARAMEL NUT THUMBPRINTS

✦

Yield: 4 dozen cookies;
Prep Time: 1 hour 30 minutes

Gooey caramel makes a nice filling for a crisp, nutty cookie. For a change of pace, fill the centers with a bit of strawberry or raspberry jelly instead of caramel.

COOKIES
3/4 cup sugar
1/2 cup margarine or butter,
    softened
1/2 cup shortening
1 teaspoon vanilla
1 egg, separated
1 3/4 cups all-purpose flour
1/2 cup unsweetened cocoa
1/2 teaspoon baking powder
1 1/2 cups finely chopped pecans

FILLING
20 caramels, unwrapped
1/4 cup half-and-half

1. Heat oven to 325°F. In large bowl, combine sugar, margarine and shortening; beat until light and fluffy. Add vanilla and egg yolk; blend well. Add flour, cocoa and baking powder; mix well.

2. In small bowl, beat egg white until foamy; place pecans in another small bowl. Shape dough into 1-inch balls. Dip in egg white; roll in pecans. Place 2 inches apart on ungreased cookie sheets. With thumb, make indentation in center of each cookie.

3. Bake at 325°F. for 12 to 14 minutes or until cookies are set. Immediately remove cookies from cookie sheets; place on wire racks.

4. In small saucepan, combine caramels and half-and-half; cook over medium-low heat until caramels are melted, stirring occasionally. Spoon 1/2 teaspoon warm caramel mixture into center of each cookie. Cool 15 minutes or until caramel is set.

High Altitude (Above 3,500 feet): Increase flour to 2 cups. Bake as directed above.

Nutrition per Serving: Serving Size: 1 Cookie. Calories 110; Calories from Fat 60; Total Fat 7g; Saturated Fat 1g; Cholesterol 5mg; Sodium 40mg; Dietary Fiber 1g

Dietary Exchange: 1/2 Starch, 1 1/2 Fat OR 1/2 Carbohydrate, 1 1/2 Fat

LEMON-GLAZED CASHEW SHORTBREAD

Yield: 4 dozen cookies;
Prep Time: 30 minutes
(Ready in 1 hour 30 minutes)

Finely chopped cashews add crumbly texture to melt-in-your-mouth cookies.

COOKIES
¾ cup powdered sugar
1¼ cups butter, softened
3 cups all-purpose flour
½ cup finely chopped cashews
1 teaspoon ginger
½ cup coarsely chopped cashews

GLAZE
1 cup powdered sugar
1 teaspoon grated lemon peel
4 to 6 teaspoons lemon juice

1. Heat oven to 325°F. In large bowl, combine ¾ cup powdered sugar and butter; beat until light and fluffy. Add flour, ½ cup finely chopped cashews and ginger; mix well. Press dough evenly into ungreased 15×10×1-inch baking pan. Sprinkle with coarsely chopped cashews; press lightly into dough.

2. Bake at 325°F. for 20 to 30 minutes or until edges are light

Lemon-Glazed Cashew Shortbread

golden brown. Place pan on wire rack. Immediately cut into 2 1/2-inch squares. Cut each square diagonally in half. Cool in pan 30 minutes or until completely cooled.

3. In small bowl, combine all glaze ingredients, adding enough lemon juice for desired drizzling consistency. Remove cooled cookies from pan; place on waxed paper. Drizzle with glaze.

High Altitude (Above 3,500 feet): Decrease flour to 2 3/4 cups. Bake as directed above.

Nutrition per Serving: Serving Size: 1 Cookie. Calories 100; Calories from Fat 50; Total Fat 6g; Saturated Fat 3g; Cholesterol 15mg; Sodium 65mg; Dietary Fiber 0g

Dietary Exchange: 1 Fruit, 1 Fat OR 1 Carbohydrate, 1 Fat

ALMOND KISS COKIES

♦

Yield: 4 dozen cookies; **Prep Time:** 1 hour
(Ready in 2 hours)

These pretty cookies, with the distinctive candy kiss center, are best-sellers at bake sales.

COOKIES
1/2 cup sugar
1/2 cup firmly packed brown sugar
1/2 cup margarine or butter, softened
1/2 cup shortening
1 teaspoon almond extract
1 egg

2 cups all-purpose flour
1 teaspoon baking soda
1/4 teaspoon salt
Sugar
48 almond-filled milk chocolate candy kisses, unwrapped

GLAZE
1/4 cup seedless raspberry preserves or red currant jelly
1/4 teaspoon almond extract

1. In large bowl, combine sugar, brown sugar, margarine and shortening; beat until light and fluffy. Add 1 teaspoon almond extract and egg; blend well. Add flour, baking soda and salt; mix well. Cover with plastic wrap; refrigerate 1 hour for easier handling.

2. Heat oven to 325°F. Shape dough into 1-inch balls; roll in sugar. Place 2 inches apart on ungreased cookie sheets.

3. Bake at 325°F. for 7 to 12 minutes or until light golden brown. Immediately top each cookie with a candy kiss, pressing down gently. Remove from cookie sheets.

4. In small bowl, combine glaze ingredients; blend well. Drizzle over warm cookies. Cool 15 minutes or until glaze is set.

High Altitude (Above 3,500 feet): No change.

Nutrition per Serving: Serving Size: 1 Cookie. Calories 110; Calories from Fat 50; Total Fat 6g; Saturated Fat 2g; Cholesterol 5mg; Sodium 65mg; Dietary Fiber 0g

Dietary Exchange: 1 Fruit, 1 Fat OR 1 Carbohydrate, 1 Fat

SPRITZ COOKIES

Yield: 5 dozen cookies; **Prep Time:** 1 hour

Cookie-press cookies are just the thing when you want fancy decorative shapes but don't have the time for a rolling pin and cookie cutters.

1 cup powdered sugar
1 cup butter, softened
1/2 teaspoon vanilla
1 egg
2 1/3 cups all-purpose flour
1/4 teaspoon salt

1. Heat oven to 400°F. In large bowl, combine powdered sugar, butter, vanilla and egg; beat until light and fluffy. Add flour and salt; mix well. Fit cookie press with desired template. Fill cookie press; press dough onto ungreased cookie sheets.

2. Bake at 400°F. for 5 to 7 minutes or until edges are firm but not brown. Immediately remove from cookie sheets.

High Altitude (Above 3,500 feet): No change.

Nutrition per Serving: Serving Size: 1 Cookie. Calories 50; Calories from Fat 25; Total Fat 3g; Saturated Fat 2g; Cholesterol 10mg; Sodium 40mg; Dietary Fiber 0g

Dietary Exchange: 1/2 Starch, 1/2 Fat OR 1/2 Carbohydrate, 1/2 Fat

VARIATION

Chocolate Spritz Cookies: Prepare dough as directed in recipe, adding 2 oz. melted unsweetened chocolate to powdered sugar mixture.

CHOCOLATE-ORANGE CRESCENT COOKIES

◆

Yield: 24 cookies; Prep Time: 1 hour

With their delicate texture and fancy chocolate-dipped appearance, these orange-flavored crescents are excellent for an elegant dessert buffet or gift plate.

½ cup sugar
½ cup butter, softened
1 teaspoon finely grated orange peel
2 tablespoons orange juice
1 ¼ cups all-purpose flour
3 oz. semi-sweet chocolate, chopped
1 teaspoon shortening

1. Heat oven to 375°F. In small bowl, combine sugar and butter; beat well. Add orange peel and orange juice; blend well. Add flour; mix well. For each cookie, with hands, roll 1 scant tablespoon of dough into 3-inch strip. Taper ends and form into crescent shape on ungreased cookie sheet.

2. Bake at 375°F. for 6 to 10 minutes or until cookies are firm to the touch. Cool 1 minute; remove from cookie sheets. Cool 15 minutes or until completely cooled.

3. Meanwhile, in small saucepan, melt chocolate and shortening; stir until smooth. Dip 1 end of each cookie in chocolate; lightly scrape excess chocolate from bottom on edge of pan. Place on waxed paper to set. Store between sheets of waxed paper in loosely covered container.

High Altitude (Above 3,500 feet): No change.

Nutrition per Serving: Serving Size: 1 Cookie. Calories 100; Calories from Fat 45; Total Fat 5g; Saturated Fat 3g; Cholesterol 10mg; Sodium 40mg; Dietary Fiber 0g

Dietary Exchange: 1 Fruit, 1 Fat OR 1 Carbohydrate, 1 Fat

DOUBLE CHOCOLATE-ORANGE BISCOTTI

◆

Yield: 6 ½ dozen cookies;
Prep Time: 1 hour 45 minutes
(Ready in 2 hours)

Just as Americans have begun to discover Italy's espresso and cappuccino in recent years, biscotti—another Italian staple—are turning up in more and more places, too. The name means "twice cooked." First, the dough bakes in a log. Then it's cut into diagonal slices and baked again, yielding a crisp-textured cookie that's ideal for dunking.

COOKIES
3 cups all-purpose flour
½ cup sugar
½ cup firmly packed brown sugar
3 teaspoons baking powder
½ teaspoon salt
4 oz. unsweetened chocolate, melted, cooled
1 tablespoon grated orange peel
⅓ cup olive or vegetable oil
¼ cup orange juice
2 teaspoons vanilla
3 eggs
6 oz. white chocolate baking bar, chopped

TOPPING
4 oz. white chocolate baking bar, chopped
1 tablespoon shortening

1. Heat oven to 350°F. Lightly grease 2 cookie sheets. In large bowl, combine flour, sugar, brown sugar, baking powder and salt; mix well. Add melted chocolate, orange peel, oil, orange juice, vanilla and eggs; blend well. (Dough will be stiff.) Add 6 oz. chopped baking bar; gently knead into dough.

2. Divide dough into 4 equal parts; shape each part into roll 14 inches long. Place 2 rolls on each cookie sheet; flatten each roll to 2 ½-inch width. Bake at 350°F. for 18 to 20 minutes or until firm to the touch.

Double Chocolate-Orange Biscotti

3. Remove cookie sheets from oven. Reduce oven temperature to 300° F. Cool rolls on cookie sheets for 10 minutes.

4. Cut rolls diagonally into 1/2-inch-thick slices. Place slices, cut side up, on same cookie sheets. Bake at 300° F. for 7 to 9 minutes or until top surface is dry.

5. Turn cookies over; bake an additional 7 to 9 minutes. Remove from cookie sheets. Cool 15 minutes or until completely cooled.

6. In small saucepan over low heat, melt topping ingredients, stirring until smooth. Drizzle over cookies.

High Altitude (Above 3,500 feet): No change.

Nutrition per Serving: Serving Size: 1 Cookie. Calories 70; Calories from Fat 25; Total Fat 3g; Saturated Fat 1g; Cholesterol 10mg; Sodium 40mg; Dietary Fiber 0g

Dietary Exchange: 1/2 Starch, 1/2 Fat OR 1/2 Carbohydrate, 1/2 Fat

DRIED CHERRY BISCOTTI

PICTURED ON PAGE 232.

Yield: 24 cookies; **Prep Time:** 45 minutes
(Ready in 1 hour 15 minutes)

Drying cherries concentrates their natural sweetness; their chewy texture is a pleasant surprise in crisp biscotti. If you can't find dried cherries in your market, substitute chopped dried apricots or sweetened dried cranberries.

3 cups all-purpose flour
1 cup sugar
¾ teaspoon baking soda
½ cup chopped almonds, toasted*
1 (3.5-oz.) pkg. (¾ cup) dried
    cherries
2 tablespoons margarine or butter,
    melted
1 teaspoon almond extract
2 eggs
2 egg whites

1. Heat oven to 350°F. Spray large cookie sheet with nonstick cooking spray. In large bowl, combine flour, sugar, baking soda, almonds and cherries; mix well. Add all remaining ingredients; blend well.

2. Turn dough out onto lightly floured surface. Knead dough about 8 times. Shape dough into roll 16 inches long. Place roll on sprayed cookie sheet; flatten to 1-inch thickness. Bake at 350°F. for 20 to 30 minutes or until golden brown. Cool roll on cookie sheet for 10 minutes.

3. Cut roll diagonally into ½-inch-thick slices. Place slices, cut side up, on same cookie sheet. Return to oven; bake an additional 8 minutes or until light golden brown.

4. Turn cookies over; bake an additional 8 minutes or until cookies are golden brown. Remove from cookie sheet. Cool 15 minutes or until completely cooled.

*Tip: To toast almonds, spread on cookie sheet; bake at 350°F. for 5 to 7 minutes or until golden brown, stirring occasionally.

High Altitude (Above 3,500 feet): Increase flour to 3¼ cups. Bake as directed above.

Nutrition per Serving: Serving Size: 1 Cookie. Calories 140; Calories from Fat 25; Total Fat 3g; Saturated Fat 0g; Cholesterol 20mg; Sodium 60mg; Dietary Fiber 1g

Dietary Exchange: 1 Starch, ½ Fruit, ½ Fat OR 1½ Carbohydrate, ½ Fat

OATMEAL CRUNCH BARS

Yield: 48 bars; **Prep Time:** 10 minutes
(Ready in 1 hour 35 minutes)

So easy, so good! These crunchy bars make an excellent take-along snack.

4 cups quick-cooking rolled oats
1½ cups chopped nuts
1 cup firmly packed brown sugar
1 cup coconut
1 teaspoon salt
¾ cup margarine or butter, melted
¾ cup orange marmalade

1. Heat oven to 400°F. Grease 15×10×1-inch baking pan. In large bowl, combine all ingredients; mix well. Press in greased pan.

2. Bake at 400°F. for 18 to 22 minutes or until golden brown. Cool 1 hour or until completely cooled. Cut into bars.

High Altitude (Above 3,500 feet): No change.

Nutrition per Serving: Serving Size: 1 Bar. Calories 120; Calories from Fat 50; Total Fat 6g; Saturated Fat 1g; Cholesterol 0mg; Sodium 85mg; Dietary Fiber 1g

Dietary Exchange: 1 Starch, 1 Fat OR 1 Carbohydrate, 1 Fat

CURRANT-PUMPKIN BARS

✦

Yield: 48 bars; **Prep Time:** 15 minutes
(Ready in 1 hour 45 minutes)

Translate the spice-scented flavors of pumpkin pie into a satisfying bar cookie spread with luscious cream cheese frosting.

BARS

2 cups all-purpose flour
2 cups sugar
½ cup dried currants or raisins
2 teaspoons baking powder
1 teaspoon baking soda
1 teaspoon cinnamon
1 teaspoon nutmeg
½ teaspoon salt
½ teaspoon cloves
1 cup oil
1 (16-oz.) can pumpkin
4 eggs

FROSTING

2 cups powdered sugar
⅓ cup margarine or butter, softened
1 (3-oz.) pkg. cream cheese, softened
1 tablespoon milk
1 teaspoon vanilla
½ teaspoon grated orange peel

1. Heat oven to 350°F. Grease 15×10×1-inch baking pan. In large bowl, combine all bar ingredients at low speed until moistened; beat 2 minutes at medium speed. Pour into greased pan.

2. Bake at 350°F. for 25 to 30 minutes or until toothpick inserted in center comes out clean. Cool 1 hour or until completely cooled.

3. In small bowl, combine all frosting ingredients; beat until smooth. Spread over cooled bars. Cut into bars. Store in refrigerator.

High Altitude (Above 3,500 feet): Decrease baking soda to ½ teaspoon. Bake at 375°F. for 30 to 35 minutes.

Nutrition per Serving: Serving Size: 1 Bar. Calories 140; Calories from Fat 60; Total Fat 7g; Saturated Fat 1g; Cholesterol 20mg; Sodium 95mg; Dietary Fiber 1g

Dietary Exchange: ½ Starch, 1 Fruit, 1 Fat OR 1½ Carbohydrate, 1 Fat

PINEAPPLE-CRANBERRY BARS

✦

Yield: 36 bars; **Prep Time:** 30 minutes
(Ready in 2 hours)

Tropical pineapple meets northern cranberries for a filling that's as pretty as it is tasty, spread onto a nutty crust.

FILLING

1 cup fresh or frozen cranberries
3 tablespoons brown sugar
1½ teaspoons cornstarch
1 (8-oz.) can crushed pineapple in its own juice, undrained

CRUMB MIXTURE

1½ cups all-purpose flour
1 cup rolled oats
1 cup firmly packed brown sugar
½ cup chopped nuts
¼ teaspoon salt
¾ cup margarine or butter

1. Heat oven to 350°F. Grease 13×9-inch pan. In medium saucepan, combine all filling ingredients. Bring to a boil over medium heat, stirring constantly. Reduce heat; cover and simmer 10 to 15 minutes or until cranberry skins pop and mixture thickens, stirring occasionally. Remove from heat.

2. Meanwhile, in large bowl, combine flour, rolled oats, 1 cup brown sugar, nuts and salt; mix well. With pastry blender or fork, cut in margarine until mixture resembles coarse crumbs. Reserve 2 cups crumb mixture for topping. Press remaining crumb mixture firmly in bottom of greased pan.

3. Drop cranberry mixture by tablespoonfuls evenly over crumb mixture in pan; spread evenly. Sprinkle with reserved crumb mixture; press lightly.

4. Bake at 350°F. for 20 to 30 minutes or until golden brown. Cool 1 hour or until completely cooled. Cut into bars.

High Altitude (Above 3,500 feet): No change.

Nutrition per Serving: Serving Size: 1 Bar. Calories 110; Calories from Fat 45; Total Fat 5g; Saturated Fat 1g; Cholesterol 0mg; Sodium 65mg; Dietary Fiber 1g

Dietary Exchange: ½ Starch, ½ Fruit, 1 Fat OR 1 Carbohydrate, 1 Fat

CHOCOLATE-MAPLE BAKLAVA

Yield: 28 bars; **Prep Time:** 30 minutes
(Ready in 2 hours 10 minutes)

Baklava, a signature Greek sweet, gets updated with chocolate and maple. Like the original, this recipe features layers of crisp phyllo dough.

1 (8-oz.) pkg. frozen phyllo (filo) pastry sheets, thawed
3/4 cup butter, melted
2 cups coarsely chopped walnuts
1 cup miniature semi-sweet chocolate chips
2 tablespoons brown sugar
1/2 cup sugar
1/4 cup firmly packed brown sugar
1/2 cup water
1/2 cup light corn syrup
1 teaspoon maple flavor

1. Unroll pastry sheets; cover with damp paper towels and plastic wrap.

2. Heat oven to 350°F. Place 1 sheet of phyllo in 13×9-inch pan; brush with melted butter. Continue layering half of phyllo sheets (about 10) and melted butter. Sprinkle with walnuts, chocolate chips and 2 tablespoons brown sugar.

3. Layer remaining half of phyllo sheets over walnut mixture, brushing each sheet with melted butter. Press down around edges.

4. With a knife, cut through top layers of phyllo making 6 lengthwise strips. Measure and mark 9 inches on long side of pan. Cut diagonally from 9-inch mark to opposite corner of pan (see diagram). Make parallel cuts on each side of diagonal cut every 1 1/2 inches.

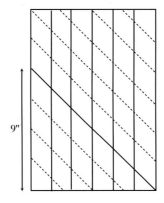

9"

5. Bake at 350°F. for 35 to 40 minutes or until puffed and golden brown.

6. Meanwhile, in small saucepan, combine sugar, 1/4 cup brown sugar, water and corn syrup. Cook over medium heat until mixture boils, stirring constantly; boil 5 minutes. Remove from heat; stir in maple flavor. Refrigerate syrup until baklava is baked.

7. Remove baklava from oven; immediately pour cooled syrup over hot bars. Cool 1 hour or until completely cooled. Cut along original perforations, cutting through all layers.

Nutrition per Serving: Serving Size: 1 Bar. Calories 160; Calories from Fat 90; Total Fat 10g; Saturated Fat 4g; Cholesterol 10mg; Sodium 80mg; Dietary Fiber 1g

Dietary Exchange: 1/2 Starch, 1/2 Fruit, 2 Fat OR 1 Carbohydrate, 2 Fat

APPLE-DATE BARS

Yield: 36 bars; **Prep Time:** 30 minutes
(Ready in 2 hours)

A crumbly crust of rolled oats holds a moist apple-date filling. To boost texture even more, stir 1/2 cup of chopped walnuts into the filling.

FILLING
1/4 cup sugar
1 cup water
2 cups chopped peeled apples
1 (8-oz.) pkg. chopped dates

CRUMB MIXTURE
1 3/4 cups all-purpose flour
1/2 teaspoon baking soda
1/4 teaspoon salt
3/4 cup margarine or butter
1 1/2 cups rolled oats
1 cup firmly packed brown sugar

1. In medium saucepan, combine all filling ingredients; mix well. Bring to a boil. Reduce heat to low; cook about 10 minutes or until thickened, stirring occasionally. Cool slightly.

2. Meanwhile, heat oven to 375°F. Grease and flour 13×9-inch pan. In large bowl, combine flour, baking soda and salt; mix well. With pastry blender or fork, cut in margarine until mixture resembles coarse crumbs. Add oats and brown sugar; mix well.

Apple-Date Bars

3. Press 3 cups crumb mixture evenly in greased and floured pan. Spread evenly with filling. Sprinkle with remaining crumb mixture; press lightly.

4. Bake at 375°F. for 18 to 28 minutes or until golden brown. Cool 1 hour or until completely cooled. Cut into bars.

High Altitude (Above 3,500 feet): No change.

Nutrition per Serving: Serving Size: 1 Bar. Calories 120; Calories from Fat 35; Total Fat 4g; Saturated Fat 1g; Cholesterol 0mg; Sodium 80mg; Dietary Fiber 1g

Dietary Exchange: ½ Starch, ½ Fruit, 1 Fat OR 1 Carbohydrate, 1 Fat

CHERRY SHORTBREAD BITES

◆

Yield: 80 bars; **Prep Time:** 20 minutes
(Ready in 50 minutes)

Candied cherries impart holiday color to these bars, which have the butter-rich flavor and so-smooth texture of traditional Scottish shortbread. For an authentic decorative touch, prick the tops of the bars with the tines of a fork prior to baking.

BARS
¾ cup sugar
1 cup margarine or butter, softened
2 ¼ cups all-purpose flour
2 tablespoons orange juice or water
½ teaspoon almond extract
½ teaspoon vanilla
20 red or green candied cherries, quartered

GLAZE
¼ cup semi-sweet chocolate chips

1. Heat oven to 300° F. In large bowl, combine sugar and margarine; beat until light and fluffy. Add flour, orange juice, almond extract and vanilla; mix well. Press dough in bottom of ungreased 13×9-inch pan. With knife, score or mark dough into squares, 10 rows across and 8 down. Press 1 cherry piece into each square.

2. Bake at 300° F. for 25 to 30 minutes or until light golden brown. DO NOT OVERBAKE. Immediately cut through scoring to separate bars.

3. Place chocolate chips in small resealable plastic bag. Close tightly. Place in bowl of very hot water. (Bag will float.) Knead occasionally until chocolate is melted. Dry plastic bag with paper towel. Snip very small opening in corner of plastic bag. Drizzle melted chocolate over warm shortbread in a zigzag pattern.

High Altitude (Above 3,500 feet): No change.

Nutrition per Serving: Serving Size: 1 Bar. Calories 40; Calories from Fat 20; Total Fat 2g; Saturated Fat 1g; Cholesterol 0mg; Sodium 30mg; Dietary Fiber 0g

Dietary Exchange: ½ Fruit, ½ Fat OR ½ Carbohydrate, ½ Fat

**Cherry Shortbread Bites,
Hazelnut Melting Moments, page 301**

RED, WHITE AND BLUEBERRY BARS

◆

Yield: 48 bars; Prep Time: 25 minutes
(Ready in 2 hours)

Use Independence Day as an excuse, if you must, but these cherry-blueberry bars are delicious anytime.

BARS
2 cups all-purpose flour

1 1/2 cups sugar

2 teaspoons baking powder

1 teaspoon salt

1 cup milk

1/2 cup shortening

4 egg whites

1/2 teaspoon almond extract

1 cup fresh or frozen blueberries

FROSTING
3 cups powdered sugar

1/4 cup margarine or butter, softened

3 to 5 tablespoons cherry liquid or milk

1/3 cup chopped maraschino cherries

1. Heat oven to 350°F. Grease 15 × 10 × 1-inch baking pan. In large bowl, combine flour, sugar, baking powder, salt, milk and shortening; beat at low speed until moistened. Add egg whites and almond extract; beat 2 minutes at medium speed. Fold in blueberries. Pour into greased pan.

2. Bake at 350°F. for 23 to 33 minutes or until toothpick inserted in center comes out clean. Cool 1 hour or until completely cooled.

3. In medium bowl, combine powdered sugar, margarine and enough cherry liquid for desired spreading consistency; beat until smooth. Fold in cherries. Spread over cooled bars. Cut into bars.

High Altitude (Above 3,500 feet): Increase flour to 2 1/4 cups. Bake as directed above.

Nutrition per Serving: Serving Size: 1 Bar. Calories 110; Calories from Fat 25; Total Fat 3g; Saturated Fat 1g; Cholesterol 0mg; Sodium 85mg; Dietary Fiber 0g

Dietary Exchange: 1/2 Starch, 1 Fruit, 1/2 Fat OR 1 1/2 Carbohydrate, 1/2 Fat

GRASSHOPPER SQUARES

◆

Yield: 48 bars; Prep Time: 20 minutes
(Ready in 1 hour 30 minutes)

Great for an after-school treat or a mid-afternoon pick-up. For Valentine's Day, tint the icing pink and top with heart-shaped sprinkles.

BASE
3/4 cup powdered sugar

3/4 cup margarine or butter, softened

2 oz. unsweetened chocolate, melted, cooled

1 1/2 cups all-purpose flour

1/2 teaspoon baking powder

1/4 teaspoon salt

1 tablespoon milk

1/4 teaspoon mint extract

TOPPING
4 cups powdered sugar

1 (3-oz.) pkg. cream cheese, softened

1/4 cup margarine or butter, softened

3 tablespoons milk

1 teaspoon vanilla

1/4 teaspoon mint extract

6 drops green food color

1 tablespoon chocolate sprinkles, if desired

1. Heat oven to 325°F. Grease 13 × 9-inch pan. In large bowl, combine 3/4 cup powdered sugar and 3/4 cup margarine; beat until light and fluffy. Stir in cooled melted chocolate. Add all remaining base ingredients; mix well. (Dough will be stiff.) Press dough in bottom of greased pan.

2. Bake at 325°F. for 15 to 25 minutes or until center is set. Cool 30 minutes or until completely cooled.

3. In large bowl, combine all topping ingredients except chocolate sprinkles; beat until smooth. Spread over base. Sprinkle with chocolate sprinkles. Refrigerate 15 minutes or until firm. Cut into bars. Store in refrigerator.

High Altitude (Above 3,500 feet): No change.

Nutrition per Serving: Serving Size: 1 Bar. Calories 110; Calories from Fat 45; Total Fat 5g; Saturated Fat 2g; Cholesterol 2mg; Sodium 65mg; Dietary Fiber 0g

Dietary Exchange: 1/2 Starch, 1/2 Fruit, 1 Fat OR 1 Carbohydrate, 1 Fat

ZUCCHINI BARS WITH PENUCHE FROSTING

Yield: 45 bars; **Prep Time:** 25 minutes
(Ready in 2 hours 5 minutes)

Doesn't it seem mysterious that zucchini, which pairs so well with the likes of peppers and onions, contributes wonderful moisture and depth of flavor to desserts, too? Old-fashioned penuche (puh-NOO-chee) frosting, made on the stove-top with butter, brown sugar and milk, brings back sweet memories.

BARS
1 cup sugar
¾ cup margarine or butter, softened
1 teaspoon vanilla
2 eggs
2 cups all-purpose flour
1½ teaspoons baking powder
½ teaspoon salt
2 cups shredded zucchini
¾ cup coconut
1 cup raisins

FROSTING
3 tablespoons margarine or butter
½ cup firmly packed brown sugar
¼ cup milk
2 to 2½ cups powdered sugar

1. Heat oven to 350°F. Grease 15 × 10 × 1-inch baking pan. In large bowl, combine sugar and ¾ cup margarine; beat until light and fluffy. Add vanilla and eggs; blend well. Add flour, baking powder and salt; mix well. Stir in zucchini, coconut and raisins. Spread in greased pan.

2. Bake at 350°F. for 20 to 30 minutes or until light golden brown. Cool 1 hour or until completely cooled.

3. In medium saucepan, combine 3 tablespoons margarine and brown sugar. Bring to a boil. Cook over medium heat for 1 minute or until slightly thickened, stirring constantly. Cool 10 minutes. Add milk; beat until smooth. Beat in enough powdered sugar for desired spreading consistency. Frost cooled bars. Cut into bars.

High Altitude (Above 3,500 feet): Decrease sugar in bars to ¾ cup. Bake as directed above.

Nutrition per Serving: Serving Size: 1 Bar. Calories 130; Calories from Fat 45; Total Fat 5g; Saturated Fat 1g; Cholesterol 10mg; Sodium 90mg; Dietary Fiber 0g

Dietary Exchange: 1½ Fruit, 1 Fat OR 1½ Carbohydrate, 1 Fat

ALL-TIME FAVORITE LEMON BARS

◆

Yield: 24 bars; **Prep Time:** 30 minutes
(Ready in 2 hours)

Prebaking the simple three-ingredient crust yields a crisp base for a rich, lemony filling.

CRUST
1 cup all-purpose flour
¼ cup powdered sugar
½ cup margarine or butter

FILLING
2 eggs
1 cup sugar
2 tablespoons all-purpose flour
2 to 3 teaspoons grated lemon peel
½ teaspoon baking powder
2 tablespoons lemon juice

1. Heat oven to 350°F. In large bowl, combine 1 cup flour and powdered sugar. With pastry blender or fork, cut in margarine until mixture resembles coarse crumbs. Press crumb mixture in bottom of ungreased 8 or 9-inch square pan. Bake at 350°F. for 15 minutes.

2. Meanwhile, in small bowl, combine eggs and sugar; blend well. Stir in all remaining filling ingredients. Pour filling over partially baked crust.

3. Return to oven; bake an additional 18 to 25 minutes or until light golden brown. Cool 1 hour or until completely cooled. Cut into bars.

High Altitude (Above 3,500 feet): No change.

Nutrition per Serving: Serving Size: 1 Bar. Calories 100; Calories from Fat 35; Total Fat 4g; Saturated Fat 1g; Cholesterol 20mg; Sodium 60mg; Dietary Fiber 0g

Dietary Exchange: 1 Fruit, 1 Fat OR 1 Carbohydrate, 1 Fat

CHOCOLATE-CARAMEL CASHEW CHEWIES

◆

Yield: 36 bars; **Prep Time:** 35 minutes
(Ready in 1 hour 45 minutes)

For maximum texture, choose old-fashioned rolled oats for the crust; quick-cooking oats will give a slightly smoother base. If you're making these chewy bars for a children's party, substitute peanuts for the cashews.

CRUST
¾ cup firmly packed brown sugar
¾ cup margarine or butter, softened
1 egg
1 ½ cups all-purpose flour
1 cup rolled oats

FILLING
1 (14-oz.) pkg. caramels, unwrapped
⅓ cup half-and-half

TOPPING
1 cup large cashew pieces
1 cup semi-sweet chocolate chunks (from 10-oz. pkg.)

1. Heat oven to 350°F. Grease 13×9-inch pan. In large bowl, combine brown sugar and margarine; beat until light and fluffy. Add egg; beat well. Add flour and oats; mix well. Press in bottom of greased pan.

2. Bake at 350°F. for 15 to 18 minutes or until light golden brown.

3. Meanwhile, in medium saucepan, combine caramels and half-and-half; cook over low heat until caramels are melted and mixture is smooth, stirring occasionally. Pour caramel mixture over partially baked crust. Sprinkle with cashews and chocolate chunks.

4. Return to oven; bake an additional 8 to 10 minutes or until chocolate is softened and caramel just begins to bubble around edges. If desired, swirl softened chocolate chunks with knife. Cool 1 hour or until completely cooled. If desired, refrigerate bars to set chocolate. Cut into bars.

High Altitude (Above 3,500 feet): No change.

Nutrition per Serving: Serving Size: 1 Bar. Calories 170; Calories from Fat 70; Total Fat 8g; Saturated Fat 3g; Cholesterol 10mg; Sodium 100mg; Dietary Fiber 1g

Dietary Exchange: ½ Starch, 1 Fruit, 1 ½ Fat OR 1 ½ Carbohydrate, 1 ½ Fat

Chocolate-Caramel Cashew Chewies

SALTED PEANUT-CHOCOLATE-CARAMEL SQUARES

Yield: 16 bars; **Prep Time:** 30 minutes
(Ready in 1 hour 30 minutes)

These gooey, crunchy squares are paradise in a pan for lovers of caramel, chocolate and nuts.

MARSHMALLOW LAYER
2 ½ cups powdered sugar
1 (7-oz.) jar marshmallow creme

CRUST
1 cup crushed creme-filled
    chocolate sandwich cookies
    (10 cookies)
½ cup salted peanuts, finely
    chopped
¼ cup margarine or butter,
    softened

TOPPING
36 caramels, unwrapped
3 tablespoons milk
1 cup salted peanuts, coarsely
    chopped
½ cup semi-sweet chocolate
    chips, melted

1. In medium bowl, combine ½ cup of the powdered sugar and marshmallow creme; blend thoroughly. On surface sprinkled with powdered sugar, knead in remaining 2 cups powdered sugar. Shape mixture into 7 ½-inch square. Cover with plastic wrap. Set aside.

2. Heat oven to 350°F. Line 8-inch square pan with foil. In small bowl, combine all crust ingredients; mix well. Press in bottom of foil-lined pan. Bake at 350°F. for 10 minutes or until puffy. Uncover marshmallow square; immediately place over hot crust.

3. In medium saucepan over low heat, heat caramels and milk until caramels are melted, stirring occasionally. Pour melted caramels over marshmallow layer. Immediately sprinkle with 1 cup peanuts. Drizzle melted chocolate chips over peanuts. Cool 1 hour or until completely cooled. Cut into bars. Store in refrigerator

Nutrition per Serving: Serving Size: 1 Bar. Calories 360; Calories from Fat 130; Total Fat 14g; Saturated Fat 4g; Cholesterol 0mg; Sodium 240mg; Dietary Fiber 2g

Dietary Exchange: 1 ½ Starch, 2 Fruit, 2 ½ Fat OR 3 ½ Carbohydrate, 2 ½ Fat

FUDGY ORANGE-HAZELNUT BROWNIES

Yield: 24 brownies; **Prep Time:** 25 minutes
(Ready in 2 hours)

A touch of orange peel injects a bright note into chocolaty brownies.

BROWNIES
1 cup sugar
½ cup margarine or butter,
    softened
⅓ cup unsweetened cocoa
1 tablespoon grated orange peel
2 eggs
1 cup all-purpose flour
½ teaspoon baking soda
¼ teaspoon salt
1 cup coarsely chopped hazelnuts

FROSTING
1 cup powdered sugar
1 teaspoon grated orange peel
1 to 2 tablespoons milk

1. Heat oven to 350°F. Grease 9-inch square pan. In large bowl, combine sugar and margarine; beat until light and fluffy. Add cocoa, 1 tablespoon orange peel and eggs; blend well. Add flour, baking soda and salt; mix well. Stir in hazelnuts. Spread in greased pan.

2. Bake at 350°F. for 23 to 33 minutes or until firm to the touch. DO NOT OVERBAKE. Cool 1 hour or until completely cooled.

3. In small bowl, combine all frosting ingredients, adding enough milk for desired spreading consistency; blend until smooth. Spread over cooled brownies. Let stand until set. Cut into bars.

High Altitude (Above 3,500 feet): Increase flour to 1 ¼ cups. Bake as directed above.

Nutrition per Serving: Serving Size: 1 Bar. Calories 150; Calories from Fat 60; Total Fat 7g; Saturated Fat 1g; Cholesterol 20mg; Sodium 100mg; Dietary Fiber 1g

Dietary Exchange: 1 Starch, 1 ½ Fat OR 1 Carbohydrate, 1 ½ Fat

FROSTED BLOND CASHEW BROWNIES

Yield: 25 bars; **Prep Time:** 30 minutes
(Ready in 2 hours)

Caramel asserts itself sweetly in these cashew-packed bars.

BROWNIES

1 cup salted cashews
1 cup firmly packed brown sugar
1/3 cup oil
1 teaspoon vanilla
2 eggs
1 1/4 cups all-purpose flour
1 teaspoon baking powder
1/4 teaspoon salt, if desired

FROSTING

3 oz. white chocolate baking bar,
   cut into pieces
2 tablespoons margarine or butter,
   softened
2 tablespoons milk
1 cup powdered sugar

1. Heat oven to 350°F. Grease 8 or 9-inch square pan. In food processor bowl with metal blade or blender container, process 1/2 cup of the cashews until ground; place in medium bowl. Coarsely chop remaining cashews; set aside.

2. Add brown sugar, oil, vanilla and eggs to ground cashews; beat well. Add flour, baking powder, salt and chopped cashews; mix well. Spread in greased pan.

3. Bake at 350°F. for 20 to 30 minutes or until toothpick inserted in center comes out clean. Cool 1 hour or until completely cooled.

4. In small saucepan over low heat, melt baking bar, stirring constantly; remove from heat. Add margarine, milk and powdered sugar; beat until smooth. Spread evenly over cooled bars. Cut into bars.

High Altitude (Above 3,500 feet): Decrease brown sugar to 3/4 cup; increase flour to 1 1/2 cups. Bake as directed above.

Nutrition per Serving: Serving Size: 1 Bar. Calories 170; Calories from Fat 70; Total Fat 8g; Saturated Fat 2g; Cholesterol 20mg; Sodium 95mg; Dietary Fiber 0g

Dietary Exchange: 1 Starch, 1/2 Fruit, 1 1/2 Fat OR 1 1/2 Carbohydrate, 1 1/2 Fat

IRISH CREAM BROWNIES

Yield: 48 bars; **Prep Time:** 20 minutes
(Ready in 2 hours 10 minutes)

'Tis a bit of warmth that Irish cream liqueur brings to both brownies and frosting. Chocolate glaze is the icing on top of the frosting!

BROWNIES

1 (1 lb. 3.5-oz.) pkg. fudge
   brownie mix
1/4 cup Irish cream liqueur
1/2 cup oil
2 eggs

FROSTING

1/2 cup butter, softened
2 cups powdered sugar
1/2 teaspoon vanilla
2 tablespoons Irish cream liqueur
2 to 3 teaspoons milk

GLAZE

1 oz. semi-sweet chocolate,
   chopped
1 teaspoon butter

1. Heat oven to 350°F. Grease bottom only of 13×9-inch pan. In large bowl, combine all brownie ingredients; beat 50 strokes with spoon. Spread in greased pan.

2. Bake at 350°F. for 28 to 30 minutes or until set. DO NOT OVERBAKE. Cool 1 hour or until completely cooled.

3. In small bowl, beat 1/2 cup butter until light and fluffy. Beat in all remaining frosting ingredients, adding enough milk for desired spreading consistency. Spread over cooled brownies.

4. In small saucepan over low heat, melt glaze ingredients, stirring occasionally. Drizzle over frosted brownies. Refrigerate 15 minutes or until firm. Cut into bars.

High Altitude (Above 3,500 feet): See package for directions.

Nutrition per Serving: Serving Size: 1 Bar. Calories 120; Calories from Fat 50; Total Fat 6g; Saturated Fat 2g; Cholesterol 15mg; Sodium 55mg; Dietary Fiber 0g

Dietary Exchange: 1/2 Starch, 1/2 Fruit, 1 Fat OR 1 Carbohydrate, 1 Fat

VANILLA BROWNIES

Yield: 16 bars; **Prep Time:** 15 minutes
(Ready in 1 hour 10 minutes)

Vanilla chips make these "blondies" extra special.

1 cup firmly packed brown sugar
3 tablespoons margarine or butter, softened
1/3 cup refrigerated or frozen fat-free egg product, thawed
1 1/2 teaspoons vanilla
1 cup all-purpose flour
1/2 teaspoon baking powder
1/3 cup white vanilla chips

1. Heat oven to 375°F. Spray 8-inch square pan with nonstick cooking spray. In medium bowl, combine brown sugar and margarine; beat well. Add egg product and vanilla; blend well. Add flour and baking powder; stir just until dry ingredients are moistened. Spread in sprayed pan. Sprinkle evenly with chips.

2. Bake at 375°F. for 20 to 25 minutes or until brownies are golden brown and toothpick inserted in center comes out clean. Cool at least 30 minutes or until completely cooled. If desired, sprinkle with powdered sugar. Cut into bars.

High Altitude (Above 3,500 feet): Increase flour to 1 1/4 cups. Bake as directed above.

Nutrition per Serving: Serving Size: 1 Bar. Calories 120; Calories from Fat 25; Total Fat 3g; Saturated Fat 1g; Cholesterol 0mg; Sodium 55mg; Dietary Fiber 0g

Dietary Exchange: 1/2 Starch, 1 Fruit, 1/2 Fat OR 1 1/2 Carbohydrate, 1/2 Fat

OLD-FASHIONED BUTTERMILK BROWNIES

Yield: 50 bars; **Prep Time:** 20 minutes
(Ready in 1 hour 40 minutes)

Pour a tall glass of milk and sink your teeth into one of these cakelike brownies. For variety when serving a large group, prepare half of the frosting without the coconut and add 1/2 cup coconut to the remaining half of the frosting.

BROWNIES
2 cups all-purpose flour
2 cups sugar
5 teaspoons unsweetened cocoa
1 cup water
1/2 cup margarine or butter
1 teaspoon baking soda
1/2 cup buttermilk*
2 eggs

FROSTING
1/4 cup unsweetened cocoa
1/3 cup buttermilk or milk*
1/2 cup margarine or butter
4 1/2 cups powdered sugar
1 teaspoon vanilla
1 cup coconut, if desired

1. Heat oven to 375°F. Grease 15 × 10 × 1-inch baking pan. In large bowl, combine flour, sugar and 5 teaspoons cocoa; mix well.

2. In medium saucepan, combine water and 1/2 cup margarine; bring to a boil. Pour over flour mixture; beat at low speed until blended. Beat at high speed until smooth. Add baking soda, 1/2 cup buttermilk and eggs; blend well. Pour batter into greased pan.

3. Bake at 375°F. for 15 to 20 minutes or until toothpick inserted in center comes out clean. DO NOT OVERBAKE.

4. In large saucepan, combine 1/4 cup cocoa, 1/3 cup buttermilk and 1/2 cup margarine. Bring to a boil over medium heat. Remove from heat. Add powdered sugar, vanilla and coconut; mix well. Spread over warm brownies. Cool 1 hour or until completely cooled. Cut into bars.

Tip: To substitute for 1/2 cup buttermilk in brownies, use 1 1/2 teaspoons vinegar or lemon juice plus milk to make 1/2 cup. For 1/3 cup buttermilk, use 1 teaspoon vinegar or lemon juice plus milk to make 1/3 cup.

High Altitude (Above 3,500 feet): Decrease sugar to 1 3/4 cups. Bake as directed above.

Nutrition per Serving: Serving Size: 1 Bar. Calories 150; Calories from Fat 45; Total Fat 5g; Saturated Fat 1g; Cholesterol 10mg; Sodium 75mg; Dietary Fiber 0g

Dietary Exchange: 1/2 Starch, 1 Fruit, 1 Fat OR 1 1/2 Carbohydrate, 1 Fat

Old-Fashioned Buttermilk Brownies

MINT BROWNIES SUPREME

Yield: 48 bars; **Prep Time:** 35 minutes
(Ready in 3 hours 10 minutes)

A cool minty filling is sandwiched between fudgy brownies and chocolate frosting.

BROWNIES
1 (1 lb. 3.5-oz.) pkg. fudge
   brownie mix
½ cup oil
¼ cup water
2 eggs

FILLING
½ cup margarine or butter,
   softened
1 (3-oz.) pkg. cream cheese,
   softened
2 ½ cups powdered sugar
3 tablespoons creme de menthe
   syrup
Green food color, if desired

FROSTING
1 (6-oz.) pkg. (1 cup) semi-sweet
   chocolate chips
⅓ cup margarine or butter

1. Heat oven to 350°F. Grease bottom only of 13 × 9-inch pan. In large bowl, combine all brownie ingredients; beat 50 strokes with spoon. Spread in greased pan.

2. Bake at 350°F. for 28 to 30 minutes or until set. DO NOT OVERBAKE. Cool 45 minutes or until completely cooled.

3. In medium bowl, combine ½ cup margarine and cream cheese; beat until light and fluffy. Add all remaining filling ingredients; beat until smooth. Spread evenly over cooled brownies.

4. In small saucepan, combine frosting ingredients; melt over low heat, stirring constantly until smooth. Remove from heat; cool 15 minutes. Pour frosting evenly over filling; spread carefully to cover. Refrigerate 1 hour before cutting into bars. Garnish as desired. Store in refrigerator.

High Altitude (Above 3,500 feet): See package for directions.

Nutrition per Serving: Serving Size: 1 Bar. Calories 150; Calories from Fat 70; Total Fat 8g; Saturated Fat 2g; Cholesterol 10mg; Sodium 80mg; Dietary Fiber 1g

Dietary Exchange: ½ Starch, ½ Fruit, 1 ½ Fat OR 1 Carbohydrate, 1 ½ Fat

RASPBERRY-LAYERED WHITE CHOCOLATE BROWNIES

Yield: 36 bars; **Prep Time:** 25 minutes
(Ready in 2 hours)

Doctor up a packaged brownie mix with a lacing of raspberry preserves and white chocolate icing.

BROWNIES
1 (1 lb. 3.5-oz.) pkg. fudge
   brownie mix
½ cup oil
¼ cup water
2 eggs
¾ cup raspberry preserves or jam

FROSTING
6 oz. white chocolate baking bar,
   3 cubes vanilla-flavored candy
   coating or 1 cup white vanilla
   chips
¾ cup butter, softened
¼ cup powdered sugar

1. Heat oven to 350°F. Grease 13 × 9-inch pan. In large bowl, combine brownie mix, oil, water, and eggs; beat 50 strokes with spoon. Spread in greased pan.

2. Bake at 350°F. for 28 to 30 minutes or until set. DO NOT OVERBAKE. Cool 10 minutes; spread with preserves. Cool 1 hour or until completely cooled.

**Raspberry-Layered
White Chocolate Brownies**

3. In small saucepan over low heat, melt baking bar, stirring constantly. Remove from heat; cool 30 minutes. In small bowl, combine butter and powdered sugar; beat until light and fluffy. Gradually beat in cooled baking bar until smooth and fluffy. Carefully spread over preserves. Cut into bars. Store in refrigerator. Let stand at room temperature for 5 to 10 minutes before serving.

High Altitude (Above 3,500 feet): See package for directions.

Nutrition per Serving: Serving Size: 1 Bar. Calories 180; Calories from Fat 90; Total Fat 10g; Saturated Fat 4g; Cholesterol 25mg; Sodium 90mg; Dietary Fiber 1g

Dietary Exchange: ½ Starch, 2 Fat OR ½ Carbohydrate, 2 Fat

DESSERT SAUCES

❖ ❖ ❖

A sweet sauce can put the crowning touch on desserts plain or fancy, homemade or purchased. Ladle Hot Fudge Sauce over a scoop of ice cream, drizzle Raspberry Dessert Sauce on cake. A jar of your own sauce, trimmed with a ribbon, makes an easy, sweet and sure to be appreciated gift.

TOASTED PECAN SAUCE, PAGE 326

Versatile sweet sauces let you fashion elegant restaurant-style desserts from simple ingredients

SERVING THE SAUCE

I t's a simple matter, and certainly acceptable, to put a ladle in the sauce and set it on the table. For more formal presentations, consider the following:

◆ Pool sauce on a plate and set the dessert on top of the sauce.

◆ "Paint" a plate with two different sauces swirled together or spooned into distinct contrasting circles on the plate.

◆ Layer sauce, fruit and ice cream or yogurt in a sundae glass or wine goblet for a parfait.

◆ Drizzle sauce in a pattern across the top of the dessert.

◆ Pool sauce on a plate and highlight or outline it with melted chocolate. Melt semi-sweet chocolate chips in a microwave-safe self-sealing bag in the microwave. Snip off a corner of the bag and use the melted chocolate to "write" on the dessert plate with zigzags, crosshatches, swirls, dots, hearts or letters.

TOASTED PECAN SAUCE

Yield: 2 ¼ cups; Prep Time: 15 minutes

Drizzle this nutty, sweet sauce over waffles, pound cake or ice cream. The topping also works well with walnuts instead of pecans.

½ cup butter
1 ¼ cups firmly packed brown sugar
2 tablespoons light corn syrup
½ cup whipping cream
1 cup coarsely chopped pecans, toasted*

1. Melt butter in medium saucepan over medium heat. Add brown sugar and corn syrup; blend well. Bring to a boil. Boil 1 minute, stirring constantly. Gradually stir in whipping cream. Return to a boil.

2. Remove from heat; stir in pecans. Serve warm or cool. Store in refrigerator.

*Tip: To toast pecans, spread on cookie sheet; bake at 350°F. for 5 to 7 minutes or until light golden brown, stirring occasionally.

Nutrition per Serving: Serving Size: 1 Tablespoon. Calories 90; Calories from Fat 50; Total Fat 6g; Saturated Fat 3g; Cholesterol 10mg; Sodium 30mg; Dietary Fiber 0g

Dietary Exchange: ½ Fruit, 1 Fat OR ½ Carbohydrate, 1 Fat

BITTERSWEET CHOCOLATE SAUCE

Yield: 1 ¾ cups; Prep Time: 15 minutes

Adding unsweetened chocolate along with the semi-sweet gives this rich sauce intense flavor. Serve it warm over ice cream or cool with cheesecake.

1 ½ cups whipping cream
⅓ cup powdered sugar
3 oz. semi-sweet chocolate, cut into pieces
1 oz. unsweetened chocolate, cut into pieces
½ teaspoon vanilla

1. In medium saucepan, combine cream and powdered sugar. Bring to a boil over medium heat, stirring constantly. Stir in semi-sweet and unsweetened chocolate.

2. Reduce heat to low; cook 3 to 5 minutes or until mixture is smooth, stirring constantly.

3. Remove from heat; stir in vanilla. Serve warm or cool. Store in refrigerator.

Nutrition per Serving: Serving Size: 1 Tablespoon. Calories 70; Calories from Fat 50; Total Fat 6g; Saturated Fat 4g; Cholesterol 15mg; Sodium 5mg; Dietary Fiber 0g

Dietary Exchange: ½ Fruit, 1 Fat OR ½ Carbohydrate, 1 Fat

HOT FUDGE SAUCE

✦

Yield: 1 ¼ cups; **Prep Time:** 15 minutes

The quintessential American indulgence, hot fudge sauce is one of the favorite toppings for vanilla ice cream. But don't stop there. It's also great with coffee and peppermint stick ice cream—or pair it with chocolate for a true chocoholic fantasy.

3 oz. semi-sweet chocolate, cut into pieces
⅔ cup sugar
Dash salt
1 (5-oz.) can (⅔ cup) evaporated milk

1. Melt chocolate in small saucepan over very low heat, stirring constantly. Stir in sugar and salt.

2. Gradually add evaporated milk, stirring constantly. Cook until thickened and hot, stirring constantly. Serve warm. Store in refrigerator.

Nutrition per Serving: Serving Size: 1 Tablespoon. Calories 60; Calories from Fat 20; Total Fat 2g; Saturated Fat 1g; Cholesterol 2mg; Sodium 15mg; Dietary Fiber 0g

Dietary Exchange: ½ Starch, ½ Fat OR ½ Carbohydrate, ½ Fat

LITE CHOCOLATE SAUCE

✦

Yield: ¾ cup; **Prep Time:** 15 minutes

If you can't pass up sweets but are watching fat, this lower-fat chocolate sauce takes some of the guilt out of indulging. Pair it with a low-fat or nonfat ice cream or frozen yogurt or ice milk.

⅓ cup sugar
¼ cup unsweetened cocoa
⅓ cup water
3 tablespoons light corn syrup
1 teaspoon vanilla
½ teaspoon chocolate extract, if desired

1. In small saucepan, combine sugar, cocoa, water and corn syrup. Bring to a boil over medium heat, stirring constantly. Boil 2 minutes, stirring constantly until smooth and glossy.

2. Remove from heat; stir in vanilla and chocolate extract. Serve warm or cool.

Nutrition per Serving: Serving Size: 1 Tablespoon. Calories 40; Calories from Fat 0; Total Fat 0g; Saturated Fat 0g; Cholesterol 0mg; Sodium 5mg; Dietary Fiber 1g

Dietary Exchange: ½ Fruit OR ½ Carbohydrate

CARAMEL APPLE DESSERT SAUCE

✦

Yield: 1 cup; **Prep Time:** 40 minutes

Doctor up purchased caramel ice cream topping with juice and nuts to make a fantastic accompaniment for plain cake, frozen yogurt, ice cream or cut-up fresh fruit.

1 ½ cups apple juice
¼ cup sugar
2 teaspoons margarine or butter
¼ cup caramel ice cream topping
¼ cup finely chopped pecans

1. In small saucepan, combine apple juice, sugar and margarine; mix well. Bring to a boil over medium-high heat. Boil 18 to 22 minutes or until golden brown and reduced to about ⅔ cup.

2. Remove from heat; stir in ice cream topping and pecans. Cool 10 minutes. Serve warm. Store in refrigerator.

Nutrition per Serving: Serving Size: 1 Tablespoon. Calories 60; Calories from Fat 20; Total Fat 2g; Saturated Fat 0g; Cholesterol 0mg; Sodium 25mg; Dietary Fiber 0g

Dietary Exchange: ½ Fruit, ½ Fat OR ½ Carbohydrate, ½ Fat

FRESH BLUEBERRY SAUCE

◆

Yield: 3 cups; **Prep Time:** 15 minutes
(Ready in 1 hour 15 minutes)

Re-create the flavors of blueberry pie à la mode with less work by making this quick sauce and serving it over vanilla ice cream decorated with shortbread cookies. It's also a nice finishing touch for Triple Vanilla Cheesecake (page 159).

¾ cup sugar
1 tablespoon cornstarch
Dash salt
¾ cup water
3 cups fresh or frozen blueberries
1½ teaspoons grated lemon peel
4 teaspoons lemon juice

1. In medium saucepan, combine sugar, cornstarch and salt; mix well. Add water; mix well. Add blueberries. Bring to a boil. Reduce heat to medium-low; simmer 5 to 10 minutes or until thickened.

2. Remove from heat; stir in lemon peel and lemon juice. Refrigerate at least 1 hour before serving.

Nutrition per Serving: Serving Size: ¼ Cup. Calories 70; Calories from Fat 0; Total Fat 0g; Saturated Fat 0g; Cholesterol 0mg; Sodium 15mg; Dietary Fiber 1g

Dietary Exchange: 1 Fruit OR 1 Carbohydrate

FRUITY SALSA TOPPING

◆

Yield: 2 cups; **Prep Time:** 10 minutes

Improvise by substituting other fruits you might have on hand. Spoon the salsa over Baked Custard (page 132), Vanilla Pudding (page 196) or your favorite flavor of sorbet, frozen yogurt or ice cream.

½ cup coarsely chopped fresh
  strawberries
½ cup fresh blueberries
1 nectarine, coarsely chopped
1 tablespoon honey
1 teaspoon grated lime peel

In medium bowl, combine all ingredients; stir gently to mix. Serve immediately.

Tip: To make ahead, combine strawberries, blueberries and nectarine; cover tightly and refrigerate. Just before serving, add honey and lime peel; stir gently to mix.

Nutrition per Serving: Serving Size: ¼ Cup. Calories 25; Calories from Fat 0; Total Fat 0g; Saturated Fat 0g; Cholesterol 0mg; Sodium 0mg; Dietary Fiber 1g

Dietary Exchange: ½ Fruit OR ½ Carbohydrate

MARMALADE ICE CREAM SAUCE

Yield: 1¼ cups; **Prep Time:** 10 minutes

Cream sherry gives this textured sauce warmth and depth of flavor. Serve it warm over ice cream or cheesecake.

1 (10-oz.) jar orange marmalade
2 tablespoons margarine or butter
2 tablespoons dried currants
2 tablespoons slivered almonds
1 tablespoon cream sherry

1. In small saucepan, combine marmalade and margarine. Cook over low heat until mixture is melted and warm, stirring constantly.

2. Remove from heat; stir in currants, almonds and sherry. Serve warm.

Nutrition per Serving: Serving Size: 1 Tablespoon. Calories 60; Calories from Fat 20; Total Fat 2g; Saturated Fat 0g; Cholesterol 0mg; Sodium 20mg; Dietary Fiber 0g

Dietary Exchange: ½ Fruit, ½ Fat OR ½ Carbohydrate, ½ Fat

PEACH MELBA TOPPING

◆

Yield: 3 ½ cups; **Prep Time:** 20 minutes
(Ready in 1 hour 20 minutes)

Stirring raw raspberries and peaches macerated in sugar into a cooked fruit syrup retains the color and texture of the fruit. It's a pretty topping for ice cream or frozen yogurt.

2 cups fresh or frozen raspberries
2 peaches, peeled, thinly sliced
¾ cup sugar
1 tablespoon cornstarch

1. In large bowl, combine raspberries and peach slices. Sprinkle ½ cup of the sugar over fruit; let stand 1 to 2 hours.

2. Drain liquid from fruit; add water to measure 1 cup. In medium saucepan, combine remaining ¼ cup sugar and cornstarch; mix well. Add fruit liquid; blend well. Cook over medium heat for 5 minutes or until thickened and clear, stirring constantly.

3. Remove from heat; gently stir in fruit. Serve warm or cool.

Nutrition per Serving: Serving Size: ¼ Cup. Calories 60; Calories from Fat 0; Total Fat 0g; Saturated Fat 0g; Cholesterol 0mg; Sodium 0mg; Dietary Fiber 1g

Dietary Exchange: 1 Fruit OR 1 Carbohydrate

PINEAPPLE-CARAMEL SAUCE

◆

Yield: 2 ½ cups; **Prep Time:** 15 minutes

Pineapple Caramel Sauce brings back flavor memories of the topping for pineapple upside-down cake. Serve it over plain cake or sliced bananas.

1 (20-oz.) can pineapple chunks in unsweetened juice, drained, reserving ¾ cup liquid
2 tablespoons cornstarch
¼ cup butter
½ cup firmly packed brown sugar
¼ cup maraschino cherry halves, well drained

1. In small bowl, combine ¾ cup reserved pineapple liquid and cornstarch; blend well. Melt butter in medium saucepan. Add cornstarch mixture and brown sugar; blend well. Bring to a boil over medium-high heat, stirring constantly. Boil 1 minute.

2. Stir in pineapple and cherries. Cook until thoroughly heated. Serve warm.

Nutrition per Serving: Serving Size: ¼ Cup. Calories 130; Calories from Fat 45; Total Fat 5g; Saturated Fat 3g; Cholesterol 10mg; Sodium 50mg; Dietary Fiber 1g

Dietary Exchange: 1 ½ Fruit, 1 Fat OR 1 ½ Carbohydrate, 1 Fat

RASPBERRY DESSERT SAUCE

◆

Yield: 2 cups; **Prep Time:** 15 minutes
(Ready in 1 hour 15 minutes)

If you've ever wondered how they make that delicious ruby-hued raspberry sauce that graces desserts in posh restaurants, this recipe will show you how easy it is. Ladle some sauce onto a dessert plate and top with angel food cake, or spoon it over ice cream, cheesecake or bread pudding.

2 cups fresh or frozen raspberries, thawed
1 cup cranberry juice cocktail
2 tablespoons sugar
2 teaspoons cornstarch

1. In blender container or food processor bowl with metal blade, combine raspberries and juice cocktail. Cover; blend until smooth. Press mixture through strainer into medium saucepan to remove seeds; discard seeds. Add sugar and cornstarch; blend well.

2. Cook over medium heat until mixture boils and thickens slightly, stirring constantly. Remove from heat. Cool at least 1 hour before serving.

Nutrition per Serving: Serving Size: ¼ Cup. Calories 50; Calories from Fat 0; Total Fat 0g; Saturated Fat 0g; Cholesterol 0mg; Sodium 0mg; Dietary Fiber 2g

Dietary Exchange: 1 Fruit OR 1 Carbohydrate

RHUBARB-STRAWBERRY SAUCE

Yield: 2 ¾ cups; **Prep Time:** 15 minutes

Rhubarb and strawberries, a classic combination, work well in this versatile sauce that can be served warm or cool.

2 cups sliced fresh or frozen
   rhubarb
½ cup sugar
¼ cup water
1 pint (2 cups) fresh strawberries,
   sliced

1. In medium saucepan, combine rhubarb, sugar and water; mix well. Bring to a boil. Reduce heat to medium-low; simmer 5 minutes.

2. Stir in strawberries. Cook 1 minute. Serve warm or cool.

Nutrition per Serving: Serving Size: ¼ Cup. Calories 50; Calories from Fat 0; Total Fat 0g; Saturated Fat 0g; Cholesterol 0mg; Sodium 0mg; Dietary Fiber 1g

Dietary Exchange: 1 Fruit OR 1 Carbohydrate

SPICED CHERRY SAUCE

✦

Yield: 2 cups; **Prep Time:** 15 minutes

Madeira, a fortified wine, plays up the flavors of the spices and sweet cherries.

1 tablespoon sugar
1 tablespoon cornstarch
¼ teaspoon cinnamon
⅛ teaspoon ginger
1 (16-oz.) can pitted dark sweet
   cherries, drained, reserving
   liquid
1 tablespoon Madeira wine

1. In small saucepan, combine sugar, cornstarch, cinnamon and ginger; mix well. If necessary, add water to reserved cherry liquid to make 1 cup. Stir into cornstarch mixture. Cook over medium heat until mixture boils and thickens, stirring constantly.

2. Remove from heat; stir in cherries and wine. Serve warm or cool.

Nutrition per Serving: Serving Size: ¼ Cup. Calories 60; Calories from Fat 0; Total Fat 0g; Saturated Fat 0g; Cholesterol 0mg; Sodium 0mg; Dietary Fiber 1g

Dietary Exchange: 1 Fruit OR 1 Carbohydrate

CLASSIC HARD SAUCE

Yield: ¾ cup; **Prep Time:** 10 minutes

Traditional with steamed plum pudding for Christmas or New Year's celebrations, hard sauce also complements bread pudding. Or use it to embellish a purchased pound cake, warmed in the oven.

1 cup powdered sugar
¼ cup butter, softened
2 teaspoons hot water
1 tablespoon brandy, bourbon or
   rum, or 1 teaspoon brandy or
   rum extract

1. In small bowl, combine all ingredients; beat at high speed until well blended. Cover; refrigerate until serving time.

2. Serve over warm dessert. Store in refrigerator.

Nutrition per Serving: Serving Size: 1 Tablespoon. Calories 80; Calories from Fat 35; Total Fat 4g; Saturated Fat 2g; Cholesterol 10mg; Sodium 40mg; Dietary Fiber 0g

Dietary Exchange: ½ Fruit, 1 Fat OR ½ Carbohydrate, 1 Fat

DATE 'N WALNUT BRANDY SAUCE

Yield: 3 cups; **Prep Time:** 30 minutes

Try this fabulous sauce over scoops of coffee or vanilla ice cream or squares of plain coffee cake.

2 tablespoons brown sugar
2 cups water
1 cup chopped dates
2 tablespoons brandy
2 cups chopped walnuts

1. In medium saucepan, combine brown sugar and water; mix well. Bring to a boil. Stir in dates. Reduce heat to medium; simmer 20 minutes or until mixture thickens slightly, stirring occasionally.

2. Remove from heat; stir in brandy and walnuts. Serve warm. Store in refrigerator.

Nutrition per Serving: Serving Size: 1 Tablespoon. Calories 50; Calories from Fat 25; Total Fat 3g; Saturated Fat 0g; Cholesterol 0mg; Sodium 0mg, Dietary Fiber 1g

Dietary Exchange: 1/2 Fruit, 1/2 Fat OR 1/2 Carbohydrate, 1/2 Fat

MARSHMALLOW PEPPERMINT TOPPING

Yield: 2 cups; **Prep Time:** 25 minutes

Spoon the minty topping over chocolate or vanilla ice cream for a refreshing change of pace from hot fudge.

2/3 cup light corn syrup
3 tablespoons margarine or butter
1 (7-oz.) jar (1 1/2 cups) marshmallow creme
1/2 cup half-and-half
1/2 cup crushed hard peppermint candy

1. In medium saucepan, combine corn syrup and margarine. Bring to a boil over medium heat, stirring constantly. Boil 5 minutes, stirring constantly. Cool 5 minutes.

2. Stir in marshmallow creme until well blended. Gradually add half-and-half, stirring until mixture is smooth. Fold in crushed candy. Serve warm or cool. Store in refrigerator.

Nutrition per Serving: Serving Size: 1 Tablespoon. Calories 70; Calories from Fat 20; Total Fat 2g; Saturated Fat 0g; Cholesterol 0mg; Sodium 25mg; Dietary Fiber 0g

Dietary Exchange: 1 Fruit OR 1 Carbohydrate

RUM RAISIN CARAMEL SAUCE

Yield: 2 cups; **Prep Time:** 15 minutes

Scrumptious over ice cream, this amber-colored sauce makes a wonderful gift. Ladle the sauce into decorative half-pint jars and include a "store in the refrigerator" reminder on the label.

1/2 cup butter
1 1/2 cups firmly packed brown sugar
2 tablespoons light corn syrup
1/2 cup whipping cream
1/2 cup raisins
1/8 teaspoon rum extract

1. Melt butter in medium saucepan over medium heat. Add brown sugar and corn syrup; blend well. Bring to a boil. Cook until sugar is dissolved, stirring constantly. Stir in whipping cream. Return to a boil.

2. Remove from heat; stir in raisins and rum extract. Serve warm. Store in refrigerator.

Nutrition per Serving: Serving Size: 1 Tablespoon. Calories 90; Calories from Fat 35; Total Fat 4g; Saturated Fat 3g; Cholesterol 15mg; Sodium 35mg; Dietary Fiber 0g

Dietary Exchange: 1 Fruit, 1/2 Fat OR 1 Carbohydrate, 1/2 Fat

INDEX

❖ ❖ ❖

Titles by Pillsbury

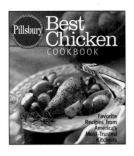

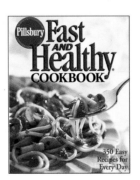

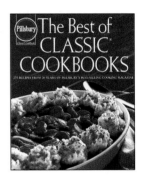

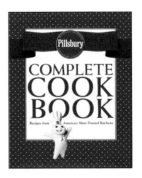